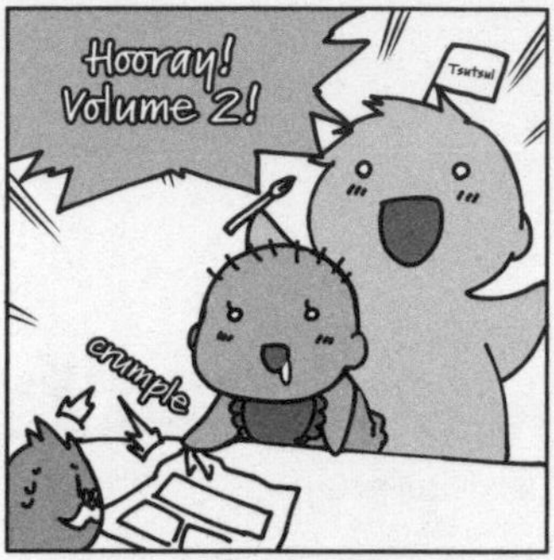
Hooray! Volume 2!
Tsutsui
crumple

Yay! Volume 2!
Thank you so much for reading the second volume of *We Never Learn*! I was a terrible student when I was prepping for entrance exams, but I remember it being really fun studying with friends and quizzing and teaching each other. It's hard being a high school senior, but there's something very special about that unusual year as well. When you're tired of studying, how about taking a break to relax and read this manga?

• Taishi Tsutsui •

We Never Learn

We Never Learn

Volume 2 • SHONEN JUMP Manga Edition

STORY AND ART **Taishi Tsutsui**

TRANSLATION Camellia Nieh

SHONEN JUMP SERIES LETTERING Snir Aharon

GRAPHIC NOVEL TOUCH-UP ART & LETTERING Erika Terriquez

DESIGN Shawn Carrico

SHONEN JUMP SERIES EDITOR John Bae

GRAPHIC NOVEL EDITOR David Brothers

Printed in the U.S.A.

Published by VIZ Media, LLC
P.O. Box 77010
San Francisco, CA 94107

10 9 8 7 6 5 4 3 2 1
First printing, February 2019

viz.com

shonenjump.com

ratings.viz.com

PARENTAL ADVISORY
WE NEVER LEARN is rated T+ for Older Teen and is recommended for ages 16 and up. This volume contains mild language and sexual themes.

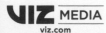

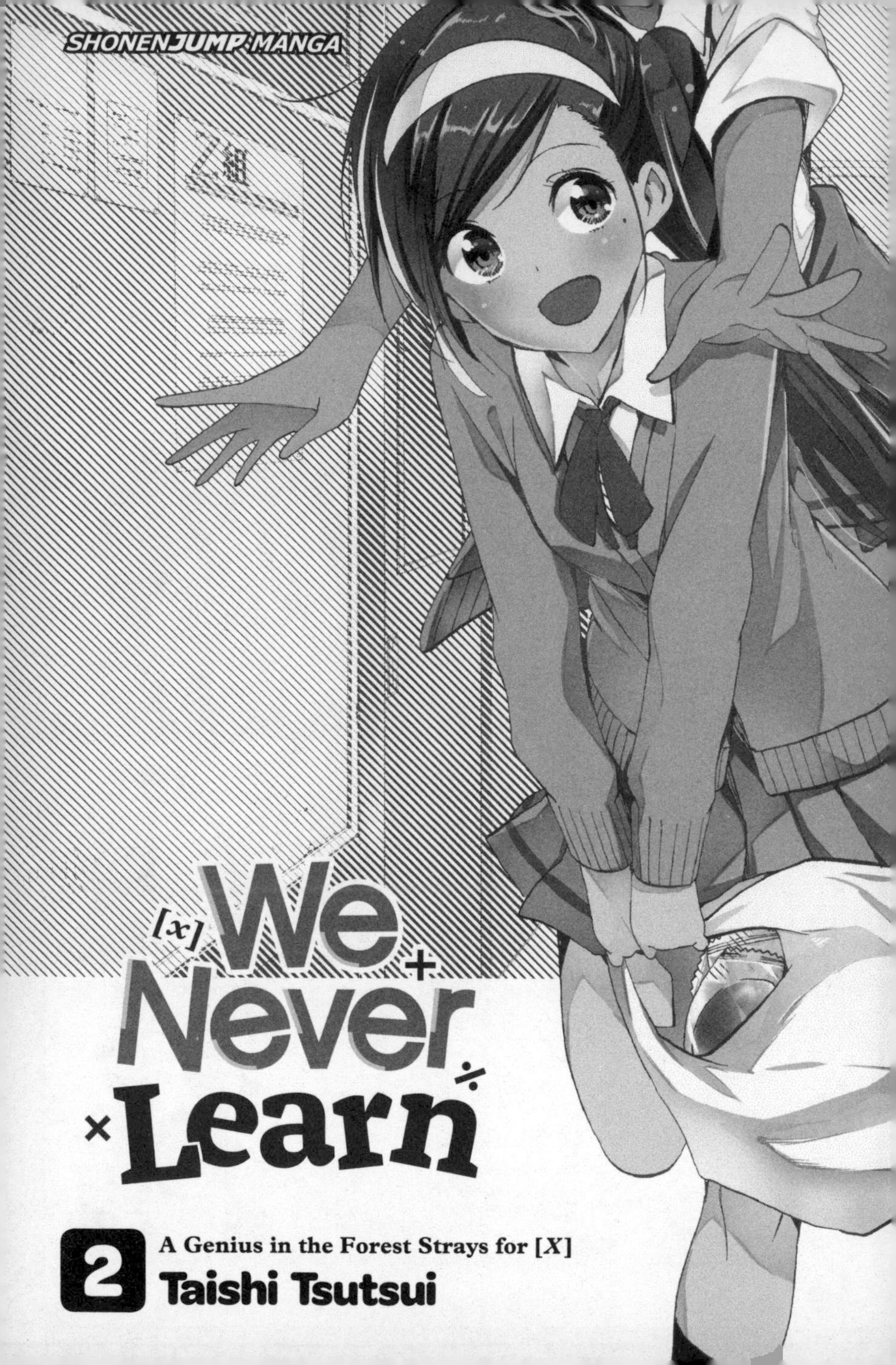

SHONEN JUMP MANGA

We Never Learn

2

A Genius in the Forest Strays for [X]

Taishi Tsutsui

We Never Learn

Nariyuki Yuiga and his family have led a humble life since his father passed away, with Yuiga doing everything he can to support his siblings. So when the principal of his school agrees to grant Nariyuki the school's special VIP recommendation for a full scholarship to college, he leaps at the opportunity. However, the principal's offer comes with one condition: Yuiga must serve as the tutor of Rizu Ogata and Fumino Furuhashi, the two girl geniuses who are the pride of Ichinose Academy!

Unfortunately, the girls have chosen academic paths not in their areas of brilliance, but in subjects where their grades are absolutely rock-bottom. Soon they are joined by superathlete Uruka, who's an ace at sports but a zero at academics. How will these three struggling students ever manage to pass their college entrance exams?!

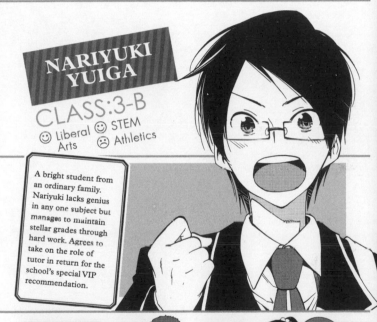

NARIYUKI YUIGA

CLASS:3-B

☺ Liberal Arts ☺ STEM
☹ Athletics

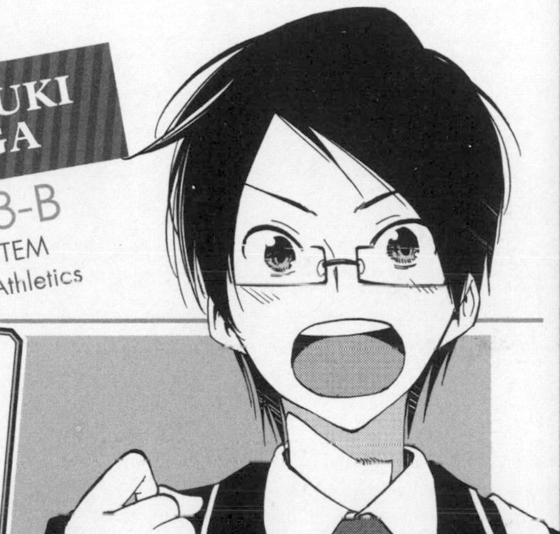

A bright student from an ordinary family. Nariyuki lacks genius in any one subject but manages to maintain stellar grades through hard work. Agrees to take on the role of tutor in return for the school's special VIP recommendation.

Kobayashi and Omori

Nariyuki's friends.

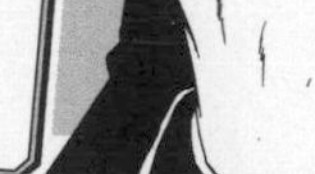

The Yuiga Family

A family of five consisting of Nariyuki, his mother and his siblings, Mizuki, Hazuki and Kazuki.

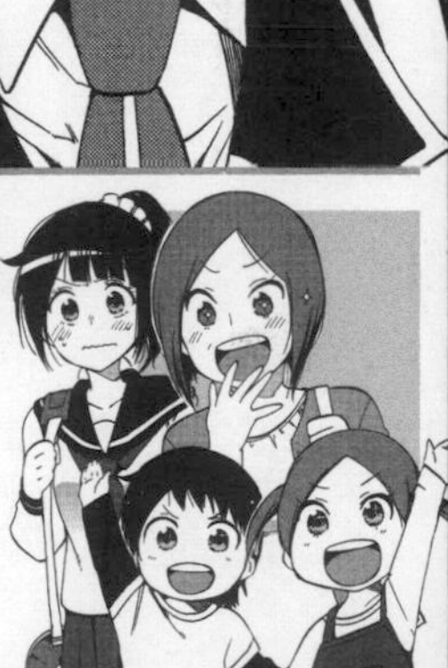

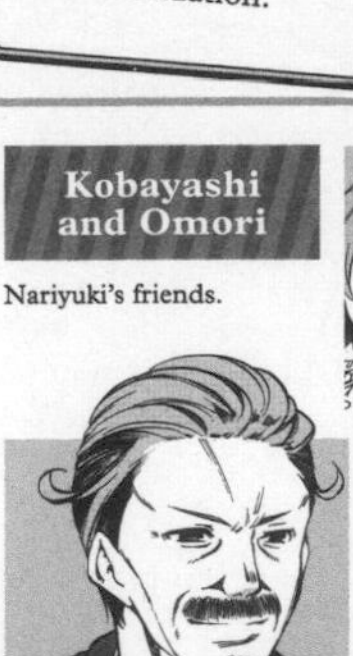

Principal

Assigns Nariyuki the role of tutor.

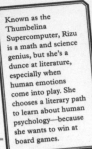

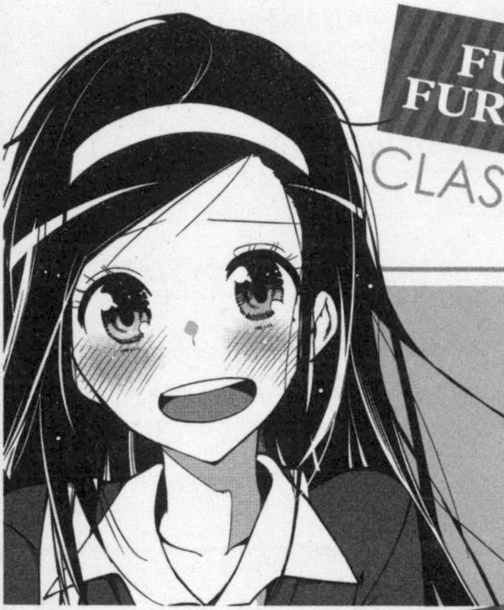

RIZU OGATA

CLASS:3-F

☹ Liberal Arts ☺ STEM ☹ Athletics

Known as the Thumbelina Supercomputer, Rizu is a math and science genius, but she's a dunce at literature, especially when human emotions come into play. She chooses a literary path to learn about human psychology—because she wants to win at board games.

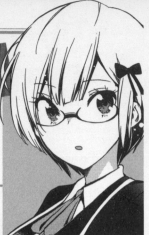

FUMINO FURUHASHI

CLASS:3-A

☺ Liberal Arts ☹ STEM ☺ Athletics

Known as the Sleeping Beauty of the Literary Forest, Fumino is a literary wiz whose mind goes completely blank when she sees numbers. She chooses a STEM path because she wants to study the stars.

URUKA TAKEMOTO

CLASS:3-D

☹ Liberal Arts ☹ STEM ☺ Athletics

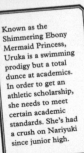

Known as the Shimmering Ebony Mermaid Princess, Uruka is a swimming prodigy but a total dunce at academics. In order to get an athletic scholarship, she needs to meet certain academic standards. She's had a crush on Nariyuki since junior high.

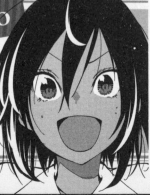

We Never Learn

CONTENTS

TITLE

VOLUME **2** A Genius in the Forest Strays for [X]

NAME **Taishi Tsutsui**

QUESTION **8** Who Does a Genius Wrestle with [X] For? 7

QUESTION **9** A Genius Resonates Emotionally with [X]? 27

QUESTION **10** A Maiden Is to Genius as [X] Is to Once a Day? 47

QUESTION **11** Said Value to a Genius Is a Consequence of [X] 67

QUESTION **12** What She Wants from a Genius Is [X] 87

QUESTION **13** Sometimes a Genius's Panic Is Inversely Related to [X] 107

QUESTION **14** A Genius in the Forest Strays for [X] 127

QUESTION **15** A Genius Boiled in Bathwater Exposes [X] 147

QUESTION **16** Thus, a Predecessor Still Relates to a Genius as [X] 167

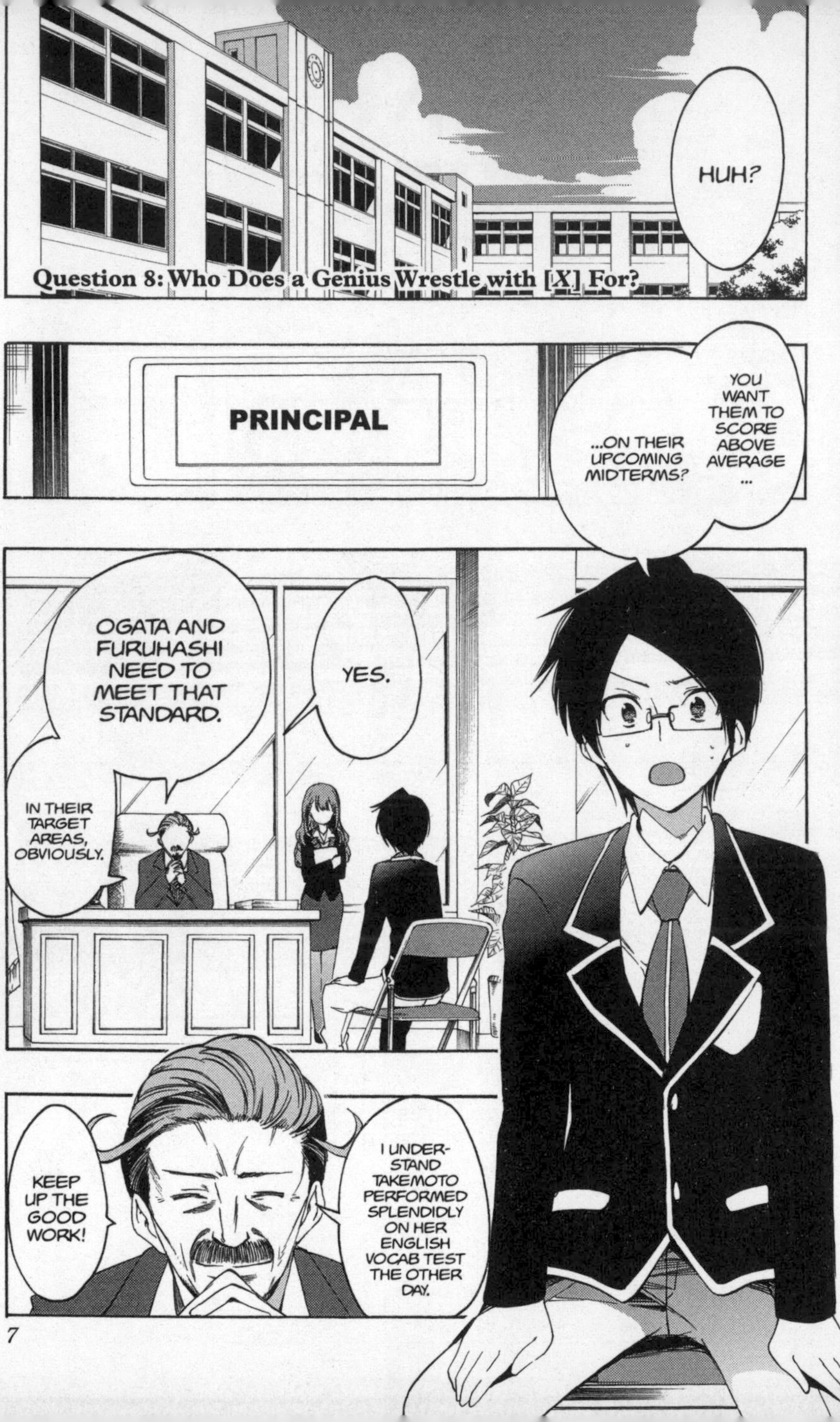
HUH?
Question 8: Who Does a Genius Wrestle with [X] For?
PRINCIPAL
YOU WANT THEM TO SCORE ABOVE AVERAGE ...
...ON THEIR UPCOMING MIDTERMS?
YES.
OGATA AND FURUHASHI NEED TO MEET THAT STANDARD.
IN THEIR TARGET AREAS, OBVIOUSLY.
I UNDER-STAND TAKEMOTO PERFORMED SPLENDIDLY ON HER ENGLISH VOCAB TEST THE OTHER DAY.
KEEP UP THE GOOD WORK!

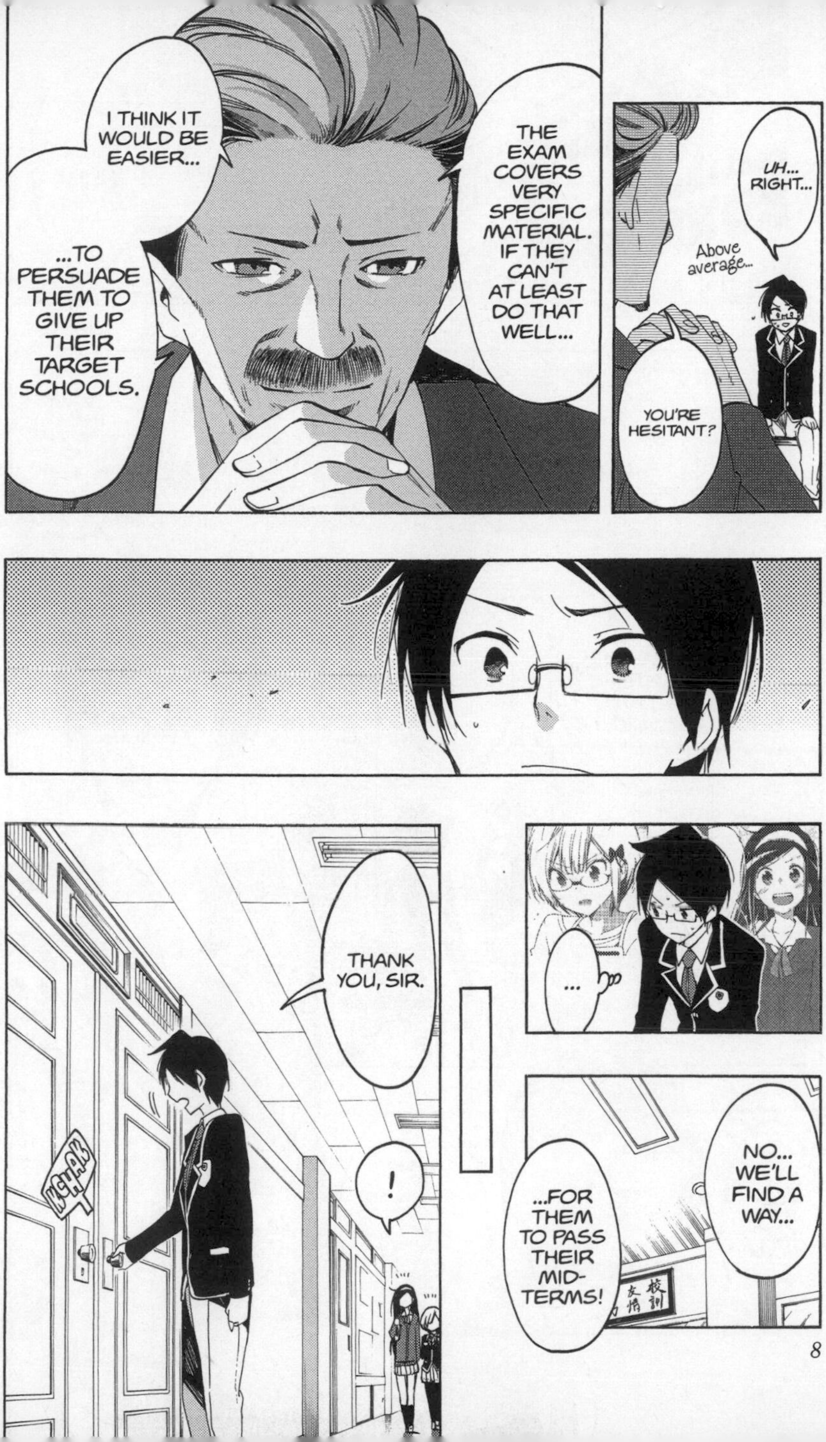
UH... RIGHT...
Above average...
YOU'RE HESITANT?
THE EXAM COVERS VERY SPECIFIC MATERIAL. IF THEY CAN'T AT LEAST DO THAT WELL...
I THINK IT WOULD BE EASIER...
...TO PERSUADE THEM TO GIVE UP THEIR TARGET SCHOOLS.
...
NO... WE'LL FIND A WAY...
...FOR THEM TO PASS THEIR MID-TERMS!
THANK YOU, SIR.
!
KCHAK

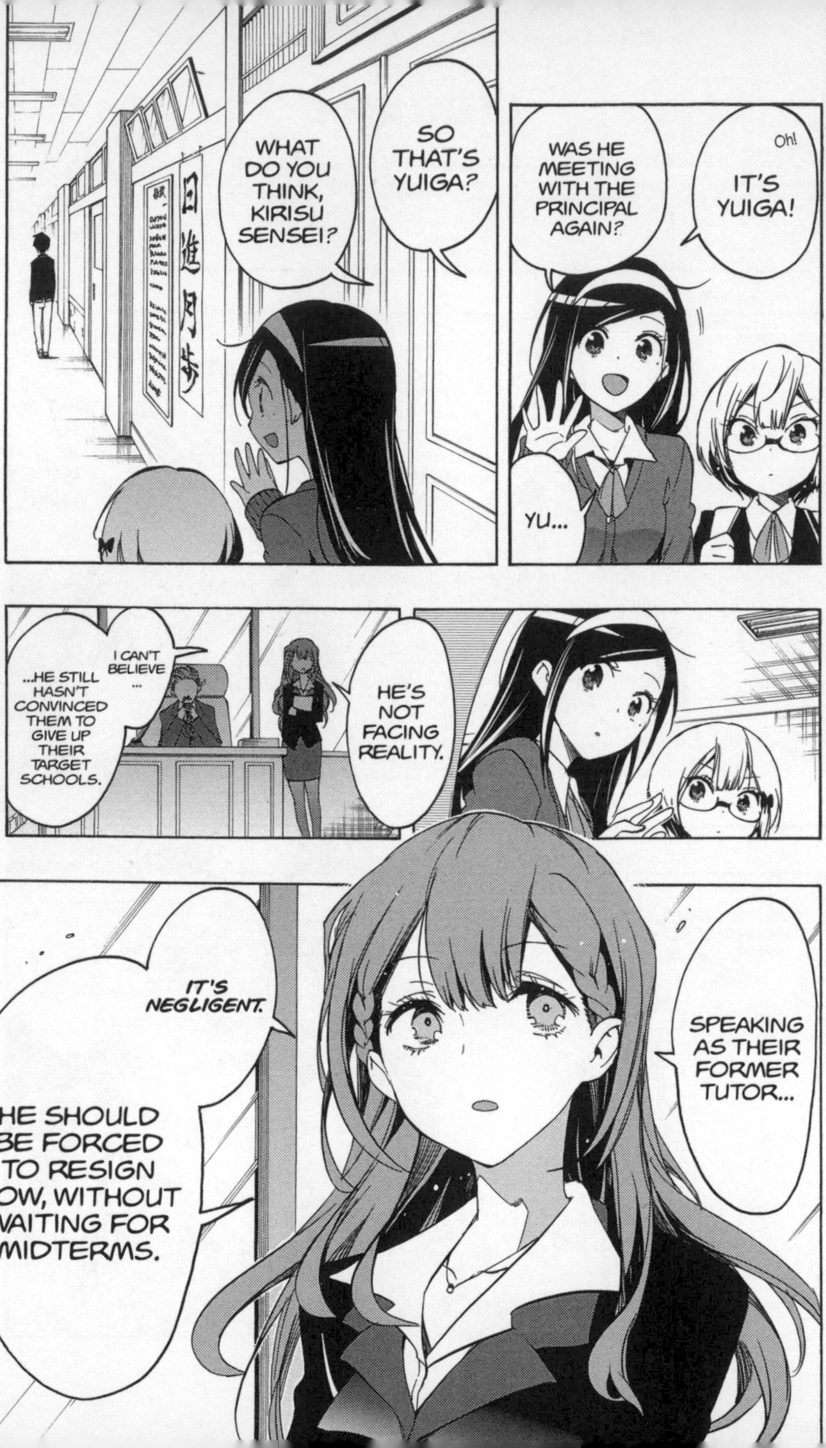
Oh!
IT'S YUIGA!
WAS HE MEETING WITH THE PRINCIPAL AGAIN?
YU...
SO THAT'S YUIGA?
WHAT DO YOU THINK, KIRISU SENSEI?
日進月歩
HE'S NOT FACING REALITY.
I CAN'T BELIEVE ...
...HE STILL HASN'T CONVINCED THEM TO GIVE UP THEIR TARGET SCHOOLS.
SPEAKING AS THEIR FORMER TUTOR...
IT'S NEGLIGENT.
HE SHOULD BE FORCED TO RESIGN NOW, WITHOUT WAITING FOR MIDTERMS.

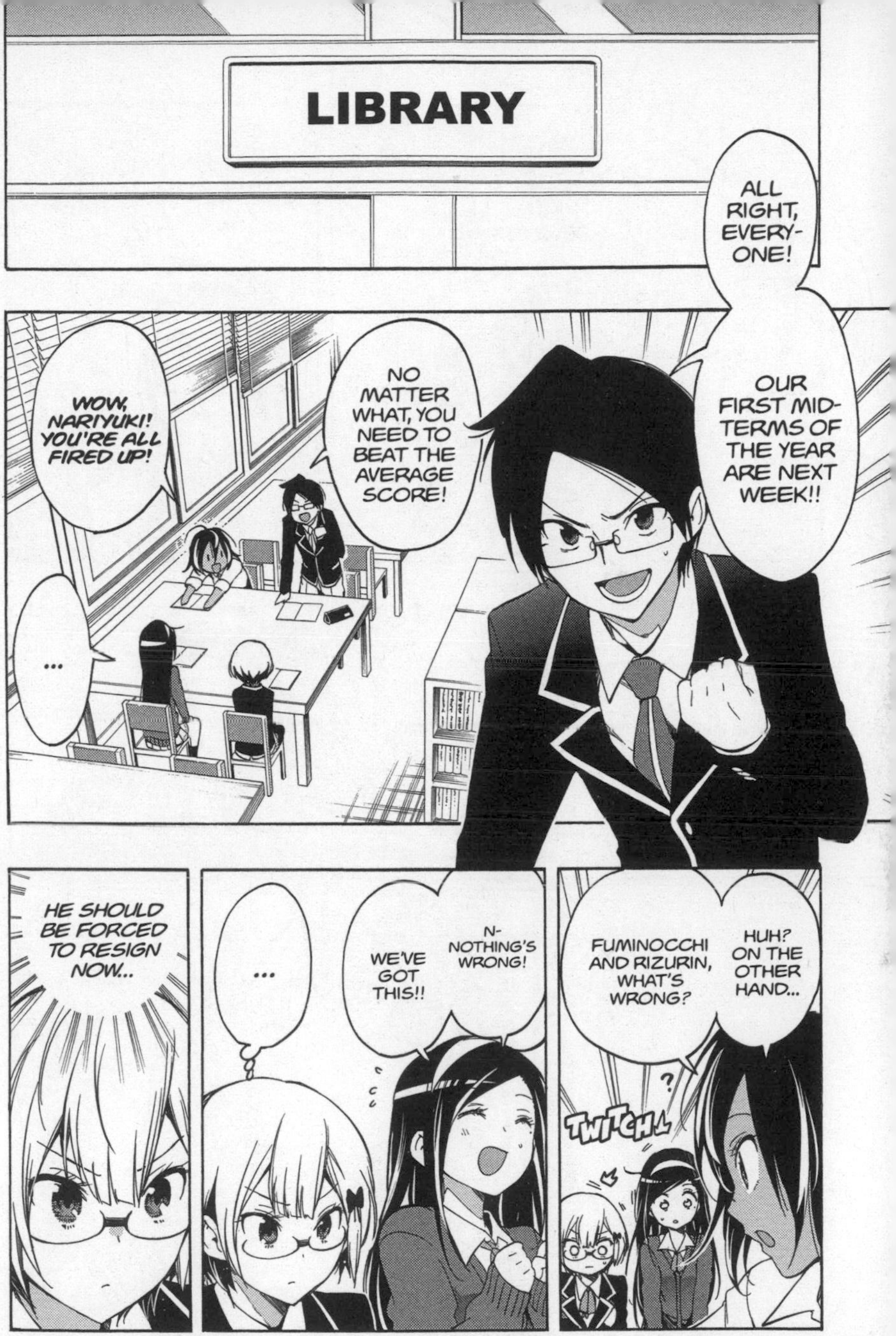
LIBRARY
ALL RIGHT, EVERYONE!
OUR FIRST MIDTERMS OF THE YEAR ARE NEXT WEEK!!
NO MATTER WHAT, YOU NEED TO BEAT THE AVERAGE SCORE!
WOW, NARIYUKI! YOU'RE ALL FIRED UP!
...
HUH? ON THE OTHER HAND...
FUMINOCCHI AND RIZURIN, WHAT'S WRONG?
TWITCH
N-NOTHING'S WRONG!
WE'VE GOT THIS!!
...
HE SHOULD BE FORCED TO RESIGN NOW...

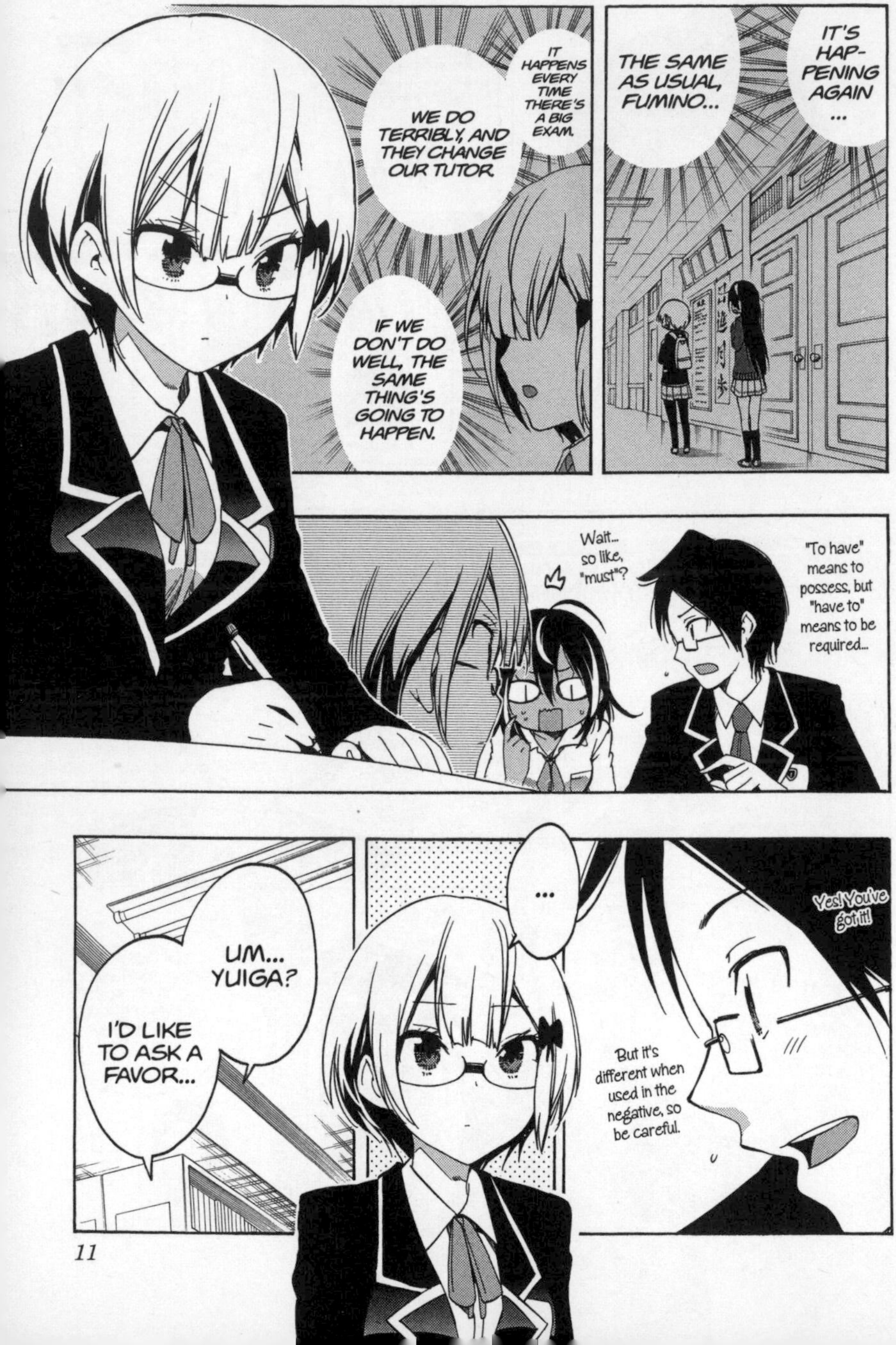
IT'S HAPPENING AGAIN...
THE SAME AS USUAL, FUMINO...
IT HAPPENS EVERY TIME THERE'S A BIG EXAM.
WE DO TERRIBLY, AND THEY CHANGE OUR TUTOR.
IF WE DON'T DO WELL, THE SAME THING'S GOING TO HAPPEN.
"To have" means to possess, but "have to" means to be required...
Wait... so like, "must"?
Yes! You've got it!
But it's different when used in the negative, so be careful.
...
UM... YUIGA?
I'D LIKE TO ASK A FAVOR...

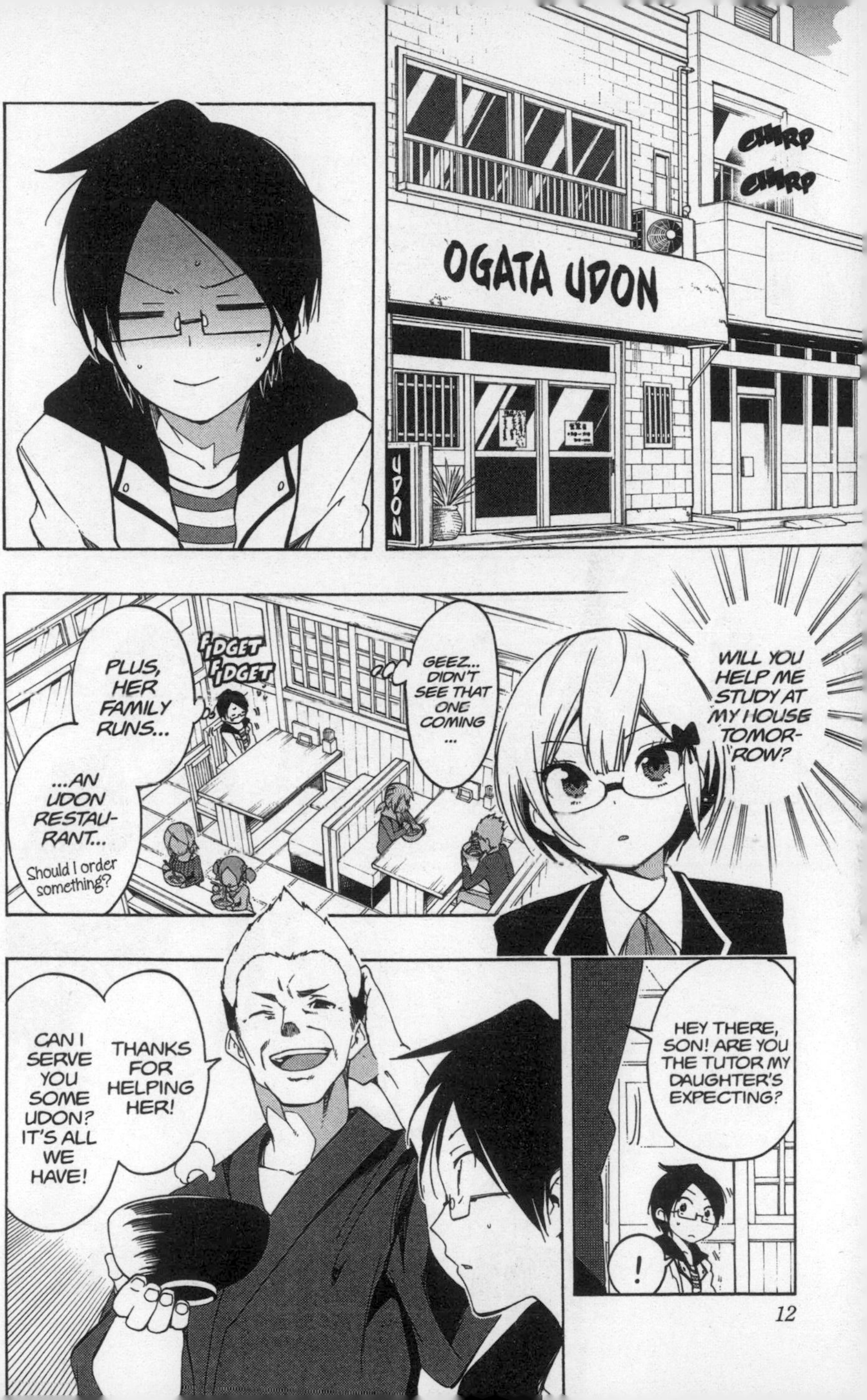
CHIRP
CHIRP
OGATA UDON
UDON
WILL YOU HELP ME STUDY AT MY HOUSE TOMORROW?
GEEZ... DIDN'T SEE THAT ONE COMING...
FIDGET FIDGET
PLUS, HER FAMILY RUNS...
...AN UDON RESTAURANT...
Should I order something?
HEY THERE, SON! ARE YOU THE TUTOR MY DAUGHTER'S EXPECTING?
!
THANKS FOR HELPING HER!
CAN I SERVE YOU SOME UDON? IT'S ALL WE HAVE!

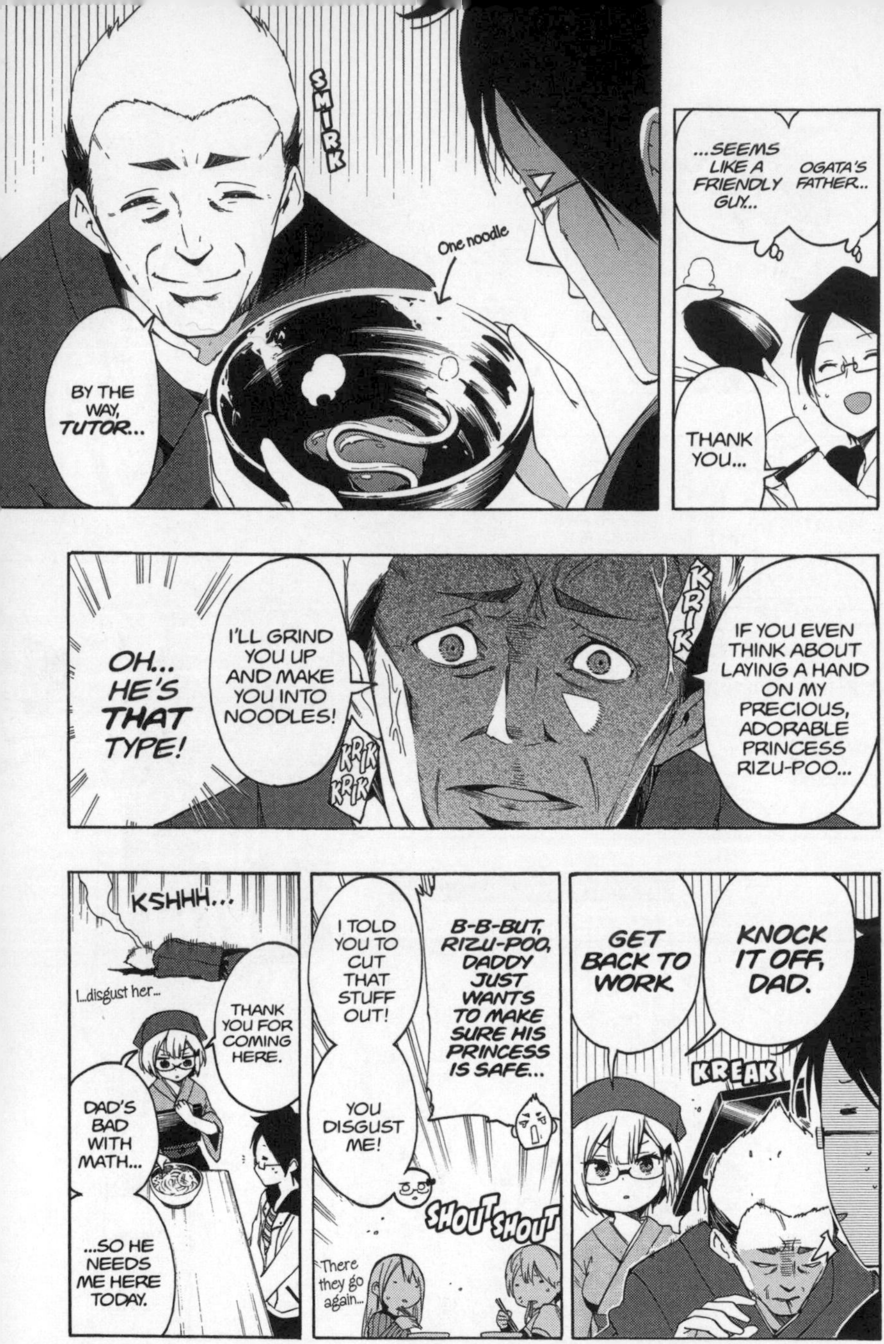
OGATA'S FATHER.. ...SEEMS LIKE A FRIENDLY GUY...
THANK YOU...
SMIRK
One noodle
BY THE WAY, TUTOR...
IF YOU EVEN THINK ABOUT LAYING A HAND ON MY PRECIOUS, ADORABLE PRINCESS RIZU-POO...
KRIK KRIK
I'LL GRIND YOU UP AND MAKE YOU INTO NOODLES!
KRIK KRIK
OH... HE'S THAT TYPE!
KNOCK IT OFF, DAD.
GET BACK TO WORK.
KREAK
B-B-BUT, RIZU-POO, DADDY JUST WANTS TO MAKE SURE HIS PRINCESS IS SAFE...
I TOLD YOU TO CUT THAT STUFF OUT!
YOU DISGUST ME!
SHOUT SHOUT
There they go again...
KSHHH...
THANK YOU FOR COMING HERE.
I...disgust her...
DAD'S BAD WITH MATH...
...SO HE NEEDS ME HERE TODAY.

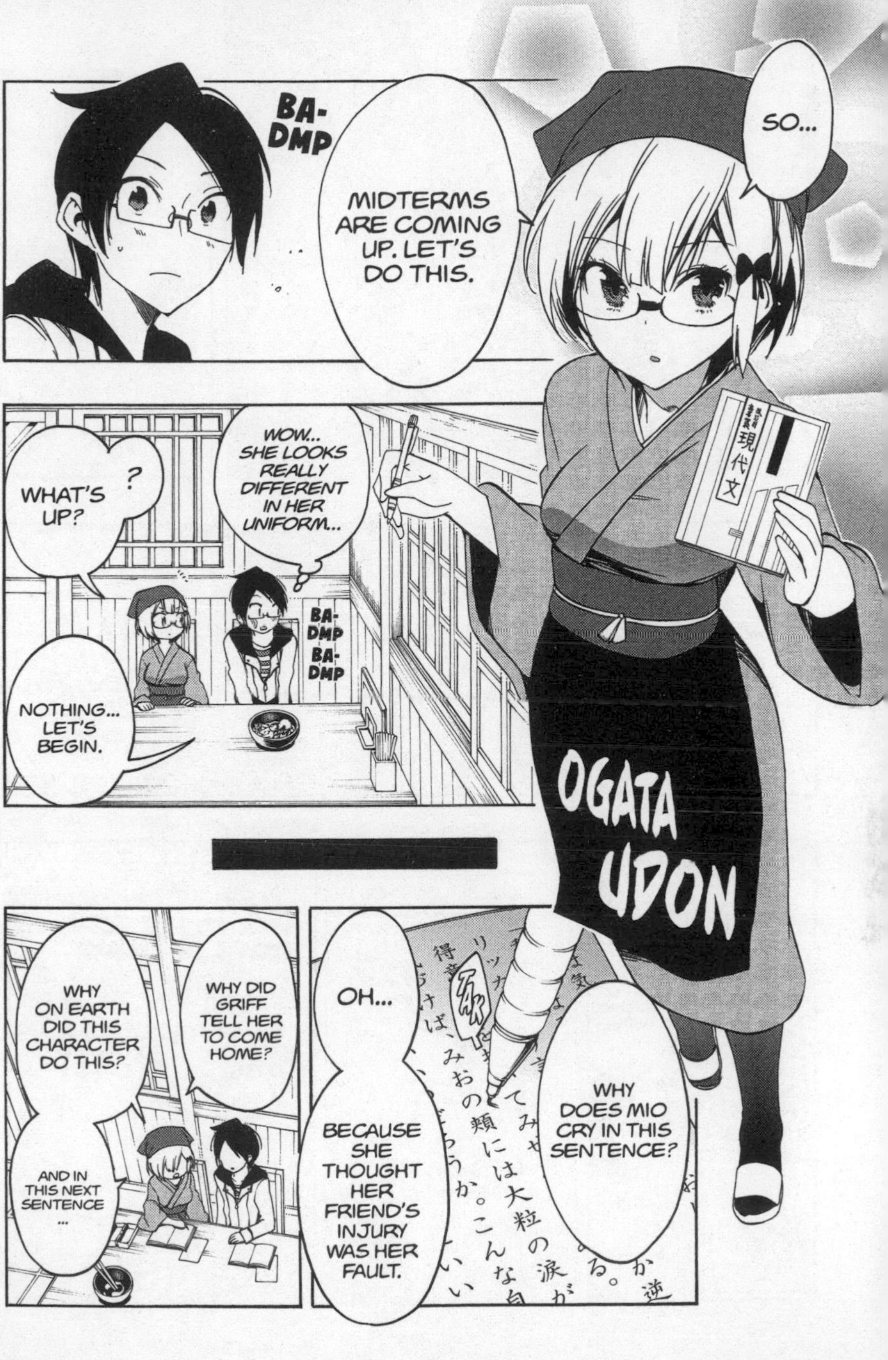
SO...
MIDTERMS ARE COMING UP. LET'S DO THIS.
BA-DMP
...
WOW... SHE LOOKS REALLY DIFFERENT IN HER UNIFORM...
WHAT'S UP?
?
BA-DMP BA-DMP
NOTHING... LET'S BEGIN.
現代文
OGATA UDON
WHY DOES MIO CRY IN THIS SENTENCE?
TAK
OH...
BECAUSE SHE THOUGHT HER FRIEND'S INJURY WAS HER FAULT.
WHY DID GRIFF TELL HER TO COME HOME?
WHY ON EARTH DID THIS CHARACTER DO THIS?
AND IN THIS NEXT SENTENCE ...

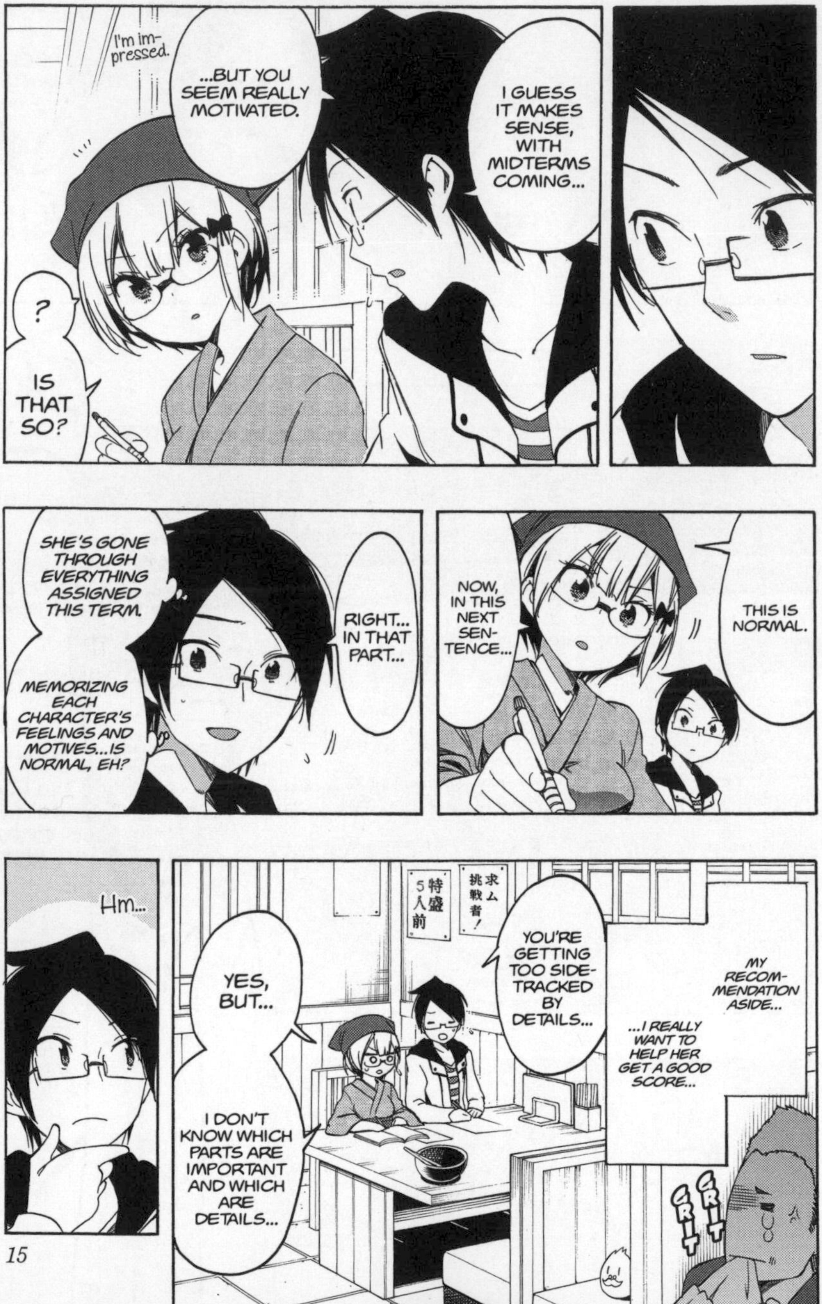
I GUESS IT MAKES SENSE, WITH MIDTERMS COMING...
...BUT YOU SEEM REALLY MOTIVATED.
I'm impressed.
?
IS THAT SO?
THIS IS NORMAL.
NOW, IN THIS NEXT SENTENCE...
RIGHT... IN THAT PART...
SHE'S GONE THROUGH EVERYTHING ASSIGNED THIS TERM.
MEMORIZING EACH CHARACTER'S FEELINGS AND MOTIVES...IS NORMAL, EH?
MY RECOMMENDATION ASIDE...
...I REALLY WANT TO HELP HER GET A GOOD SCORE...
GRIT GRIT
YOU'RE GETTING TOO SIDETRACKED BY DETAILS...
求ム挑戦者！
特盛5人前
YES, BUT...
I DON'T KNOW WHICH PARTS ARE IMPORTANT AND WHICH ARE DETAILS...
Hm...

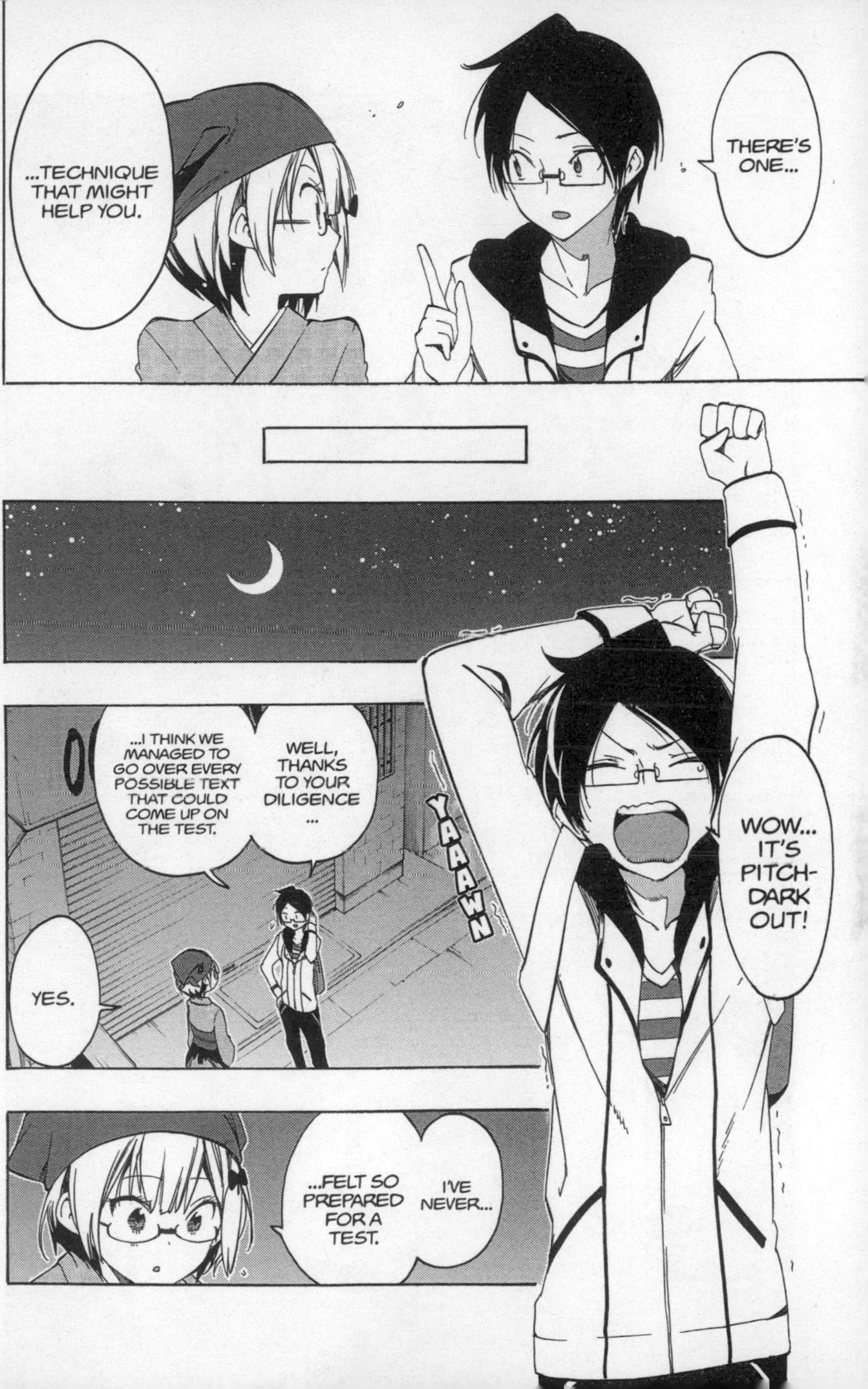
THERE'S ONE...
...TECHNIQUE THAT MIGHT HELP YOU.
WOW... IT'S PITCH-DARK OUT!
YAAAAWN
WELL, THANKS TO YOUR DILIGENCE ...
...I THINK WE MANAGED TO GO OVER EVERY POSSIBLE TEXT THAT COULD COME UP ON THE TEST.
YES.
I'VE NEVER...
...FELT SO PREPARED FOR A TEST.

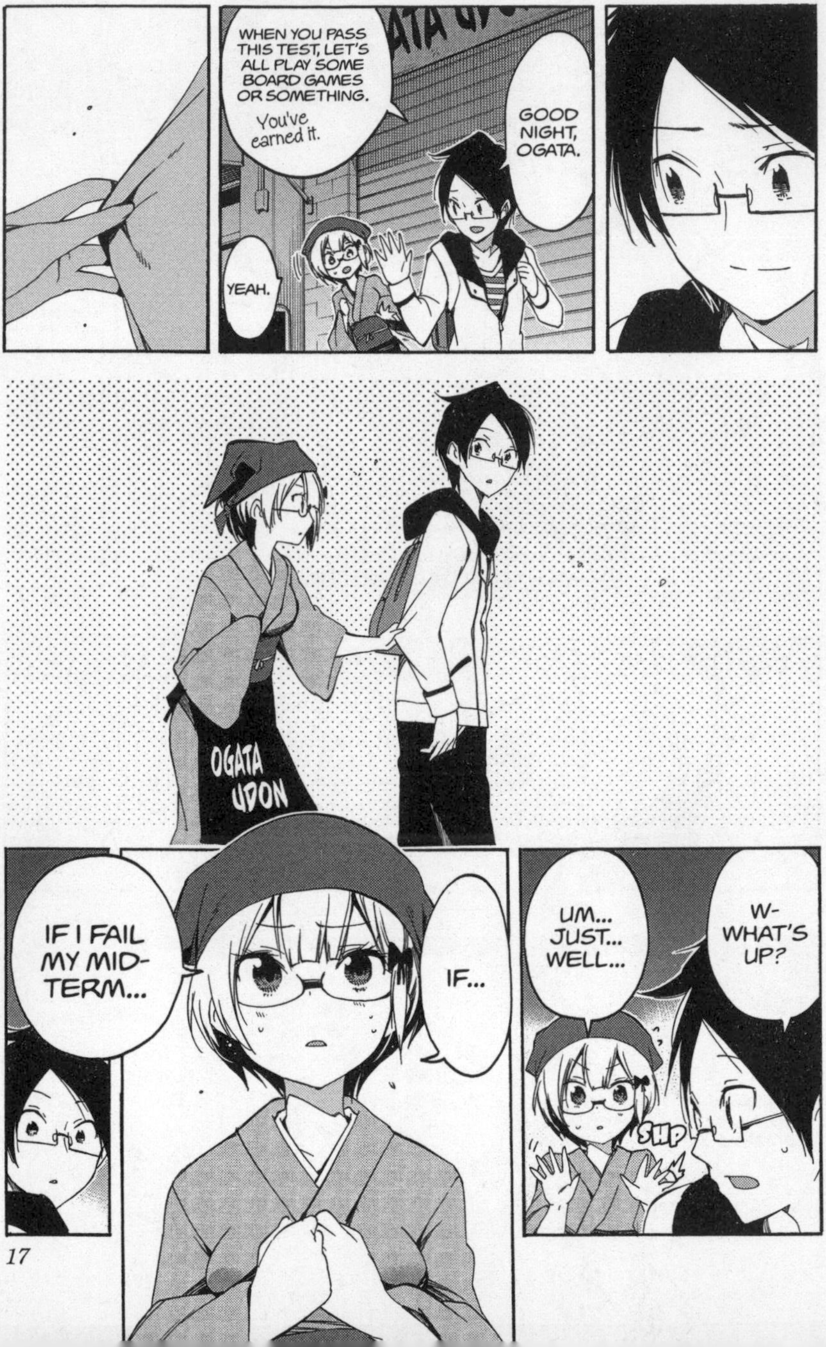
GOOD NIGHT, OGATA.
WHEN YOU PASS THIS TEST, LET'S ALL PLAY SOME BOARD GAMES OR SOMETHING.
You've earned it.
YEAH.
OGATA UDON
W- WHAT'S UP?
UM... JUST... WELL...
SHP
IF...
IF I FAIL MY MID-TERM...

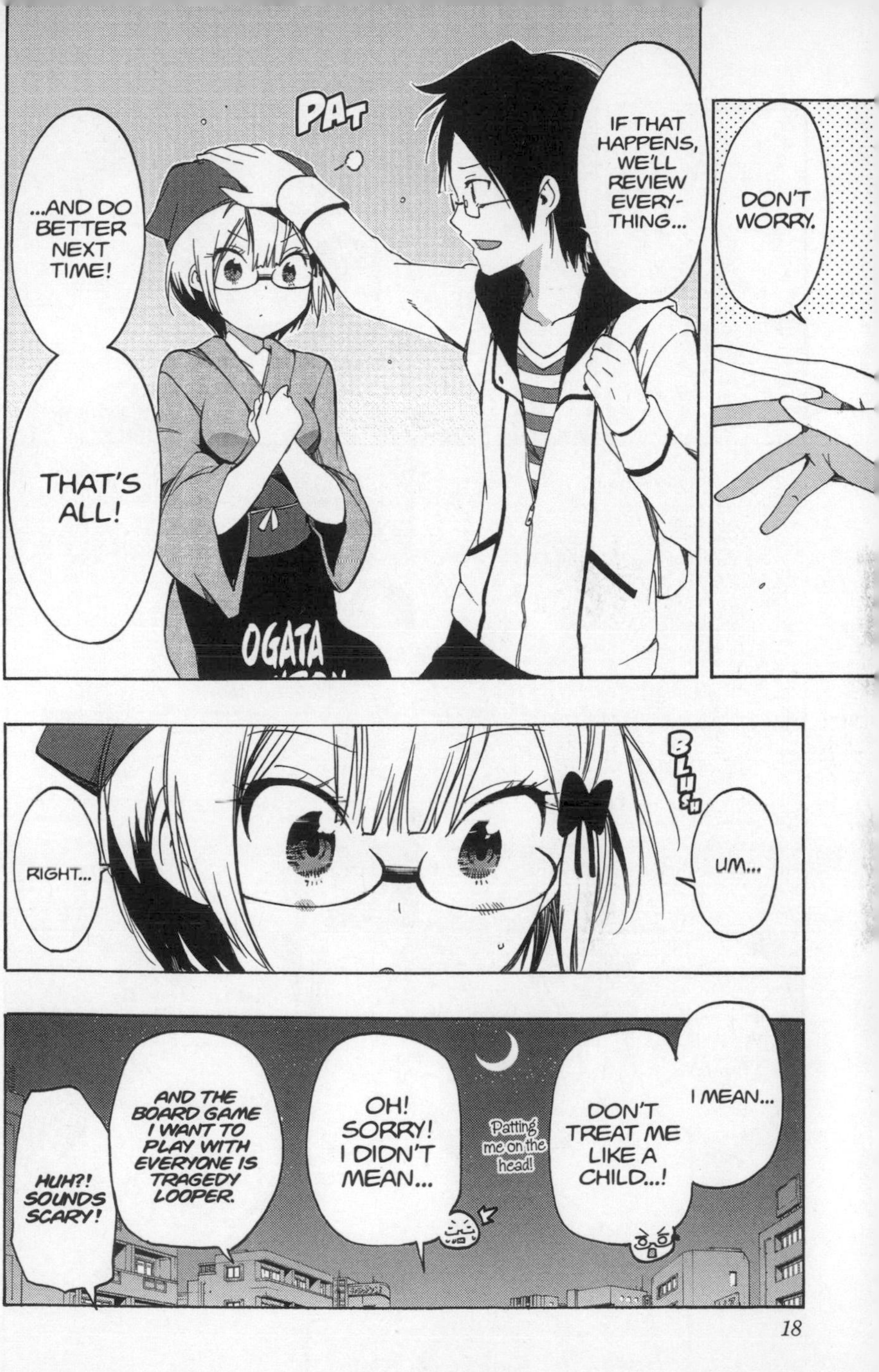
DON'T WORRY.
IF THAT HAPPENS, WE'LL REVIEW EVERYTHING...
PAT
...AND DO BETTER NEXT TIME!
THAT'S ALL!
OGATA
BLUSH
UM...
RIGHT...
I MEAN...
DON'T TREAT ME LIKE A CHILD...!
Patting me on the head!
OH! SORRY! I DIDN'T MEAN...
AND THE BOARD GAME I WANT TO PLAY WITH EVERYONE IS TRAGEDY LOOPER.
HUH?! SOUNDS SCARY!

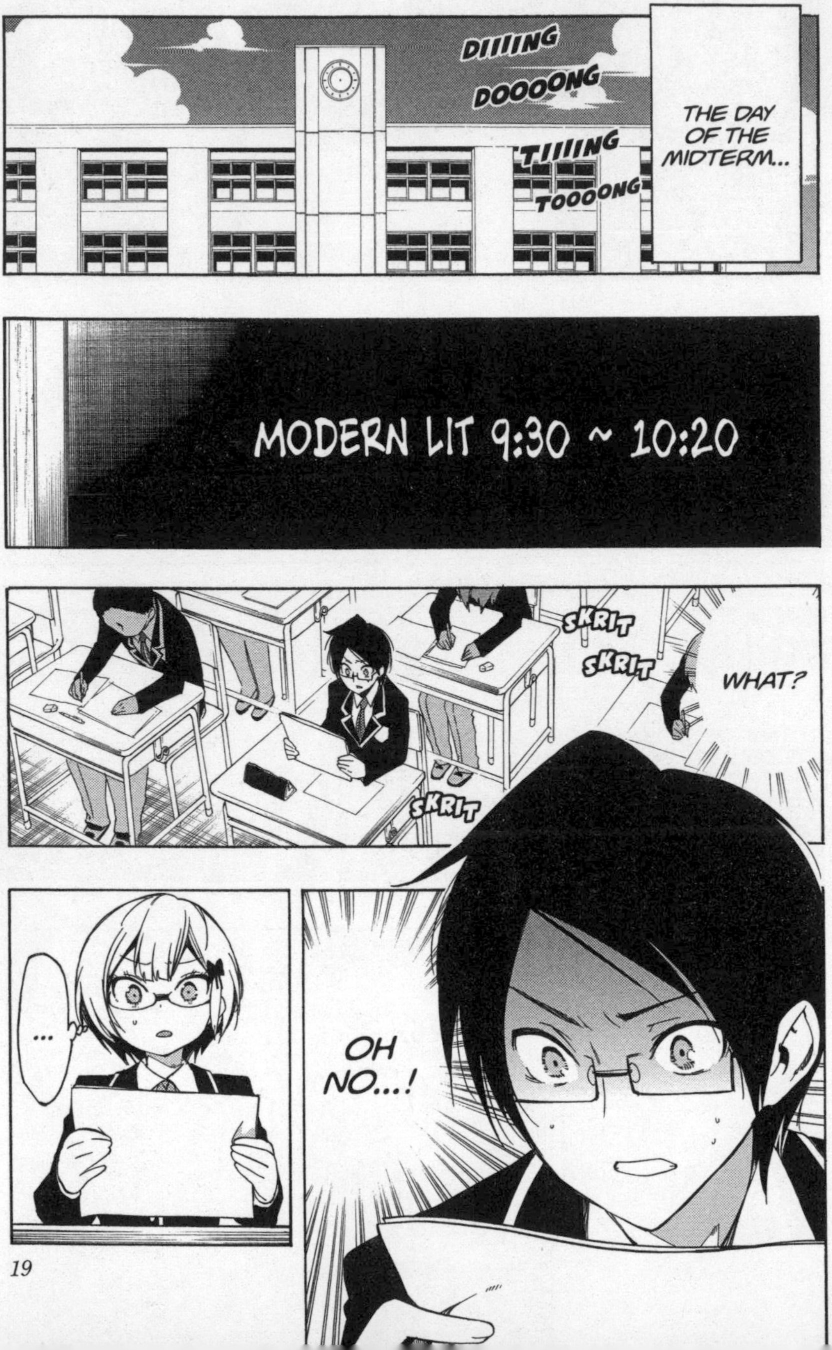
THE DAY OF THE MIDTERM...
DIIIING
DOOOOONG
TIIIIING
TOOOONG
MODERN LIT 9:30 ~ 10:20
WHAT?
SKRIT
SKRIT
SKRIT
OH NO...!
...

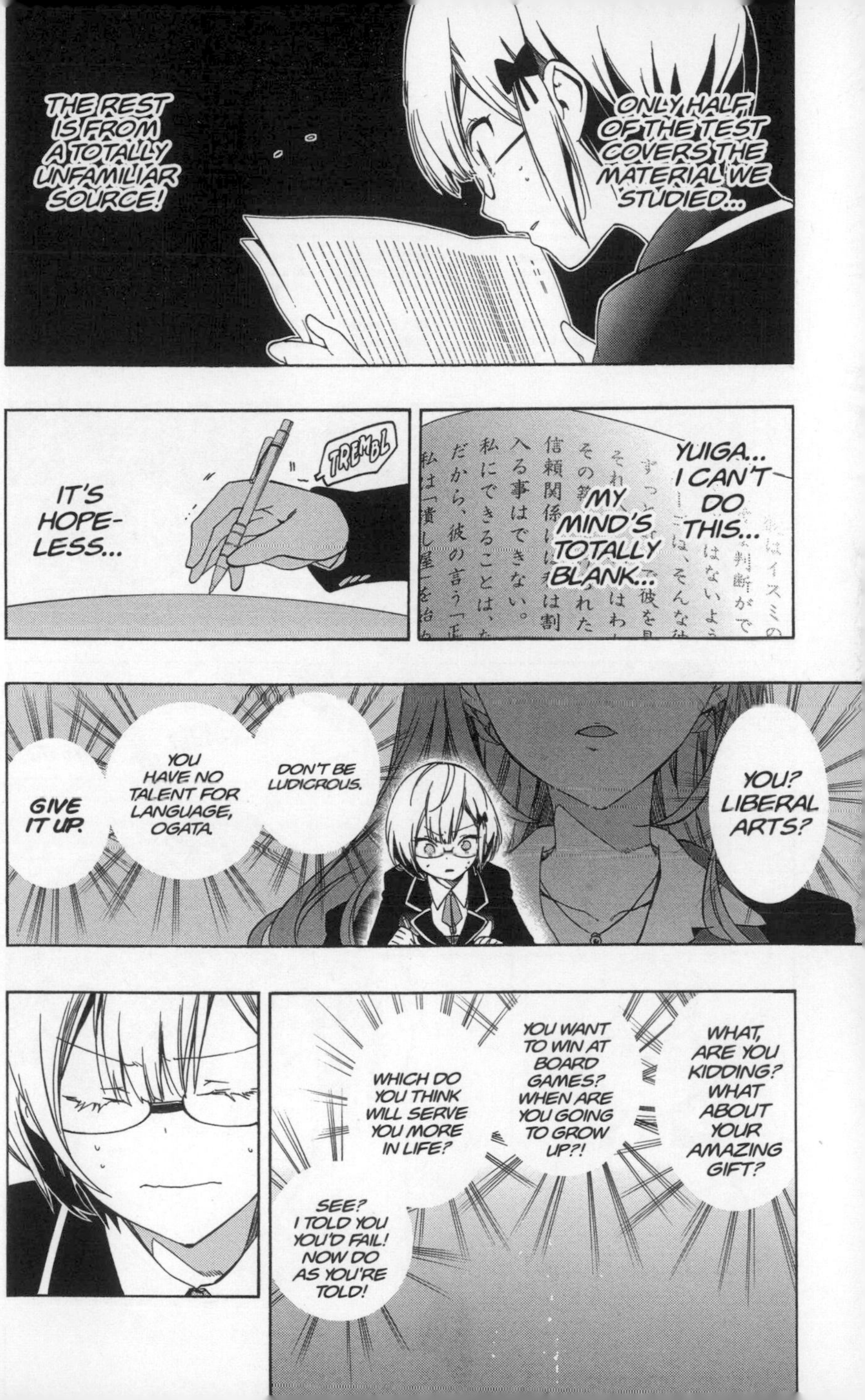
ONLY HALF OF THE TEST COVERS THE MATERIAL WE STUDIED...
THE REST IS FROM A TOTALLY UNFAMILIAR SOURCE!
YUIGA... I CAN'T DO THIS...
MY MIND'S TOTALLY BLANK...
TREMBL
IT'S HOPE-LESS...
YOU? LIBERAL ARTS?
DON'T BE LUDICROUS.
YOU HAVE NO TALENT FOR LANGUAGE, OGATA.
GIVE IT UP.
WHAT, ARE YOU KIDDING? WHAT ABOUT YOUR AMAZING GIFT?
YOU WANT TO WIN AT BOARD GAMES? WHEN ARE YOU GOING TO GROW UP?!
WHICH DO YOU THINK WILL SERVE YOU MORE IN LIFE?
SEE? I TOLD YOU YOU'D FAIL! NOW DO AS YOU'RE TOLD!

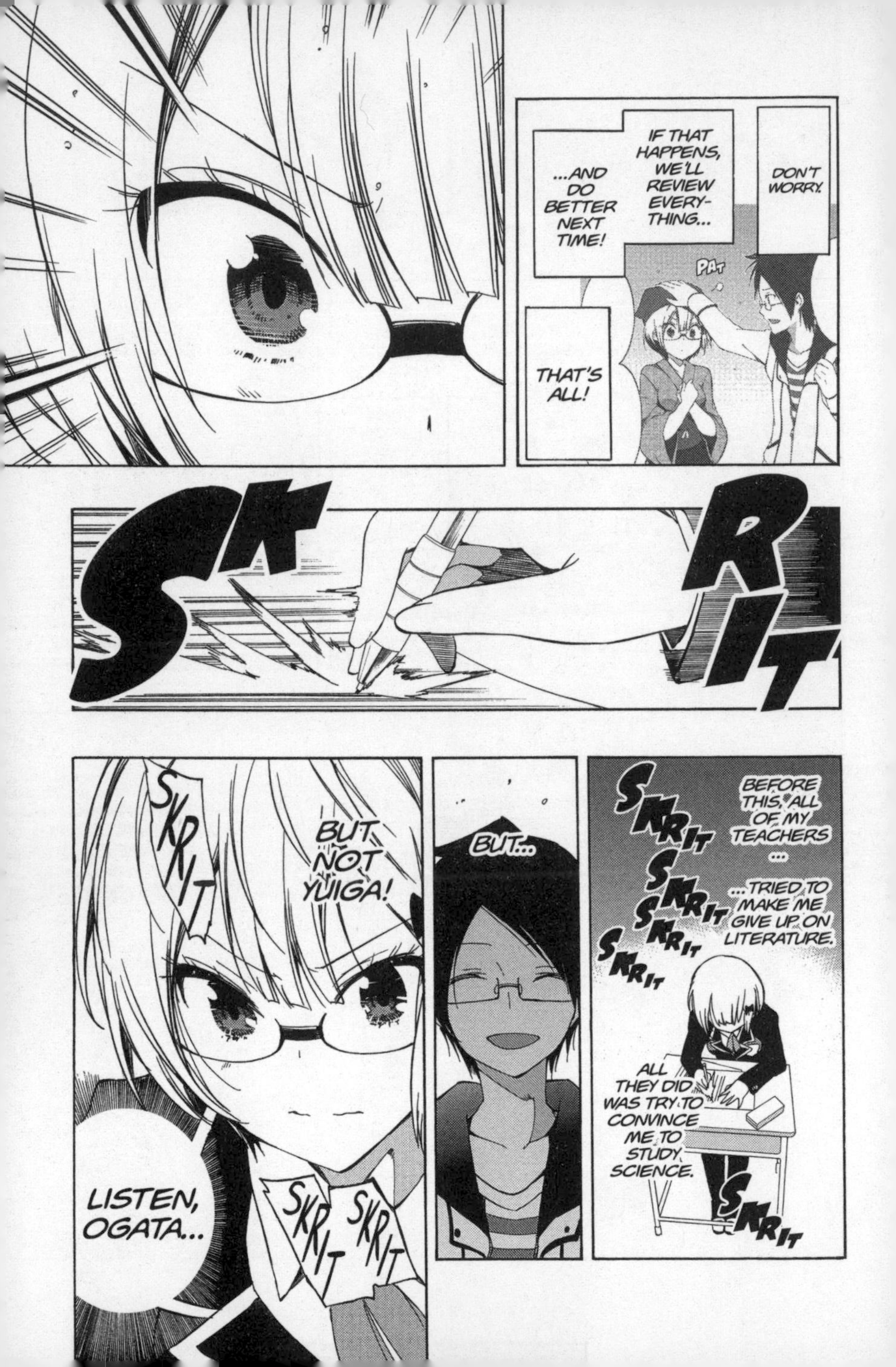
DON'T WORRY.
IF THAT HAPPENS, WE'LL REVIEW EVERYTHING...
...AND DO BETTER NEXT TIME!
PAT
THAT'S ALL!
SKRIT
BEFORE THIS, ALL OF MY TEACHERS ...
...TRIED TO MAKE ME GIVE UP ON LITERATURE.
SKRIT
SKRIT
SKRIT
SKRIT
ALL THEY DID WAS TRY TO CONVINCE ME TO STUDY SCIENCE.
SKRIT
BUT...
SKRIT
BUT NOT YUIGA!
LISTEN, OGATA...
SKRIT
SKRIT

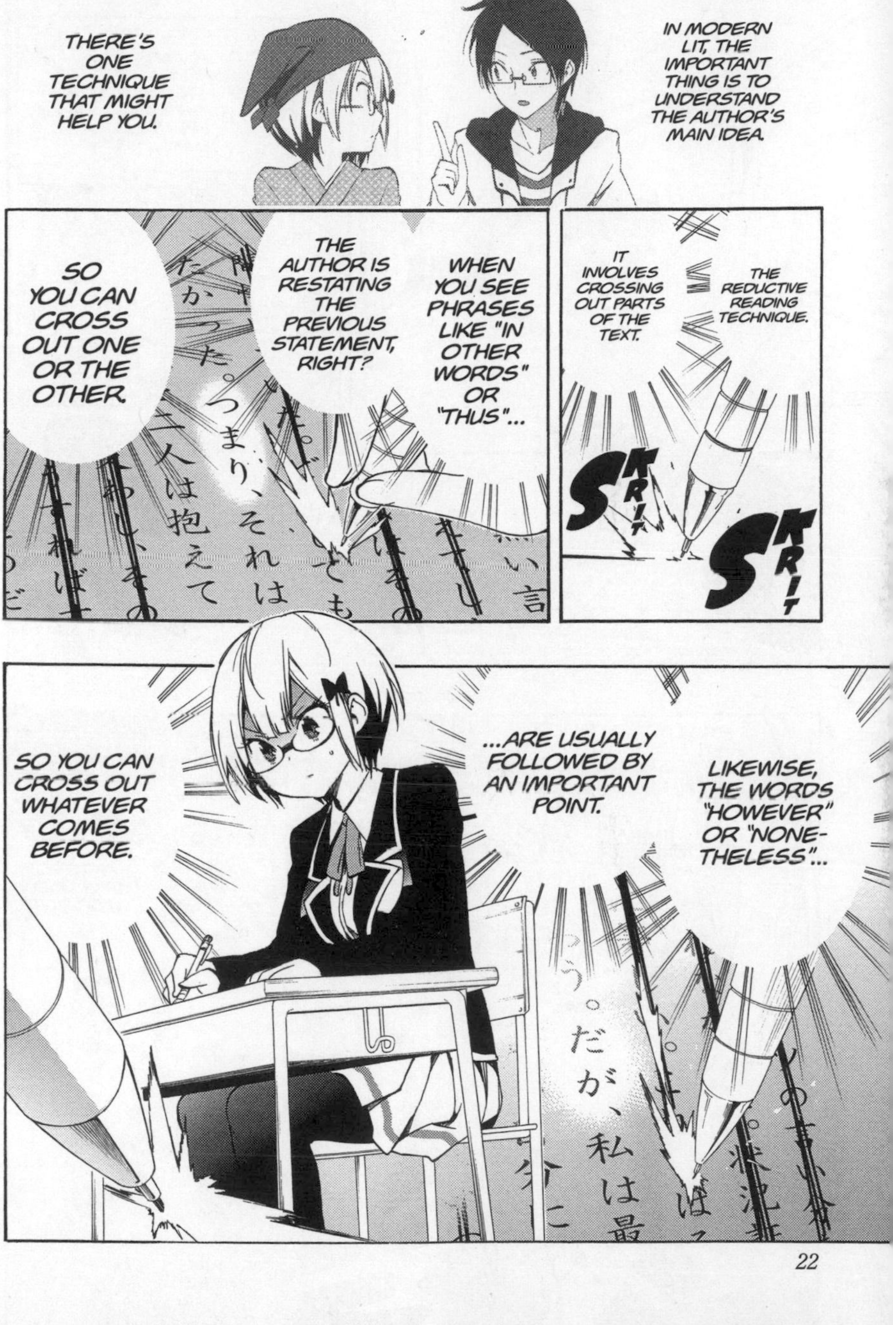
IN MODERN LIT, THE IMPORTANT THING IS TO UNDERSTAND THE AUTHOR'S MAIN IDEA.
THERE'S ONE TECHNIQUE THAT MIGHT HELP YOU.
THE REDUCTIVE READING TECHNIQUE.
IT INVOLVES CROSSING OUT PARTS OF THE TEXT.
SKRIT
SKRIT
WHEN YOU SEE PHRASES LIKE "IN OTHER WORDS" OR "THUS"...
THE AUTHOR IS RESTATING THE PREVIOUS STATEMENT, RIGHT?
SO YOU CAN CROSS OUT ONE OR THE OTHER.
LIKEWISE, THE WORDS "HOWEVER" OR "NONE-THELESS"...
...ARE USUALLY FOLLOWED BY AN IMPORTANT POINT.
SO YOU CAN CROSS OUT WHATEVER COMES BEFORE.

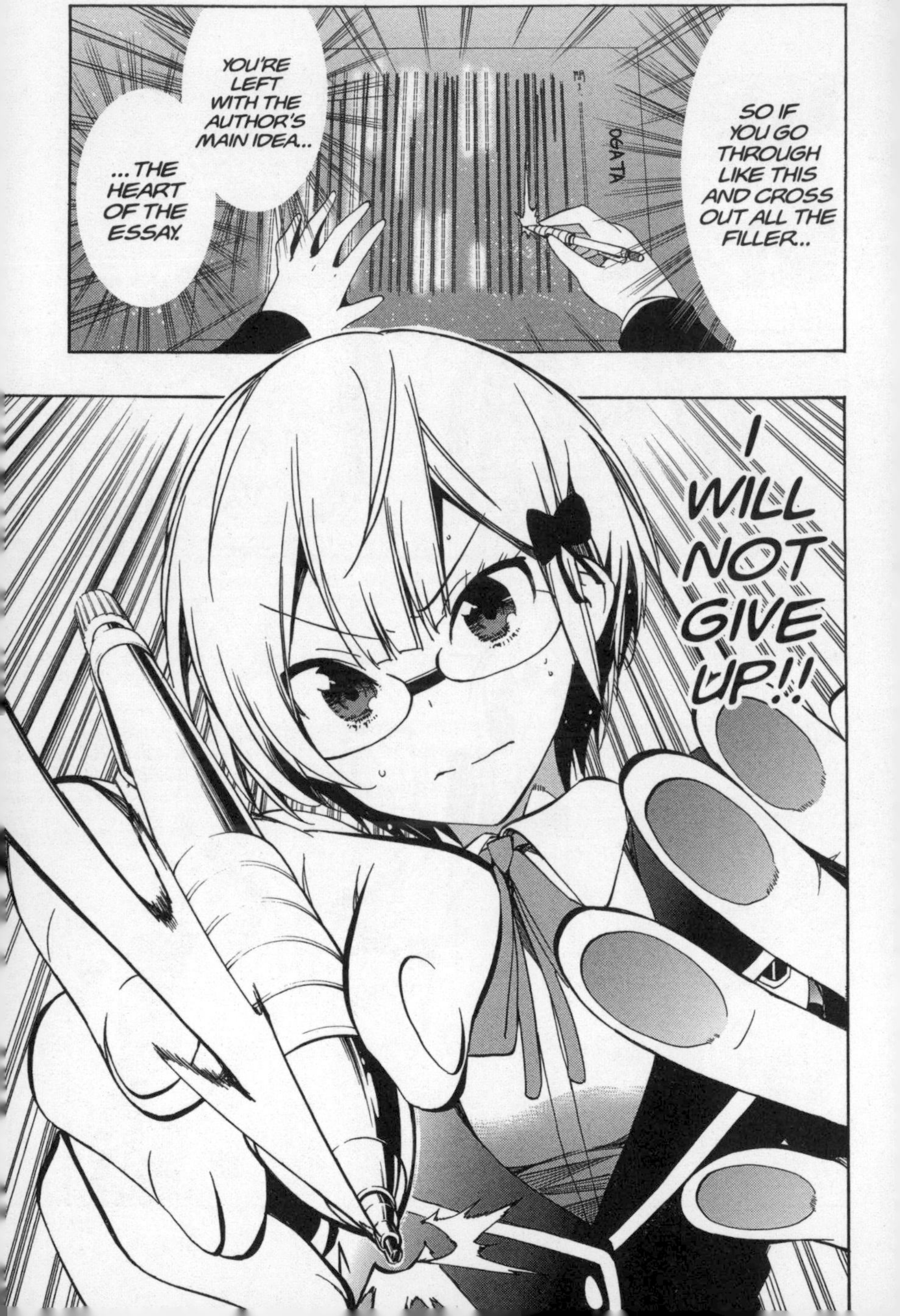
SO IF YOU GO THROUGH LIKE THIS AND CROSS OUT ALL THE FILLER...
OGATA
YOU'RE LEFT WITH THE AUTHOR'S MAIN IDEA...
...THE HEART OF THE ESSAY.
I WILL NOT GIVE UP!!

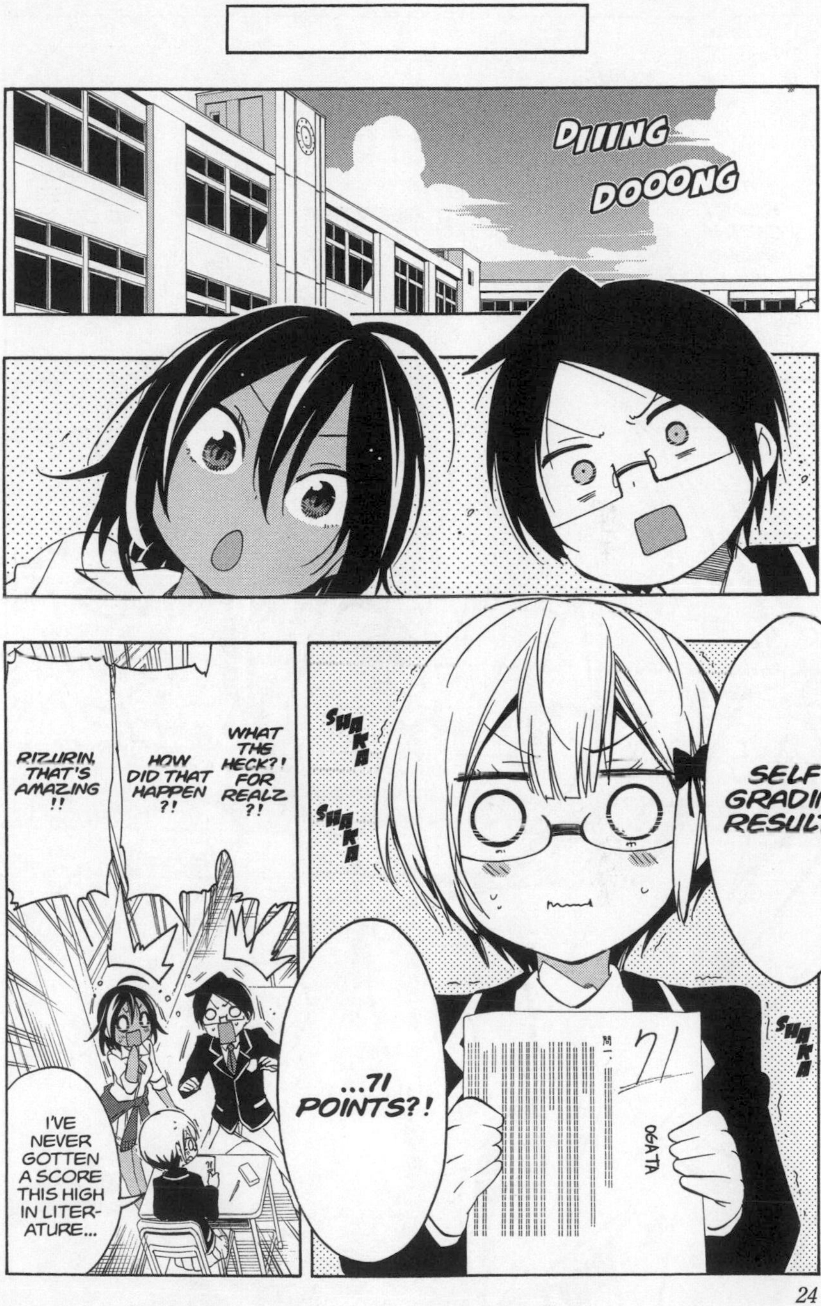
DIIING
DOOONG
SELF-GRADING RESULT...
SHAKA
SHAKA
SHAKA
...71 POINTS?!
71
OGATA
WHAT THE HECK?! FOR REALZ?!
HOW DID THAT HAPPEN?!
RIZURIN, THAT'S AMAZING!!
I'VE NEVER GOTTEN A SCORE THIS HIGH IN LITERATURE...

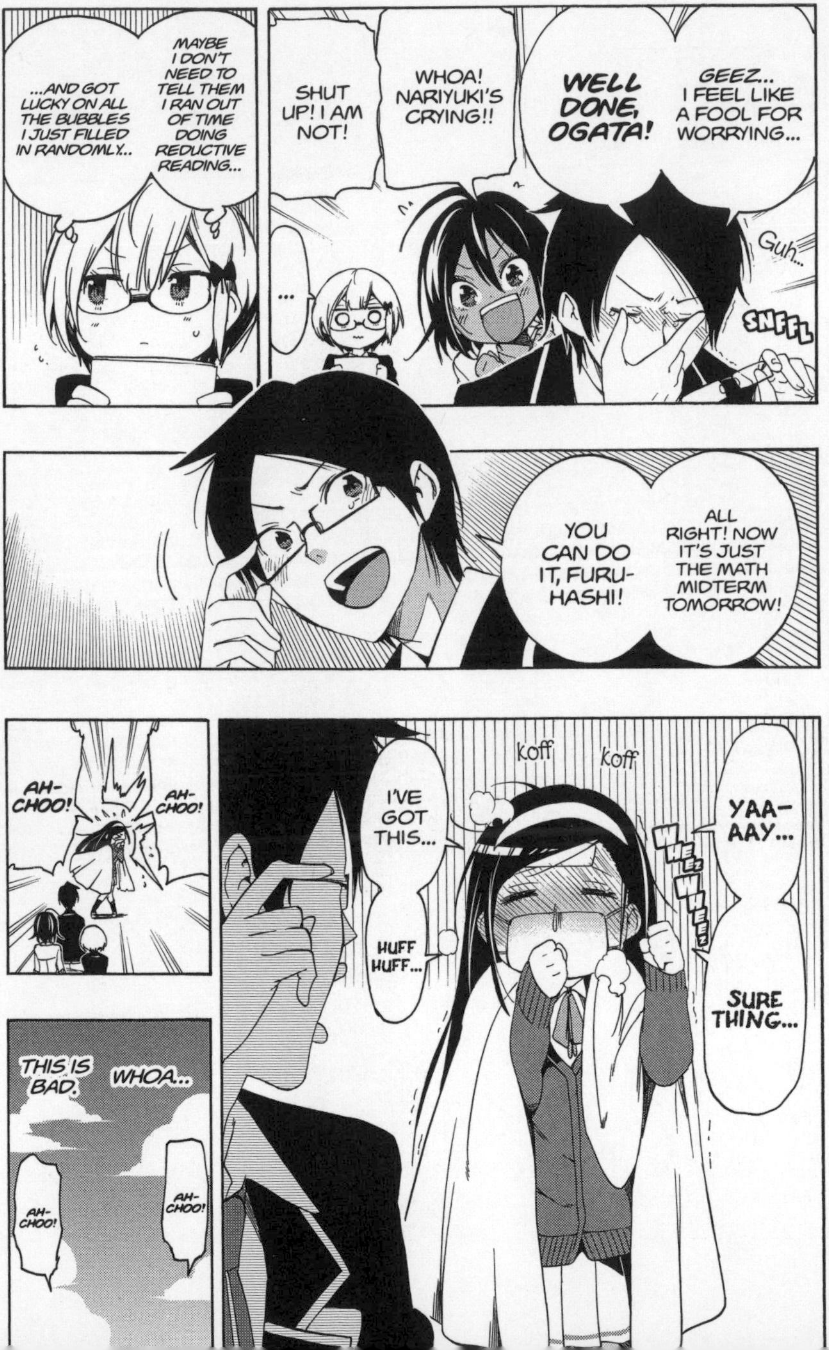
GEEZ... I FEEL LIKE A FOOL FOR WORRYING...
WELL DONE, OGATA!
WHOA! NARIYUKI'S CRYING!!
SHUT UP! I AM NOT!
Guh...
SNFFL
...
MAYBE I DON'T NEED TO TELL THEM I RAN OUT OF TIME DOING REDUCTIVE READING...
...AND GOT LUCKY ON ALL THE BUBBLES I JUST FILLED IN RANDOMLY...
ALL RIGHT! NOW IT'S JUST THE MATH MIDTERM TOMORROW!
YOU CAN DO IT, FURU-HASHI!
YAAA-AAY...
WHEEZ WHEEZ
SURE THING...
koff
koff
I'VE GOT THIS...
HUFF HUFF...
AH-CHOO!
AH-CHOO!
WHOA...
THIS IS BAD.
AH-CHOO!
AH-CHOO!

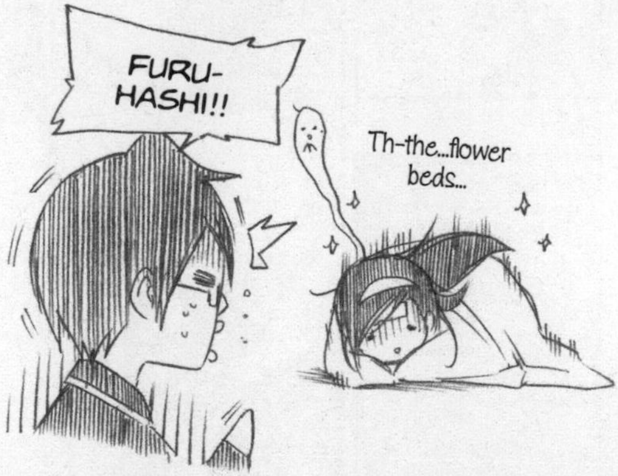
Th-the...flower beds...
FURU-HASHI!!

Question 9:
A Genius Resonates Emotionally with [*X*]?

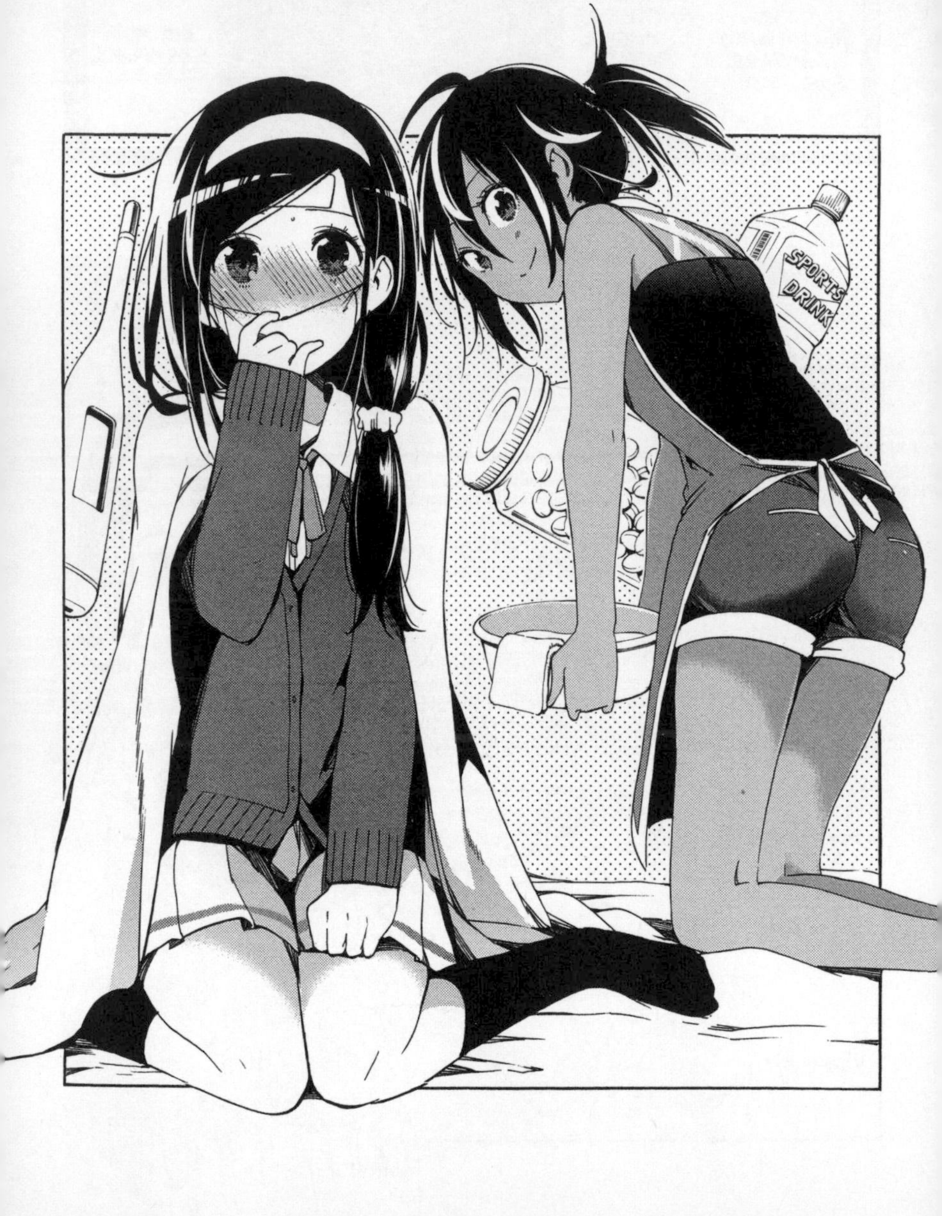
SPORTS
DRINK

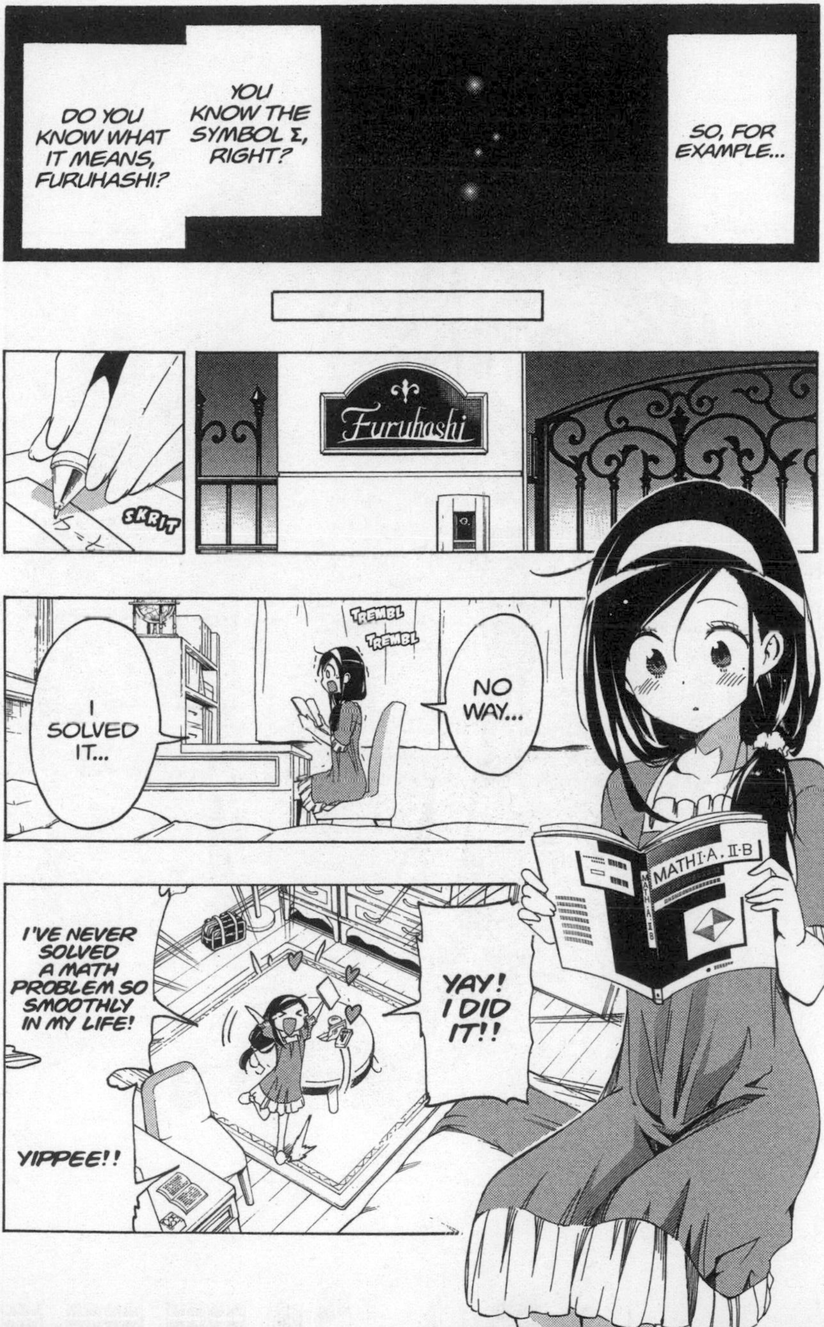
SO, FOR EXAMPLE...
YOU KNOW THE SYMBOL Σ, RIGHT?
DO YOU KNOW WHAT IT MEANS, FURUHASHI?
Furuhashi
SKRIT
MATH I·A, II·B
TREMBL
TREMBL
NO WAY...
I SOLVED IT...
YAY! I DID IT!!
I'VE NEVER SOLVED A MATH PROBLEM SO SMOOTHLY IN MY LIFE!
YIPPEE!!

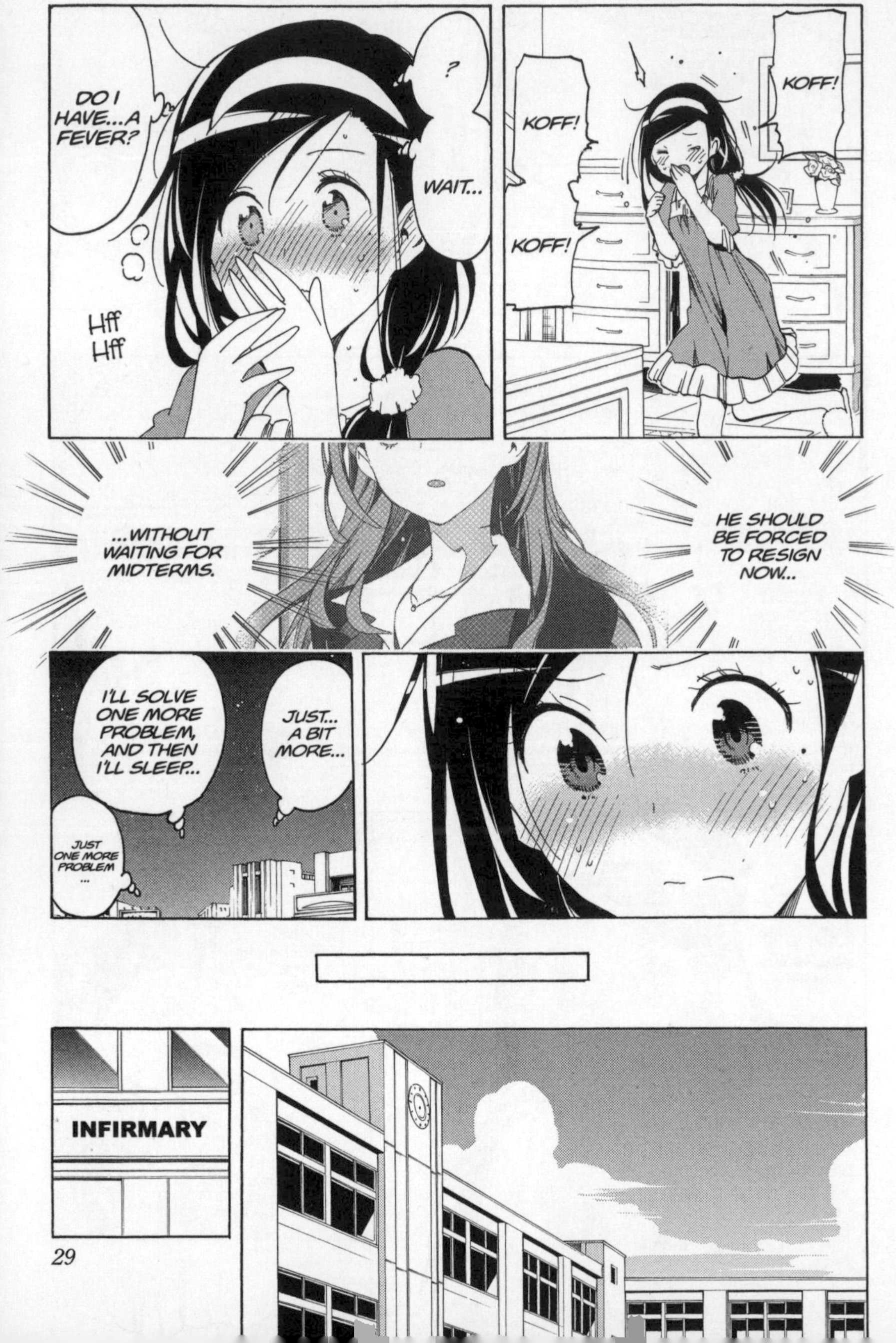
KOFF!
KOFF!
KOFF!
?
WAIT...
DO I HAVE...A FEVER?
Hff Hff
HE SHOULD BE FORCED TO RESIGN NOW...
...WITHOUT WAITING FOR MIDTERMS.
JUST... A BIT MORE...
I'LL SOLVE ONE MORE PROBLEM, AND THEN I'LL SLEEP...
JUST ONE MORE PROBLEM ...
INFIRMARY

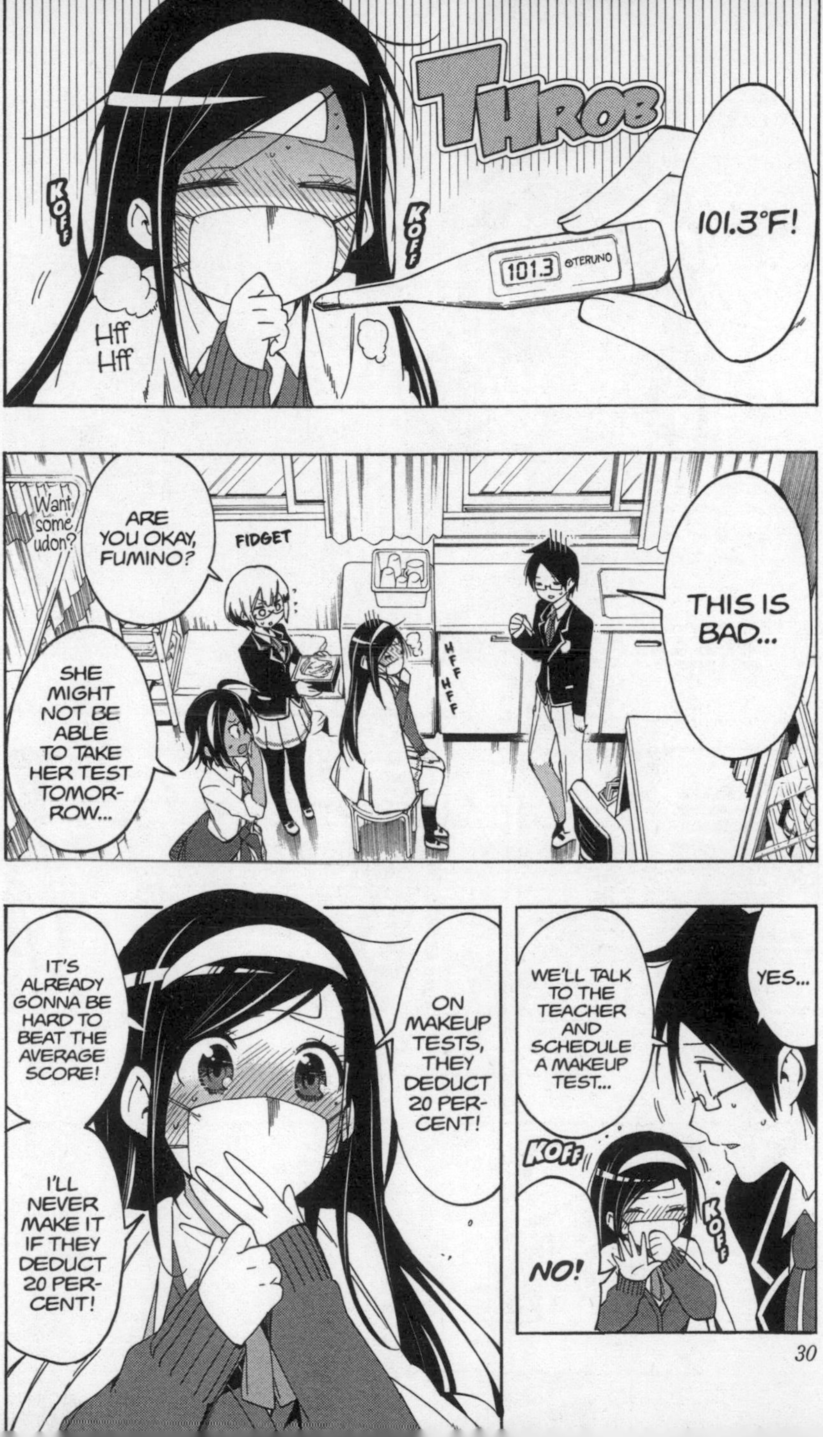
101.3°F!
THROB
101.3 ©TERUNO
KOFF
KOFF
Hff Hff
THIS IS BAD...
HFF HFF
FIDGET
ARE YOU OKAY, FUMINO?
Want some udon?
SHE MIGHT NOT BE ABLE TO TAKE HER TEST TOMORROW...
YES...
WE'LL TALK TO THE TEACHER AND SCHEDULE A MAKEUP TEST...
KOFF
KOFF
NO!
ON MAKEUP TESTS, THEY DEDUCT 20 PERCENT!
IT'S ALREADY GONNA BE HARD TO BEAT THE AVERAGE SCORE!
I'LL NEVER MAKE IT IF THEY DEDUCT 20 PERCENT!

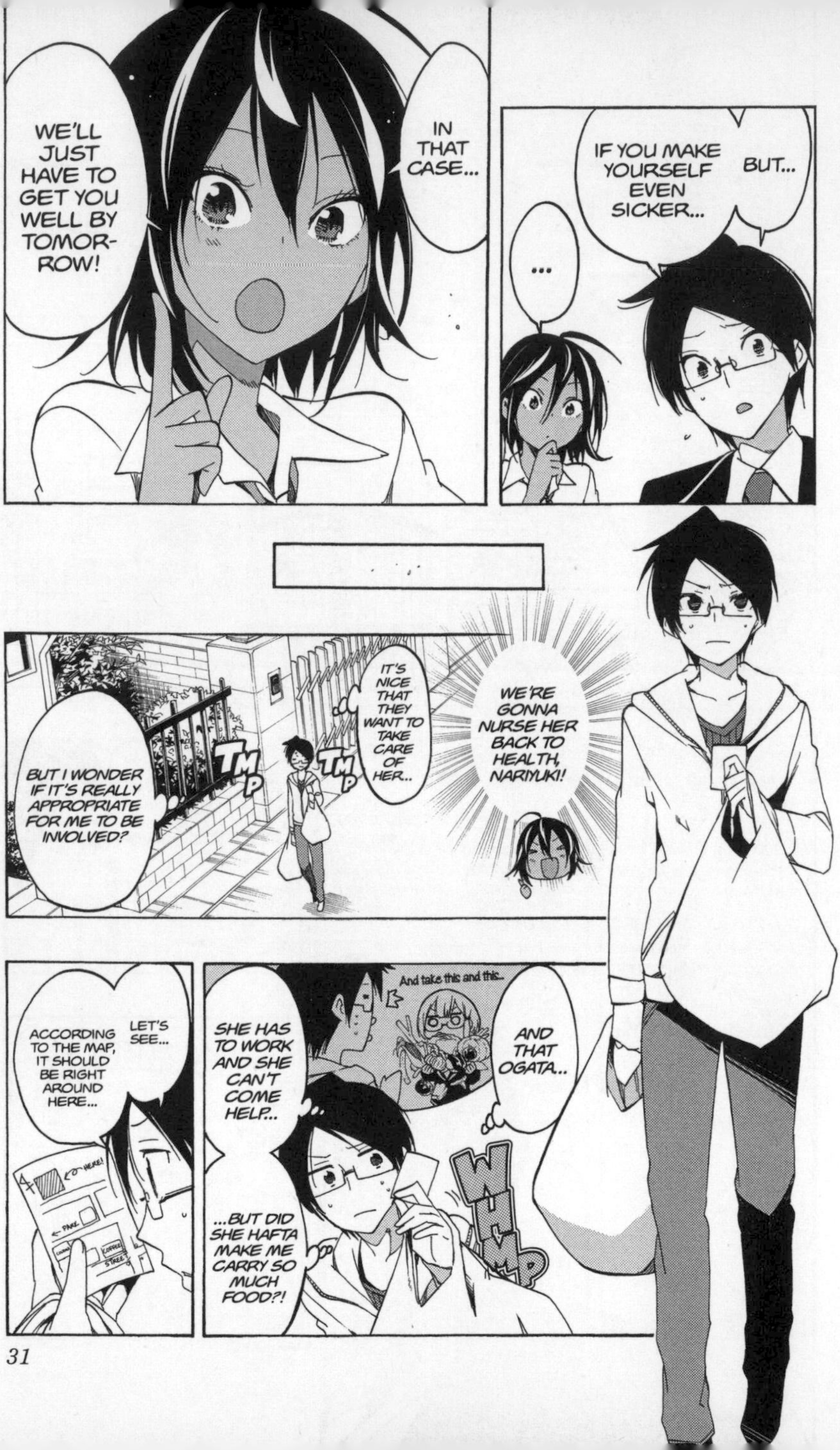

BUT...
IF YOU MAKE YOURSELF EVEN SICKER...
...
IN THAT CASE...
WE'LL JUST HAVE TO GET YOU WELL BY TOMORROW!
...
WE'RE GONNA NURSE HER BACK TO HEALTH, NARIYUKI!
IT'S NICE THAT THEY WANT TO TAKE CARE OF HER..
TMP
TMP
BUT I WONDER IF IT'S REALLY APPROPRIATE FOR ME TO BE INVOLVED?
AND THAT OGATA..
And take this and this..
SHE HAS TO WORK AND SHE CAN'T COME HELP...
WHUMP
...BUT DID SHE HAFTA MAKE ME CARRY SO MUCH FOOD?!
LET'S SEE...
ACCORDING TO THE MAP, IT SHOULD BE RIGHT AROUND HERE...
HERE!
PARK
COFFEE

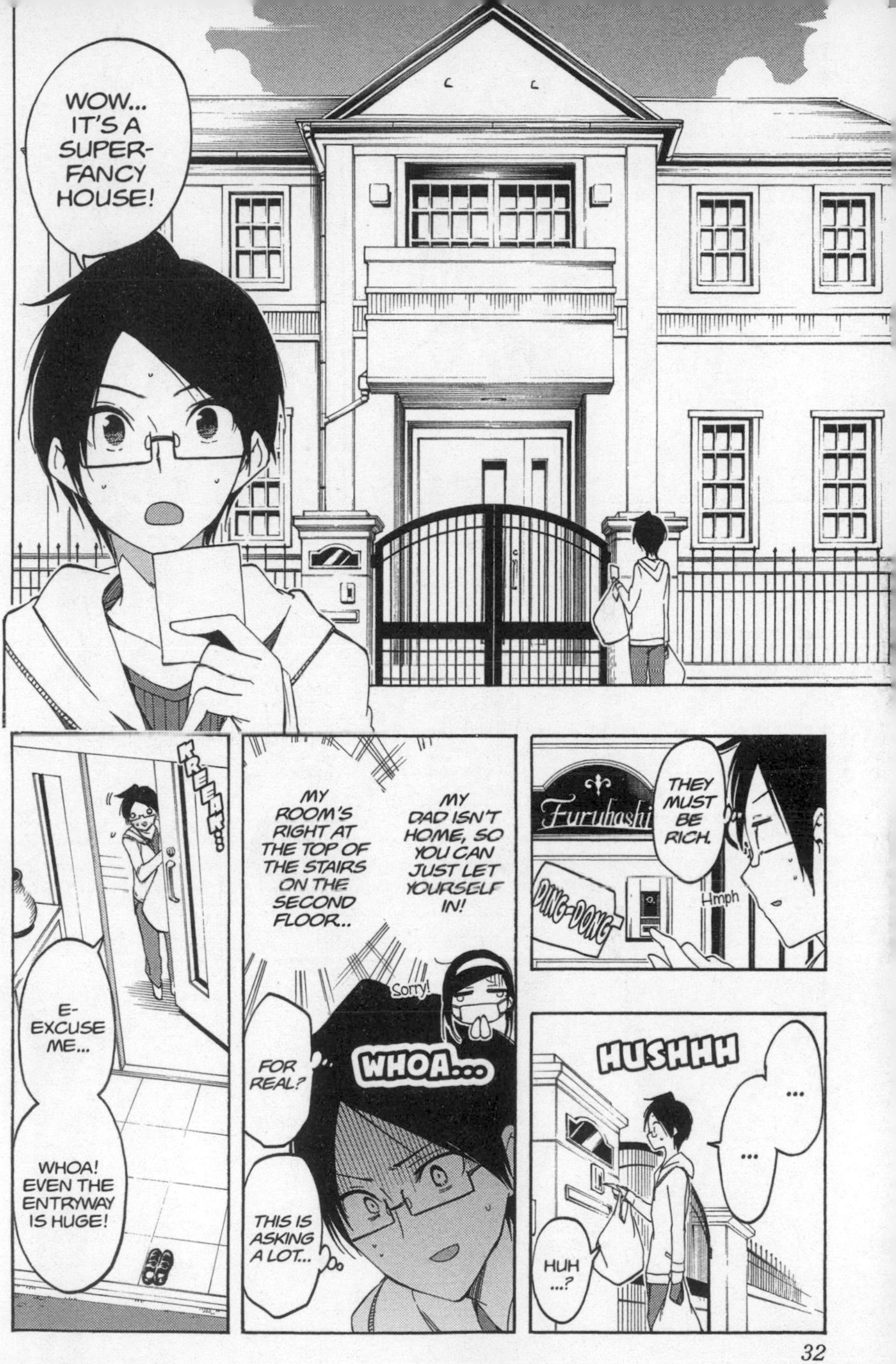
WOW... IT'S A SUPER-FANCY HOUSE!
Furuhashi
THEY MUST BE RICH.
Hmph
DING-DONG
HUSHHH
...
...
HUH ...?
MY DAD ISN'T HOME, SO YOU CAN JUST LET YOURSELF IN!
MY ROOM'S RIGHT AT THE TOP OF THE STAIRS ON THE SECOND FLOOR...
Sorry!
WHOA...
FOR REAL?
THIS IS ASKING A LOT...
KREEAK...
E-EXCUSE ME...
WHOA! EVEN THE ENTRYWAY IS HUGE!

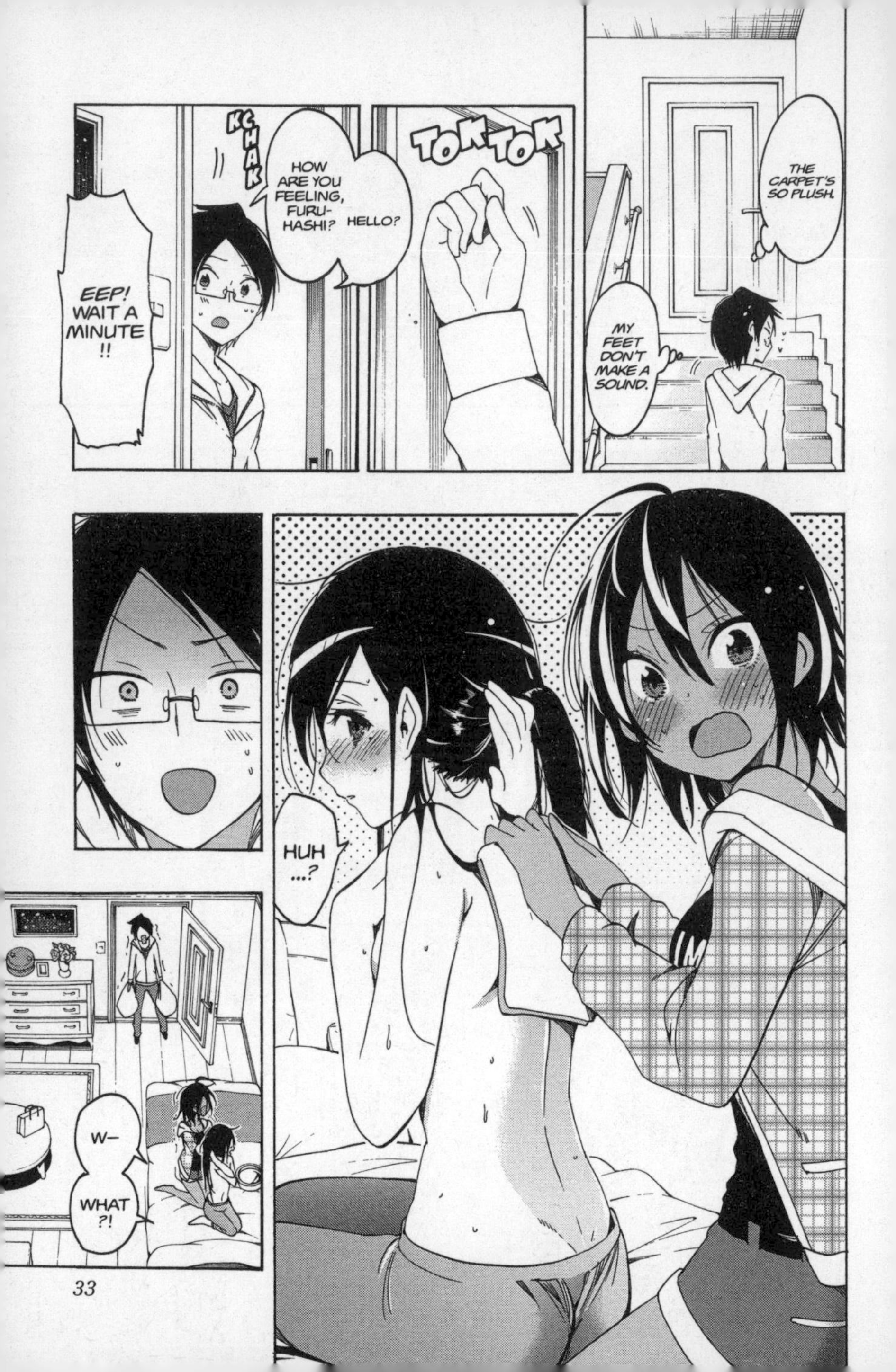
THE CARPET'S SO PLUSH.
MY FEET DON'T MAKE A SOUND.
TOK TOK
HELLO?
HOW ARE YOU FEELING, FURU-HASHI?
KCHAK
EEP! WAIT A MINUTE !!
HUH ...?
W—
WHAT ?!

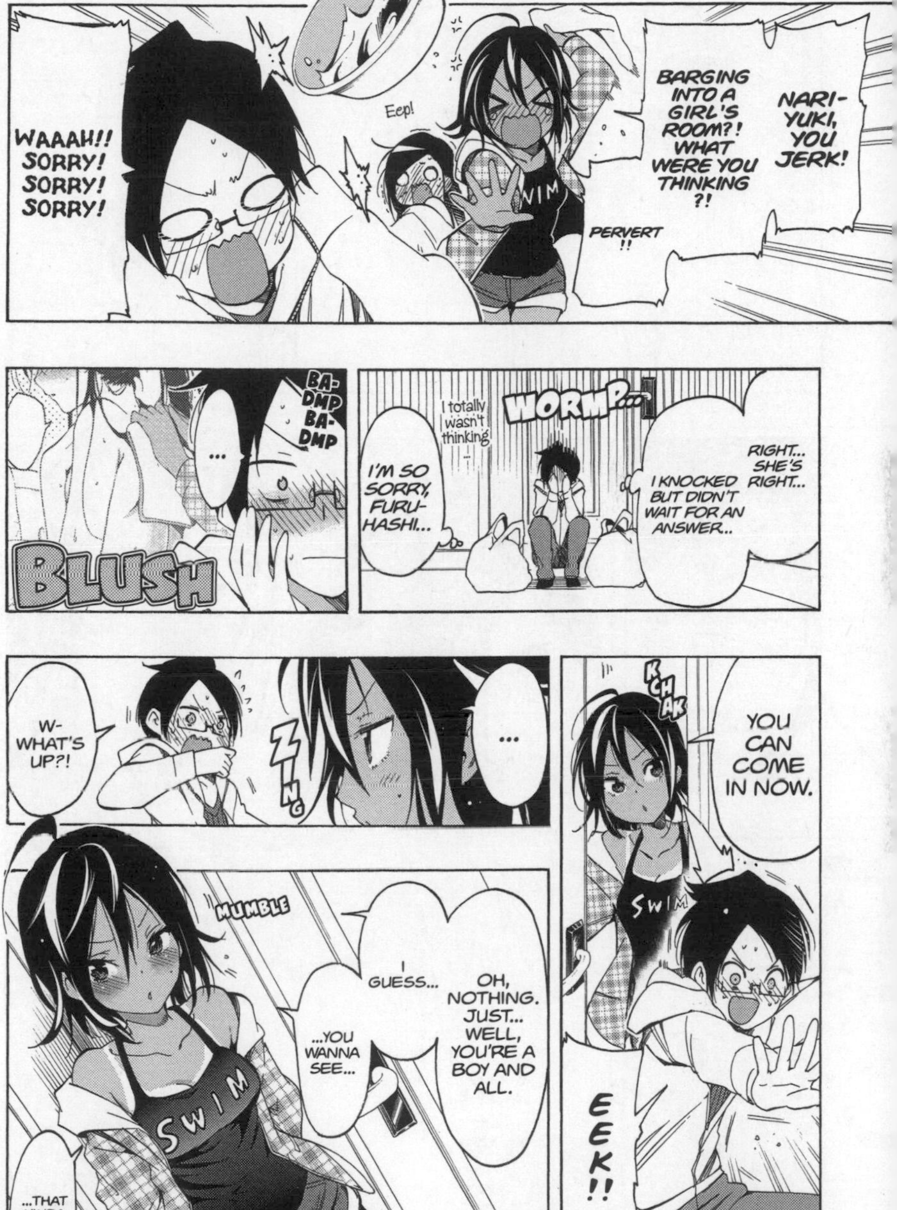
NARI-YUKI, YOU JERK!
BARGING INTO A GIRL'S ROOM?! WHAT WERE YOU THINKING ?!
PERVERT !!
Eep!
WAAAH!! SORRY! SORRY! SORRY!
RIGHT... SHE'S RIGHT...
I KNOCKED BUT DIDN'T WAIT FOR AN ANSWER...
WORMP...
I totally wasn't thinking ...
I'M SO SORRY, FURU-HASHI...
BA-DMP BA-DMP
...
BLUSH
KCHAK
YOU CAN COME IN NOW.
EEK!!
...
ZING
W-WHAT'S UP?!
OH, NOTHING. JUST... WELL, YOU'RE A BOY AND ALL.
I GUESS...
MUMBLE
...YOU WANNA SEE...
...THAT KINDA STUFF?

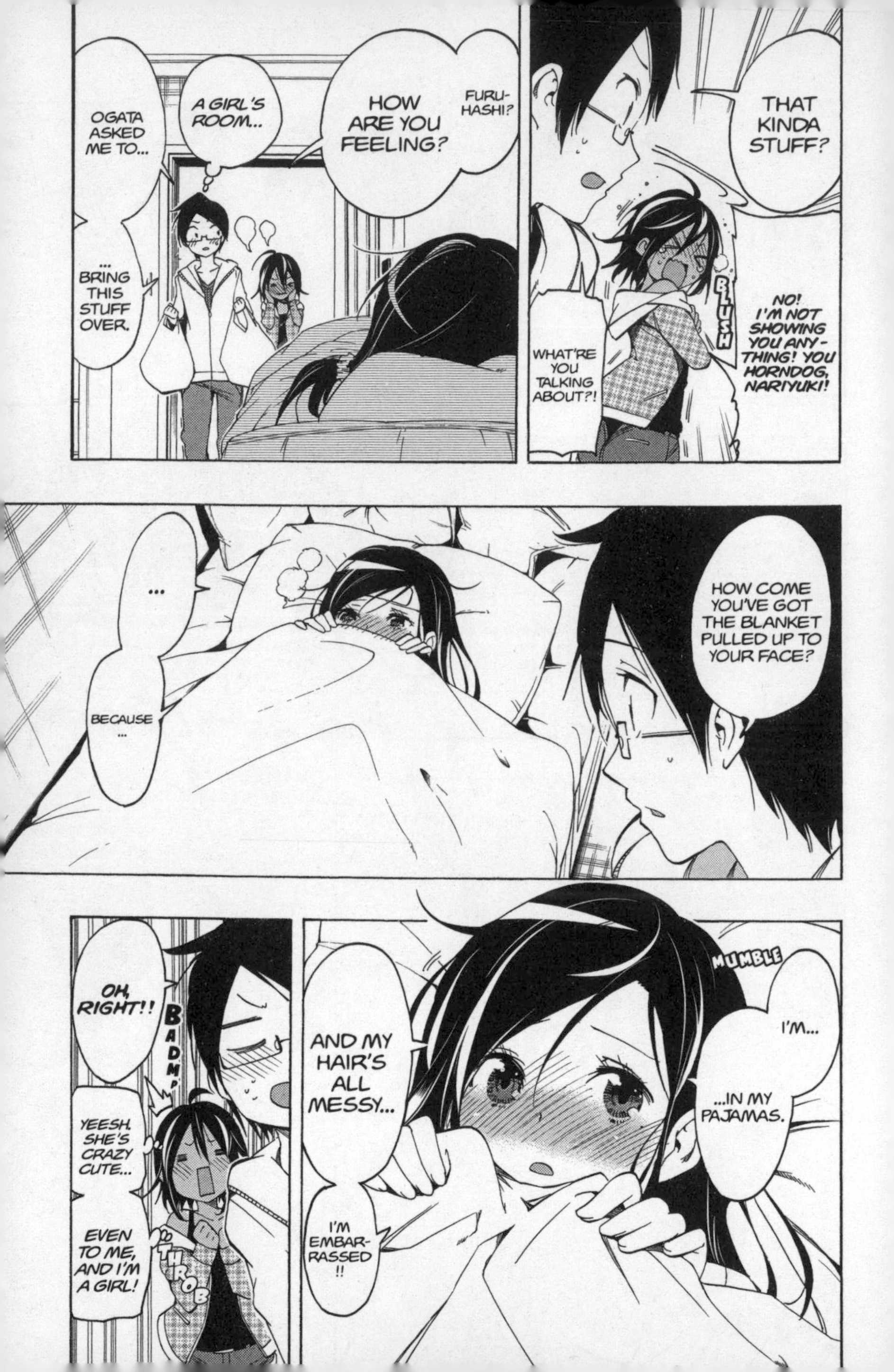
THAT KINDA STUFF?
NO! I'M NOT SHOWING YOU ANY-THING! YOU HORNDOG, NARIYUKI!
BLUSH
WHAT'RE YOU TALKING ABOUT?!
FURU-HASHI?
HOW ARE YOU FEELING?
A GIRL'S ROOM...
OGATA ASKED ME TO...
... BRING THIS STUFF OVER.
HOW COME YOU'VE GOT THE BLANKET PULLED UP TO YOUR FACE?
...
BECAUSE ...
MUMBLE
I'M...
...IN MY PAJAMAS.
AND MY HAIR'S ALL MESSY...
I'M EMBAR-RASSED!!
OH, RIGHT!!
BADMP
YEESH. SHE'S CRAZY CUTE...
EVEN TO ME, AND I'M A GIRL!
THROB

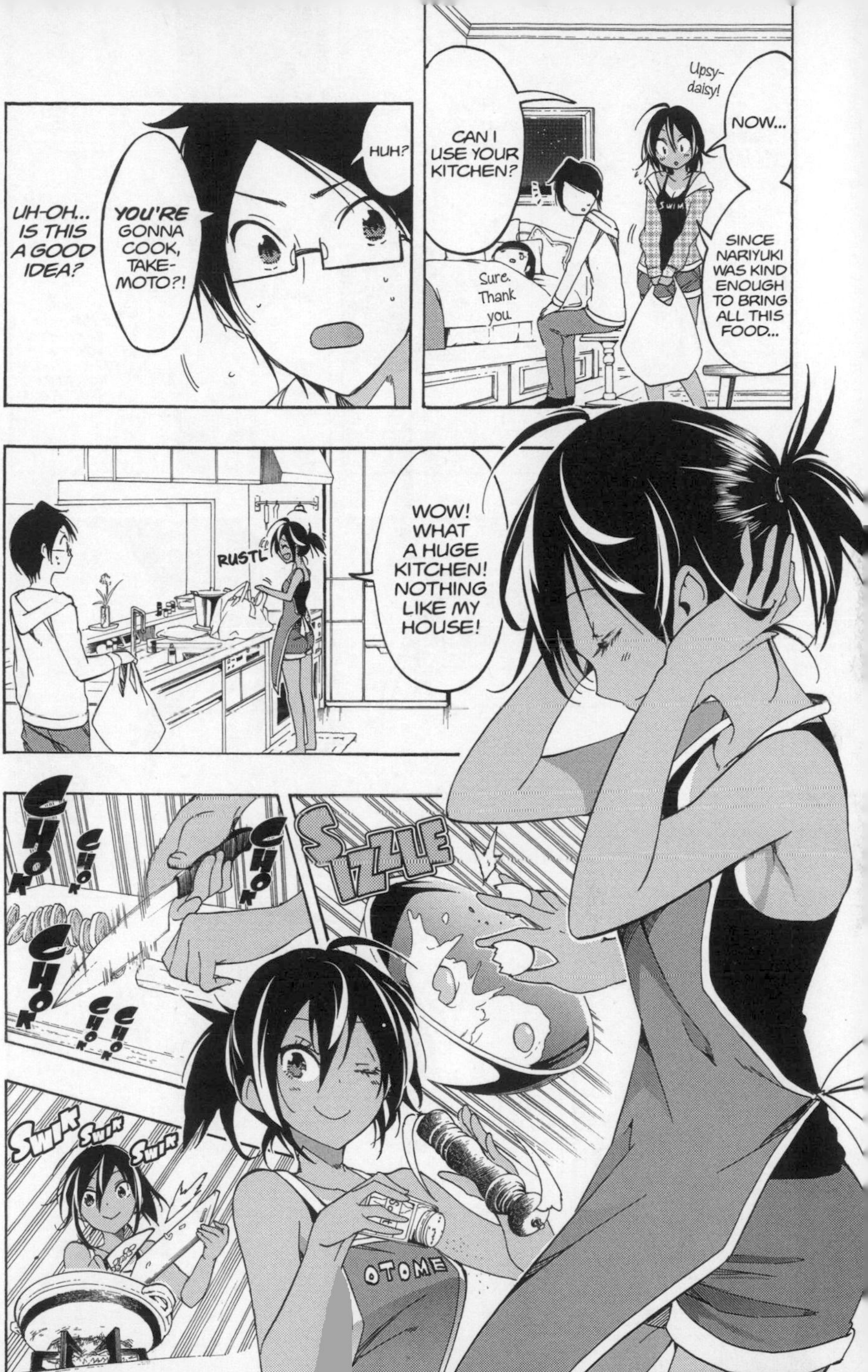
Upsy-daisy!
NOW...
SINCE NARIYUKI WAS KIND ENOUGH TO BRING ALL THIS FOOD...
CAN I USE YOUR KITCHEN?
Sure. Thank you.
HUH?
YOU'RE GONNA COOK, TAKEMOTO?!
UH-OH... IS THIS A GOOD IDEA?
WOW! WHAT A HUGE KITCHEN! NOTHING LIKE MY HOUSE!
RUSTL
SIZZLE
CHOK CHOK CHOK
CHOK CHOK CHOK CHOK
SWIR SWIR SWIR
OTOME

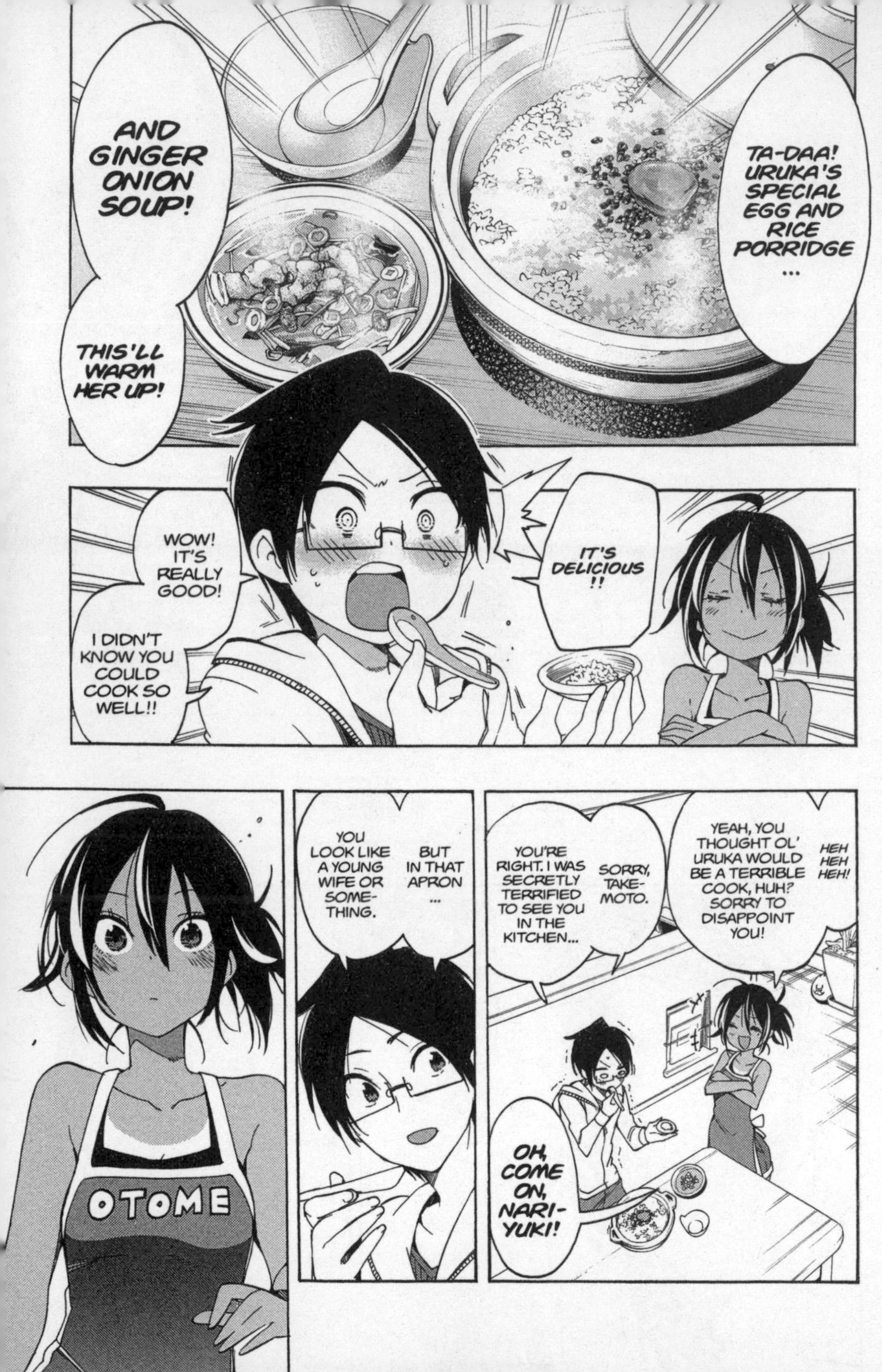
TA-DAA! URUKA'S SPECIAL EGG AND RICE PORRIDGE ...
AND GINGER ONION SOUP!
THIS'LL WARM HER UP!
IT'S DELICIOUS !!
WOW! IT'S REALLY GOOD!
I DIDN'T KNOW YOU COULD COOK SO WELL!!
YEAH, YOU THOUGHT OL' URUKA WOULD BE A TERRIBLE COOK, HUH? SORRY TO DISAPPOINT YOU!
HEH HEH HEH!
SORRY, TAKE-MOTO.
YOU'RE RIGHT. I WAS SECRETLY TERRIFIED TO SEE YOU IN THE KITCHEN...
OH, COME ON, NARI-YUKI!
BUT IN THAT APRON ...
YOU LOOK LIKE A YOUNG WIFE OR SOME-THING.
OTOME

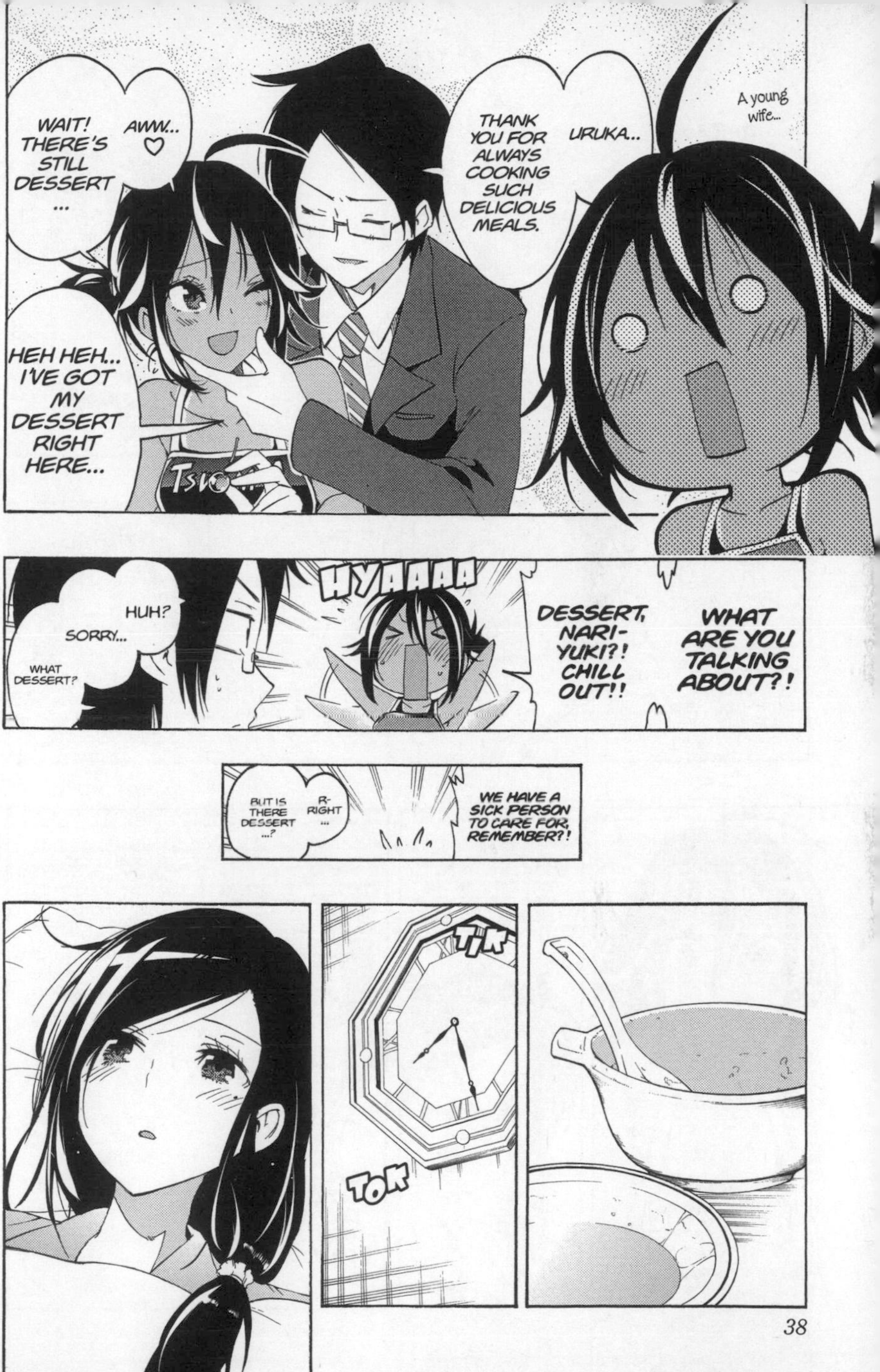
A young wife...
URUKA...
THANK YOU FOR ALWAYS COOKING SUCH DELICIOUS MEALS.
AWW... ♡
WAIT! THERE'S STILL DESSERT...
HEH HEH... I'VE GOT MY DESSERT RIGHT HERE...
WHAT ARE YOU TALKING ABOUT?!
DESSERT, NARI-YUKI?! CHILL OUT!!
HYAAAA
HUH?
SORRY...
WHAT DESSERT?
WE HAVE A SICK PERSON TO CARE FOR, REMEMBER?!
R-RIGHT...
BUT IS THERE DESSERT...?
TIK
TOK

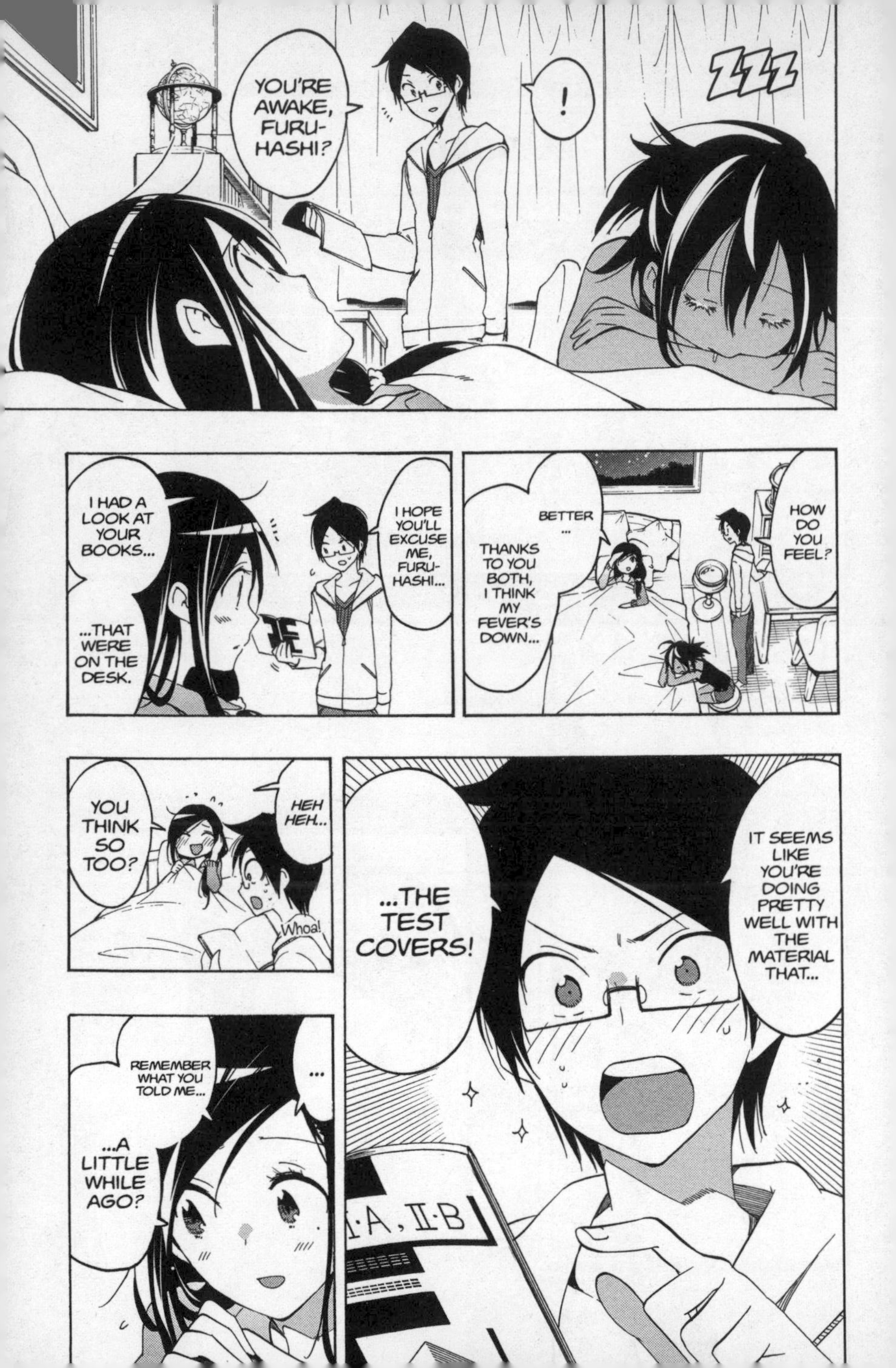
ZZZ
!
YOU'RE AWAKE, FURUHASHI?
HOW DO YOU FEEL?
BETTER ...
THANKS TO YOU BOTH, I THINK MY FEVER'S DOWN...
I HOPE YOU'LL EXCUSE ME, FURUHASHI...
I HAD A LOOK AT YOUR BOOKS...
...THAT WERE ON THE DESK.
IT SEEMS LIKE YOU'RE DOING PRETTY WELL WITH THE MATERIAL THAT...
...THE TEST COVERS!
I·A, II·B
HEH HEH...
YOU THINK SO TOO?
Whoa!
...
REMEMBER WHAT YOU TOLD ME...
...A LITTLE WHILE AGO?

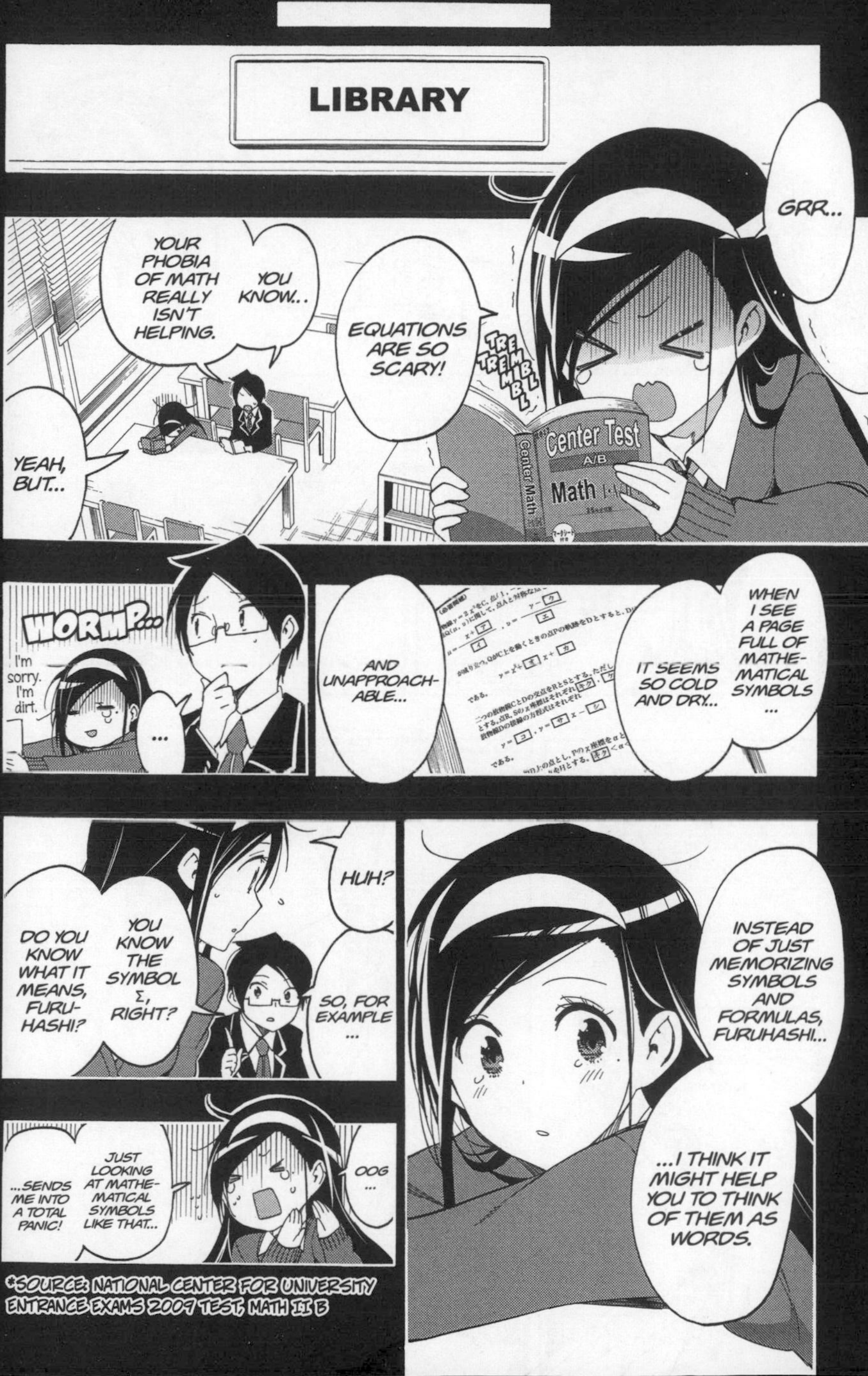
LIBRARY
GRR...
TREMBL TREMBL
EQUATIONS ARE SO SCARY!
Center Test A/B Math
Center Math
YOU KNOW...
YOUR PHOBIA OF MATH REALLY ISN'T HELPING.
YEAH, BUT...
WHEN I SEE A PAGE FULL OF MATHE-MATICAL SYMBOLS...
IT SEEMS SO COLD AND DRY...
AND UNAPPROACH-ABLE...
WORMP...
I'm sorry. I'm dirt.
...
INSTEAD OF JUST MEMORIZING SYMBOLS AND FORMULAS, FURUHASHI...
...I THINK IT MIGHT HELP YOU TO THINK OF THEM AS WORDS.
HUH?
SO, FOR EXAMPLE...
YOU KNOW THE SYMBOL Σ, RIGHT?
DO YOU KNOW WHAT IT MEANS, FURU-HASHI?
OOG...
JUST LOOKING AT MATHE-MATICAL SYMBOLS LIKE THAT...
...SENDS ME INTO A TOTAL PANIC!

*SOURCE: NATIONAL CENTER FOR UNIVERSITY ENTRANCE EXAMS 2009 TEST, MATH II B

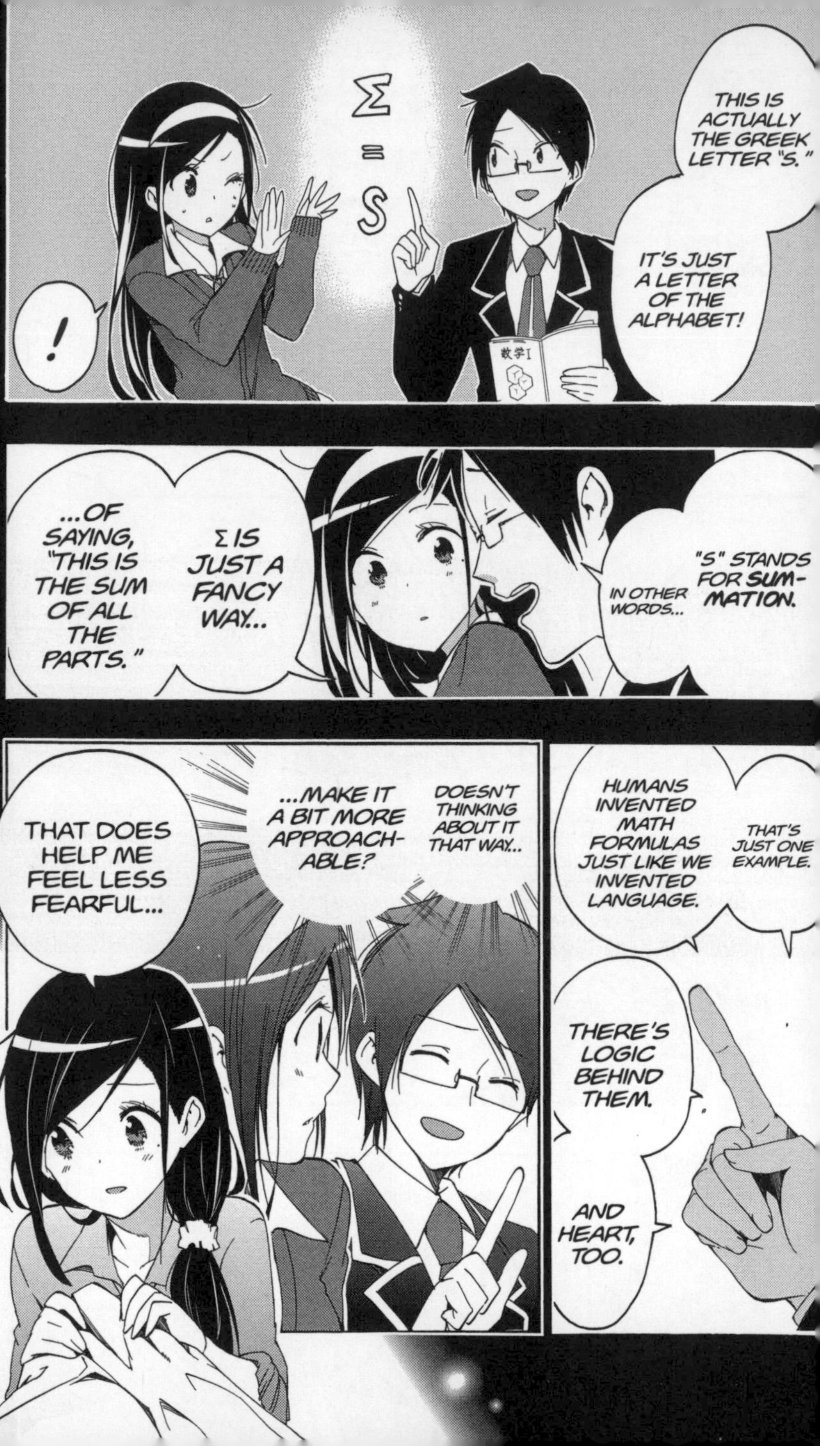
THIS IS ACTUALLY THE GREEK LETTER "S."
IT'S JUST A LETTER OF THE ALPHABET!
数学I
Σ = S
!
"S" STANDS FOR **SUMMATION.**
IN OTHER WORDS...
Σ IS JUST A FANCY WAY...
...OF SAYING, "THIS IS THE SUM OF ALL THE PARTS."
THAT'S JUST ONE EXAMPLE.
HUMANS INVENTED MATH FORMULAS JUST LIKE WE INVENTED LANGUAGE.
THERE'S LOGIC BEHIND THEM.
AND HEART, TOO.
DOESN'T THINKING ABOUT IT THAT WAY...
...MAKE IT A BIT MORE APPROACHABLE?
THAT DOES HELP ME FEEL LESS FEARFUL...

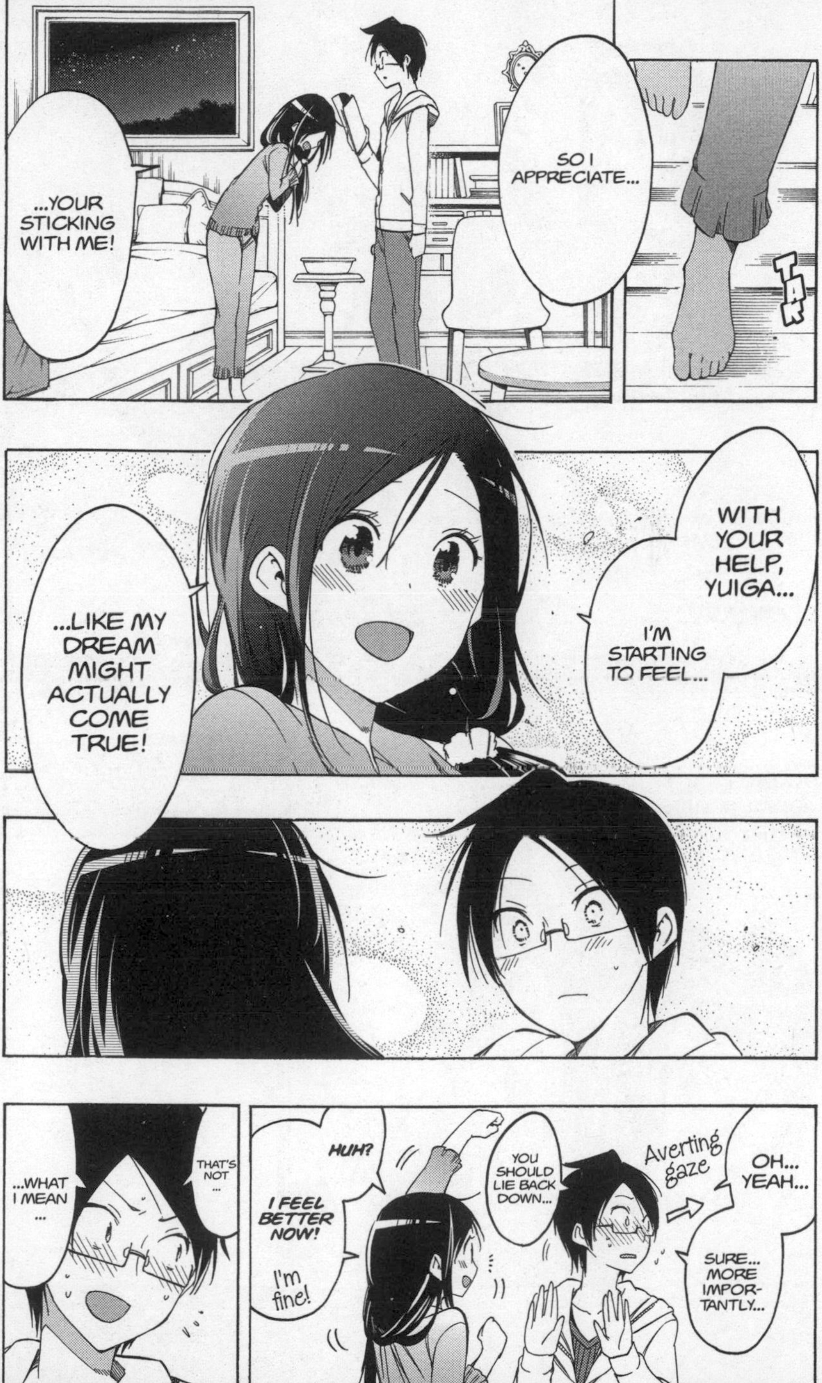
TAK
SO I APPRECIATE...
...YOUR STICKING WITH ME!
WITH YOUR HELP, YUIGA...
I'M STARTING TO FEEL...
...LIKE MY DREAM MIGHT ACTUALLY COME TRUE!
OH... YEAH...
Averting gaze
SURE... MORE IMPORTANTLY...
YOU SHOULD LIE BACK DOWN...
HUH?
I FEEL BETTER NOW!
I'm fine!
THAT'S NOT ...
...WHAT I MEAN ...

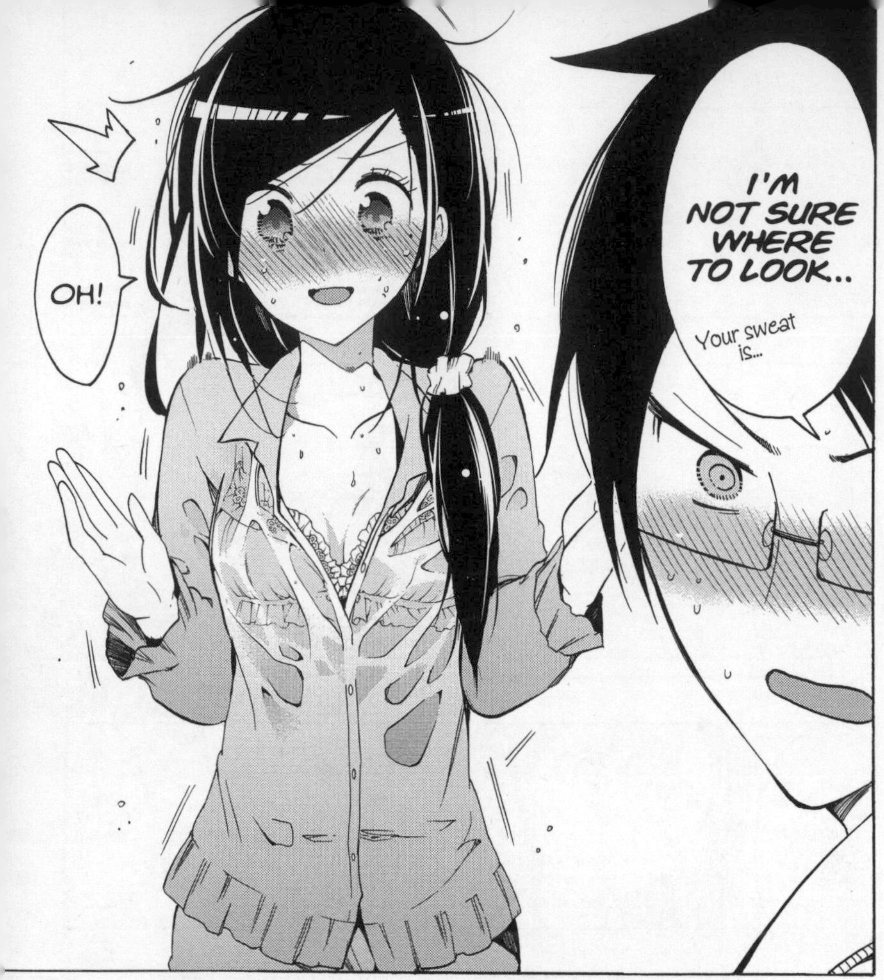
I'M NOT SURE WHERE TO LOOK...
Your sweat is...
OH!

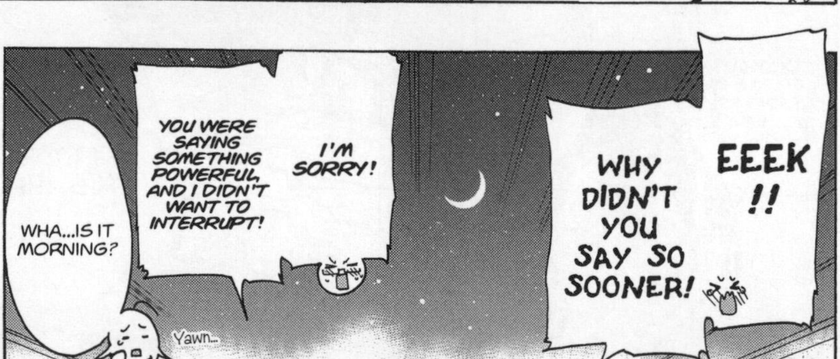
EEEK !!
WHY DIDN'T YOU SAY SO SOONER!
I'M SORRY!
YOU WERE SAYING SOMETHING POWERFUL, AND I DIDN'T WANT TO INTERRUPT!
WHA...IS IT MORNING?
Yawn...

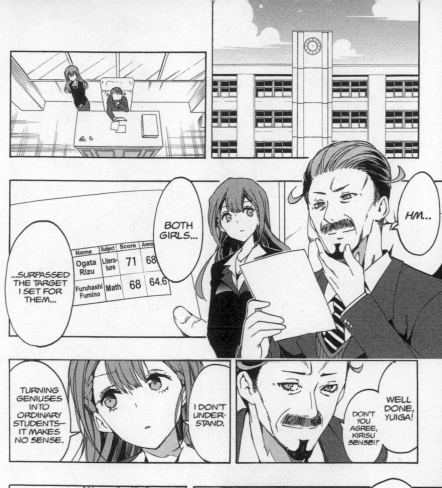

BOTH GIRLS...

...SURPASSED THE TARGET I SET FOR THEM...

Name	Subject	Score	Avera
Ogata Rizu	Literature	71	68
Furuhashi Fumino	Math	68	64.6

HM...

TURNING GENIUSES INTO ORDINARY STUDENTS— IT MAKES NO SENSE.

I DON'T UNDERSTAND.

DON'T YOU AGREE, KIRISU SENSEI?!

WELL DONE, YUIGA!

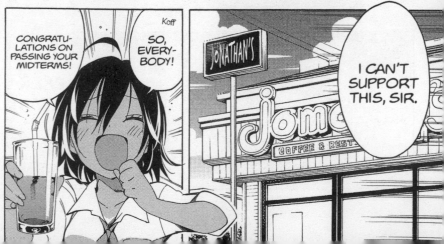

CONGRATULATIONS ON PASSING YOUR MIDTERMS!

Koff

SO, EVERYBODY!

I CAN'T SUPPORT THIS, SIR.

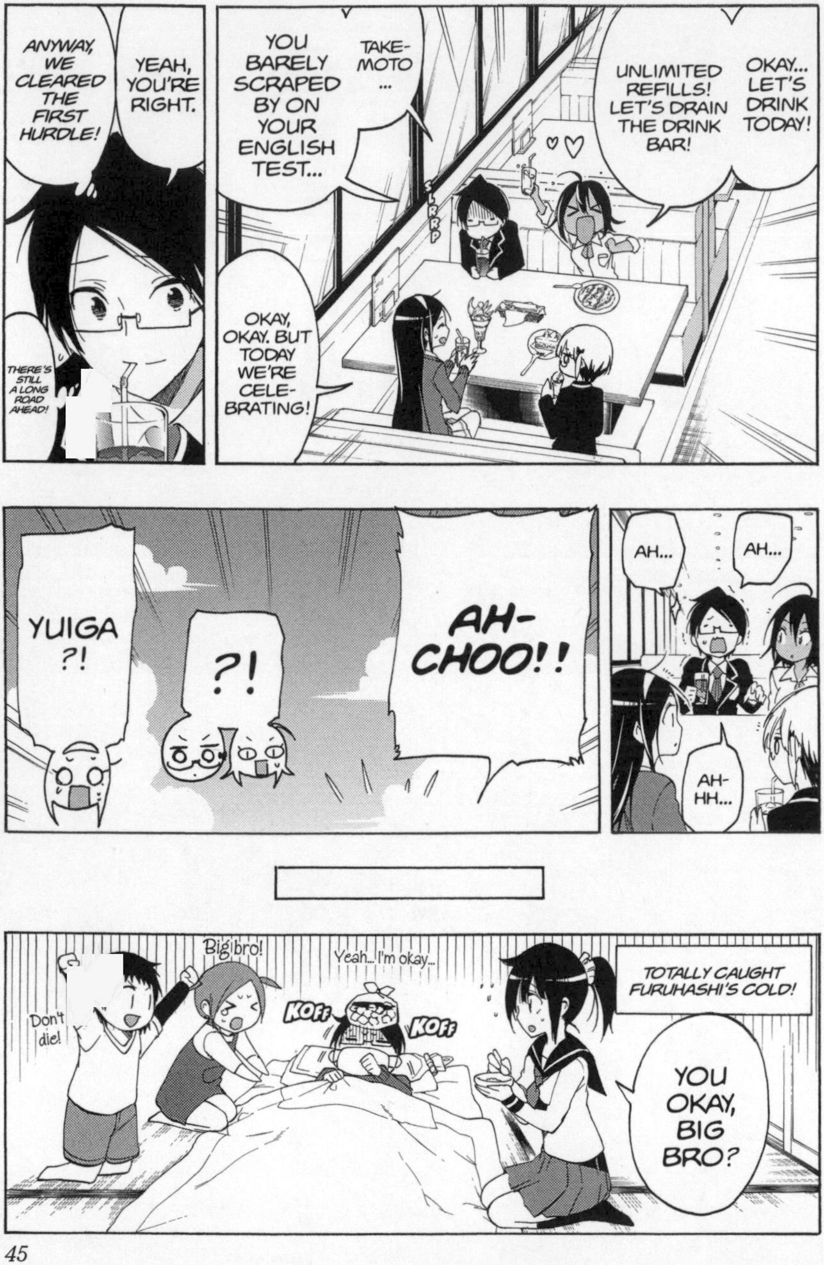
OKAY... LET'S DRINK TODAY!
UNLIMITED REFILLS! LET'S DRAIN THE DRINK BAR!
TAKE-MOTO ...
YOU BARELY SCRAPED BY ON YOUR ENGLISH TEST...
SLRRP
OKAY, OKAY. BUT TODAY WE'RE CELE-BRATING!
YEAH, YOU'RE RIGHT.
ANYWAY, WE CLEARED THE FIRST HURDLE!
THERE'S STILL A LONG ROAD AHEAD!
AH...
AH...
AH-HH...
AH-CHOO!!
?!
YUIGA ?!
TOTALLY CAUGHT FURUHASHI'S COLD!
YOU OKAY, BIG BRO?
KOFF
Yeah... I'm okay...
KOFF
Big bro!
Don't die!

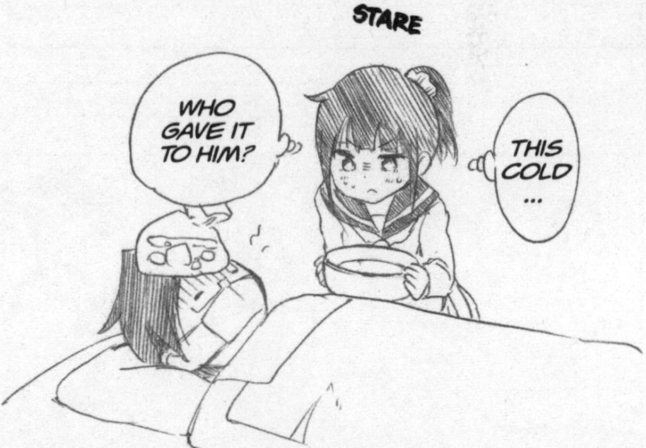
STARE
THIS COLD ...
WHO GAVE IT TO HIM?

Question 10: A Maiden Is to Genius as [X] Is to Once a Day?

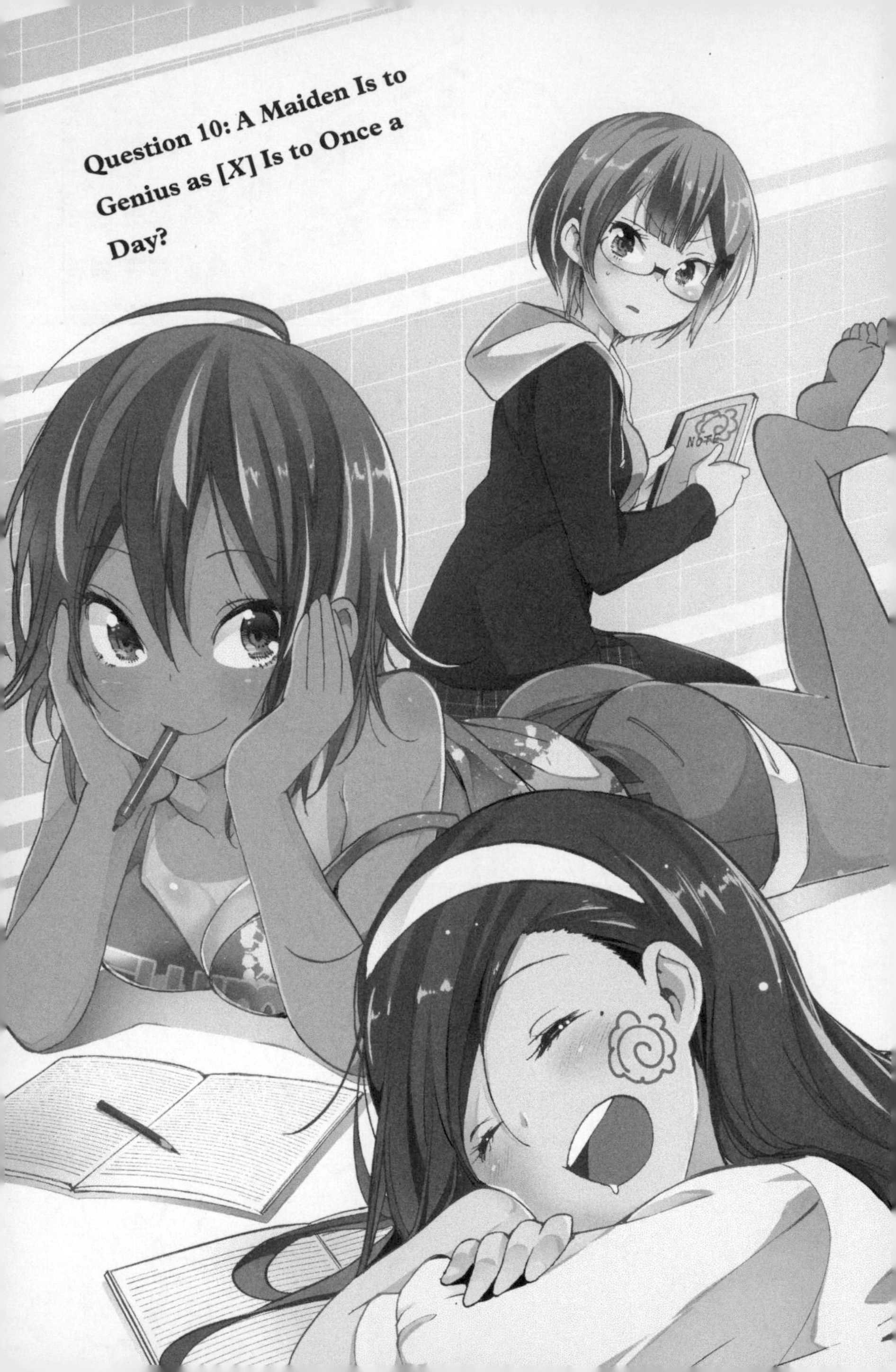
NOTE

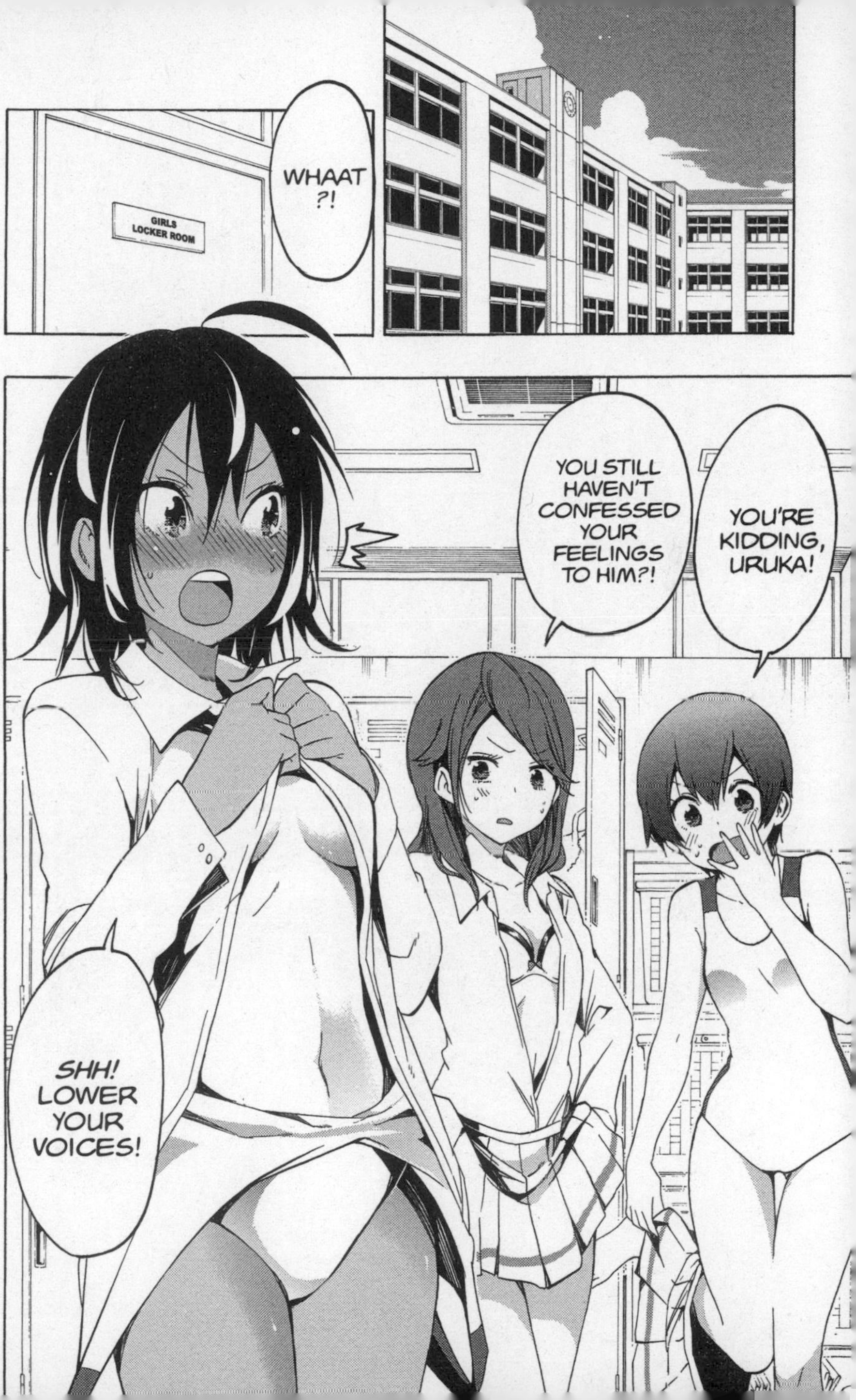
GIRLS LOCKER ROOM
WHAAT ?!
YOU'RE KIDDING, URUKA!
YOU STILL HAVEN'T CONFESSED YOUR FEELINGS TO HIM?!
SHH! LOWER YOUR VOICES!

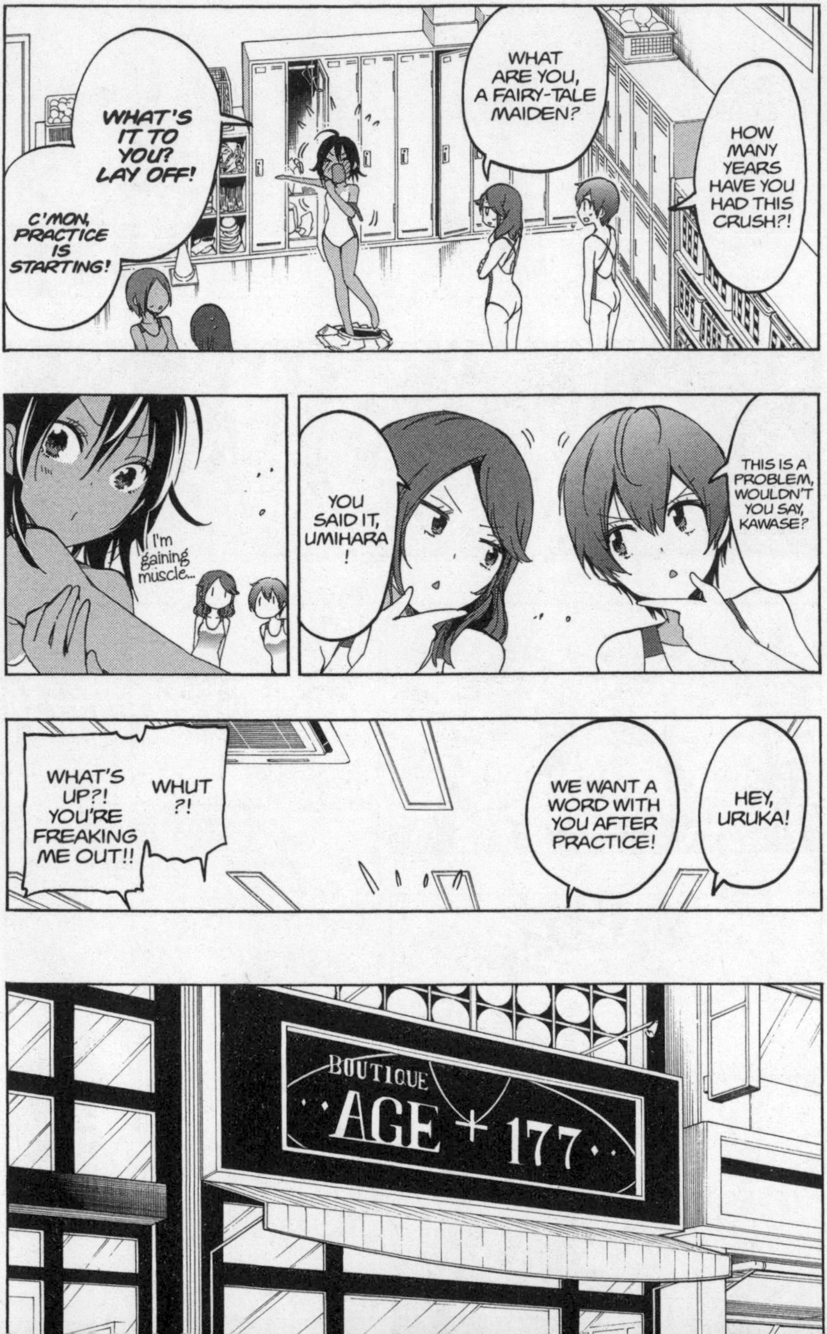
HOW MANY YEARS HAVE YOU HAD THIS CRUSH?!
WHAT ARE YOU, A FAIRY-TALE MAIDEN?
WHAT'S IT TO YOU? LAY OFF!
C'MON, PRACTICE IS STARTING!
THIS IS A PROBLEM, WOULDN'T YOU SAY, KAWASE?
YOU SAID IT, UMIHARA!
I'm gaining muscle...
HEY, URUKA!
WE WANT A WORD WITH YOU AFTER PRACTICE!
WHUT?!
WHAT'S UP?! YOU'RE FREAKING ME OUT!!
BOUTIQUE
AGE + 177

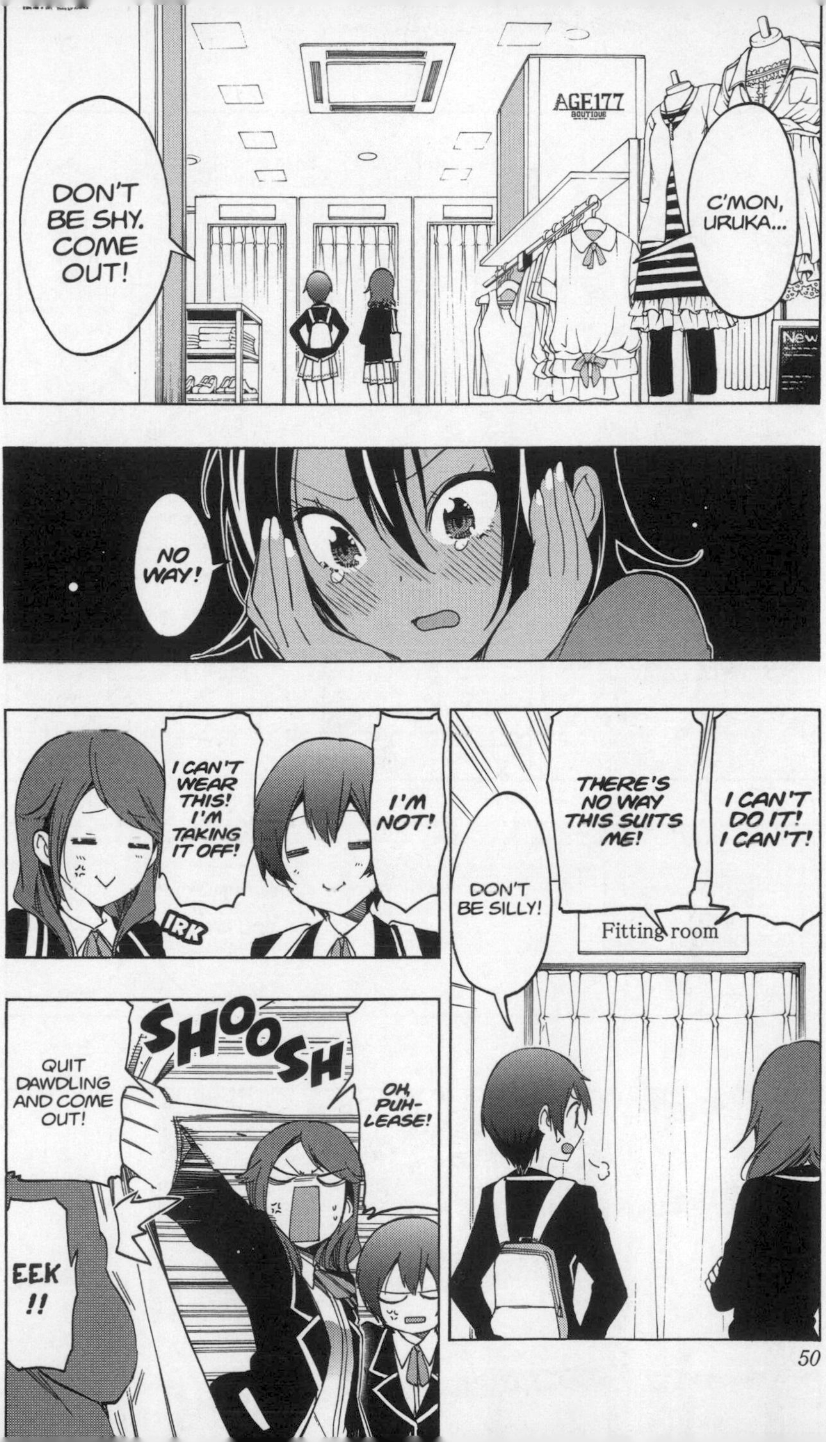
AGE177
BOUTIQUE
C'MON, URUKA...
New
DON'T BE SHY. COME OUT!
NO WAY!
I CAN'T DO IT! I CAN'T!
THERE'S NO WAY THIS SUITS ME!
DON'T BE SILLY!
Fitting room
I'M NOT!
I CAN'T WEAR THIS! I'M TAKING IT OFF!
IRK
SHOOSH
OH, PUH-LEASE!
QUIT DAWDLING AND COME OUT!
EEK !!

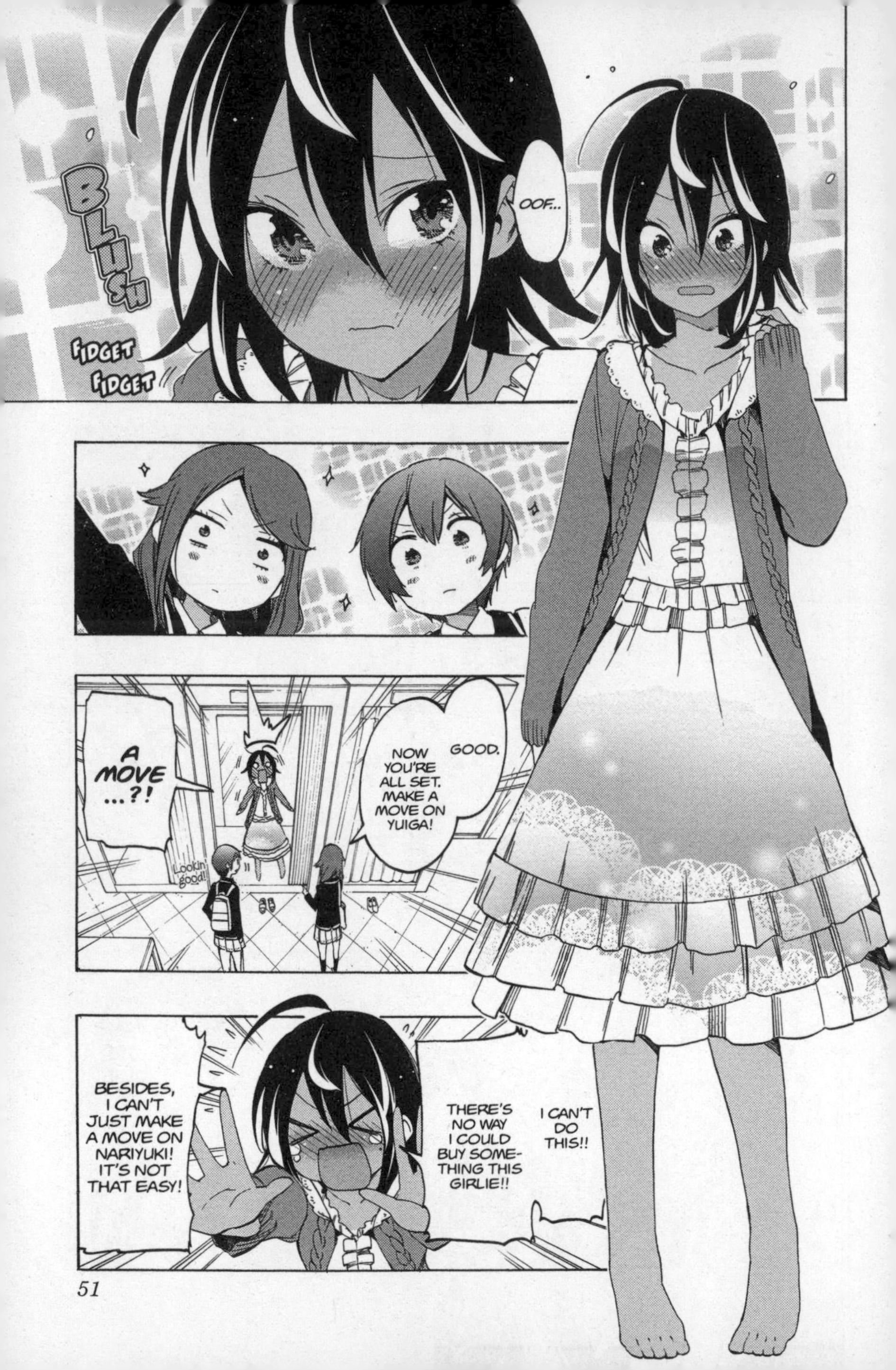
OOF...
BLUSH
FIDGET FIDGET
GOOD.
NOW YOU'RE ALL SET. MAKE A MOVE ON YUIGA!
Lookin' good!
A MOVE ...?!
I CAN'T DO THIS!!
THERE'S NO WAY I COULD BUY SOME-THING THIS GIRLIE!!
BESIDES, I CAN'T JUST MAKE A MOVE ON NARIYUKI! IT'S NOT THAT EASY!

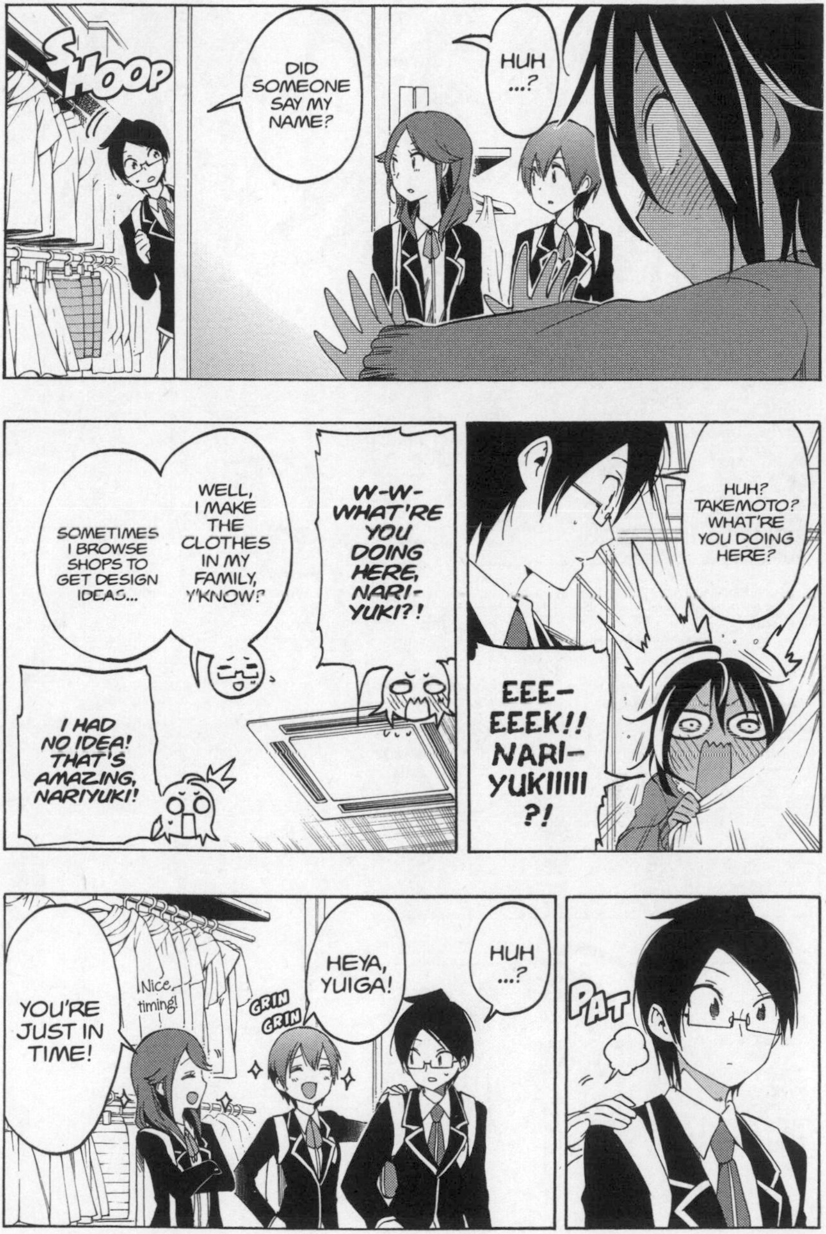
HUH ...?
DID SOMEONE SAY MY NAME?
SHOOP
HUH? TAKEMOTO? WHAT'RE YOU DOING HERE?
EEE-EEEK!! NARI-YUKIIIIII ?!
W-W-WHAT'RE YOU DOING HERE, NARI-YUKI?!
WELL, I MAKE THE CLOTHES IN MY FAMILY, Y'KNOW?
SOMETIMES I BROWSE SHOPS TO GET DESIGN IDEAS...
I HAD NO IDEA! THAT'S AMAZING, NARIYUKI!
PAT
HUH ...?
HEYA, YUIGA!
GRIN GRIN
Nice, timing!
YOU'RE JUST IN TIME!

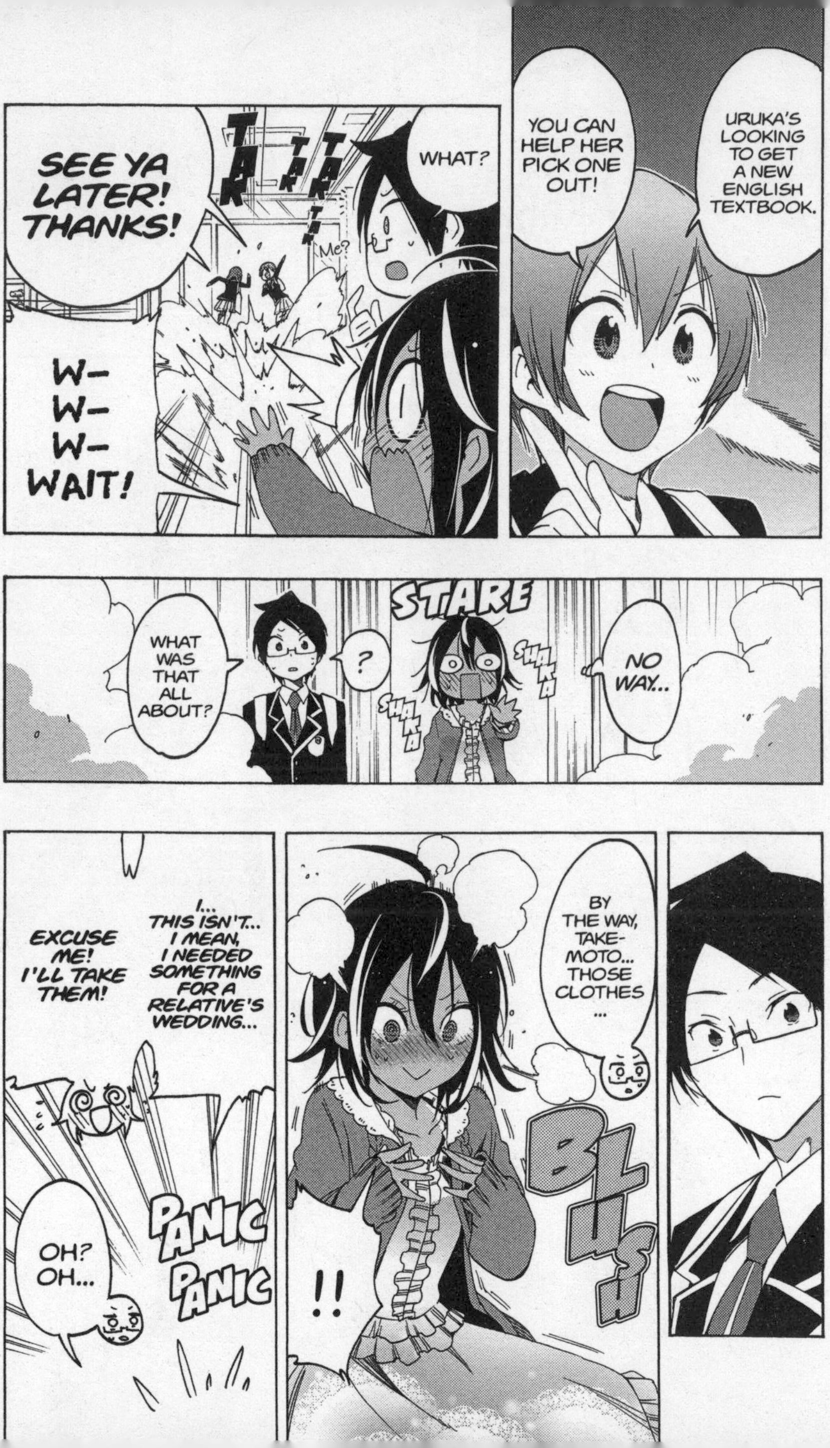
URUKA'S LOOKING TO GET A NEW ENGLISH TEXTBOOK.
YOU CAN HELP HER PICK ONE OUT!
WHAT?
Me?
TAK TAK TAK
SEE YA LATER! THANKS!
W-W-W-WAIT!
NO WAY...
STARE
SHAKA
SHAKA
?
WHAT WAS THAT ALL ABOUT?
BY THE WAY, TAKE-MOTO... THOSE CLOTHES...
BLUSH
!!
I... THIS ISN'T... I MEAN, I NEEDED SOMETHING FOR A RELATIVE'S WEDDING...
EXCUSE ME! I'LL TAKE THEM!
PANIC PANIC
OH? OH...

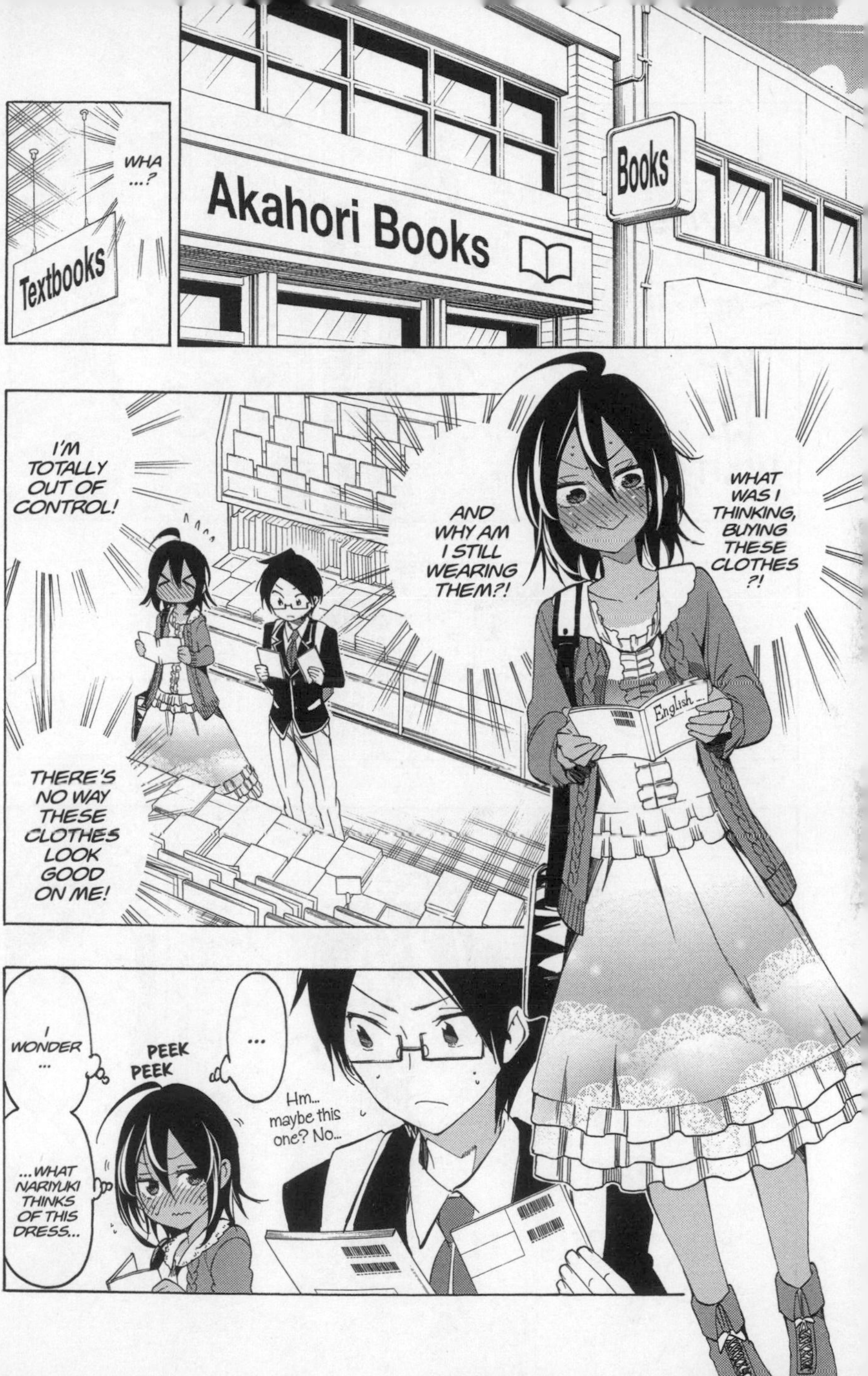
Akahori Books
Books
WHA ...?
Textbooks
WHAT WAS I THINKING, BUYING THESE CLOTHES ?!
AND WHY AM I STILL WEARING THEM?!
I'M TOTALLY OUT OF CONTROL!
English ...
THERE'S NO WAY THESE CLOTHES LOOK GOOD ON ME!
...
Hm... maybe this one? No...
I WONDER ...
PEEK PEEK
...WHAT NARIYUKI THINKS OF THIS DRESS...

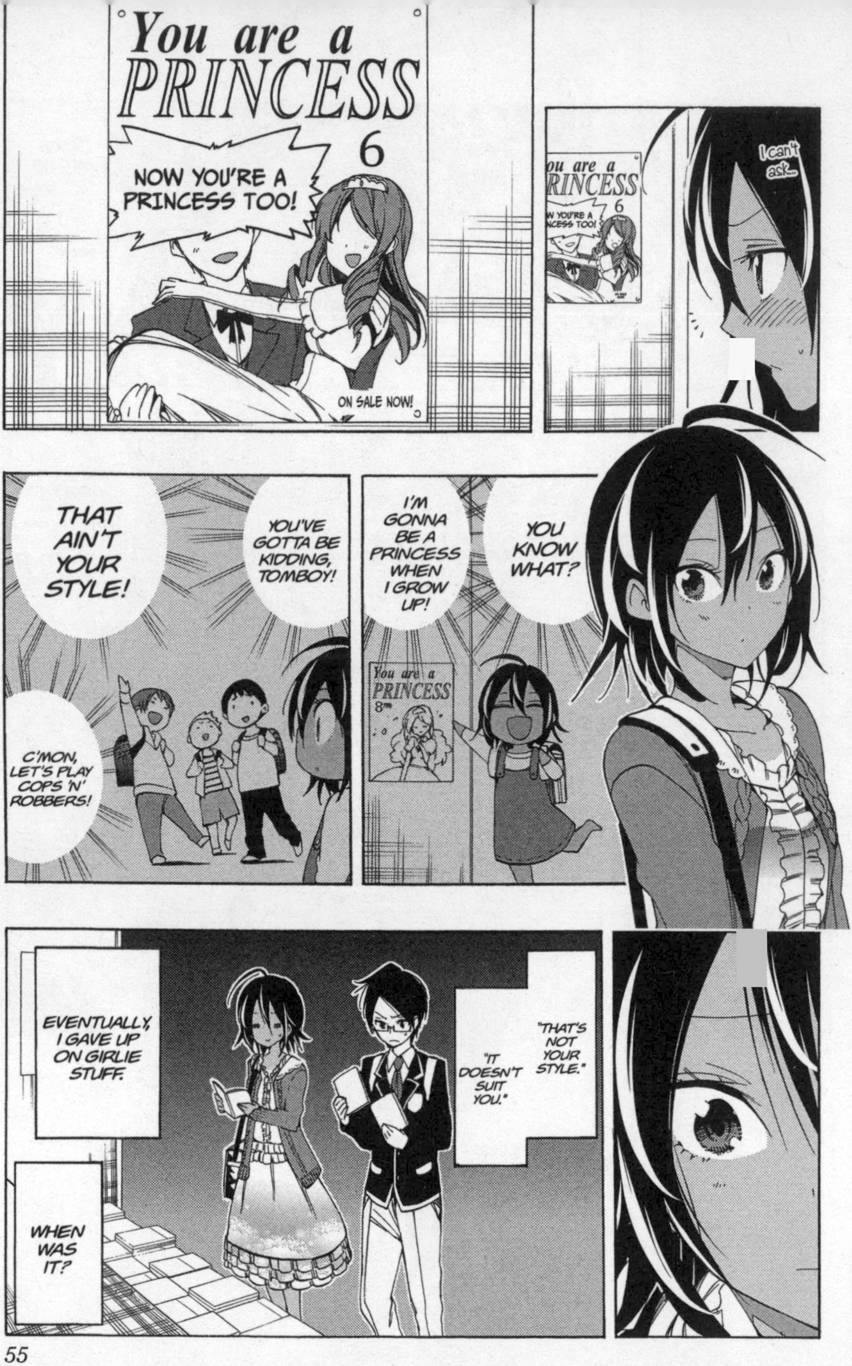
I can't ask...
You are a PRINCESS
6
NOW YOU'RE A PRINCESS TOO!
ON SALE NOW!
YOU KNOW WHAT?
I'M GONNA BE A PRINCESS WHEN I GROW UP!
You are a PRINCESS
8th
YOU'VE GOTTA BE KIDDING, TOMBOY!
THAT AIN'T YOUR STYLE!
C'MON, LET'S PLAY COPS 'N' ROBBERS!
"THAT'S NOT YOUR STYLE."
"IT DOESN'T SUIT YOU."
EVENTUALLY, I GAVE UP ON GIRLIE STUFF.
WHEN WAS IT?

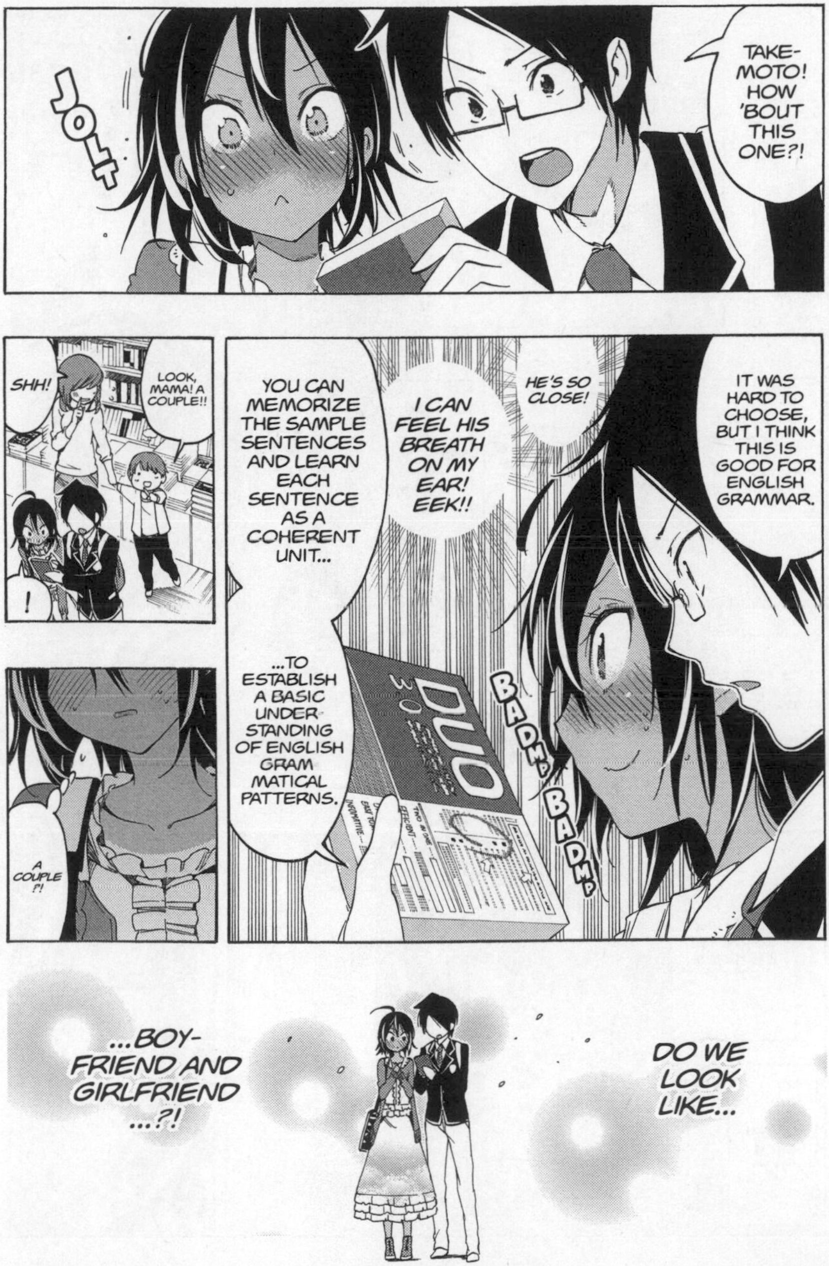
TAKE-MOTO! HOW 'BOUT THIS ONE?!
JOLT
IT WAS HARD TO CHOOSE, BUT I THINK THIS IS GOOD FOR ENGLISH GRAMMAR.
HE'S SO CLOSE!
I CAN FEEL HIS BREATH ON MY EAR! EEK!!
YOU CAN MEMORIZE THE SAMPLE SENTENCES AND LEARN EACH SENTENCE AS A COHERENT UNIT...
...TO ESTABLISH A BASIC UNDER-STANDING OF ENGLISH GRAM MATICAL PATTERNS.
DUO 3.0
BADMP BADMP
LOOK, MAMA! A COUPLE!!
SHH!
!
A COUPLE?!
DO WE LOOK LIKE...
...BOY-FRIEND AND GIRLFRIEND...?!

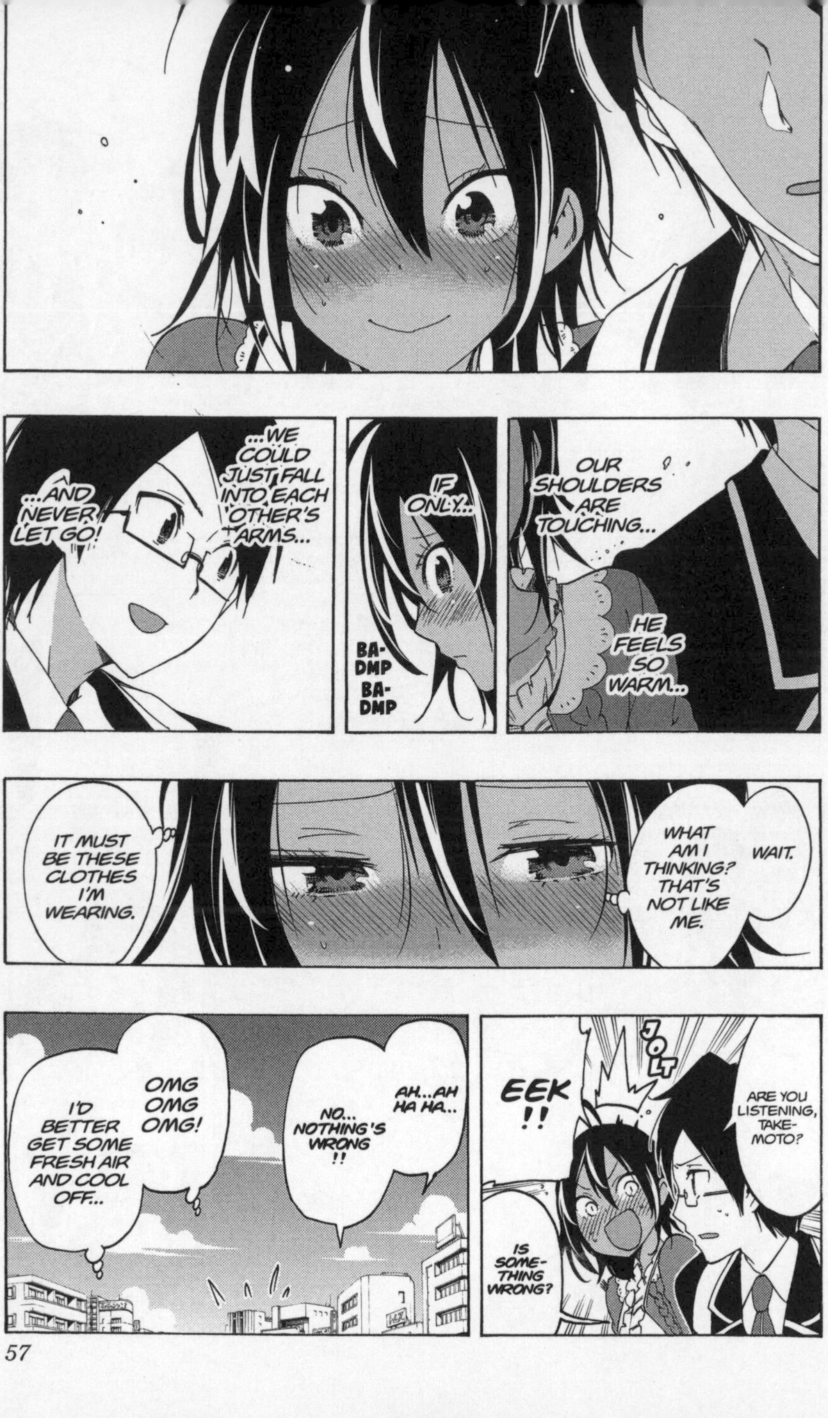
OUR SHOULDERS ARE TOUCHING...
HE FEELS SO WARM...
IF ONLY...
BA-DMP BA-DMP
...WE COULD JUST FALL INTO EACH OTHER'S ARMS...
...AND NEVER LET GO!
WAIT.
WHAT AM I THINKING? THAT'S NOT LIKE ME.
IT MUST BE THESE CLOTHES I'M WEARING.
ARE YOU LISTENING, TAKE-MOTO?
JOLT
EEK!!
IS SOME-THING WRONG?
AH...AH HA HA...
NO... NOTHING'S WRONG!!
OMG OMG OMG!
I'D BETTER GET SOME FRESH AIR AND COOL OFF...

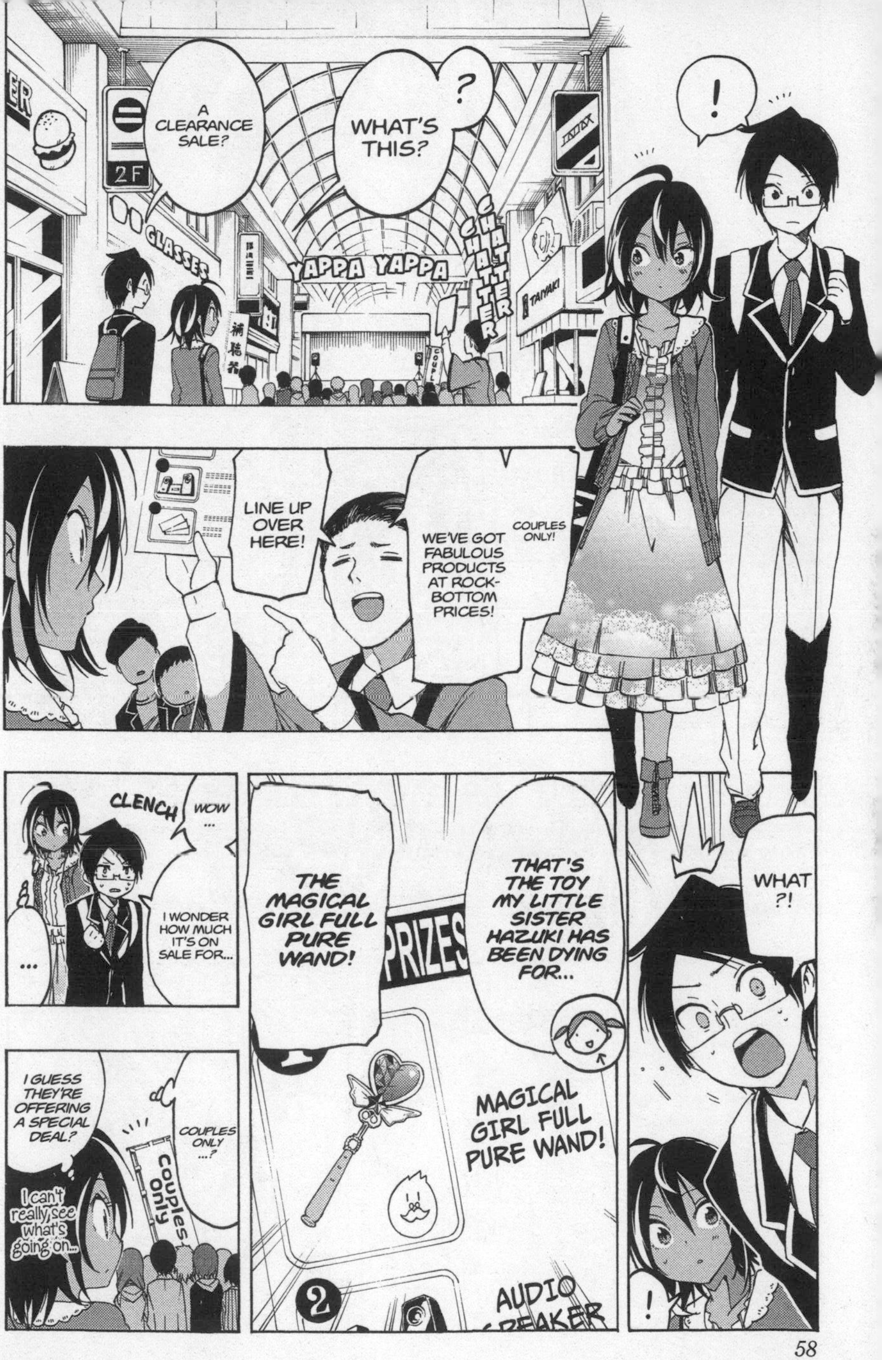
!
?
WHAT'S THIS?
A CLEARANCE SALE?
CHATTER CHATTER
TAIYAKI
YAPPA YAPPA
GLASSES
2F
COUPLES ONLY!
WE'VE GOT FABULOUS PRODUCTS AT ROCK-BOTTOM PRICES!
LINE UP OVER HERE!
WHAT ?!
!
THAT'S THE TOY MY LITTLE SISTER HAZUKI HAS BEEN DYING FOR...
THE MAGICAL GIRL FULL PURE WAND!
PRIZES
MAGICAL GIRL FULL PURE WAND!
AUDIO
WOW ...
CLENCH
I WONDER HOW MUCH IT'S ON SALE FOR...
...
COUPLES ONLY ...?
Couples Only
I GUESS THEY'RE OFFERING A SPECIAL DEAL?
I can't really see what's going on...

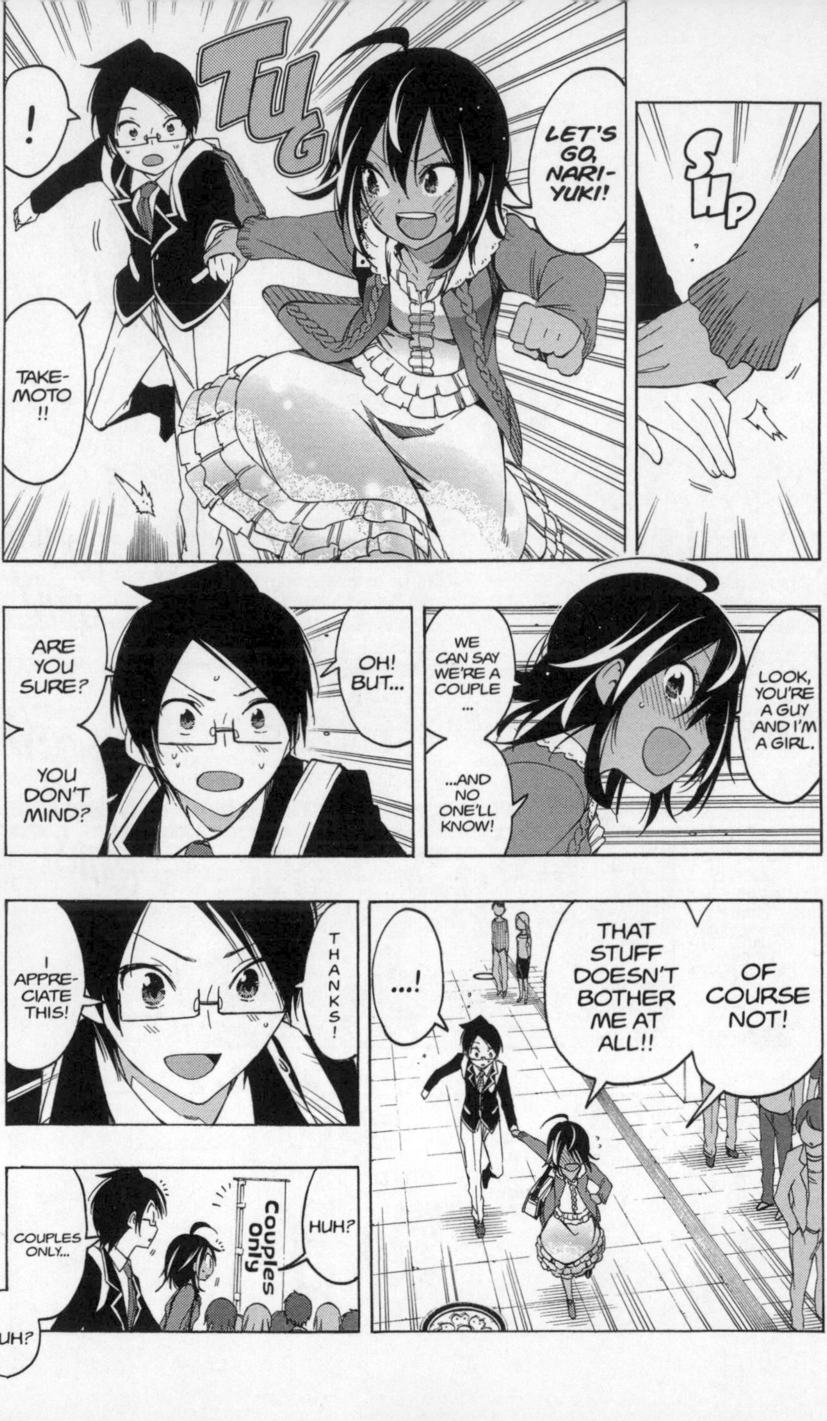
SHP
LET'S GO, NARI-YUKI!
TUG
!
TAKE-MOTO!!
LOOK, YOU'RE A GUY AND I'M A GIRL.
WE CAN SAY WE'RE A COUPLE...
...AND NO ONE'LL KNOW!
OH! BUT...
ARE YOU SURE?
YOU DON'T MIND?
OF COURSE NOT!
THAT STUFF DOESN'T BOTHER ME AT ALL!!
...!
THANKS!
I APPRE-CIATE THIS!
HUH?
Couples only
COUPLES ONLY...
HUH?

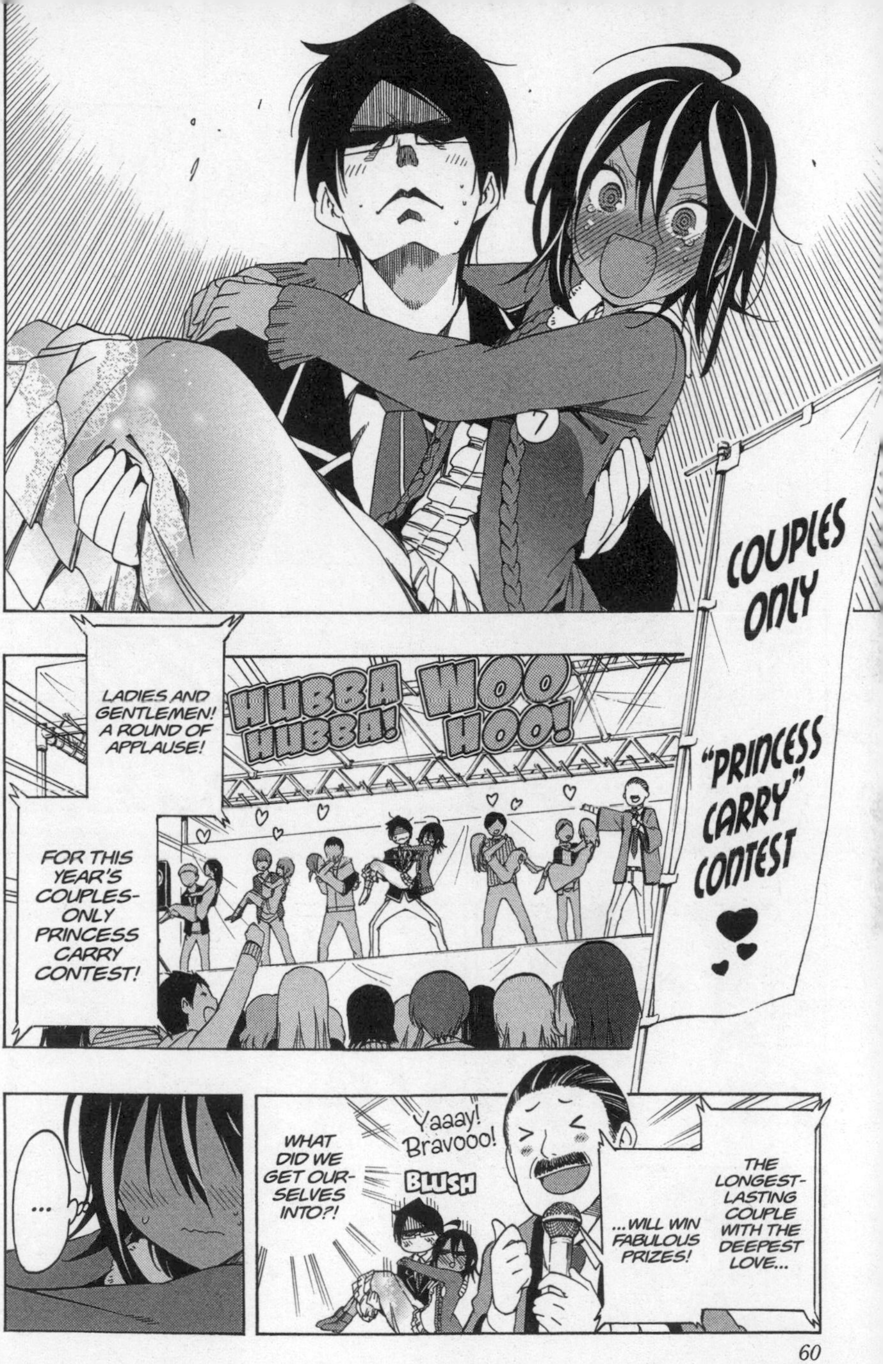
COUPLES ONLY "PRINCESS CARRY" CONTEST
WOO HOO!
HUBBA HUBBA!
LADIES AND GENTLEMEN! A ROUND OF APPLAUSE!
FOR THIS YEAR'S COUPLES-ONLY PRINCESS CARRY CONTEST!
THE LONGEST-LASTING COUPLE WITH THE DEEPEST LOVE...
...WILL WIN FABULOUS PRIZES!
Yaaay! Bravooo!
BLUSH
WHAT DID WE GET OURSELVES INTO?!
...

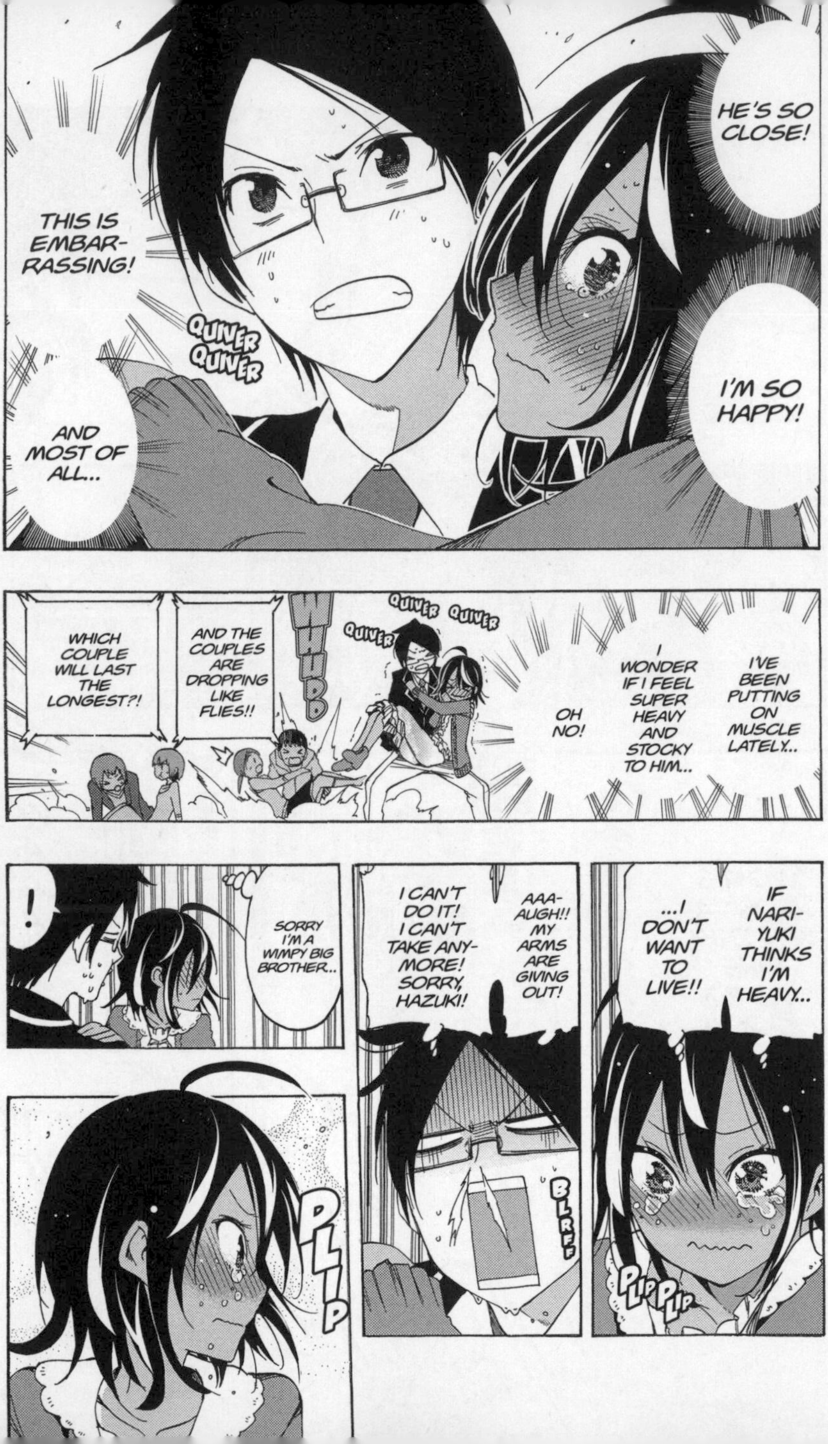
HE'S SO CLOSE!
I'M SO HAPPY!
THIS IS EMBARRASSING!
QUIVER QUIVER
AND MOST OF ALL...
I'VE BEEN PUTTING ON MUSCLE LATELY...
I WONDER IF I FEEL SUPER HEAVY AND STOCKY TO HIM...
OH NO!
QUIVER QUIVER
QUIVER
WHUD
AND THE COUPLES ARE DROPPING LIKE FLIES!!
WHICH COUPLE WILL LAST THE LONGEST?!
IF NARI-YUKI THINKS I'M HEAVY...
...I DON'T WANT TO LIVE!!
PLIP PLIP
AAA-AUGH!! MY ARMS ARE GIVING OUT!
I CAN'T DO IT! I CAN'T TAKE ANY-MORE! SORRY, HAZUKI!
BLRFF
SORRY I'M A WIMPY BIG BROTHER...
!
PLIP

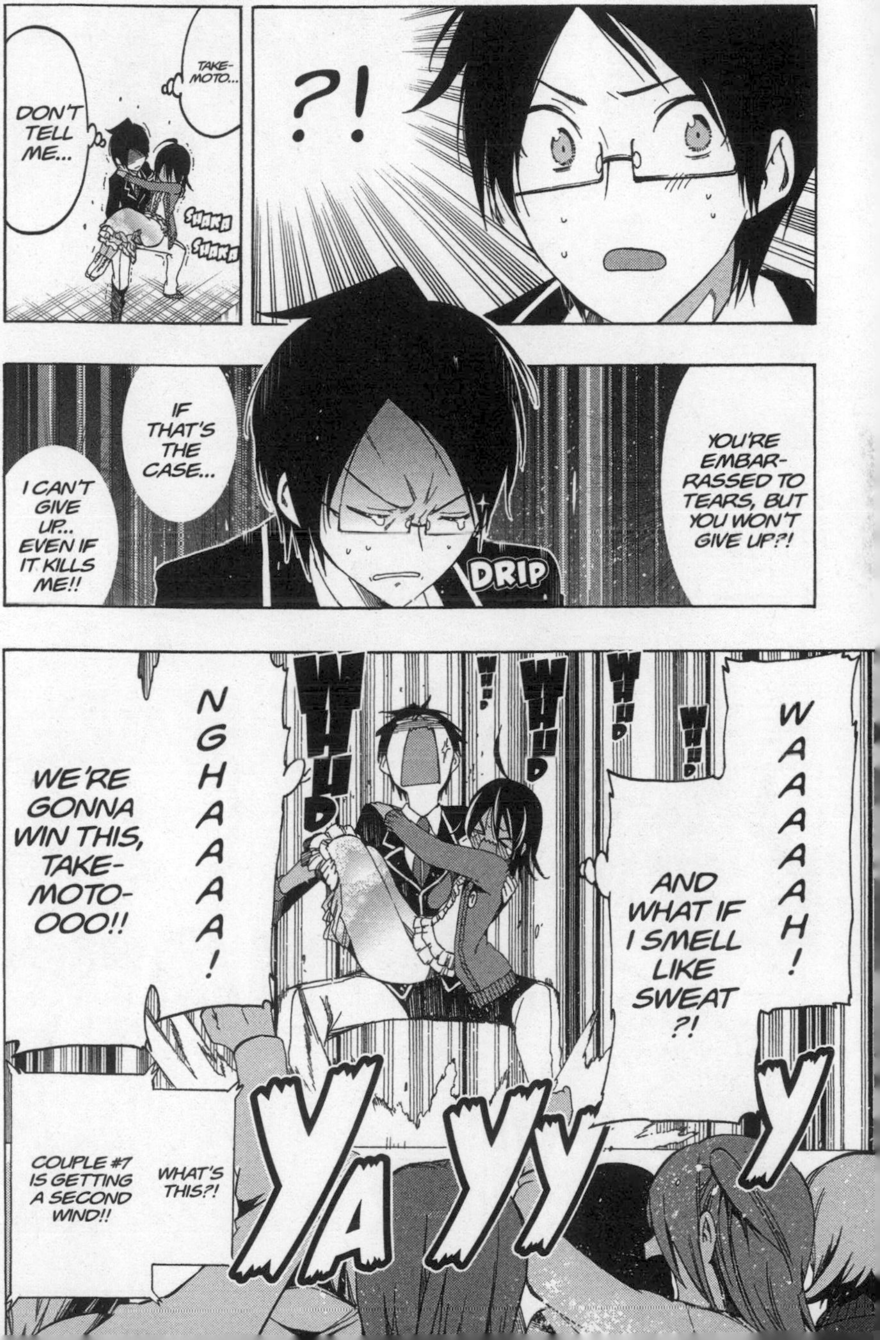
?!
TAKE-MOTO...
DON'T TELL ME...
SHAKA SHAKA
YOU'RE EMBAR-RASSED TO TEARS, BUT YOU WON'T GIVE UP?!
DRIP
IF THAT'S THE CASE...
I CAN'T GIVE UP... EVEN IF IT KILLS ME!!
WAAAAAAAH!
AND WHAT IF I SMELL LIKE SWEAT?!
WHUD WHUD WHUD WHUD WHUD WHUD
NGHAAAAAA!
WE'RE GONNA WIN THIS, TAKE-MOTO-OOO!!
YAYYY
WHAT'S THIS?!
COUPLE #7 IS GETTING A SECOND WIND!!

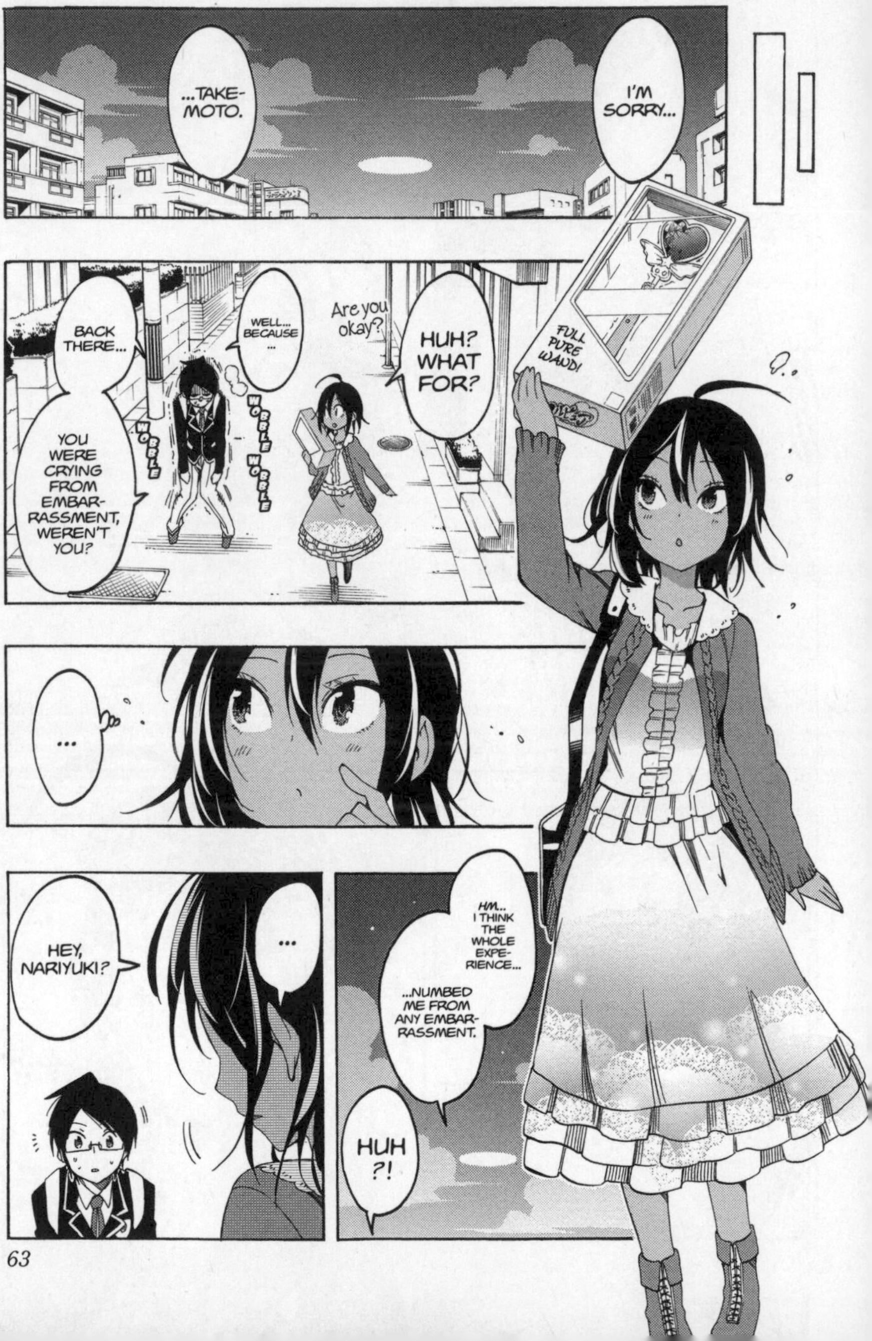
I'M SORRY...
...TAKE-MOTO.
FULL PURE WAND!
HUH? WHAT FOR?
Are you okay?
WELL... BECAUSE ...
WOBBLE WOBBLE
WOBBLE
BACK THERE...
YOU WERE CRYING FROM EMBAR-RASSMENT, WEREN'T YOU?
...
HM... I THINK THE WHOLE EXPE-RIENCE...
...NUMBED ME FROM ANY EMBAR-RASSMENT.
HUH ?!
...
HEY, NARIYUKI?

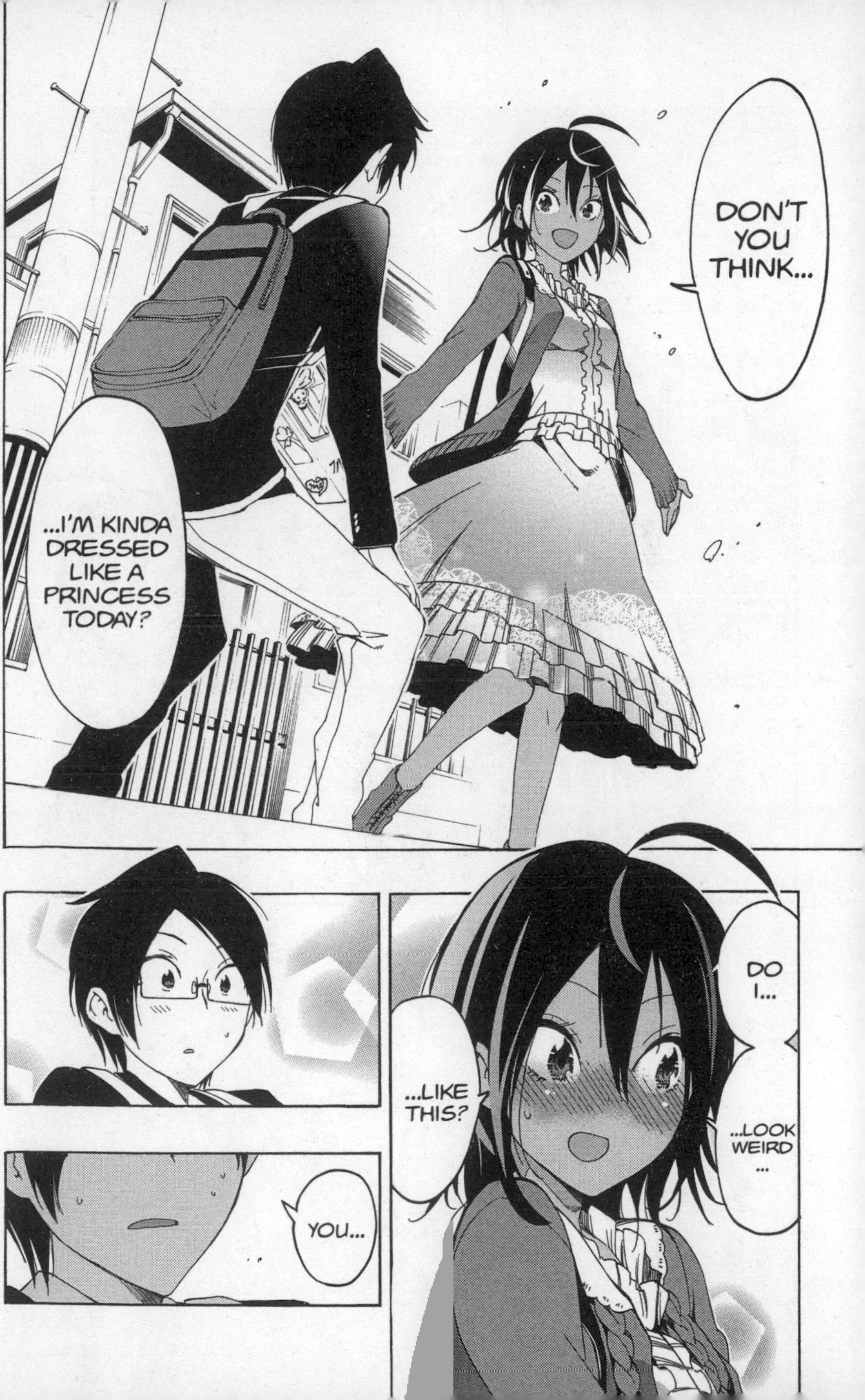
DON'T YOU THINK...
...I'M KINDA DRESSED LIKE A PRINCESS TODAY?
DO I...
...LOOK WEIRD ...
...LIKE THIS?
YOU...

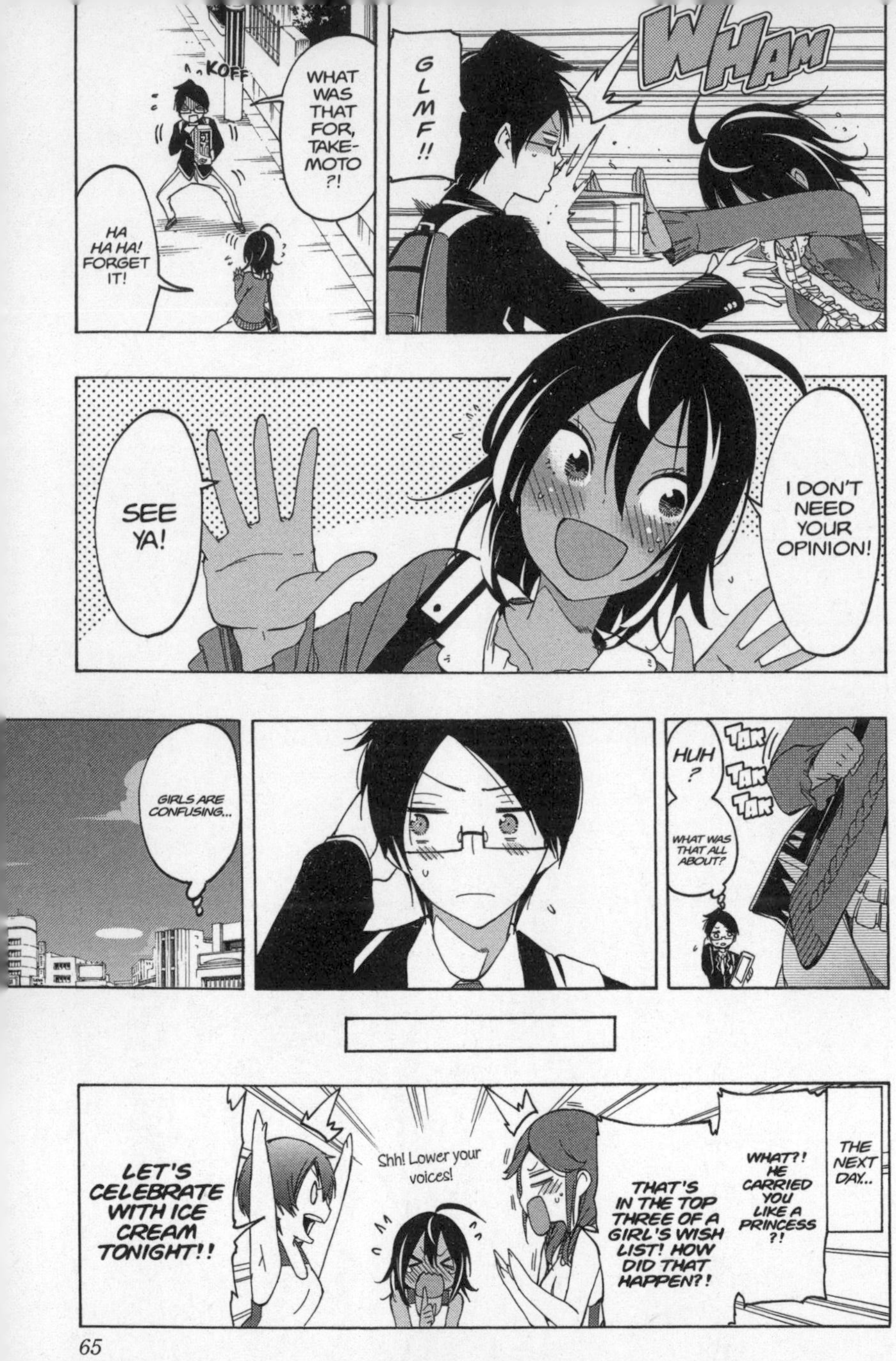
WHAM
GLMF!!
KOFF
WHAT WAS THAT FOR, TAKE-MOTO?!
HA HA HA! FORGET IT!
I DON'T NEED YOUR OPINION!
SEE YA!
TAK TAK TAK
HUH?
WHAT WAS THAT ALL ABOUT?
GIRLS ARE CONFUSING...
THE NEXT DAY...
WHAT?! HE CARRIED YOU LIKE A PRINCESS?!
THAT'S IN THE TOP THREE OF A GIRL'S WISH LIST! HOW DID THAT HAPPEN?!
Shh! Lower your voices!
LET'S CELEBRATE WITH ICE CREAM TONIGHT!!

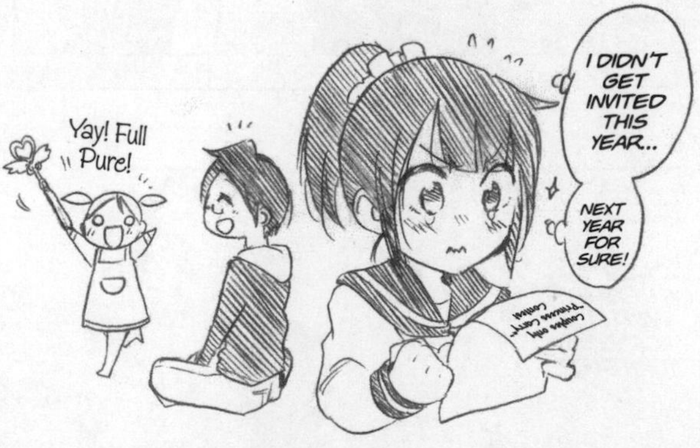
I DIDN'T GET INVITED THIS YEAR...
NEXT YEAR FOR SURE!
Couples only "Princess Carry" Contest!
Yay! Full Pure!

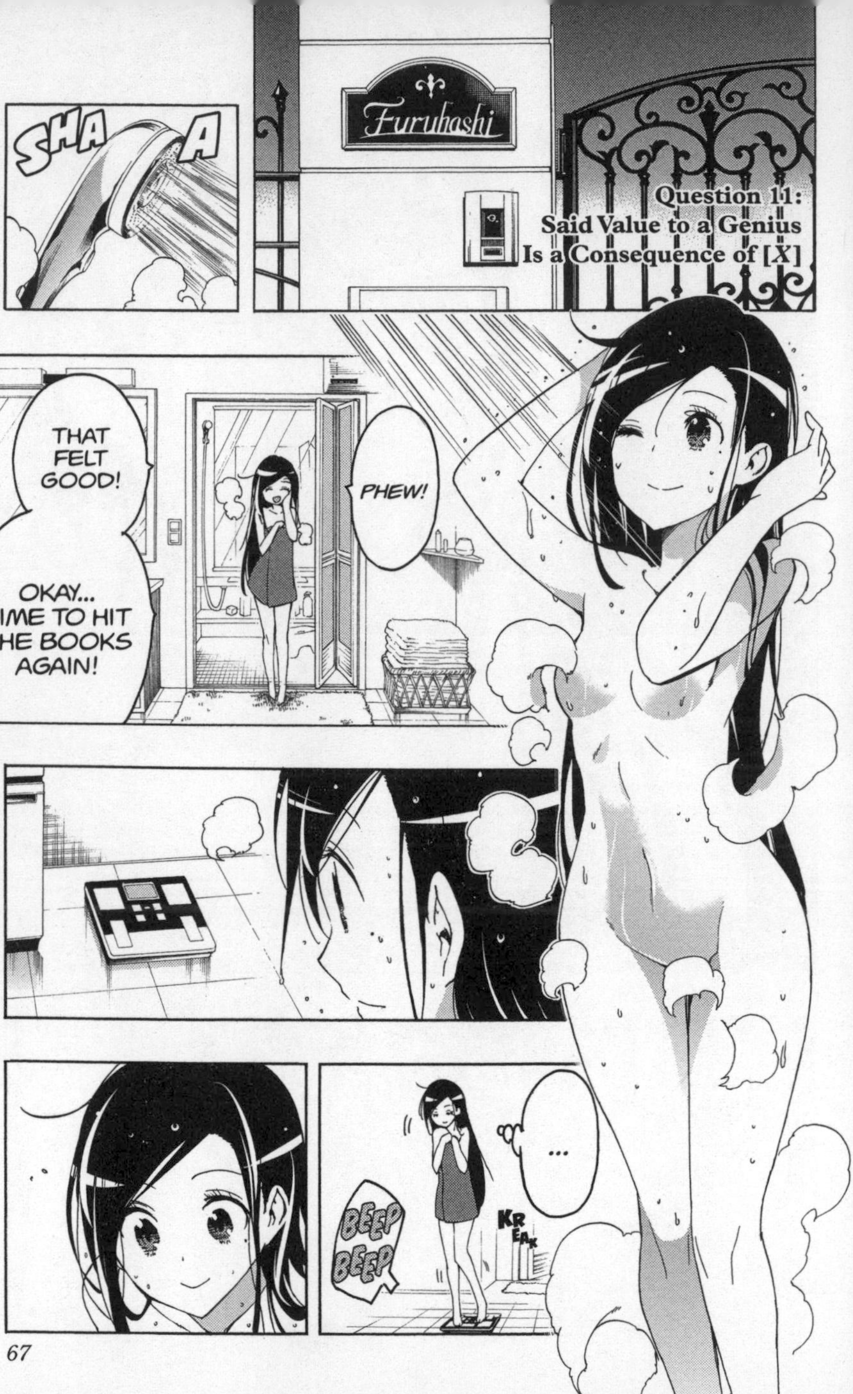
Furuhashi
Question 11:
Said Value to a Genius
Is a Consequence of [X]
SHA A
PHEW!
THAT FELT GOOD!
OKAY... TIME TO HIT THE BOOKS AGAIN!
...
KREAK
BEEP BEEP

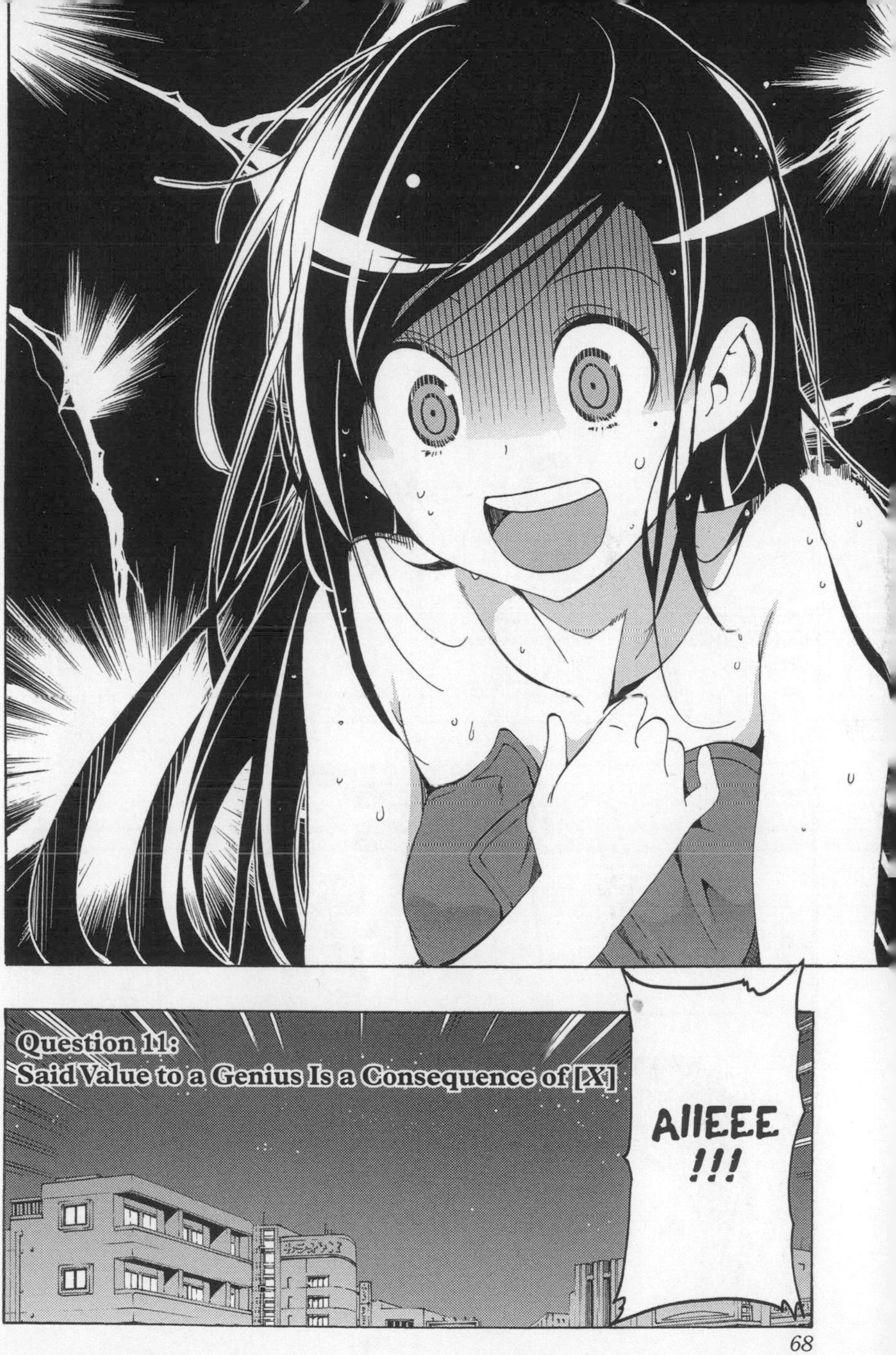
AIIEEE!!!
Question 11:
Said Value to a Genius Is a Consequence of [X]

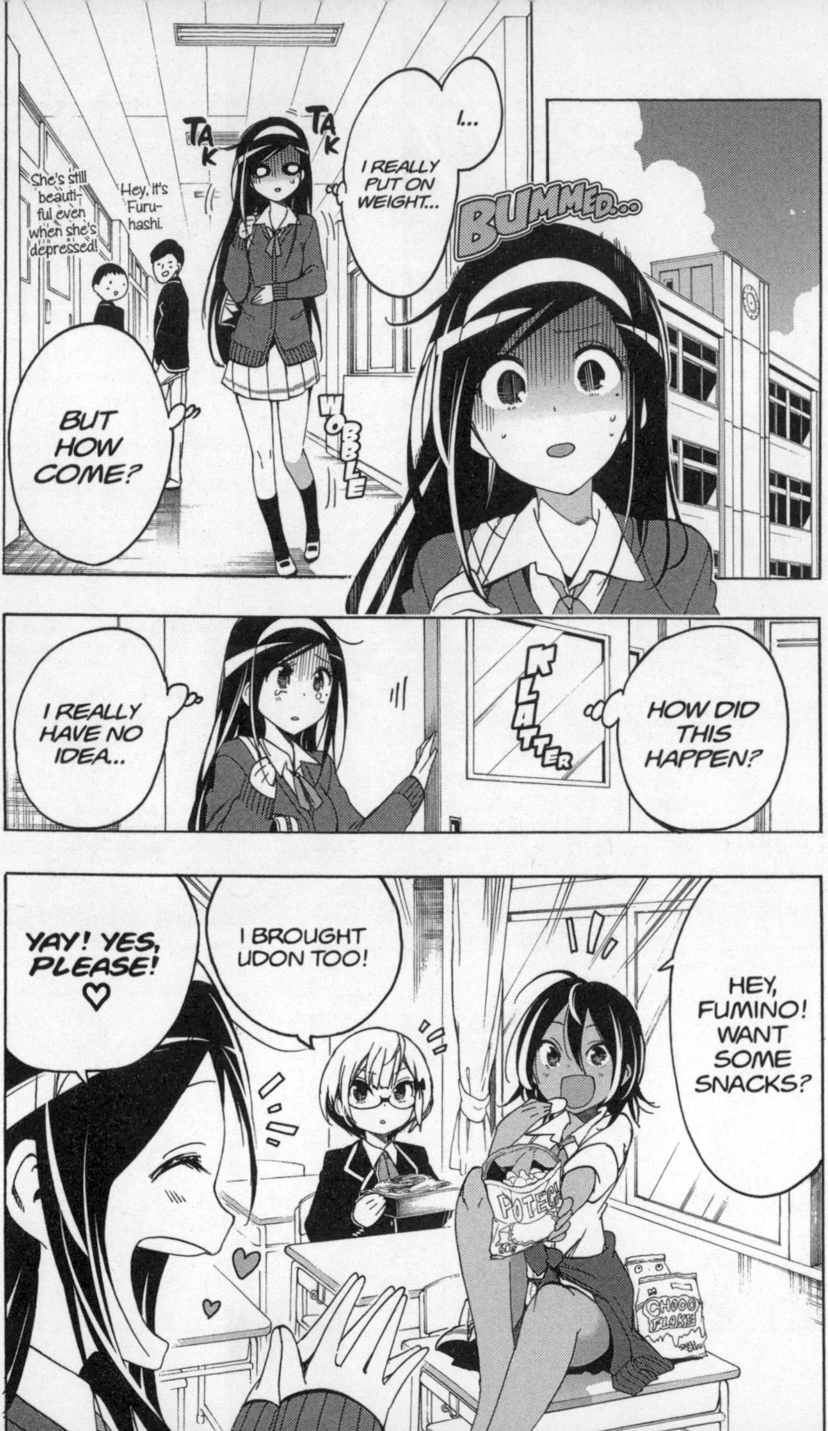
BUMMED...
I...
I REALLY PUT ON WEIGHT...
TAK
TAK
Hey, it's Furu-hashi.
She's still beauti-ful even when she's depressed!
WOBBLE
BUT HOW COME?
HOW DID THIS HAPPEN?
KLATTER
I REALLY HAVE NO IDEA...
HEY, FUMINO! WANT SOME SNACKS?
I BROUGHT UDON TOO!
YAY! YES, PLEASE! ♡
POTECH
CHOCO FLAKE

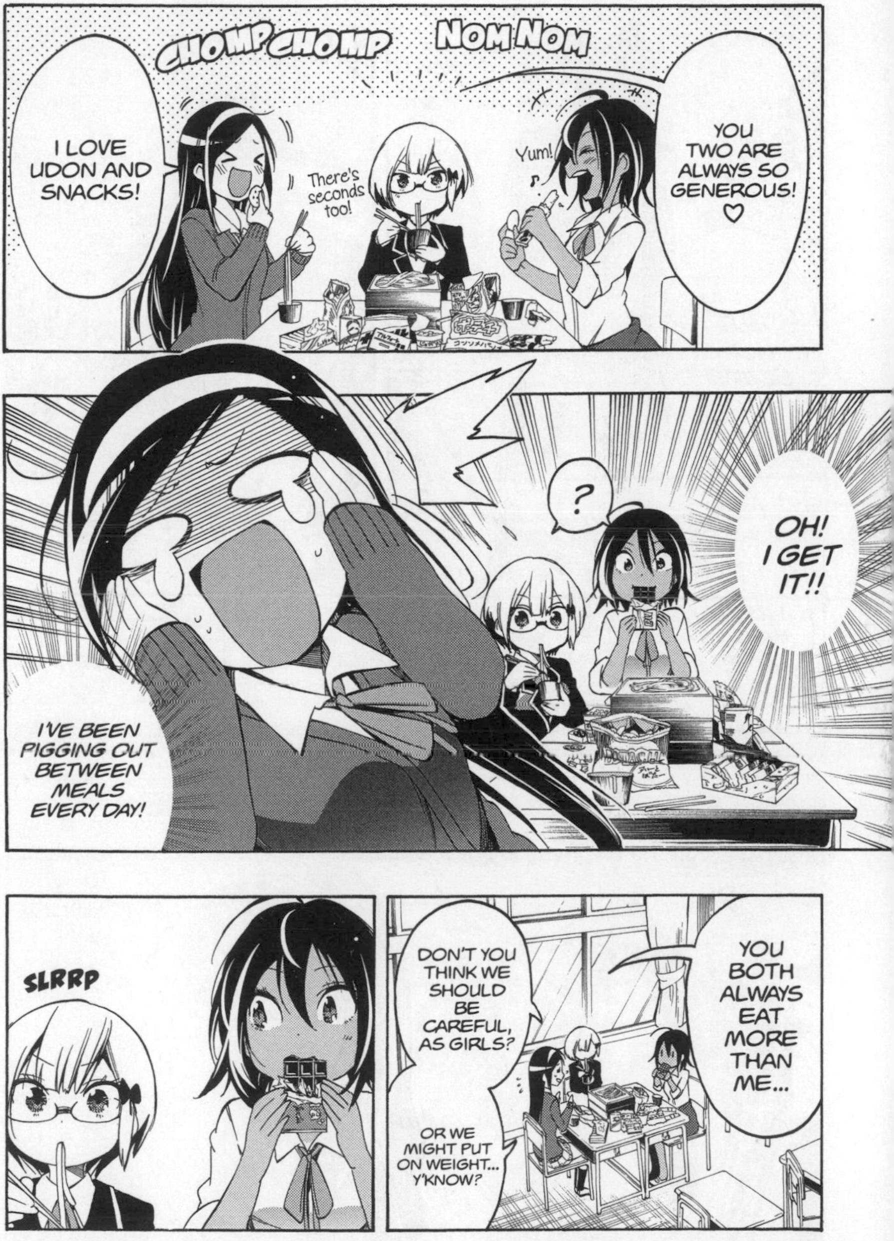
YOU TWO ARE ALWAYS SO GENEROUS! ♡
Yum!
NOM NOM
There's seconds too!
CHOMP CHOMP
I LOVE UDON AND SNACKS!
OH! I GET IT!!
?
I'VE BEEN PIGGING OUT BETWEEN MEALS EVERY DAY!
YOU BOTH ALWAYS EAT MORE THAN ME...
DON'T YOU THINK WE SHOULD BE CAREFUL, AS GIRLS?
OR WE MIGHT PUT ON WEIGHT... Y'KNOW?
SLRRP

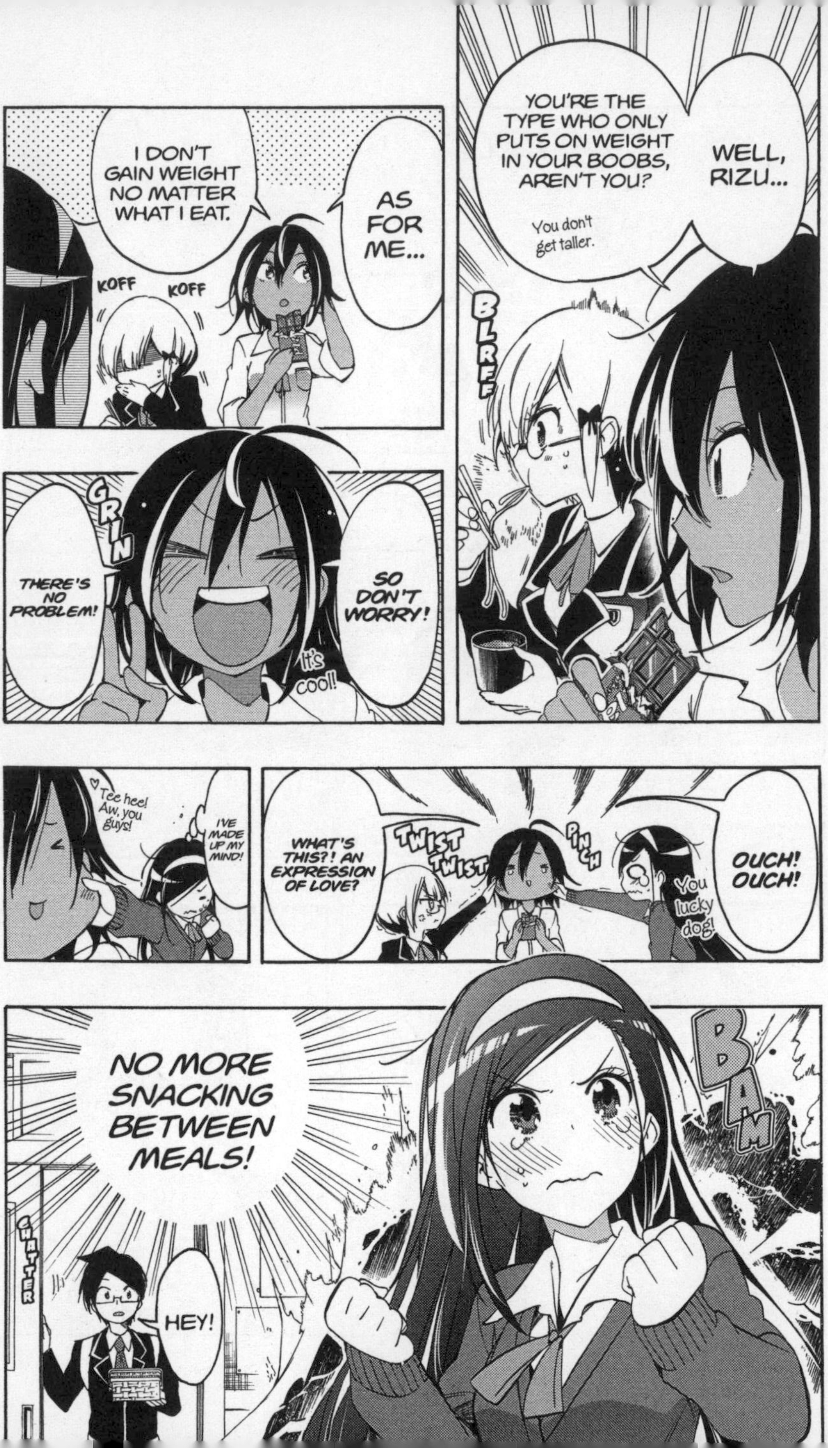
WELL, RIZU...
YOU'RE THE TYPE WHO ONLY PUTS ON WEIGHT IN YOUR BOOBS, AREN'T YOU?
You don't get taller.
BLRFF
AS FOR ME...
I DON'T GAIN WEIGHT NO MATTER WHAT I EAT.
KOFF
KOFF
SO DON'T WORRY!
GRIN
THERE'S NO PROBLEM!
It's cool!
OUCH! OUCH!
You lucky dog!
PINCH
TWIST TWIST
WHAT'S THIS?! AN EXPRESSION OF LOVE?
I'VE MADE UP MY MIND!
Tee hee! Aw, you guys!
BAM
NO MORE SNACKING BETWEEN MEALS!
HEY!
CHATTER

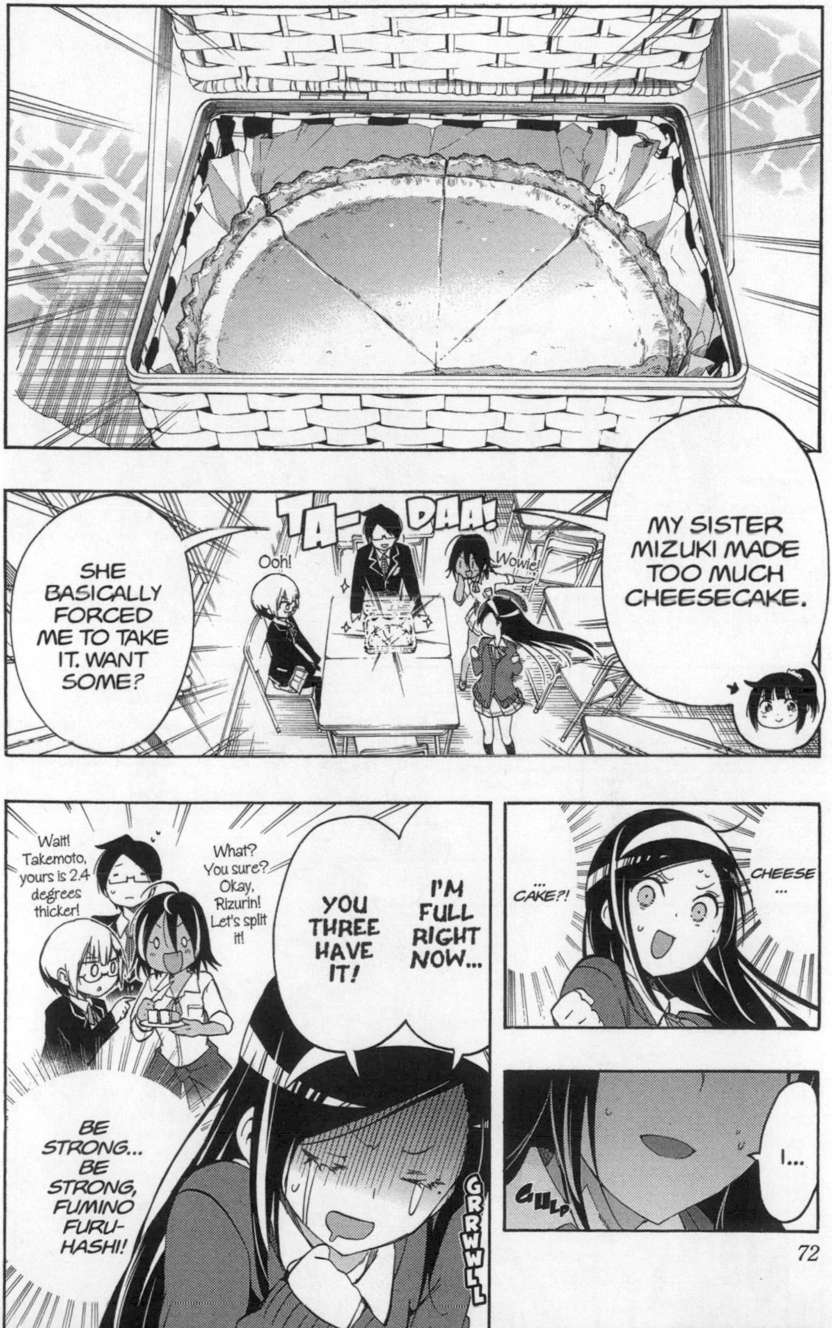
MY SISTER MIZUKI MADE TOO MUCH CHEESECAKE.
TA-DAA!
Wowie!
Ooh!
SHE BASICALLY FORCED ME TO TAKE IT. WANT SOME?
CHEESE ...
... CAKE?!
I...
GULP
I'M FULL RIGHT NOW...
YOU THREE HAVE IT!
What? You sure? Okay, Rizurin! Let's split it!
Wait! Takemoto, yours is 2.4 degrees thicker!
GRRWLL
BE STRONG... BE STRONG, FUMINO FURU-HASHI!

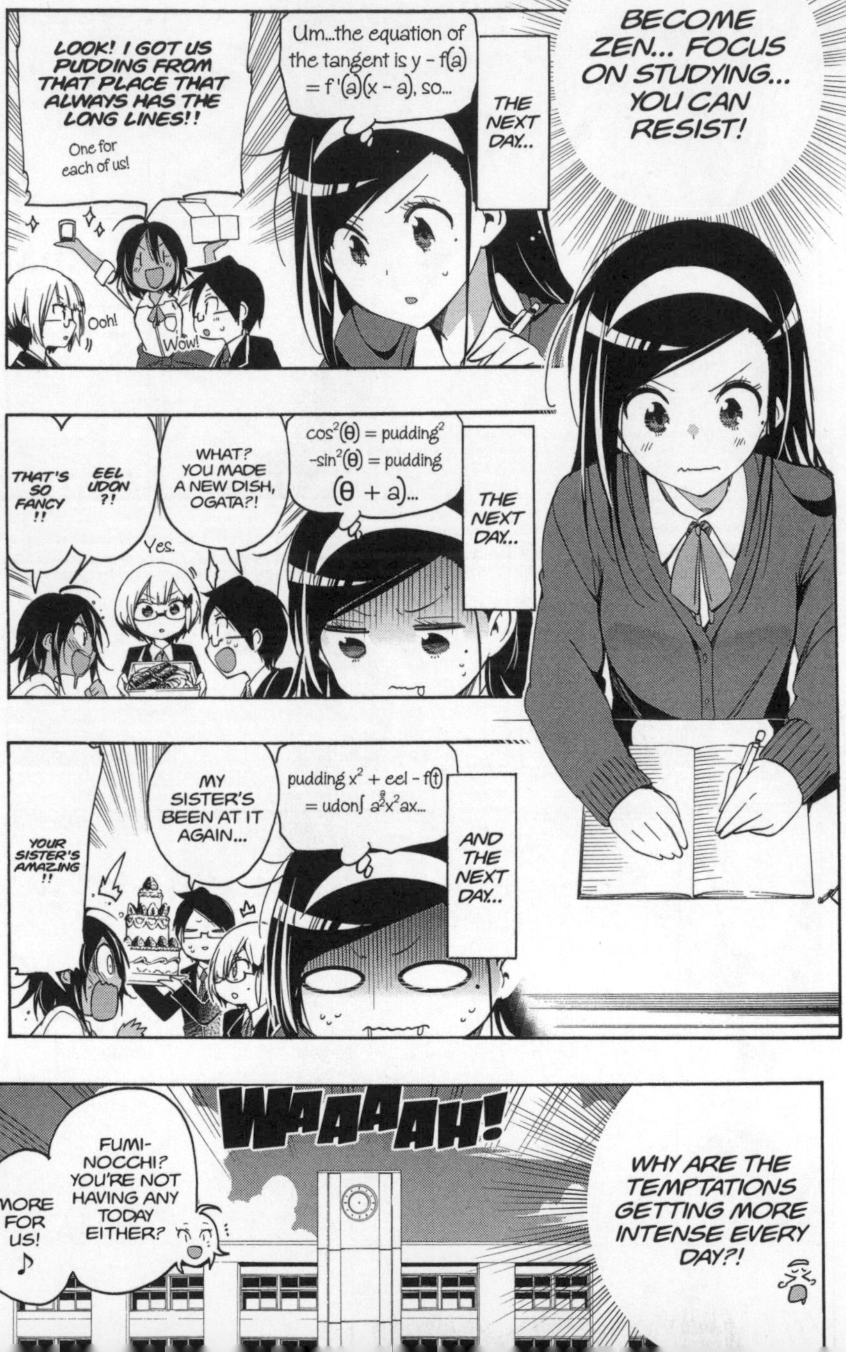
BECOME ZEN... FOCUS ON STUDYING... YOU CAN RESIST!
THE NEXT DAY...
Um...the equation of the tangent is y - f(a) = f'(a)(x - a), so...
LOOK! I GOT US PUDDING FROM THAT PLACE THAT ALWAYS HAS THE LONG LINES!!
One for each of us!
Wow!
Ooh!
THE NEXT DAY...
cos²(θ) = pudding² -sin²(θ) = pudding (θ + a)...
WHAT? YOU MADE A NEW DISH, OGATA?!
Yes.
EEL UDON?!
THAT'S SO FANCY!!
AND THE NEXT DAY...
pudding x² + eel - f(t) = udon∫ a²x²ax...
MY SISTER'S BEEN AT IT AGAIN...
YOUR SISTER'S AMAZING!!
WHY ARE THE TEMPTATIONS GETTING MORE INTENSE EVERY DAY?!
WAAAAH!
FUMI-NOCCHI? YOU'RE NOT HAVING ANY TODAY EITHER?
MORE FOR US! ♪

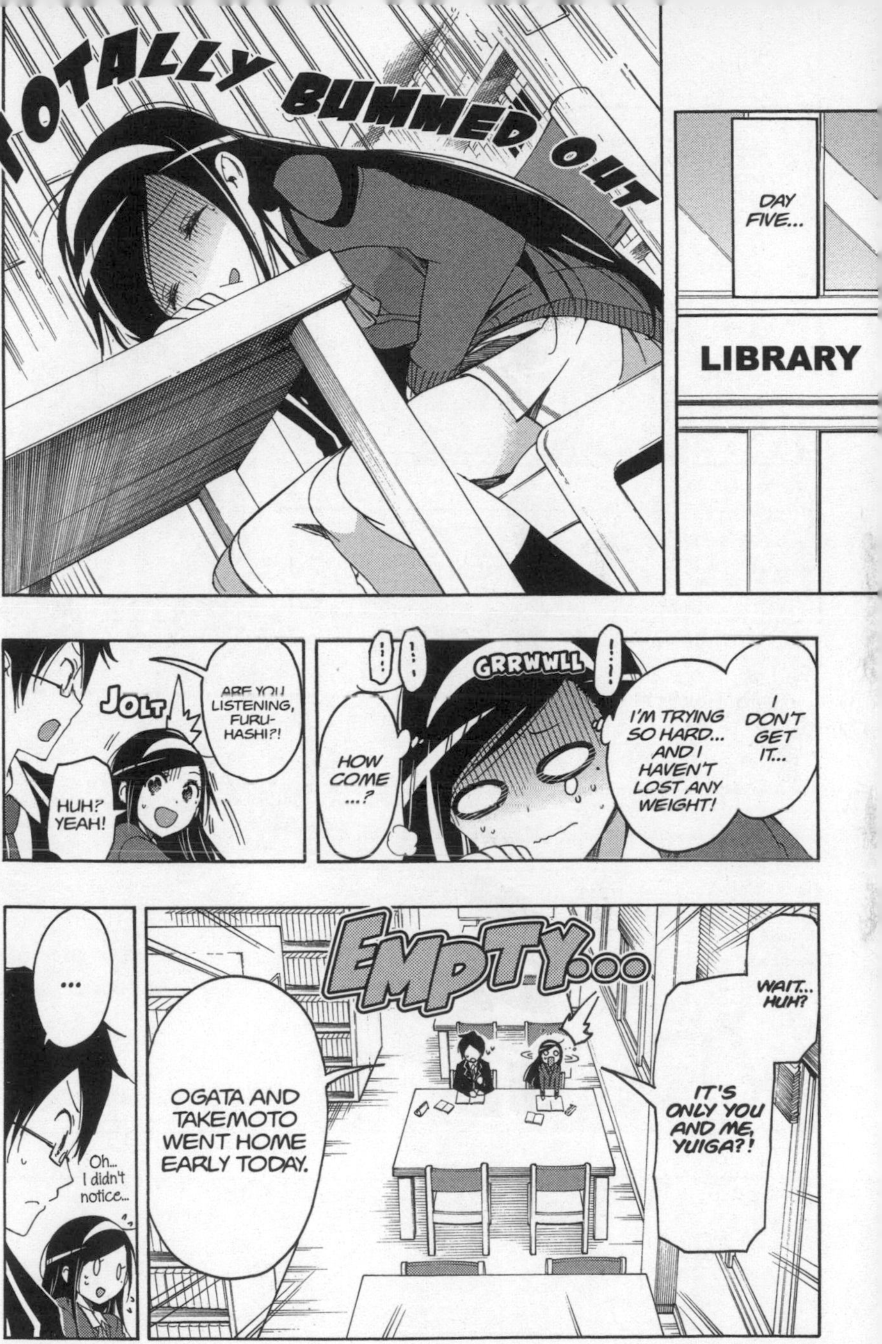
DAY FIVE...
LIBRARY
TOTALLY BUMMED OUT
I DON'T GET IT...
I'M TRYING SO HARD... AND I HAVEN'T LOST ANY WEIGHT!
GRRWWLL
HOW COME...?
ARE YOU LISTENING, FURU-HASHI?!
JOLT
HUH? YEAH!
WAIT... HUH?
EMPTY...
IT'S ONLY YOU AND ME, YUIGA?!
OGATA AND TAKEMOTO WENT HOME EARLY TODAY.
...
Oh... I didn't notice...

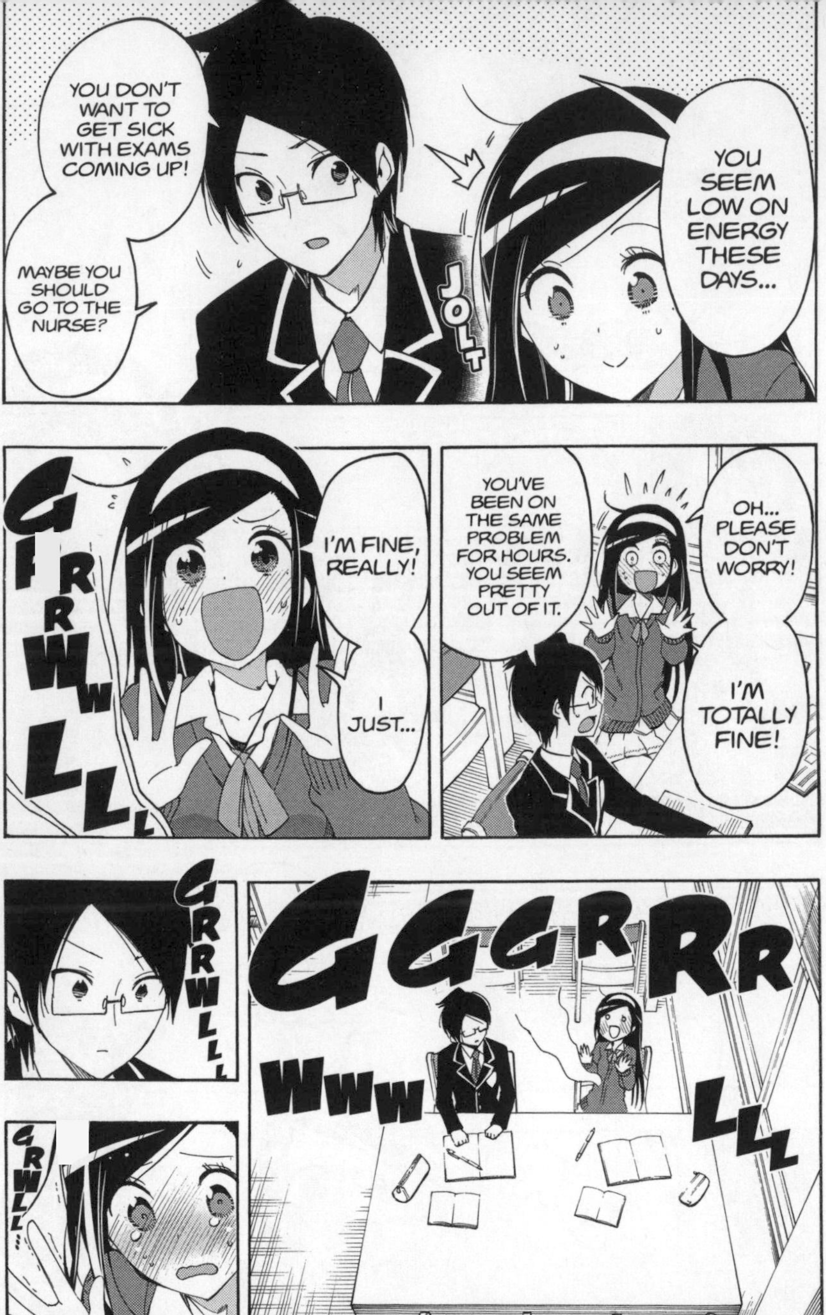
YOU SEEM LOW ON ENERGY THESE DAYS...
JOLT
YOU DON'T WANT TO GET SICK WITH EXAMS COMING UP!
MAYBE YOU SHOULD GO TO THE NURSE?
YOU'VE BEEN ON THE SAME PROBLEM FOR HOURS. YOU SEEM PRETTY OUT OF IT.
OH... PLEASE DON'T WORRY!
I'M TOTALLY FINE!
I'M FINE, REALLY!
I JUST...
GRRWWLLL
GGGRRRR WWW LLL
GRRWLLL
GRWLL!!

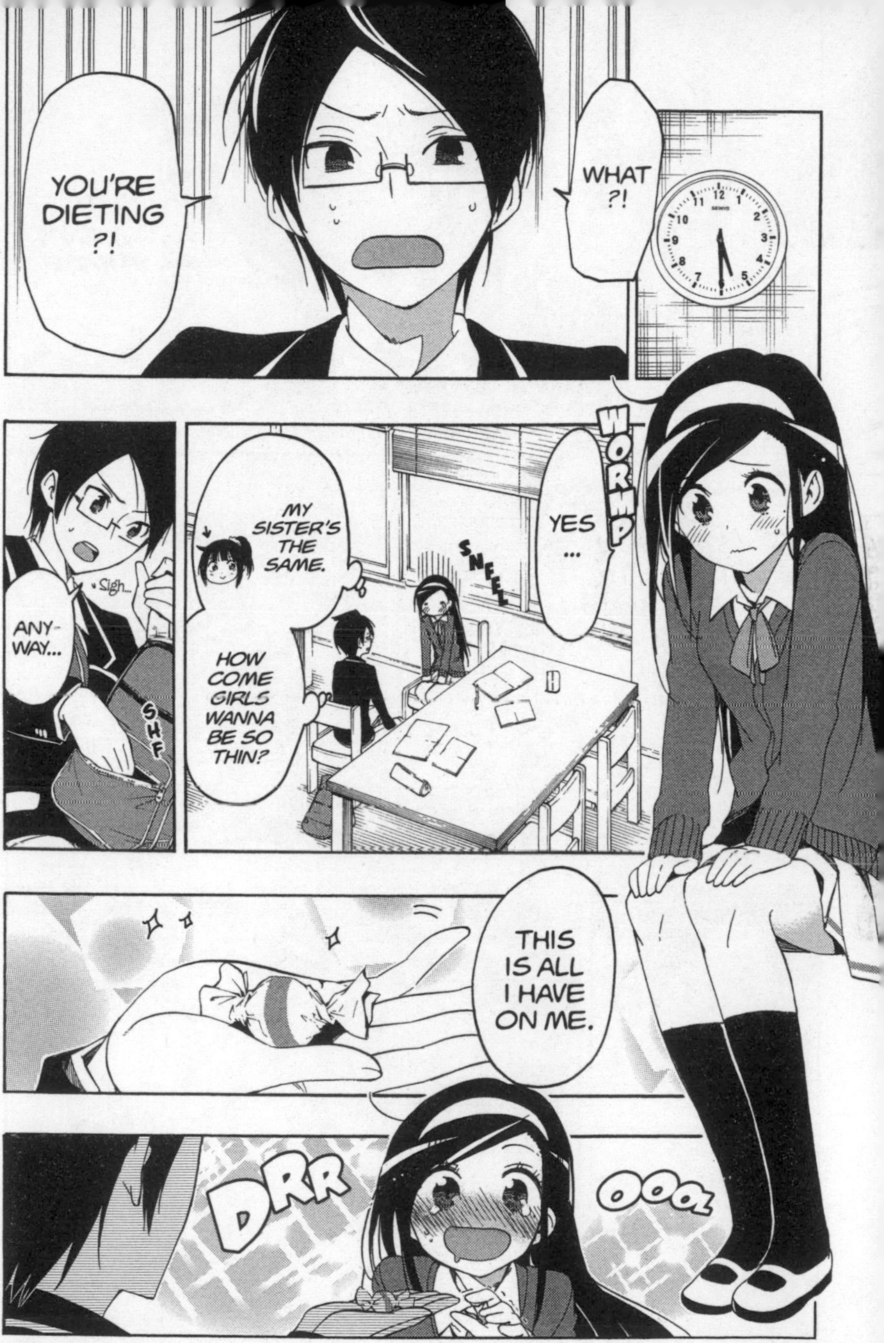
WHAT ?!
YOU'RE DIETING ?!
WORMP
YES ...
SNFEEL
MY SISTER'S THE SAME.
HOW COME GIRLS WANNA BE SO THIN?
Sigh...
ANY-WAY...
SHF
THIS IS ALL I HAVE ON ME.
DRR
OOOL

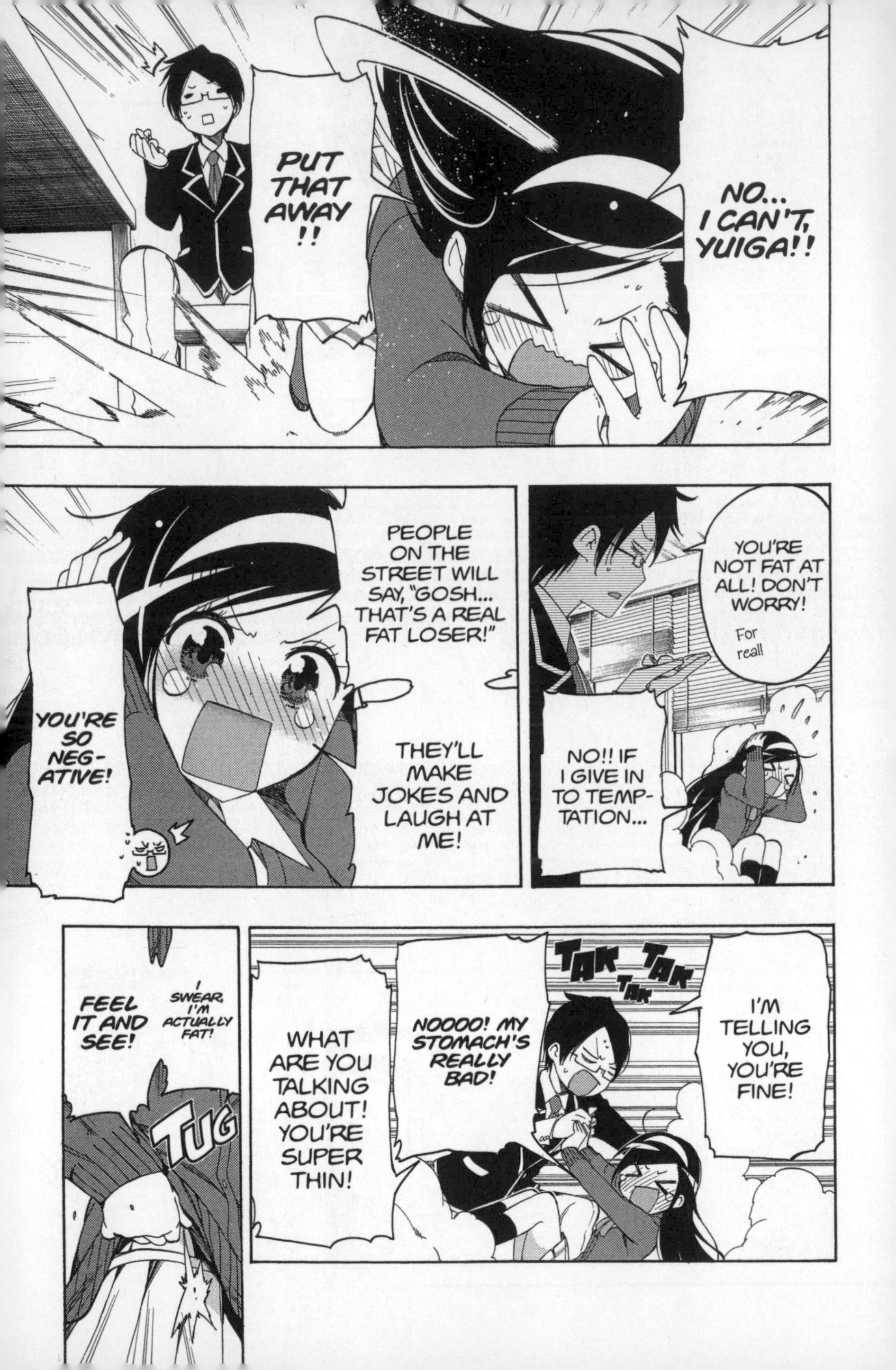
NO... I CAN'T, YUIGA!!
PUT THAT AWAY!!
YOU'RE NOT FAT AT ALL! DON'T WORRY!
For real!
NO!! IF I GIVE IN TO TEMPTATION...
PEOPLE ON THE STREET WILL SAY, "GOSH... THAT'S A REAL FAT LOSER!"
THEY'LL MAKE JOKES AND LAUGH AT ME!
YOU'RE SO NEGATIVE!
I'M TELLING YOU, YOU'RE FINE!
TAK TAK TAK
NOOOO! MY STOMACH'S REALLY BAD!
WHAT ARE YOU TALKING ABOUT! YOU'RE SUPER THIN!
I SWEAR, I'M ACTUALLY FAT!
FEEL IT AND SEE!
TUG

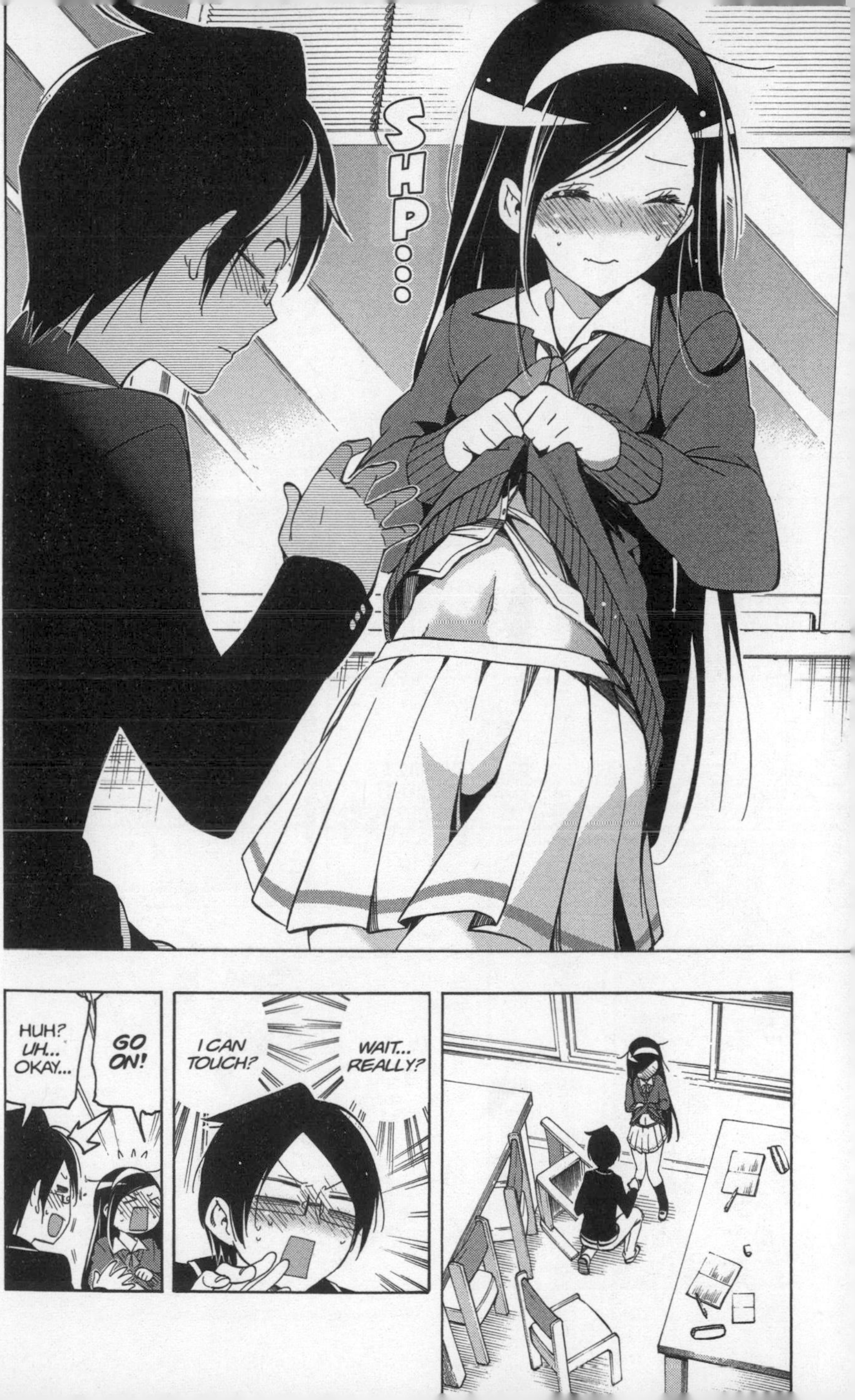
SHP...
WAIT... REALLY?
I CAN TOUCH?
GO ON!
HUH? UH... OKAY...

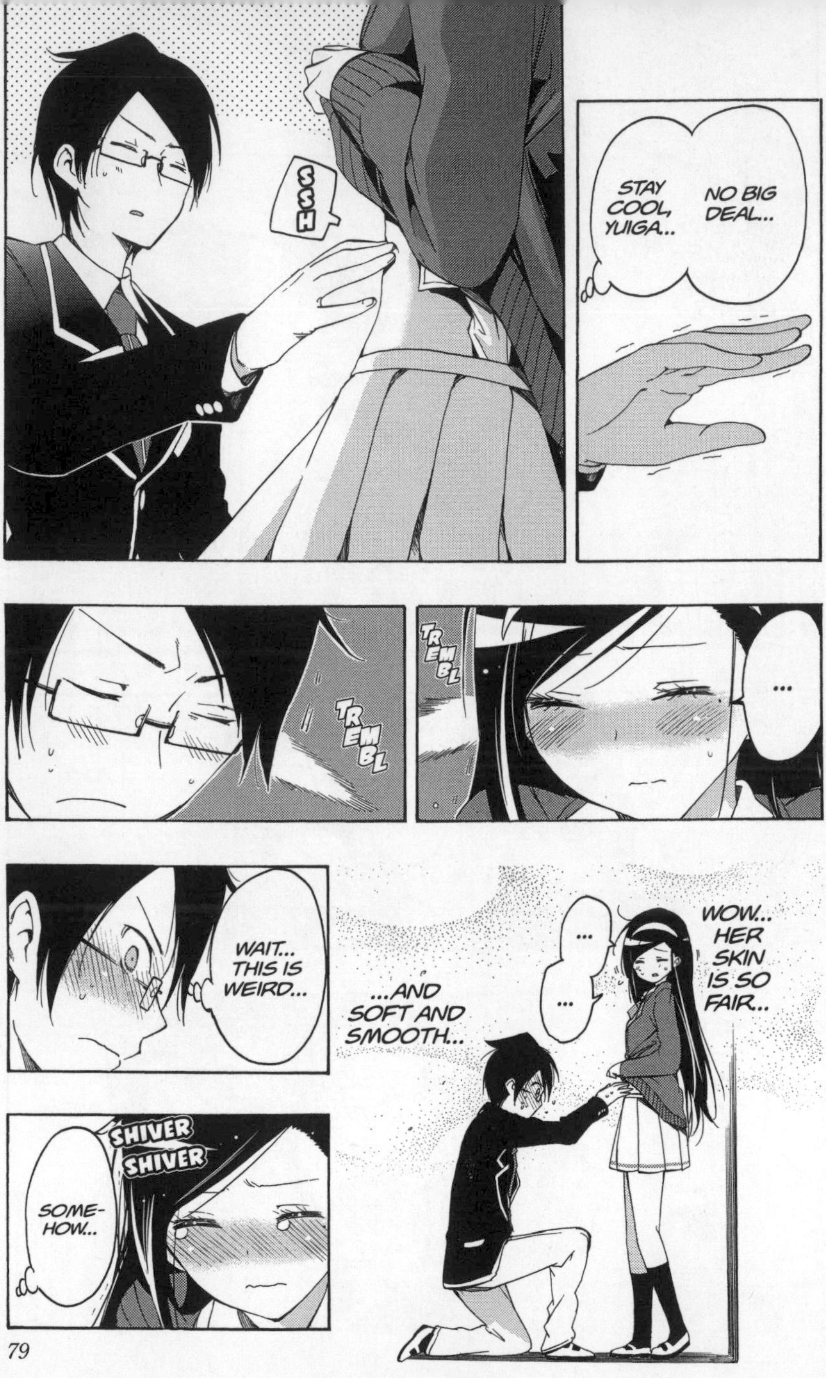
NO BIG DEAL...
STAY COOL, YUIGA...
SSH
TREMBL
...
TREMBL
WOW... HER SKIN IS SO FAIR...
...
...
...AND SOFT AND SMOOTH...
WAIT... THIS IS WEIRD...
SHIVER SHIVER
SOME-HOW...

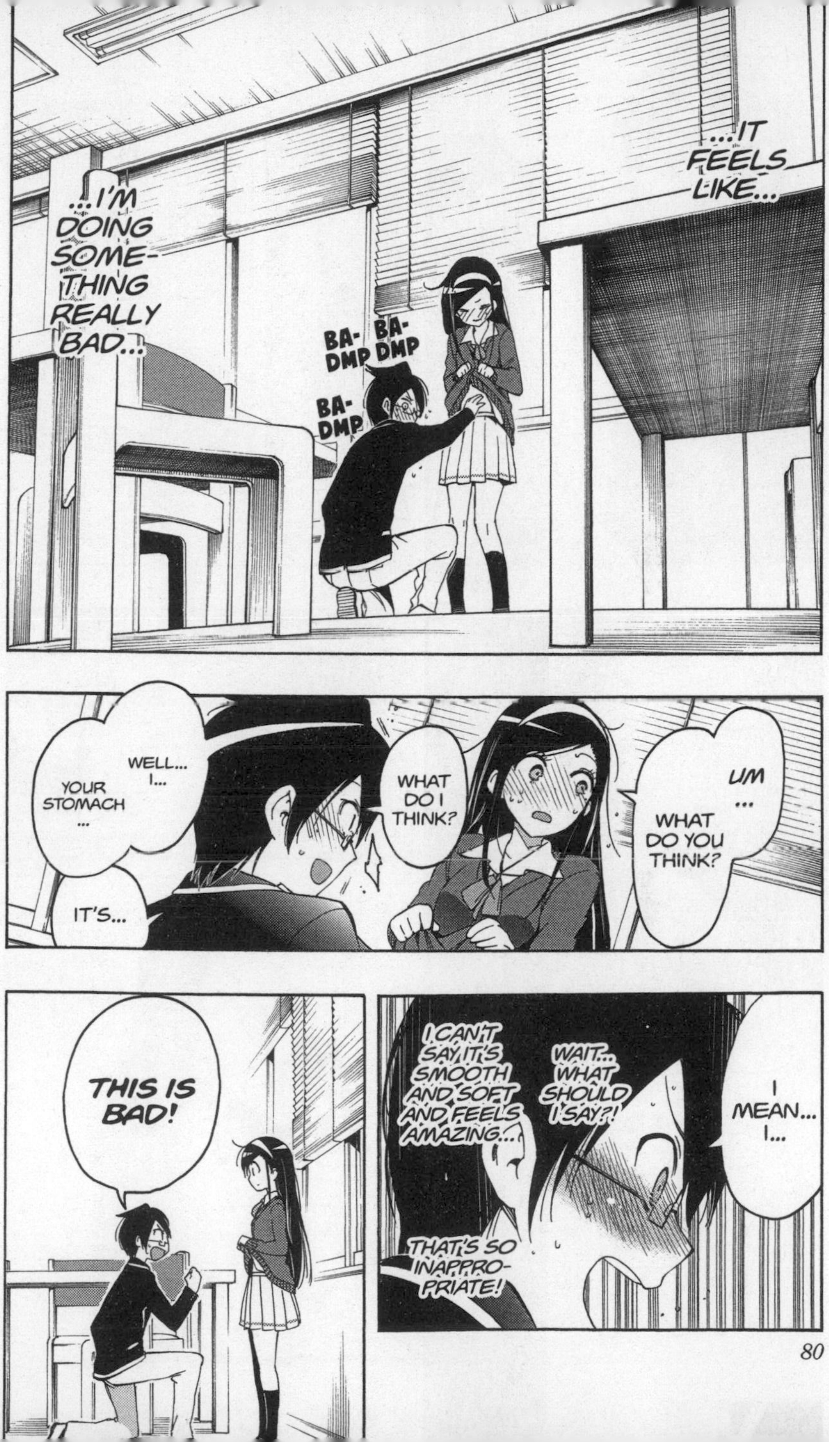
...IT FEELS LIKE...
...I'M DOING SOMETHING REALLY BAD...
BA-DMP
BA-DMP
BA-DMP
UM ... WHAT DO YOU THINK?
WHAT DO I THINK?
WELL... I...
YOUR STOMACH ...
IT'S...
I MEAN... I...
WAIT... WHAT SHOULD I SAY?!
I CAN'T SAY IT'S SMOOTH AND SOFT AND FEELS AMAZING...
THAT'S SO INAPPROPRIATE!
THIS IS BAD!

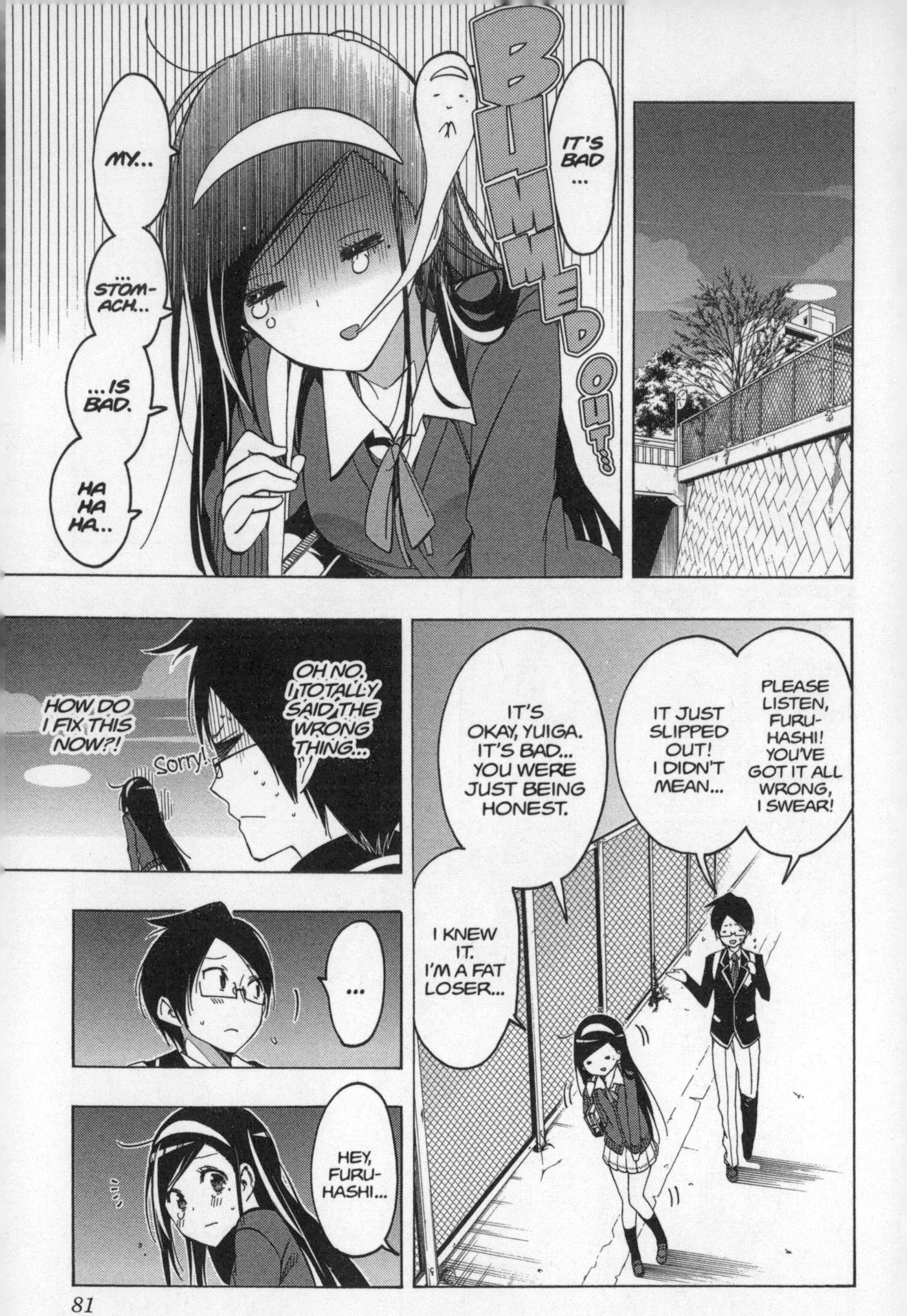
IT'S BAD ...
BUMMED OUT...
MY...
... STÖMACH...
...IS BAD.
HA HA HA...
PLEASE LISTEN, FURUHASHI! YOU'VE GOT IT ALL WRONG, I SWEAR!
IT JUST SLIPPED OUT! I DIDN'T MEAN...
IT'S OKAY, YUIGA. IT'S BAD... YOU WERE JUST BEING HONEST.
I KNEW IT. I'M A FAT LOSER...
OH NO. I TOTALLY SAID THE WRONG THING...
Sorry!
HOW DO I FIX THIS NOW?!
...
HEY, FURUHASHI...

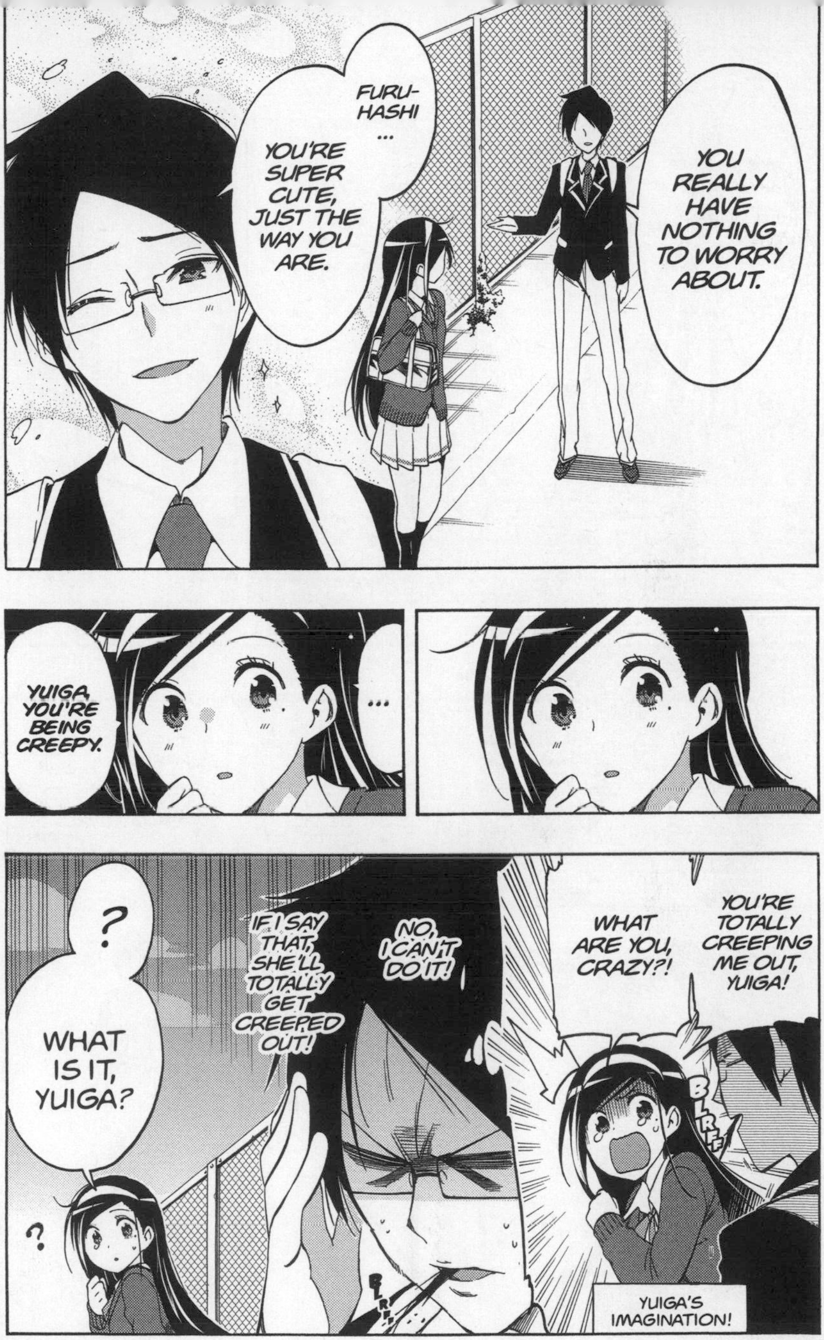
YOU REALLY HAVE NOTHING TO WORRY ABOUT.
FURU-HASHI ...
YOU'RE SUPER CUTE, JUST THE WAY YOU ARE.
...
YUIGA, YOU'RE BEING CREEPY.
YOU'RE TOTALLY CREEPING ME OUT, YUIGA!
WHAT ARE YOU, CRAZY?!
BLRFF
YUIGA'S IMAGINATION!
NO, I CAN'T DO IT!
IF I SAY THAT, SHE'LL TOTALLY GET CREEPED OUT!
?
WHAT IS IT, YUIGA?
?

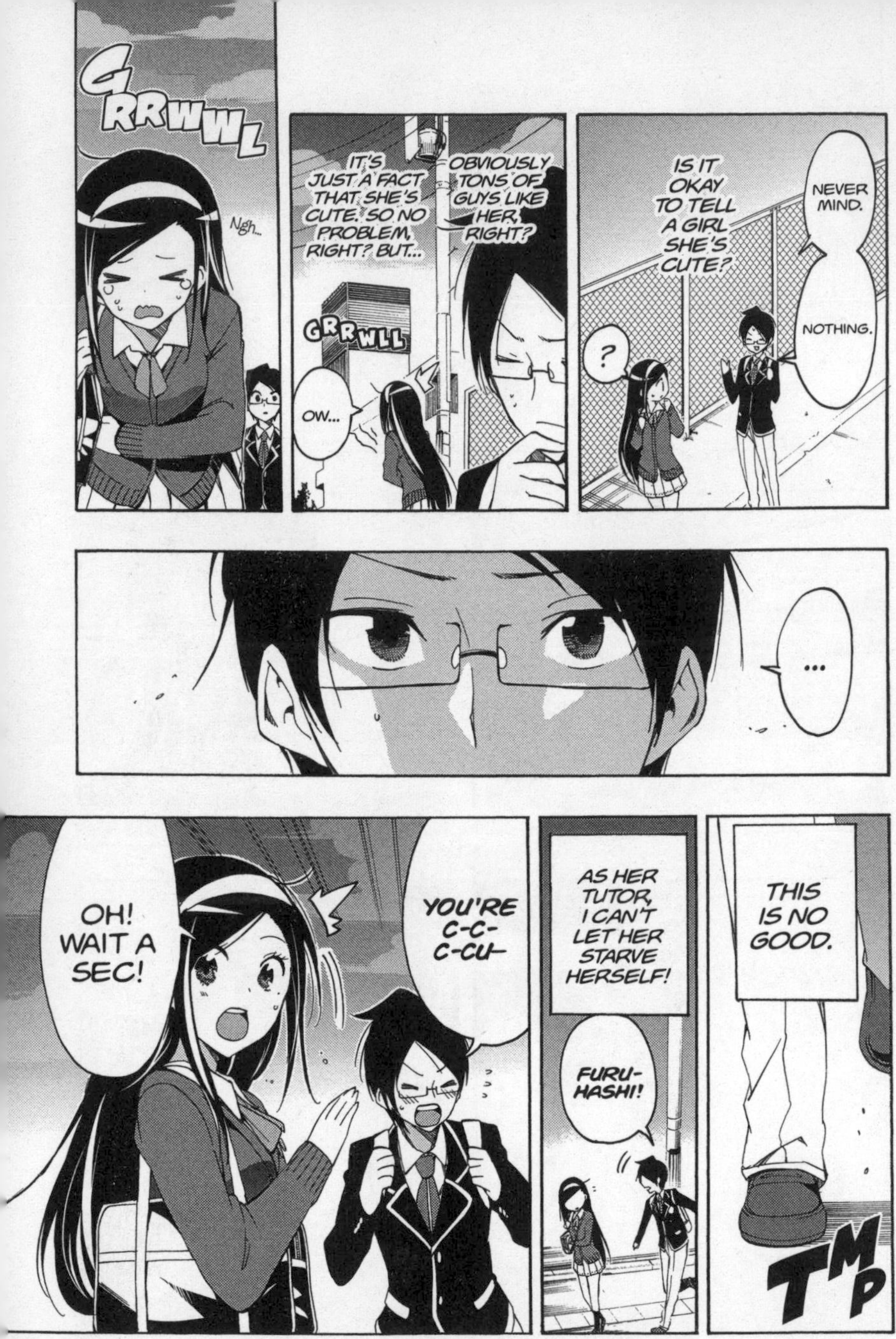
NEVER MIND.
IS IT OKAY TO TELL A GIRL SHE'S CUTE?
NOTHING.
?
OBVIOUSLY TONS OF GUYS LIKE HER, RIGHT?
IT'S JUST A FACT THAT SHE'S CUTE. SO NO PROBLEM, RIGHT? BUT...
GRRWLL
OW...
GRRWWL
Ngh...
...
THIS IS NO GOOD.
TMP
AS HER TUTOR, I CAN'T LET HER STARVE HERSELF!
FURU-HASHI!
YOU'RE C-C-C-CU—
OH! WAIT A SEC!

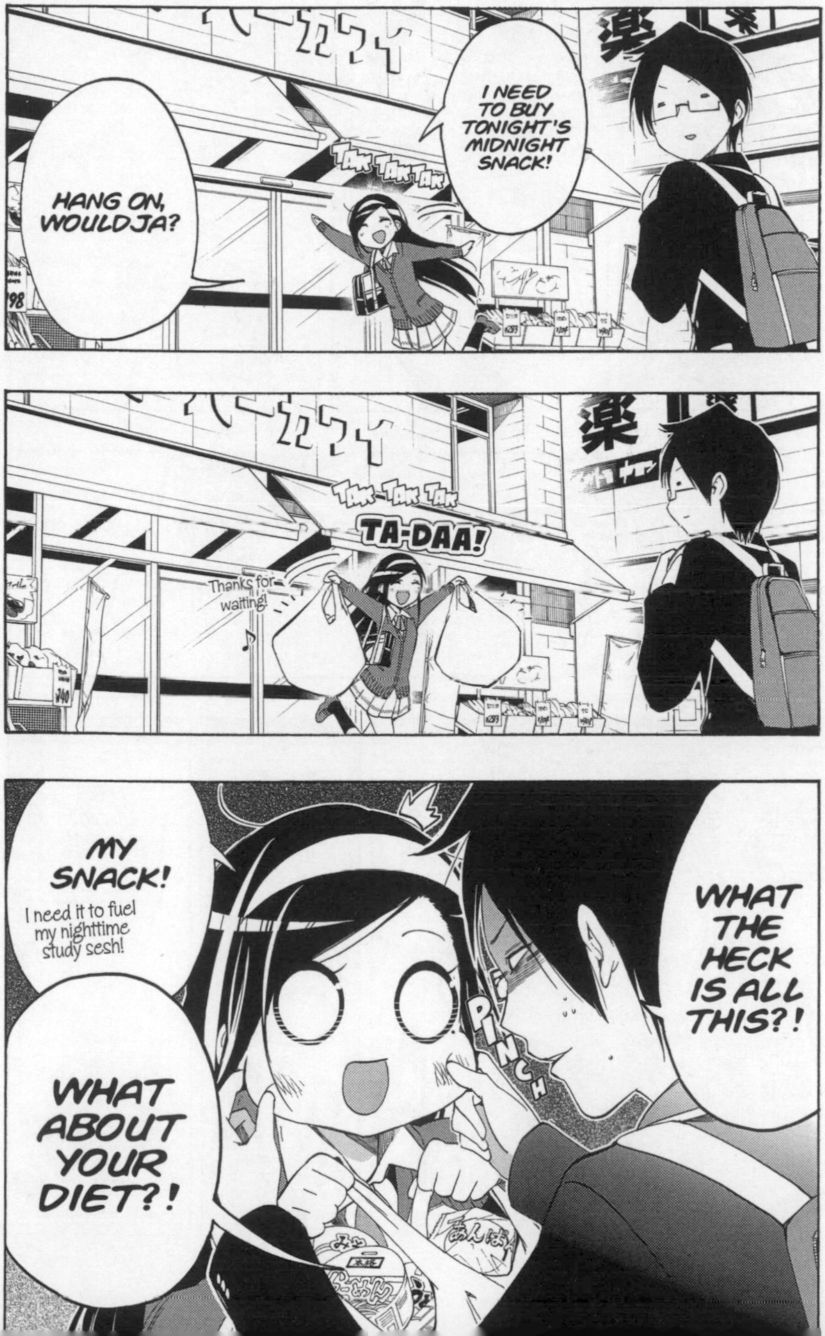
I NEED TO BUY TONIGHT'S MIDNIGHT SNACK!
TAK TAK TAK
HANG ON, WOULDJA?
TAK TAK TAK
TA-DAA!
Thanks for waiting!
WHAT THE HECK IS ALL THIS?!
MY SNACK!
I need it to fuel my nighttime study sesh!
PINCH
WHAT ABOUT YOUR DIET?!

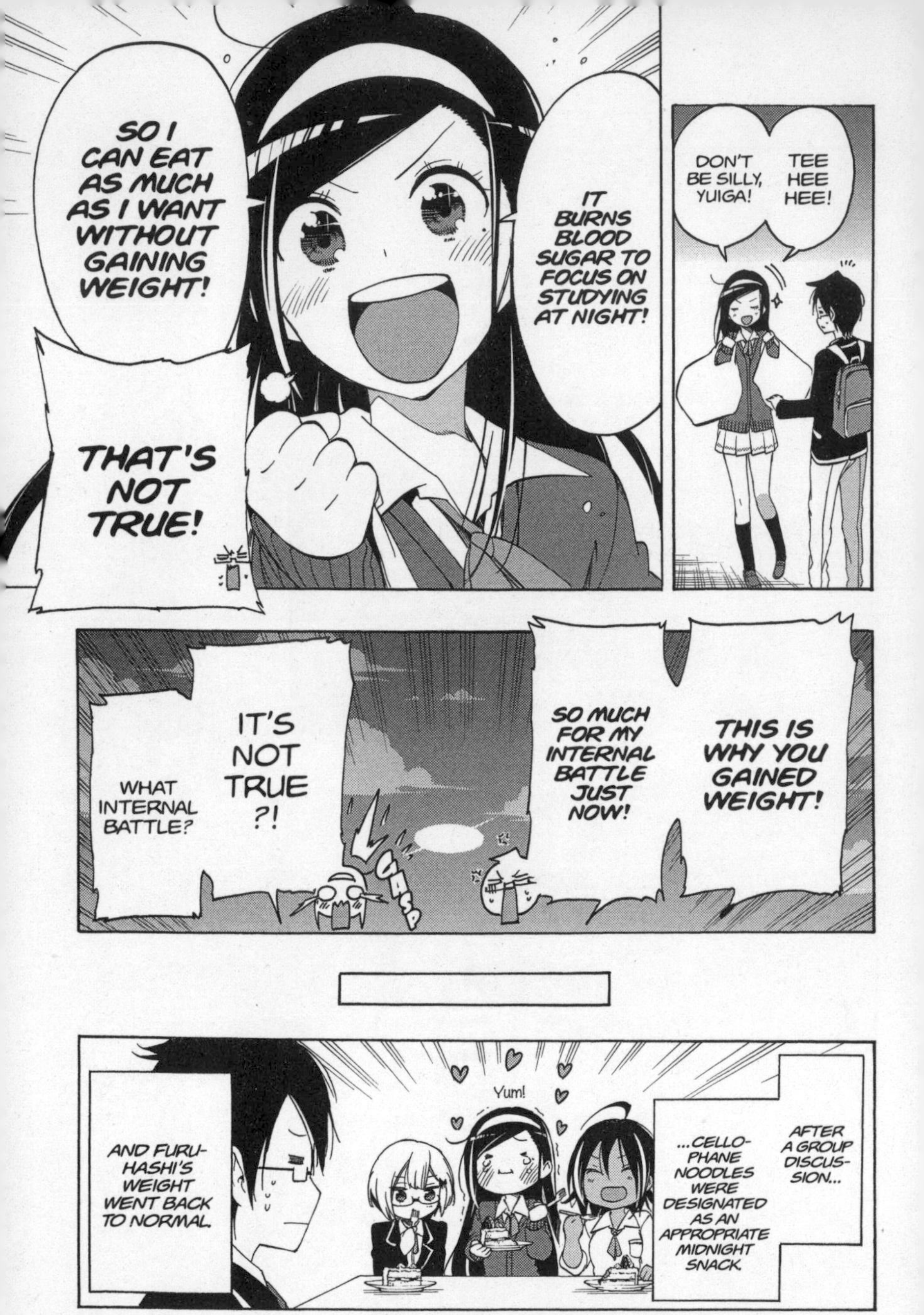
TEE HEE HEE!
DON'T BE SILLY, YUIGA!
IT BURNS BLOOD SUGAR TO FOCUS ON STUDYING AT NIGHT!
SO I CAN EAT AS MUCH AS I WANT WITHOUT GAINING WEIGHT!
THAT'S NOT TRUE!
THIS IS WHY YOU GAINED WEIGHT!
SO MUCH FOR MY INTERNAL BATTLE JUST NOW!
IT'S NOT TRUE?!
WHAT INTERNAL BATTLE?
GASA
AFTER A GROUP DISCUSSION...
...CELLOPHANE NOODLES WERE DESIGNATED AS AN APPROPRIATE MIDNIGHT SNACK.
Yum!
AND FURUHASHI'S WEIGHT WENT BACK TO NORMAL.

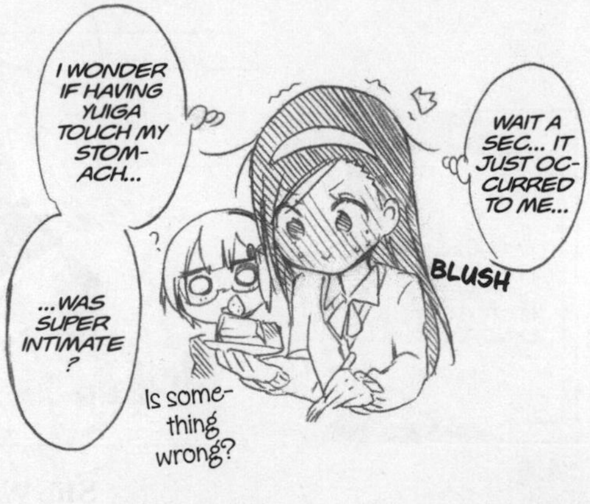
WAIT A SEC... IT JUST OC-CURRED TO ME...
BLUSH
I WONDER IF HAVING YUIGA TOUCH MY STOM-ACH...
...WAS SUPER INTIMATE ?
Is some-thing wrong?

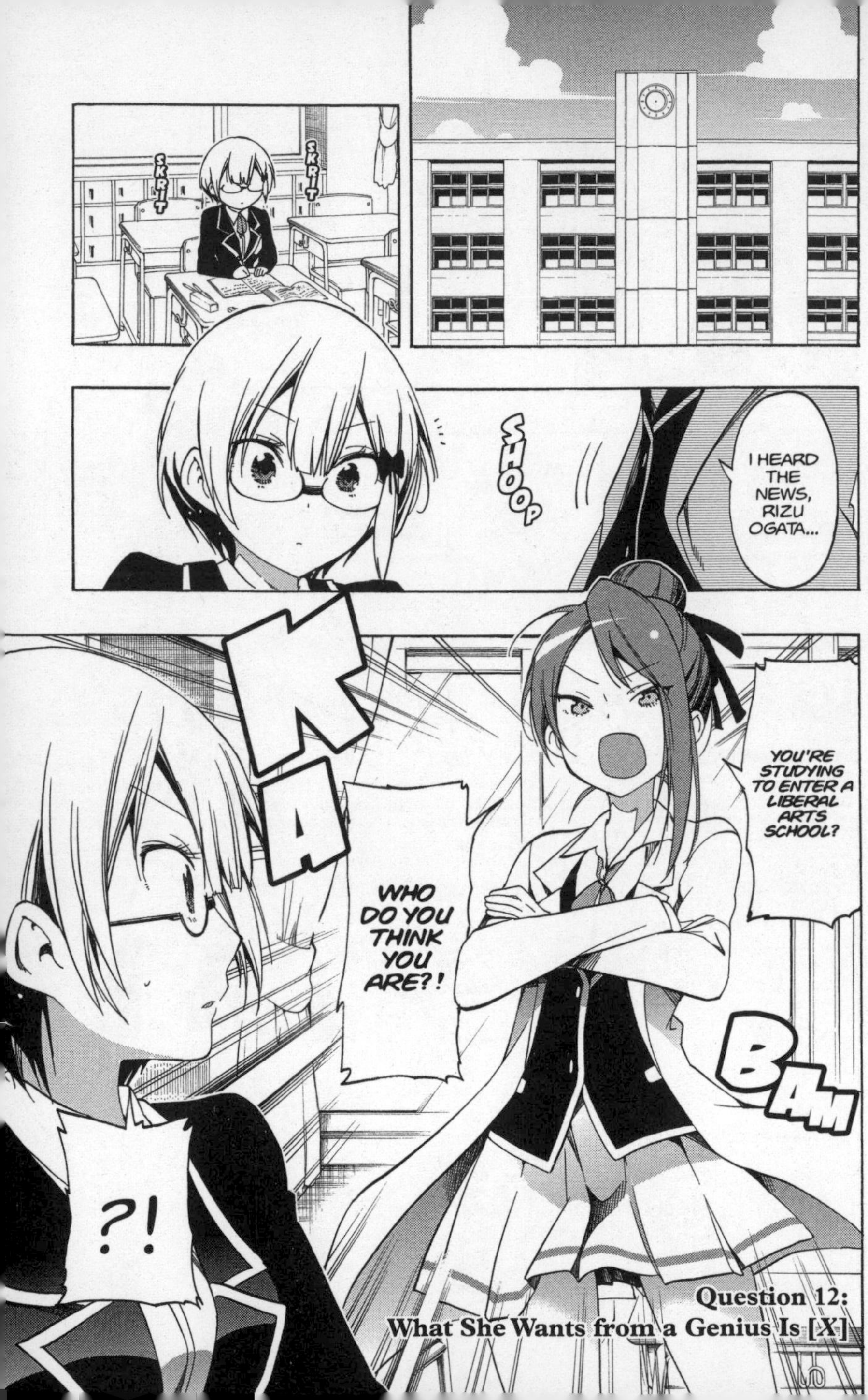
SKRIT
SKRIT
I HEARD THE NEWS, RIZU OGATA...
SHOOP
YOU'RE STUDYING TO ENTER A LIBERAL ARTS SCHOOL?
WHO DO YOU THINK YOU ARE?!
KA
BAM
?!

Question 12: What She Wants from a Genius Is [X]

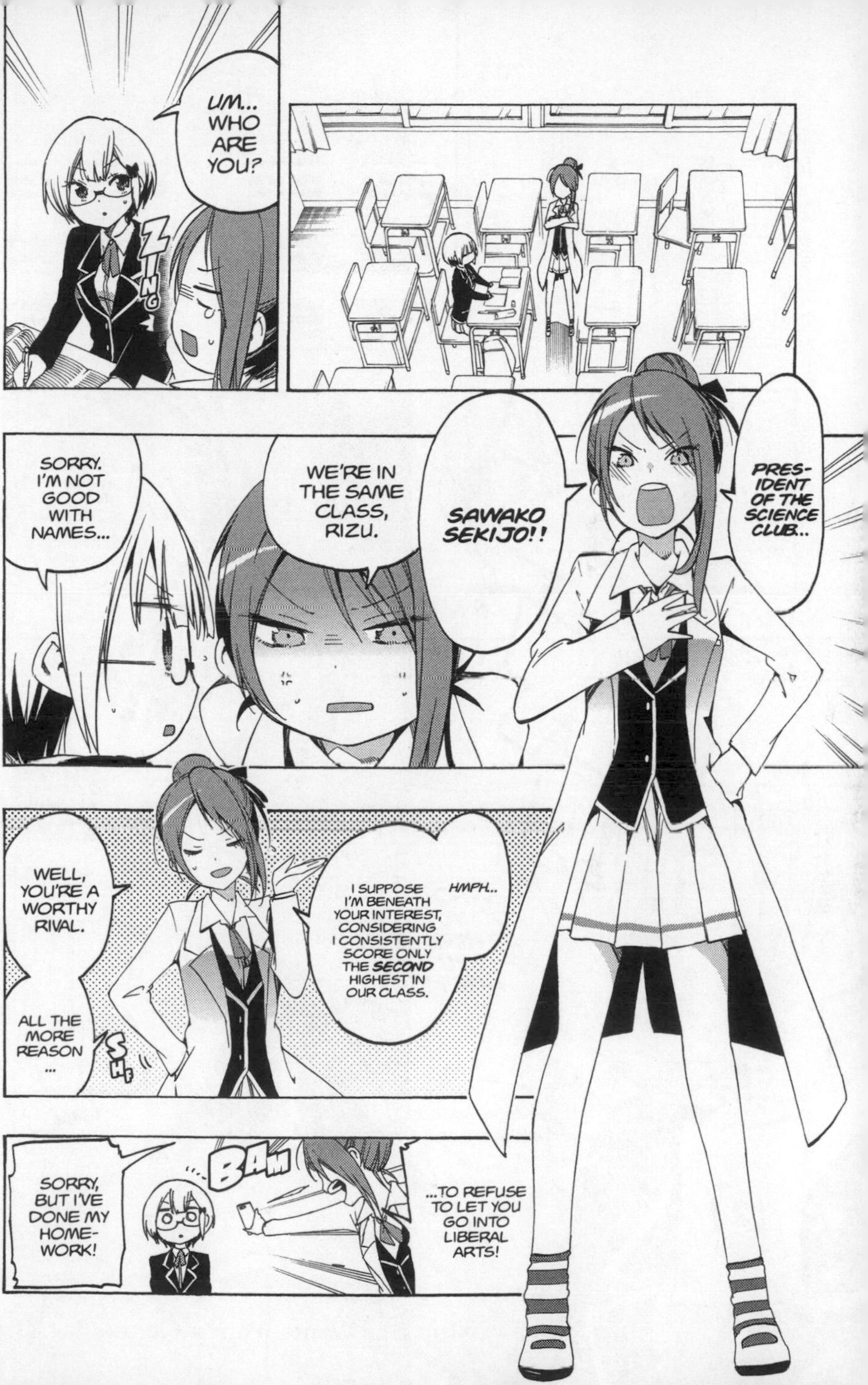
UM... WHO ARE YOU?
ZING
PRES-IDENT OF THE SCIENCE CLUB...
SAWAKO SEKIJO!!
WE'RE IN THE SAME CLASS, RIZU.
SORRY. I'M NOT GOOD WITH NAMES...
HMPH..
I SUPPOSE I'M BENEATH YOUR INTEREST, CONSIDERING I CONSISTENTLY SCORE ONLY THE SECOND HIGHEST IN OUR CLASS.
WELL, YOU'RE A WORTHY RIVAL.
ALL THE MORE REASON ...
SHF
...TO REFUSE TO LET YOU GO INTO LIBERAL ARTS!
BAM
SORRY, BUT I'VE DONE MY HOME-WORK!

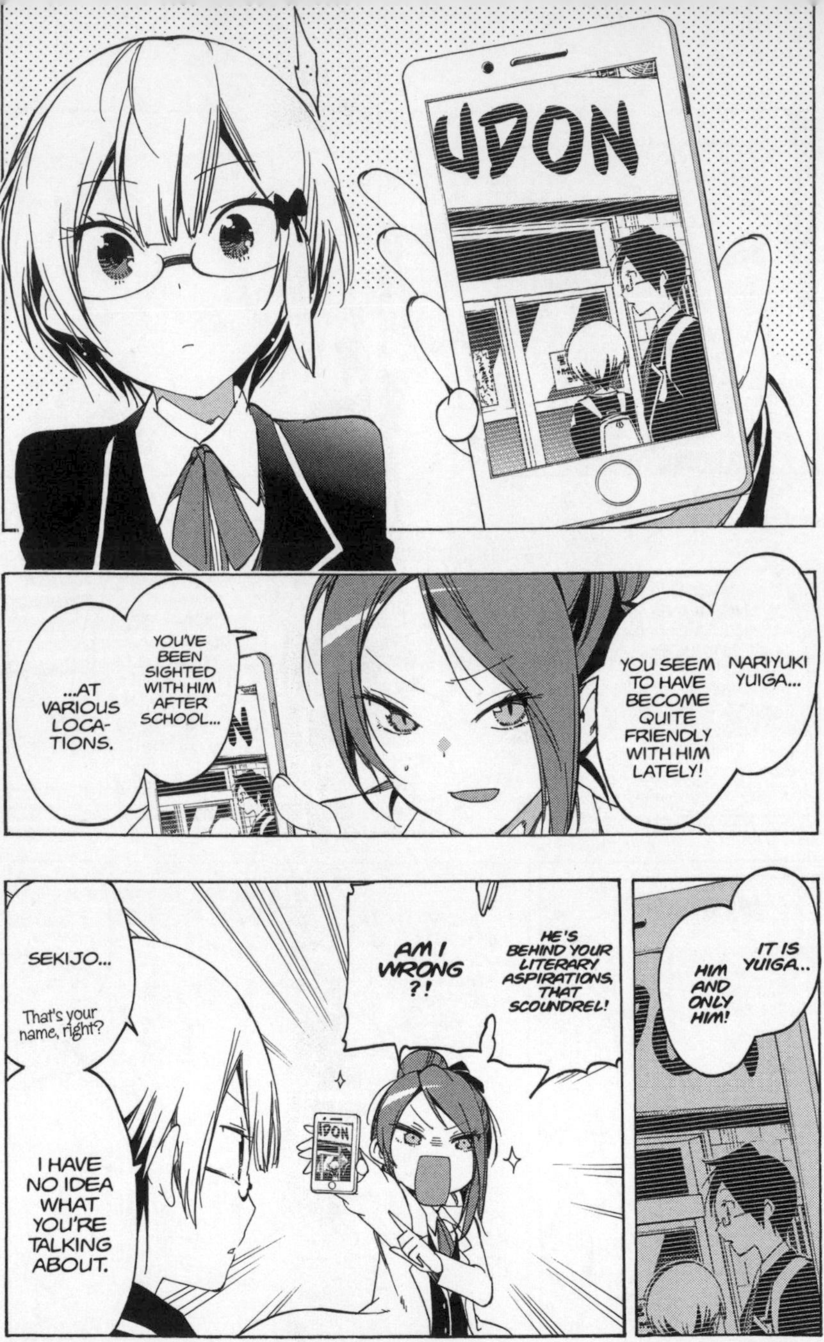
UDON
NARIYUKI YUIGA...
YOU SEEM TO HAVE BECOME QUITE FRIENDLY WITH HIM LATELY!
YOU'VE BEEN SIGHTED WITH HIM AFTER SCHOOL...
...AT VARIOUS LOCA-TIONS.
IT IS YUIGA...
HIM AND ONLY HIM!
HE'S BEHIND YOUR LITERARY ASPIRATIONS, THAT SCOUNDREL!
AM I WRONG?!
SEKIJO...
That's your name, right?
I HAVE NO IDEA WHAT YOU'RE TALKING ABOUT.

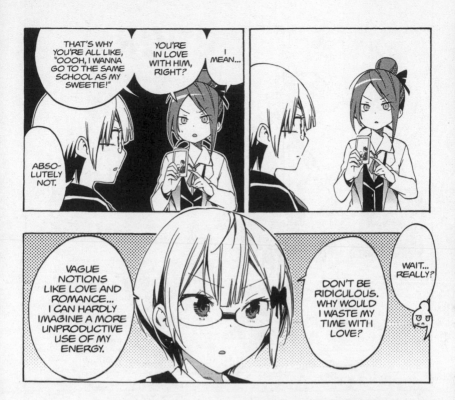

I MEAN...
YOU'RE IN LOVE WITH HIM, RIGHT?
THAT'S WHY YOU'RE ALL LIKE, "OOOH, I WANNA GO TO THE SAME SCHOOL AS MY SWEETIE!"
ABSO-LUTELY NOT.
WAIT... REALLY?
DON'T BE RIDICULOUS. WHY WOULD I WASTE MY TIME WITH LOVE?
VAGUE NOTIONS LIKE LOVE AND ROMANCE... I CAN HARDLY IMAGINE A MORE UNPRODUCTIVE USE OF MY ENERGY.
OH... IT SEEMS I WAS MISTAKEN. I WAS SO SURE...
BOW
NOW, IF YOU'LL EXCUSE ME, YUIGA IS COMING OVER TODAY.
SURE. SORRY ABOUT THAT...
KLATTER

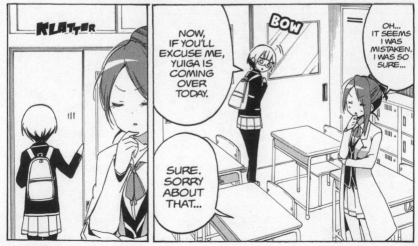

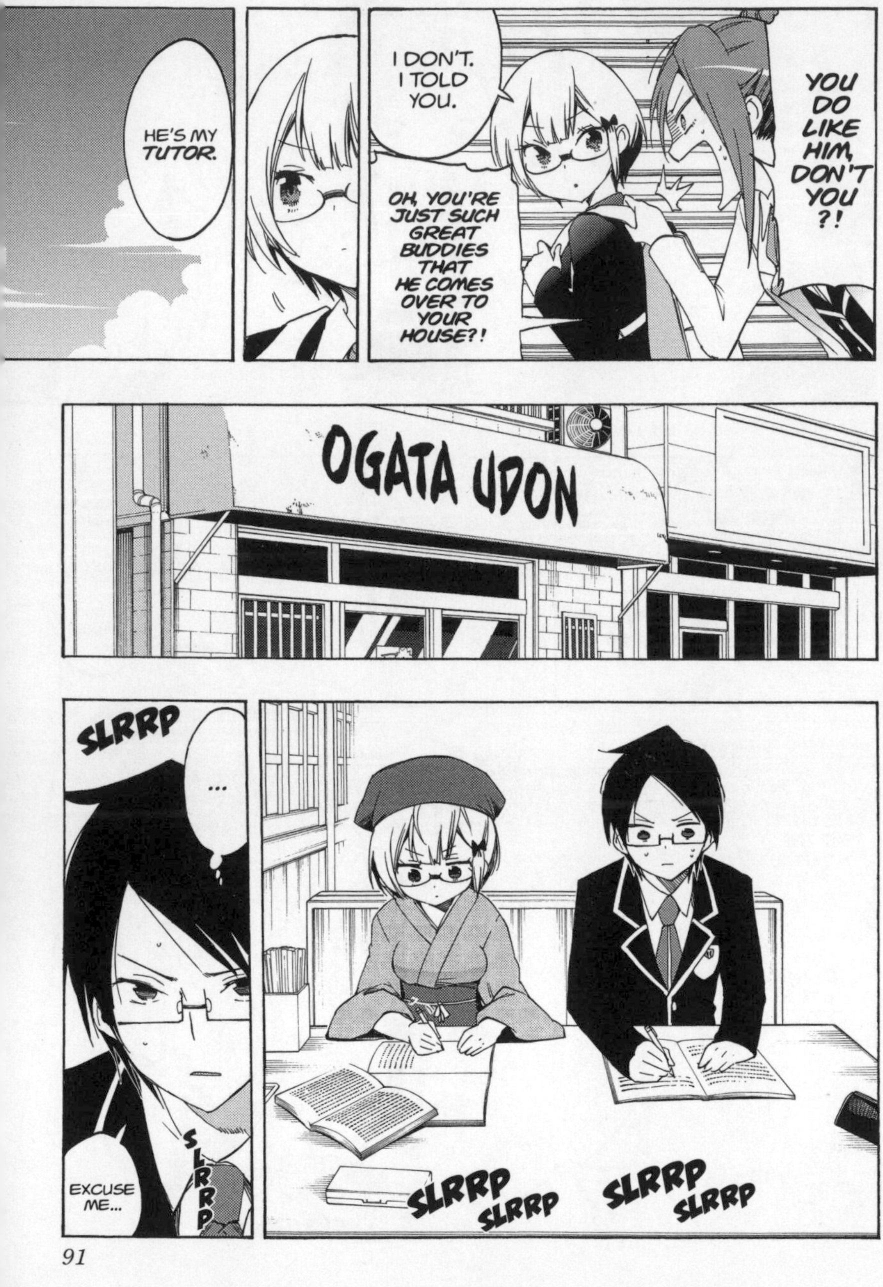
YOU DO LIKE HIM, DON'T YOU?!
I DON'T. I TOLD YOU.
OH, YOU'RE JUST SUCH GREAT BUDDIES THAT HE COMES OVER TO YOUR HOUSE?!
HE'S MY TUTOR.
OGATA UDON
SLRRP SLRRP
SLRRP SLRRP
SLRRP
...
SLRRP
EXCUSE ME...

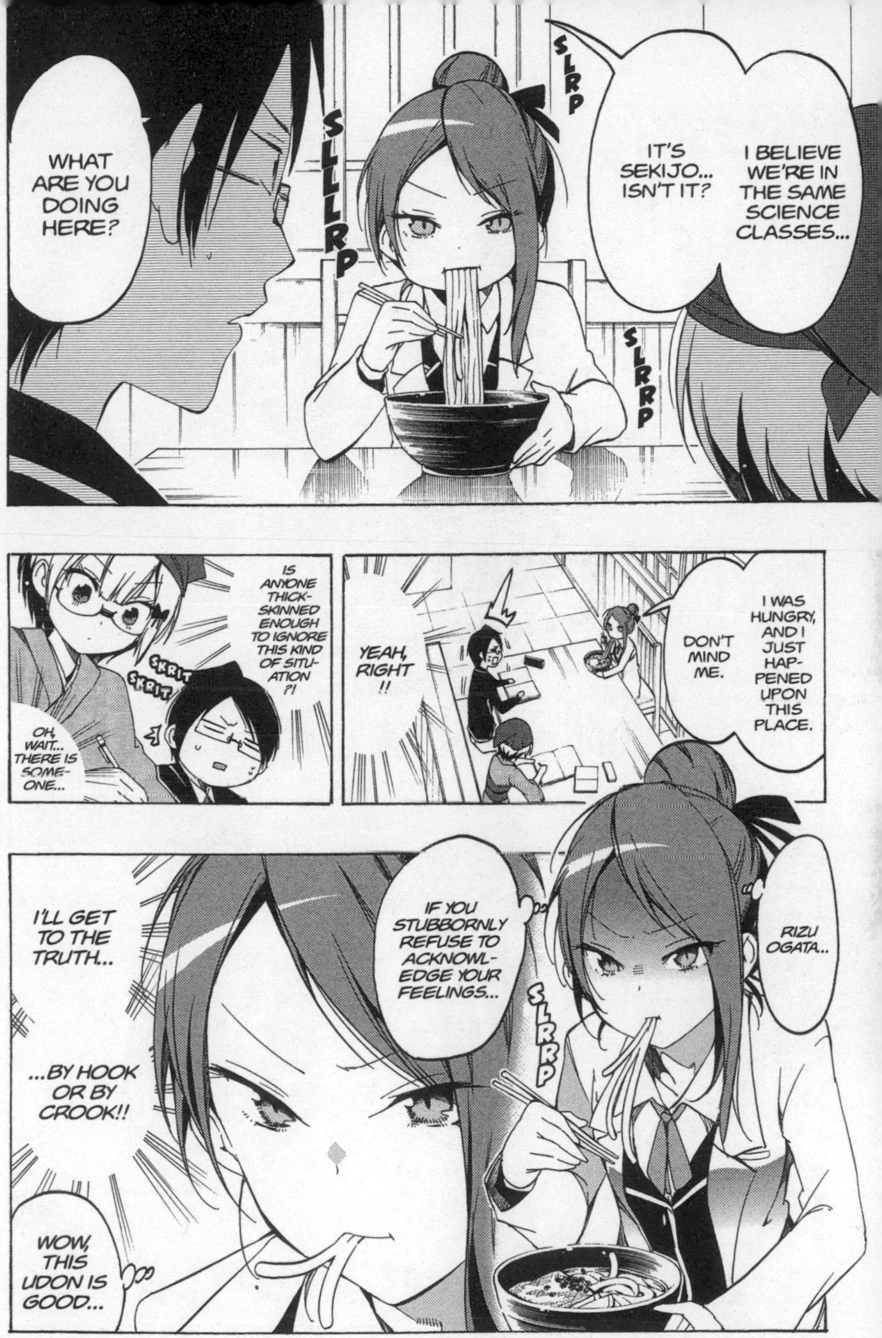
SLRP
I BELIEVE WE'RE IN THE SAME SCIENCE CLASSES...
IT'S SEKIJO... ISN'T IT?
SLRRP
SLLLRP
WHAT ARE YOU DOING HERE?
I WAS HUNGRY, AND I JUST HAPPENED UPON THIS PLACE.
DON'T MIND ME.
YEAH, RIGHT!!
IS ANYONE THICK-SKINNED ENOUGH TO IGNORE THIS KIND OF SITUATION?!
SKRIT
SKRIT
OH, WAIT... THERE IS SOMEONE...
RIZU OGATA...
SLRRP
IF YOU STUBBORNLY REFUSE TO ACKNOWLEDGE YOUR FEELINGS...
I'LL GET TO THE TRUTH...
...BY HOOK OR BY CROOK!!
WOW, THIS UDON IS GOOD...

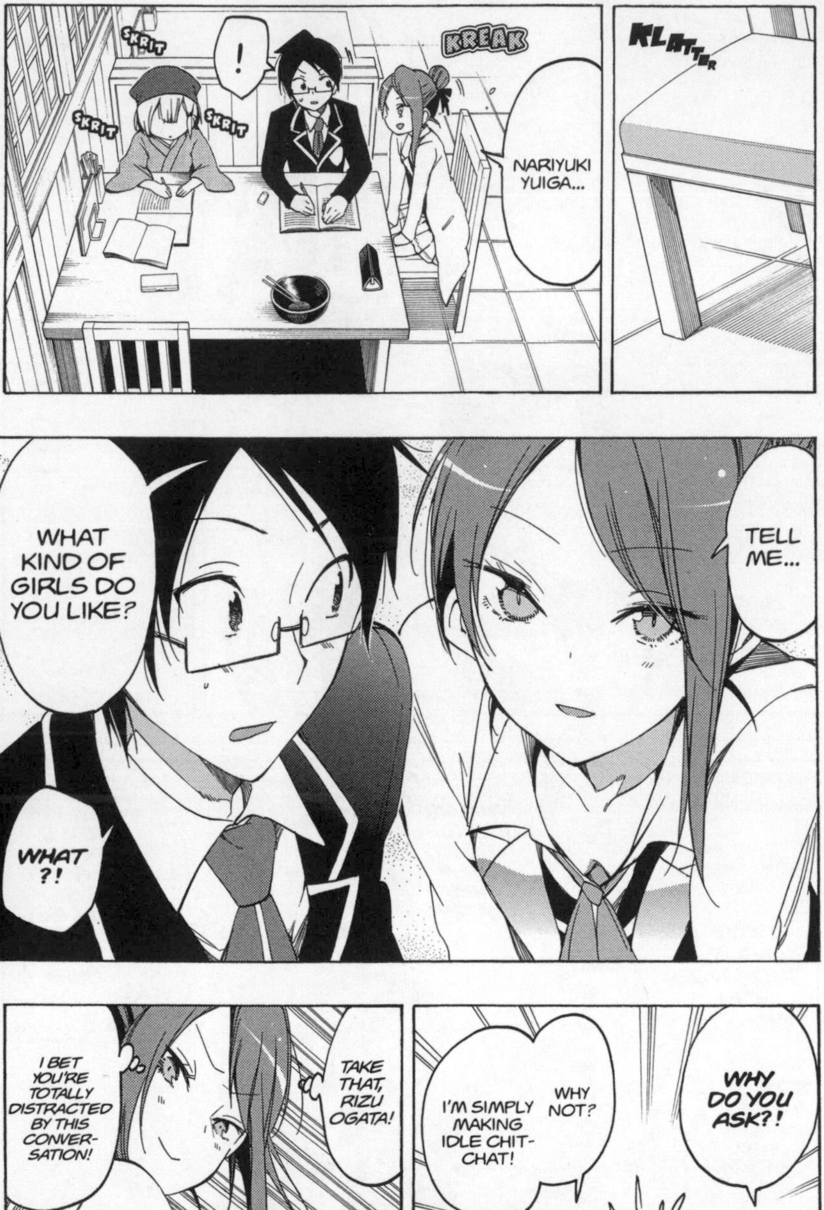
KLATTER
NARIYUKI YUIGA...
KREAK
!
SKRIT
SKRIT
SKRIT
TELL ME...
WHAT KIND OF GIRLS DO YOU LIKE?
WHAT?!
WHY DO YOU ASK?!
WHY NOT?
I'M SIMPLY MAKING IDLE CHIT-CHAT!
TAKE THAT, RIZU OGATA!
I BET YOU'RE TOTALLY DISTRACTED BY THIS CONVERSATION!

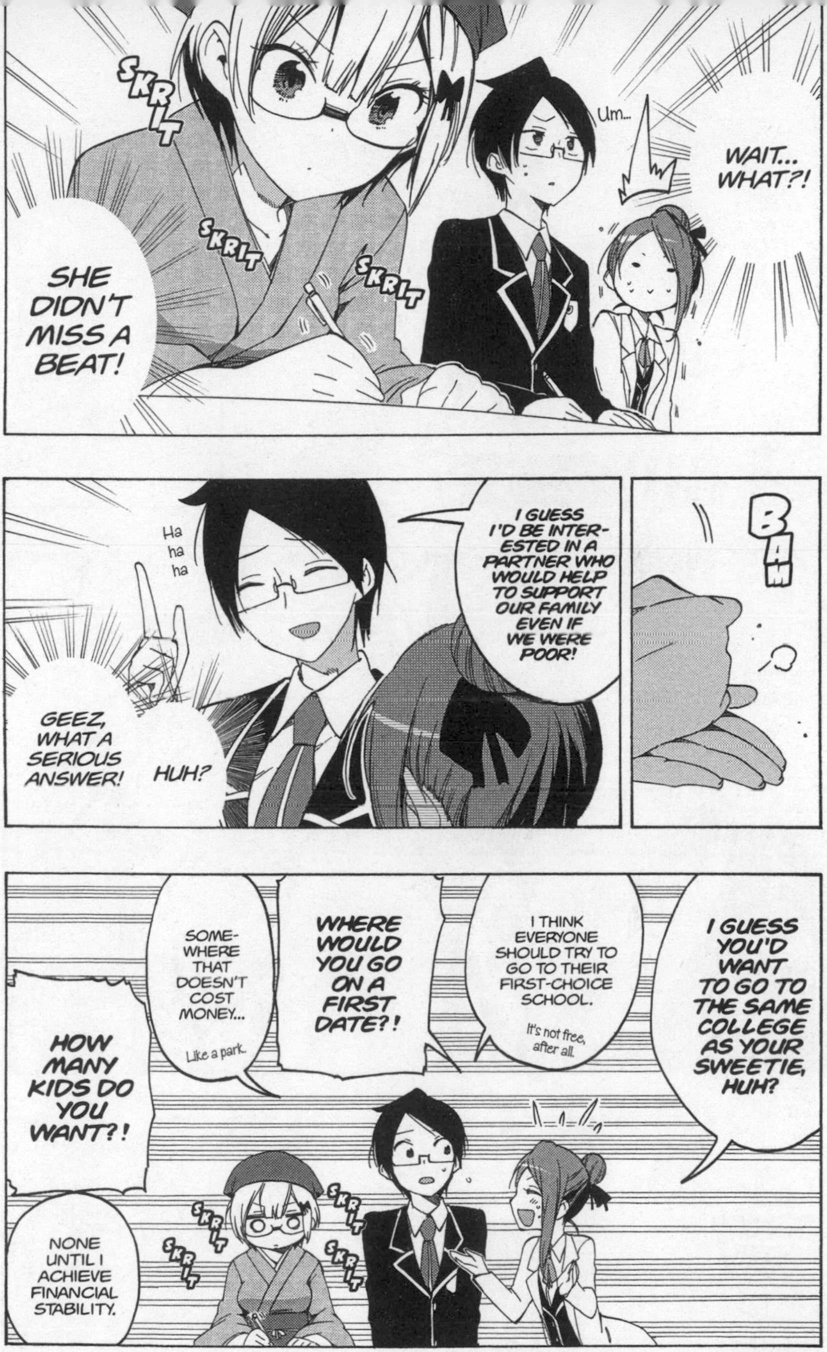
WAIT... WHAT?!
Um...
SKRIT
SKRIT
SKRIT
SHE DIDN'T MISS A BEAT!
BAM
I GUESS I'D BE INTER-ESTED IN A PARTNER WHO WOULD HELP TO SUPPORT OUR FAMILY EVEN IF WE WERE POOR!
Ha ha ha
HUH?
GEEZ, WHAT A SERIOUS ANSWER!
I GUESS YOU'D WANT TO GO TO THE SAME COLLEGE AS YOUR SWEETIE, HUH?
I THINK EVERYONE SHOULD TRY TO GO TO THEIR FIRST-CHOICE SCHOOL.
It's not free, after all.
WHERE WOULD YOU GO ON A FIRST DATE?!
SOME-WHERE THAT DOESN'T COST MONEY...
Like a park.
HOW MANY KIDS DO YOU WANT?!
SKRIT
SKRIT
SKRIT
SKRIT
NONE UNTIL I ACHIEVE FINANCIAL STABILITY.

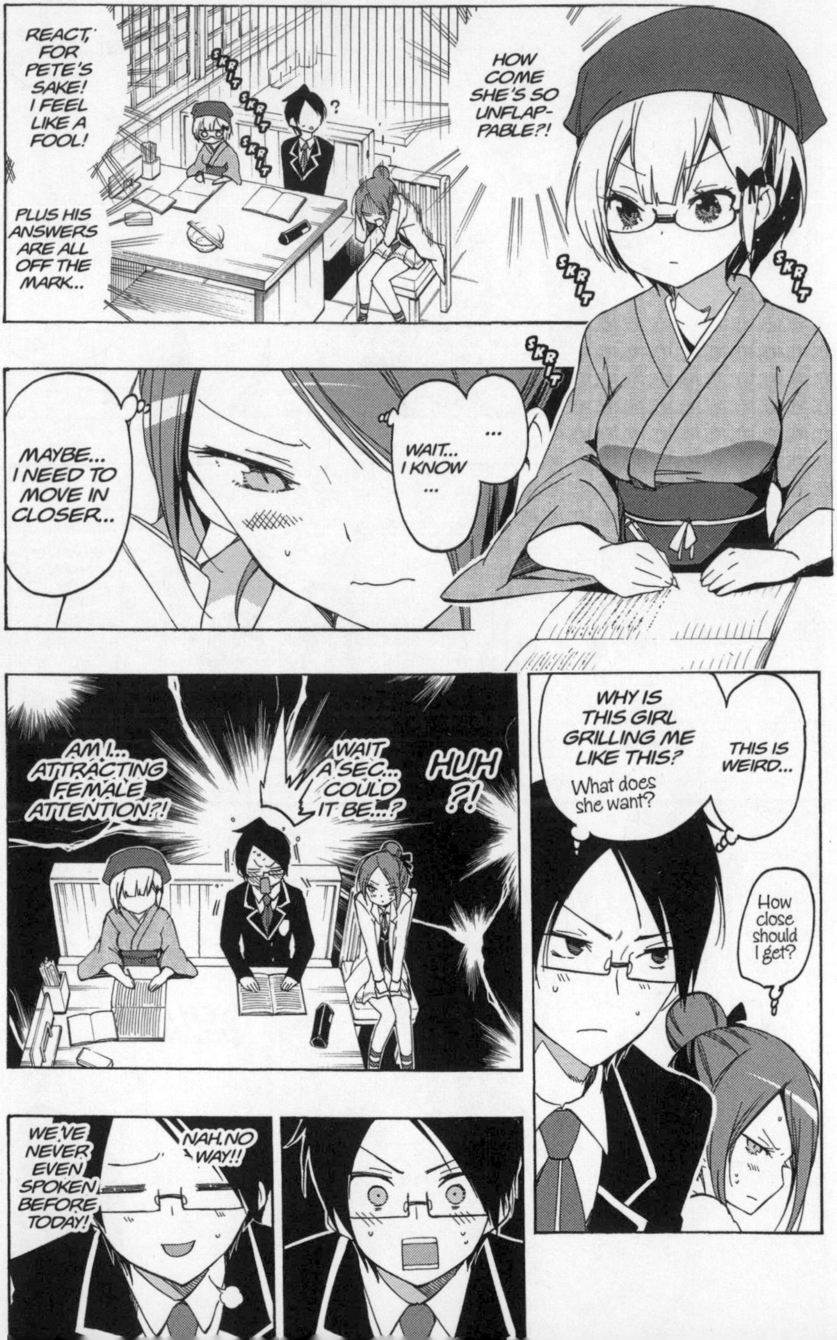
HOW COME SHE'S SO UNFLAPPABLE?!
SKRIT
SKRIT
SKRIT
REACT, FOR PETE'S SAKE! I FEEL LIKE A FOOL!
SKRIT SKRIT SKRIT
PLUS HIS ANSWERS ARE ALL OFF THE MARK...
... WAIT... I KNOW...
MAYBE... I NEED TO MOVE IN CLOSER...
WHY IS THIS GIRL GRILLING ME LIKE THIS? What does she want?
THIS IS WEIRD...
How close should I get?
HUH?!
WAIT A SEC... COULD IT BE...?
AM I... ATTRACTING FEMALE ATTENTION?!
NAH, NO WAY!!
WE'VE NEVER EVEN SPOKEN BEFORE TODAY!

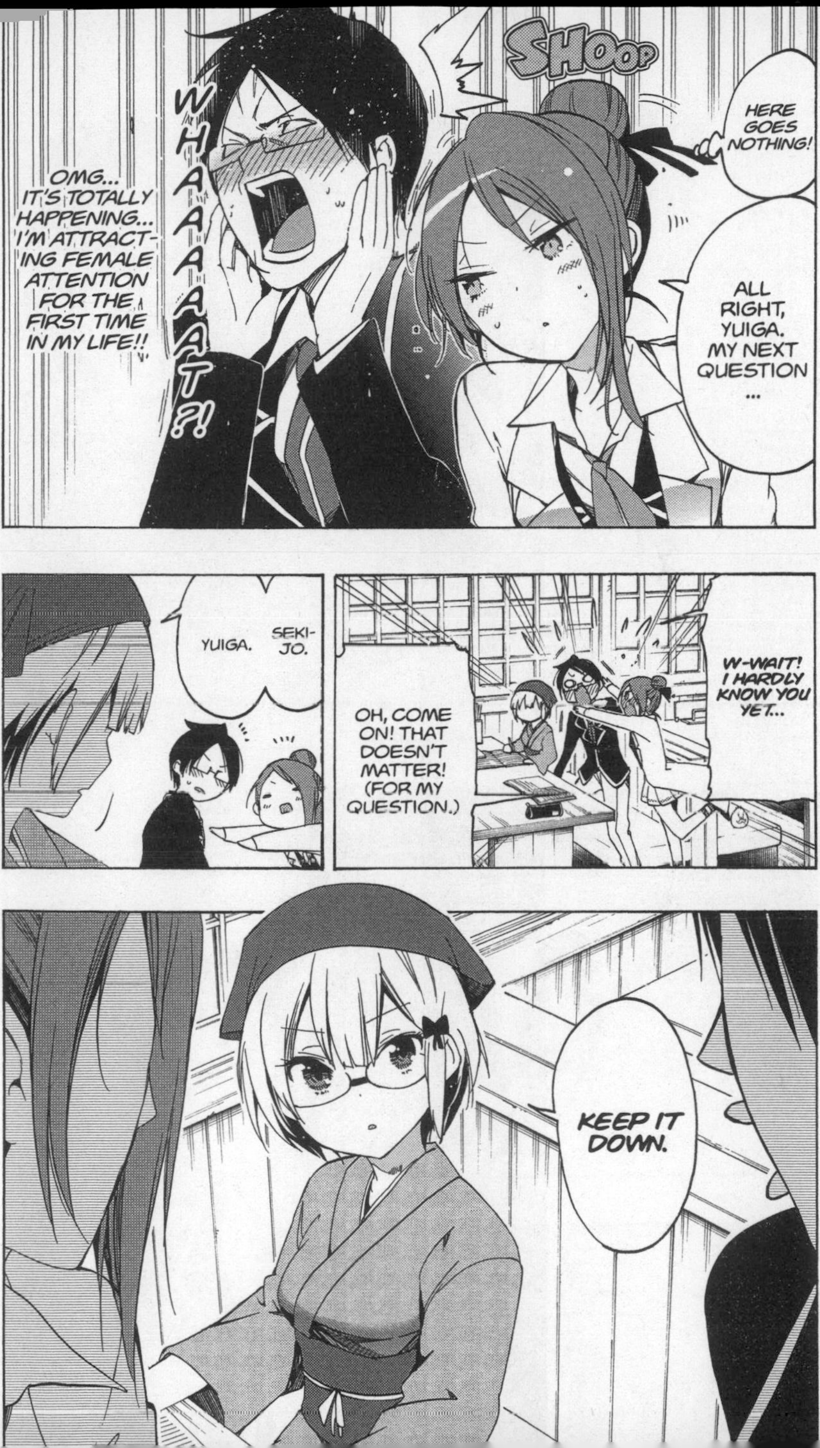
HERE GOES NOTHING!
SHOOP
ALL RIGHT, YUIGA. MY NEXT QUESTION ...
WHAAAAAAAT?!
OMG... IT'S TOTALLY HAPPENING... I'M ATTRACTING FEMALE ATTENTION FOR THE FIRST TIME IN MY LIFE!!
W-WAIT! I HARDLY KNOW YOU YET...
OH, COME ON! THAT DOESN'T MATTER! (FOR MY QUESTION.)
YUIGA. SEKI-JO.
KEEP IT DOWN.

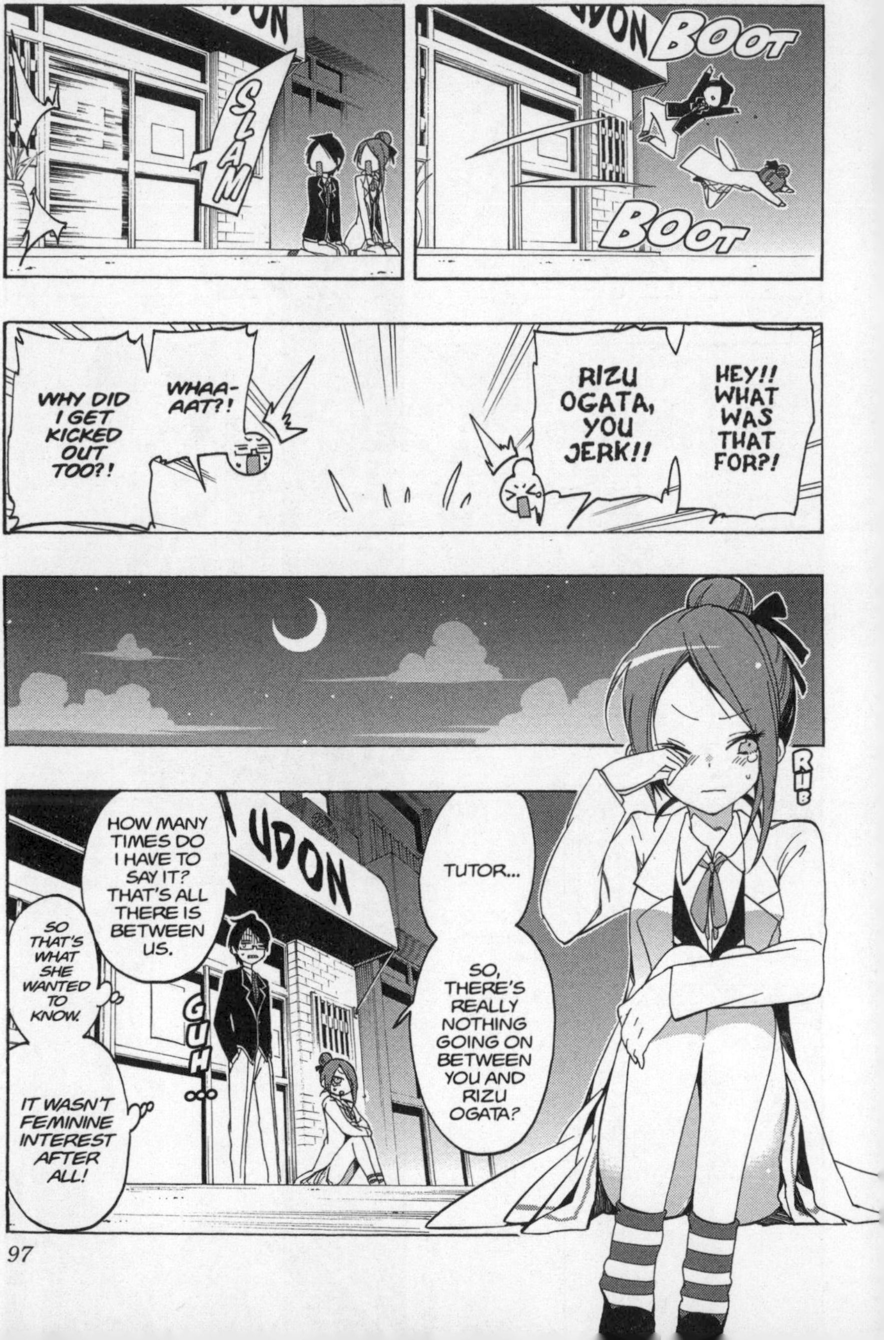
BOOT
BOOT
SLAM
HEY!! WHAT WAS THAT FOR?!
RIZU OGATA, YOU JERK!!
WHAA-AAT?!
WHY DID I GET KICKED OUT TOO?!
RUB
TUTOR...
SO, THERE'S REALLY NOTHING GOING ON BETWEEN YOU AND RIZU OGATA?
UDON
HOW MANY TIMES DO I HAVE TO SAY IT? THAT'S ALL THERE IS BETWEEN US.
GUH...
SO THAT'S WHAT SHE WANTED TO KNOW.
IT WASN'T FEMININE INTEREST AFTER ALL!

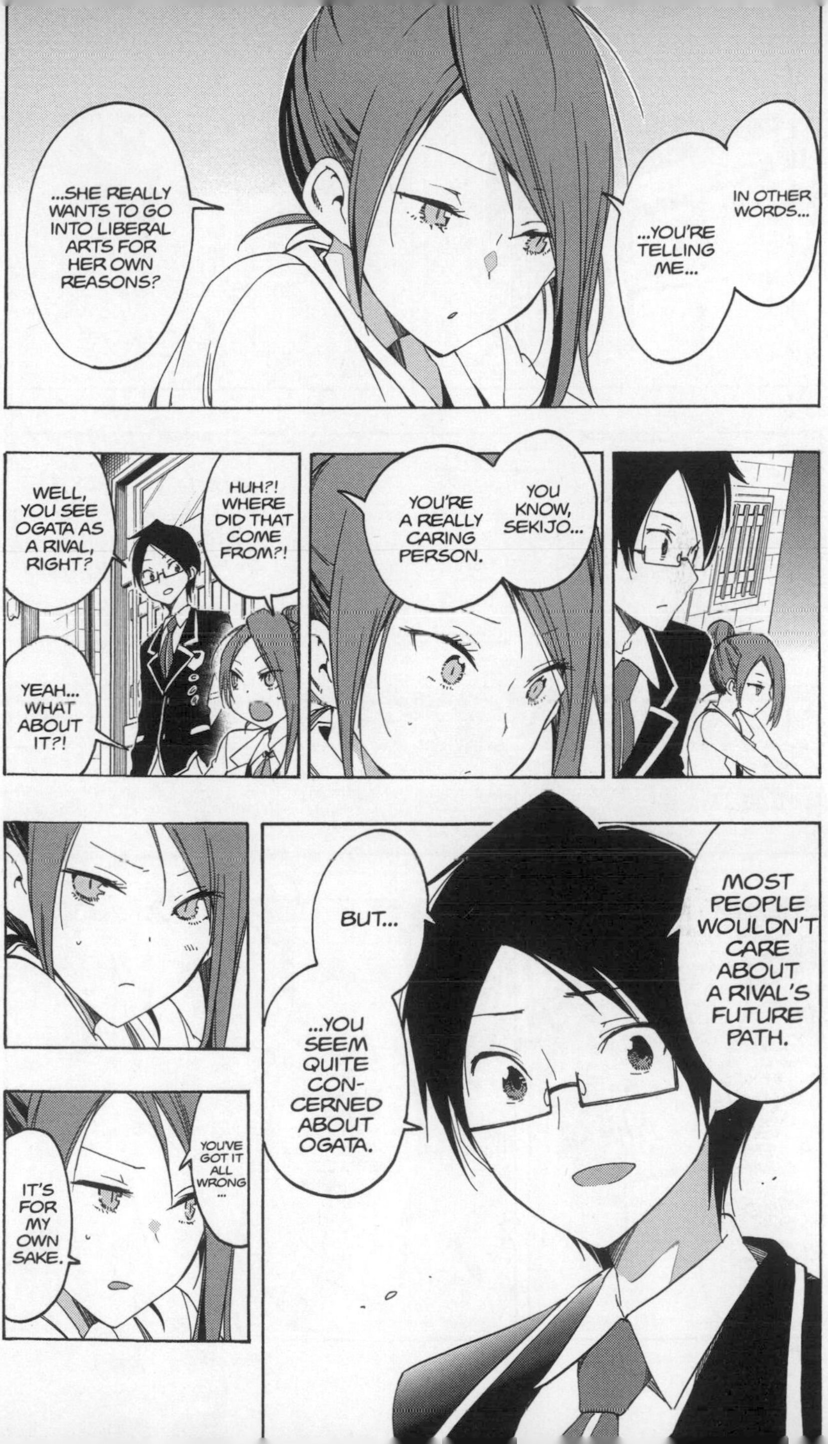
IN OTHER WORDS...
...YOU'RE TELLING ME...
...SHE REALLY WANTS TO GO INTO LIBERAL ARTS FOR HER OWN REASONS?
YOU KNOW, SEKIJO...
YOU'RE A REALLY CARING PERSON.
HUH?! WHERE DID THAT COME FROM?!
WELL, YOU SEE OGATA AS A RIVAL, RIGHT?
YEAH... WHAT ABOUT IT?!
MOST PEOPLE WOULDN'T CARE ABOUT A RIVAL'S FUTURE PATH.
BUT...
...YOU SEEM QUITE CON-CERNED ABOUT OGATA.
YOU'VE GOT IT ALL WRONG...
IT'S FOR MY OWN SAKE.

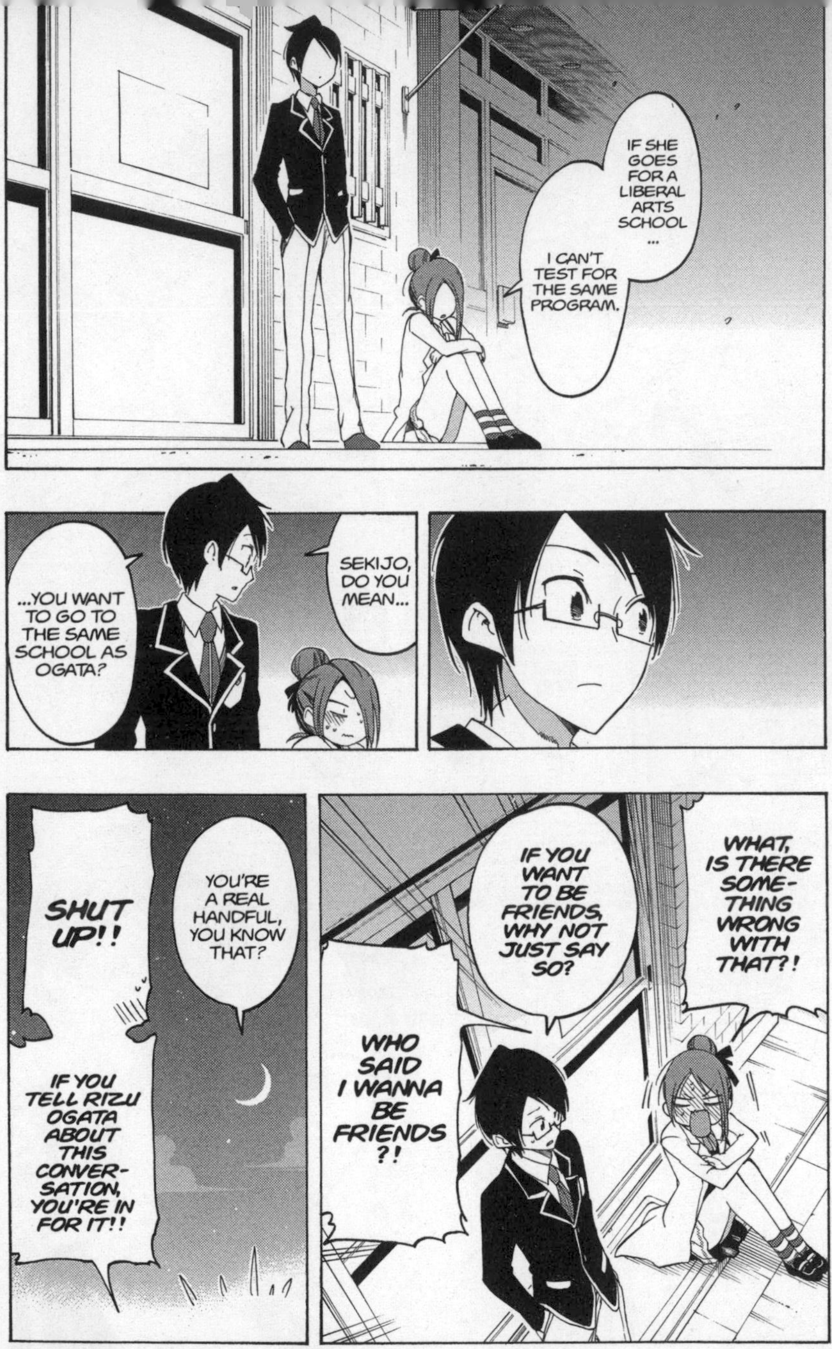
IF SHE GOES FOR A LIBERAL ARTS SCHOOL ...
I CAN'T TEST FOR THE SAME PROGRAM.
SEKIJO, DO YOU MEAN...
...YOU WANT TO GO TO THE SAME SCHOOL AS OGATA?
WHAT, IS THERE SOME-THING WRONG WITH THAT?!
IF YOU WANT TO BE FRIENDS, WHY NOT JUST SAY SO?
WHO SAID I WANNA BE FRIENDS?!
YOU'RE A REAL HANDFUL, YOU KNOW THAT?
SHUT UP!!
IF YOU TELL RIZU OGATA ABOUT THIS CONVER-SATION, YOU'RE IN FOR IT!!

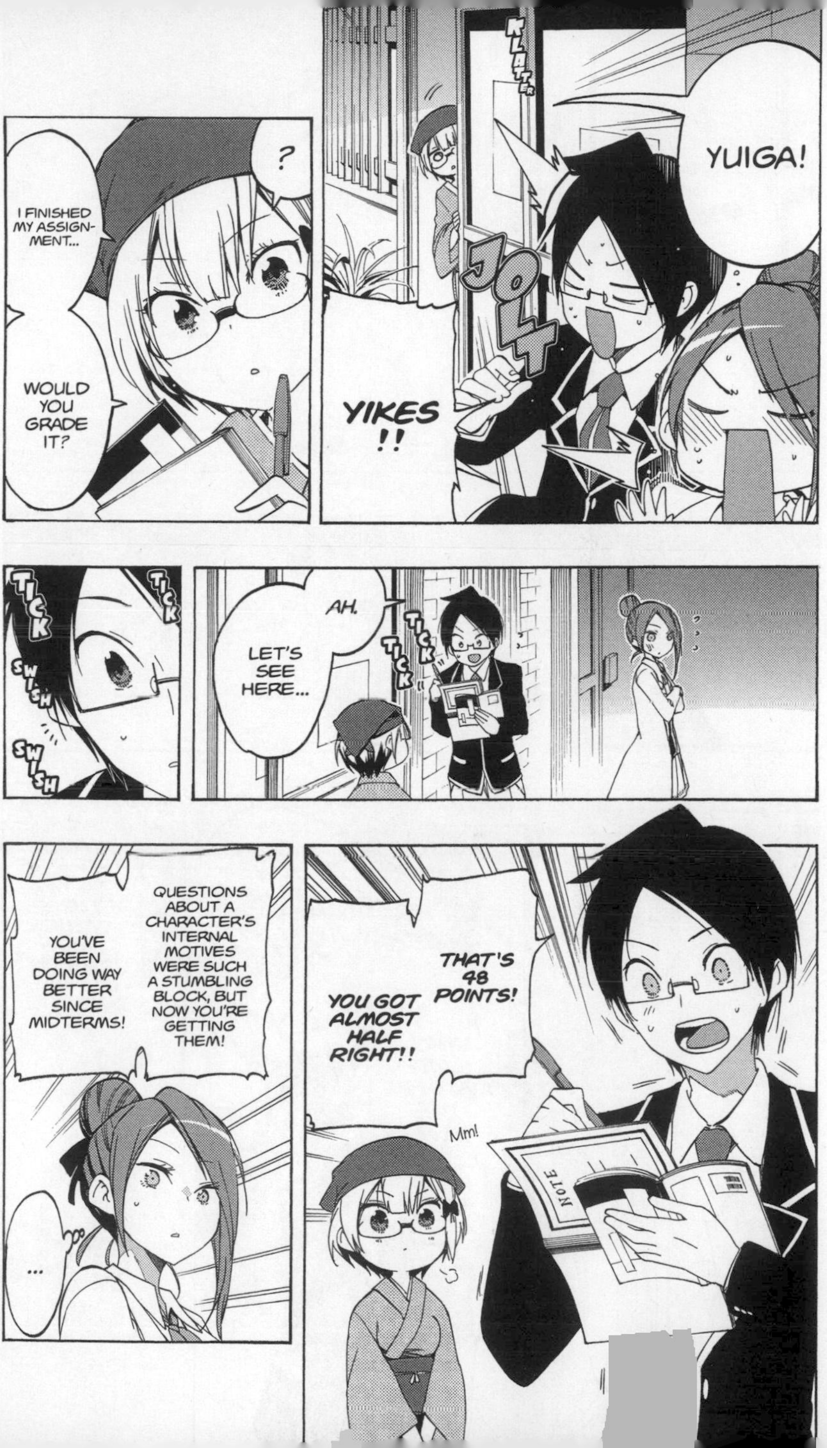
KLATTER
YUIGA!
JOLT
YIKES!!
?
I FINISHED MY ASSIGNMENT...
WOULD YOU GRADE IT?
AH.
LET'S SEE HERE...
TICK
TICK
TICK
TICK
SWISH
SWISH
THAT'S 48 POINTS!
YOU GOT ALMOST HALF RIGHT!!
Mm!
QUESTIONS ABOUT A CHARACTER'S INTERNAL MOTIVES WERE SUCH A STUMBLING BLOCK, BUT NOW YOU'RE GETTING THEM!
YOU'VE BEEN DOING WAY BETTER SINCE MIDTERMS!
...

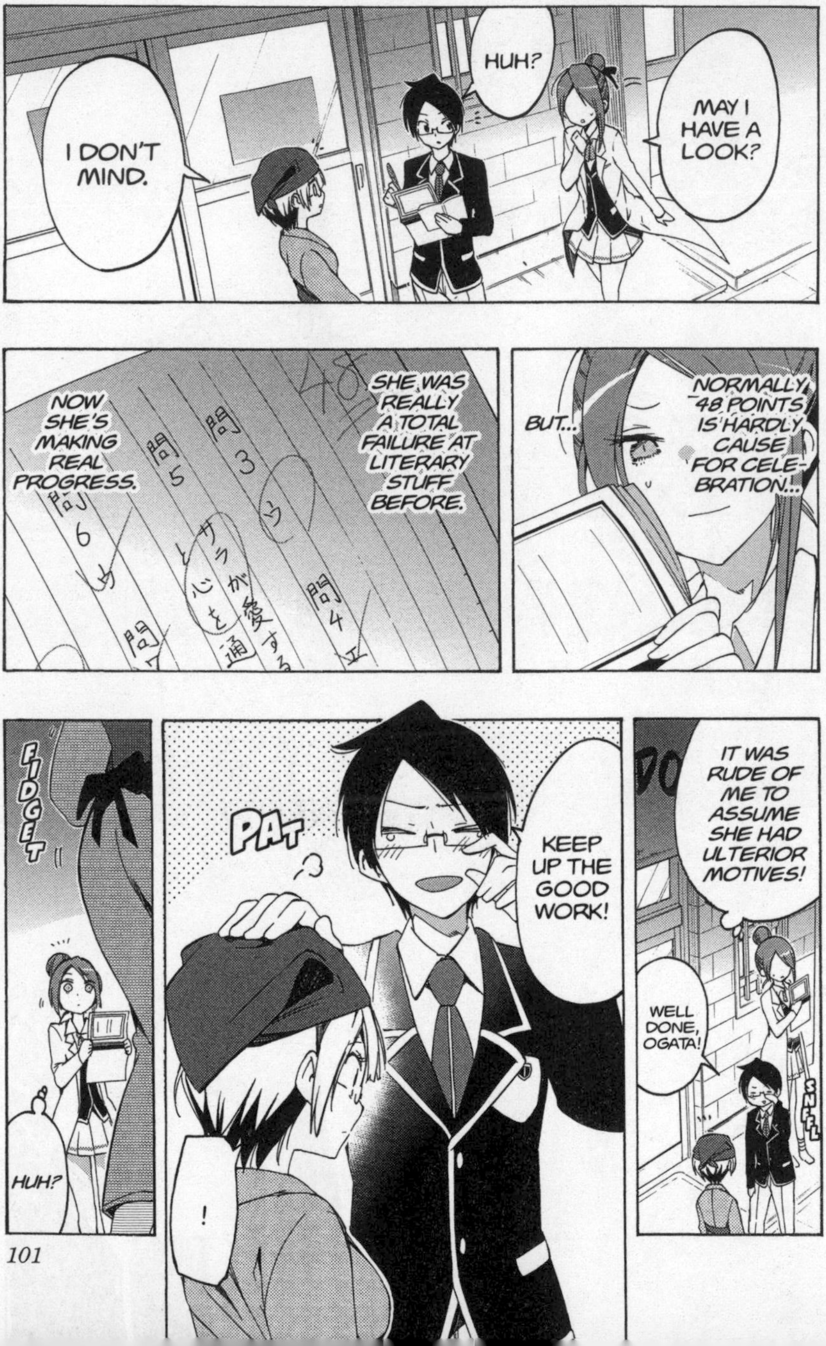

MAY I HAVE A LOOK?
HUH?
I DON'T MIND.
NORMALLY 48 POINTS IS HARDLY CAUSE FOR CELEBRATION...
BUT...
SHE WAS REALLY A TOTAL FAILURE AT LITERARY STUFF BEFORE.
NOW SHE'S MAKING REAL PROGRESS.
IT WAS RUDE OF ME TO ASSUME SHE HAD ULTERIOR MOTIVES!
WELL DONE, OGATA!
KEEP UP THE GOOD WORK!
PAT
!
FIDGET
HUH?

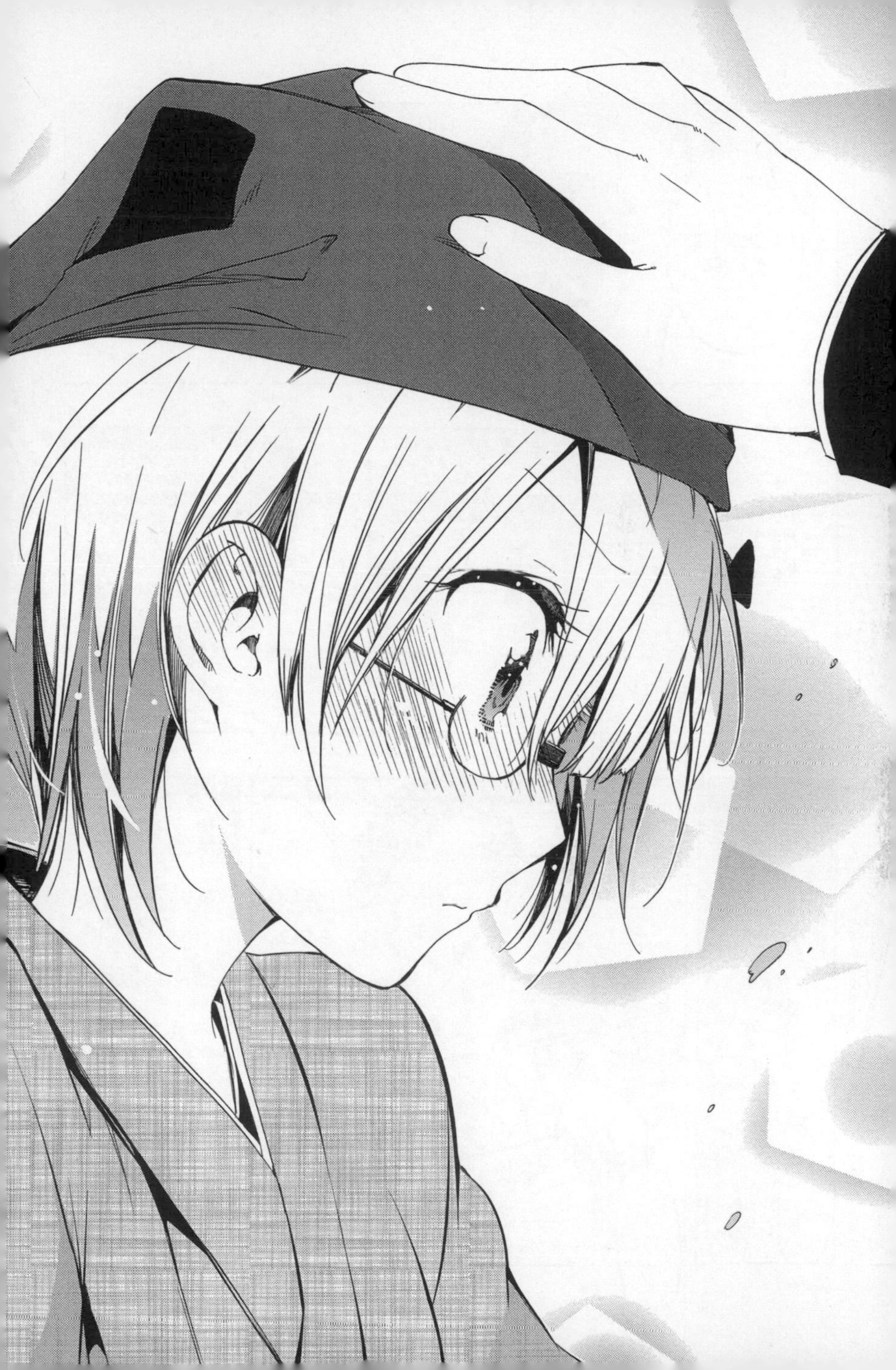

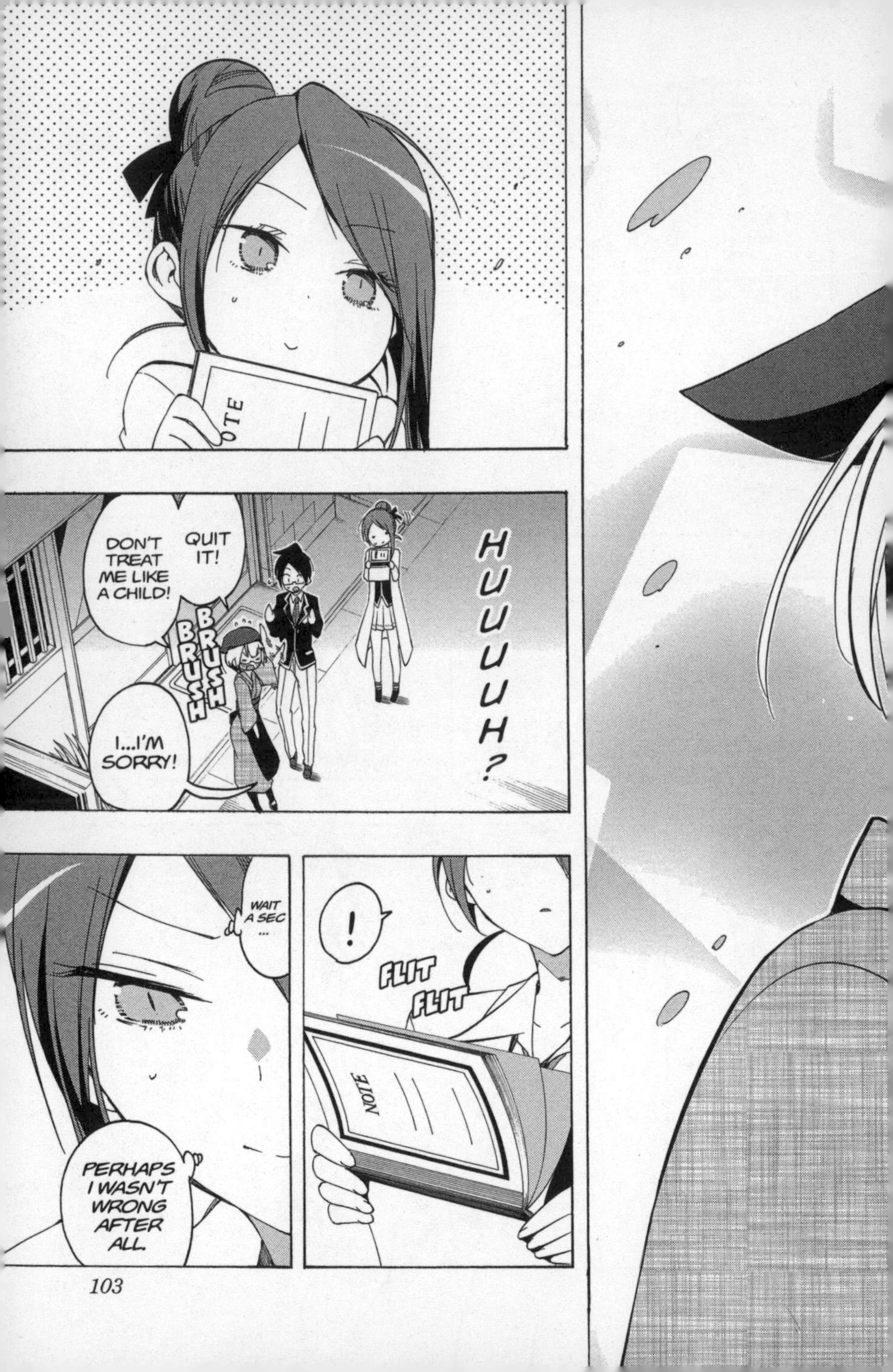
NOTE
HUUUUUH?
QUIT IT!
DON'T TREAT ME LIKE A CHILD!
BRUSH BRUSH
I...I'M SORRY!
!
FLIT FLIT
NOTE
WAIT A SEC...
PERHAPS I WASN'T WRONG AFTER ALL.

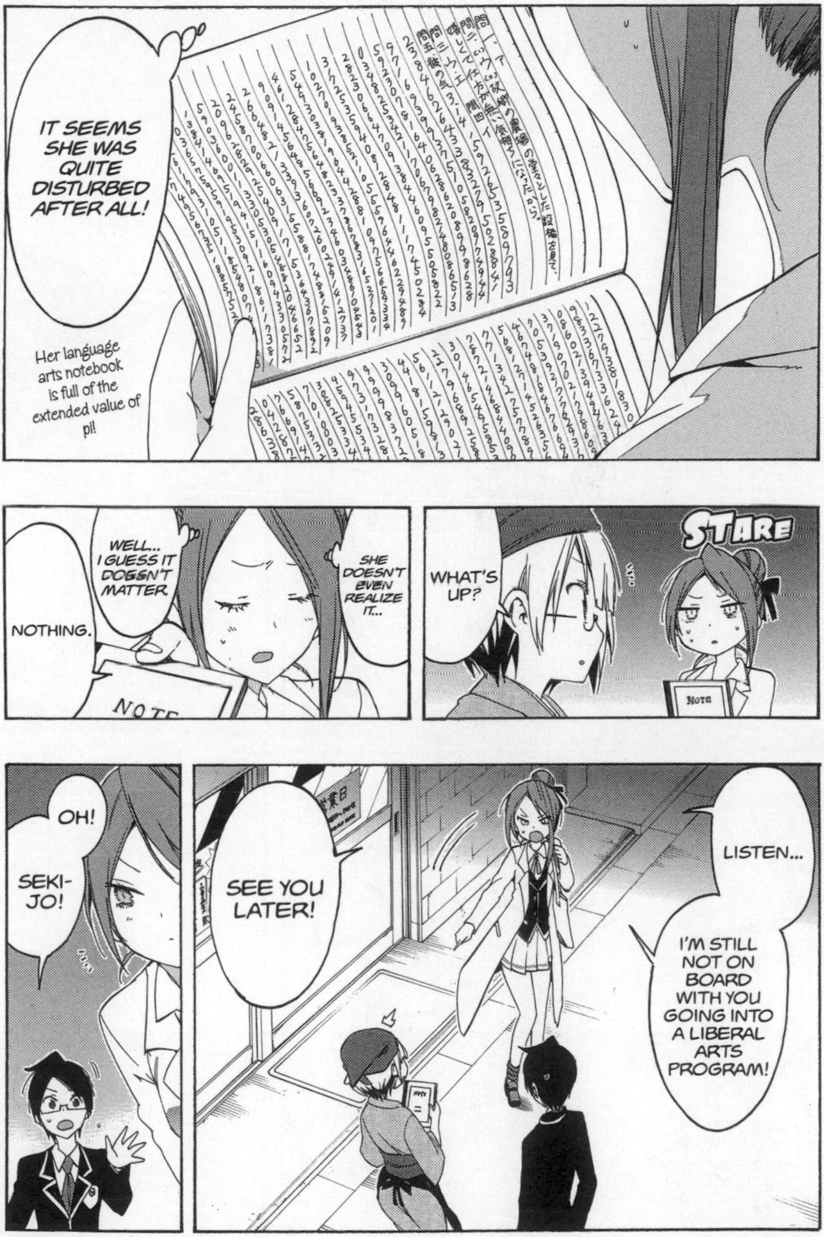
IT SEEMS SHE WAS QUITE DISTURBED AFTER ALL!
Her language arts notebook is full of the extended value of pi!
STARE
WHAT'S UP?
SHE DOESN'T EVEN REALIZE IT...
WELL... I GUESS IT DOESN'T MATTER.
NOTHING.
LISTEN...
I'M STILL NOT ON BOARD WITH YOU GOING INTO A LIBERAL ARTS PROGRAM!
SEE YOU LATER!
OH!
SEKI-JO!

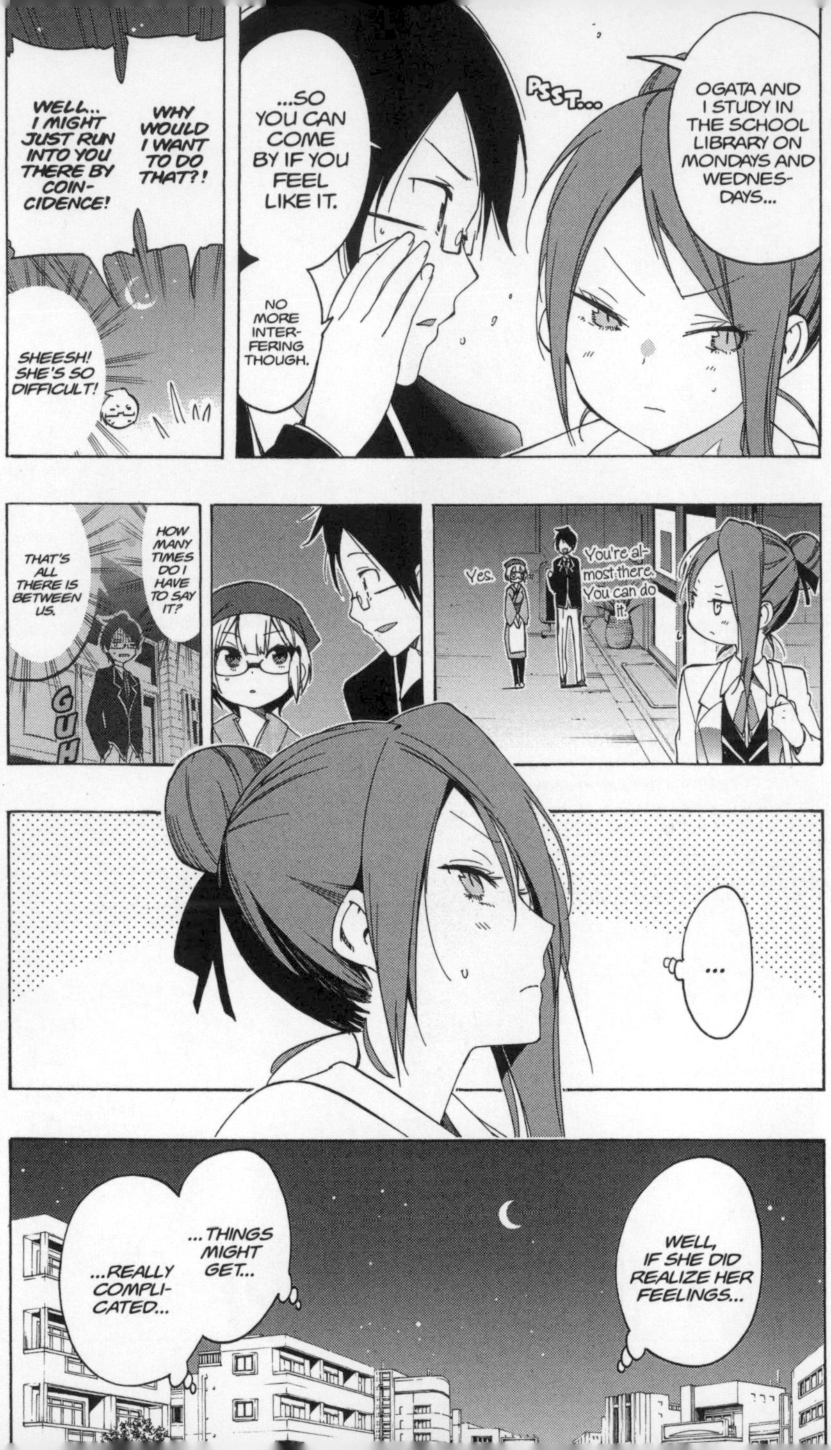
OGATA AND I STUDY IN THE SCHOOL LIBRARY ON MONDAYS AND WEDNESDAYS...
PSST...
...SO YOU CAN COME BY IF YOU FEEL LIKE IT.
NO MORE INTERFERING THOUGH.
WHY WOULD I WANT TO DO THAT?!
WELL... I MIGHT JUST RUN INTO YOU THERE BY COINCIDENCE!
SHEESH! SHE'S SO DIFFICULT!
You're almost there. You can do it.
Yes.
HOW MANY TIMES DO I HAVE TO SAY IT?
THAT'S ALL THERE IS BETWEEN US.
GUH
...
WELL, IF SHE DID REALIZE HER FEELINGS...
...THINGS MIGHT GET...
...REALLY COMPLICATED...

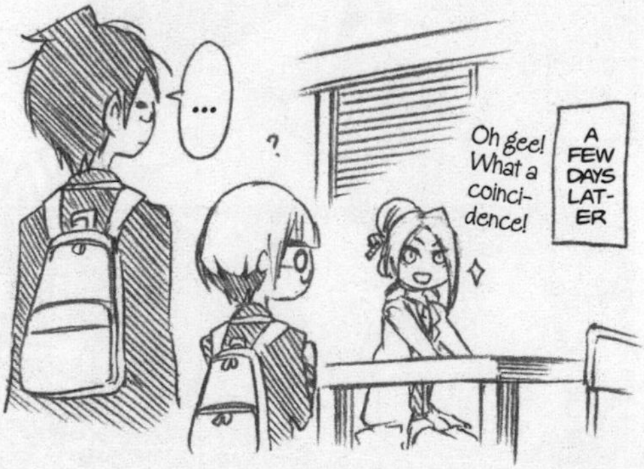
A FEW DAYS LAT-ER
Oh gee! What a coinci-dence!
?
...

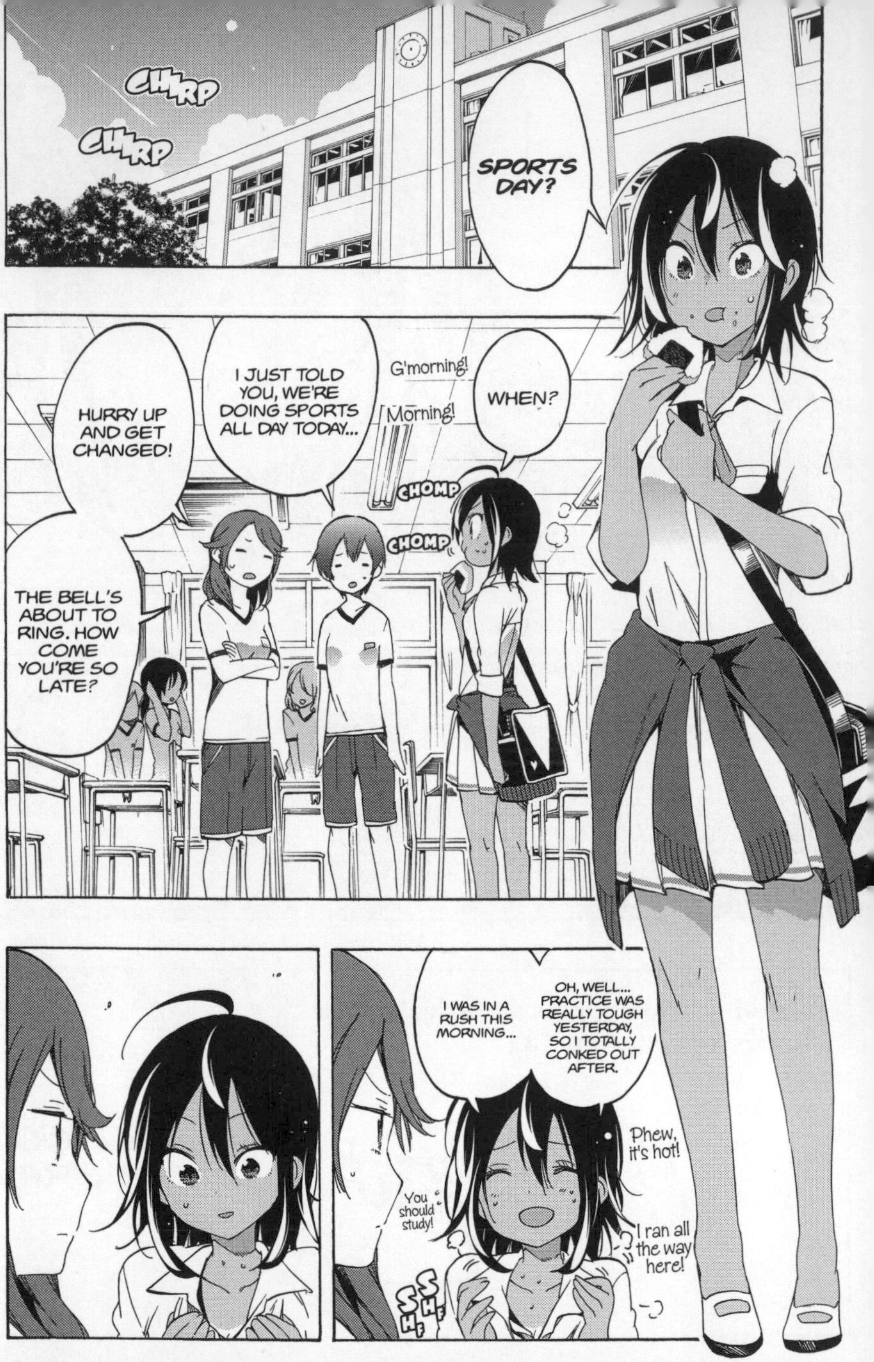
SPORTS DAY?
CHIRP
CHIRP
WHEN?
G'morning!
Morning!
I JUST TOLD YOU, WE'RE DOING SPORTS ALL DAY TODAY...
HURRY UP AND GET CHANGED!
CHOMP
CHOMP
THE BELL'S ABOUT TO RING. HOW COME YOU'RE SO LATE?
OH, WELL... PRACTICE WAS REALLY TOUGH YESTERDAY, SO I TOTALLY CONKED OUT AFTER.
I WAS IN A RUSH THIS MORNING...
Phew, it's hot!
I ran all the way here!
You should study!
SHF
SHF

Question 13: Sometimes a Genius's Panic Is Inversely Related to [*X*]

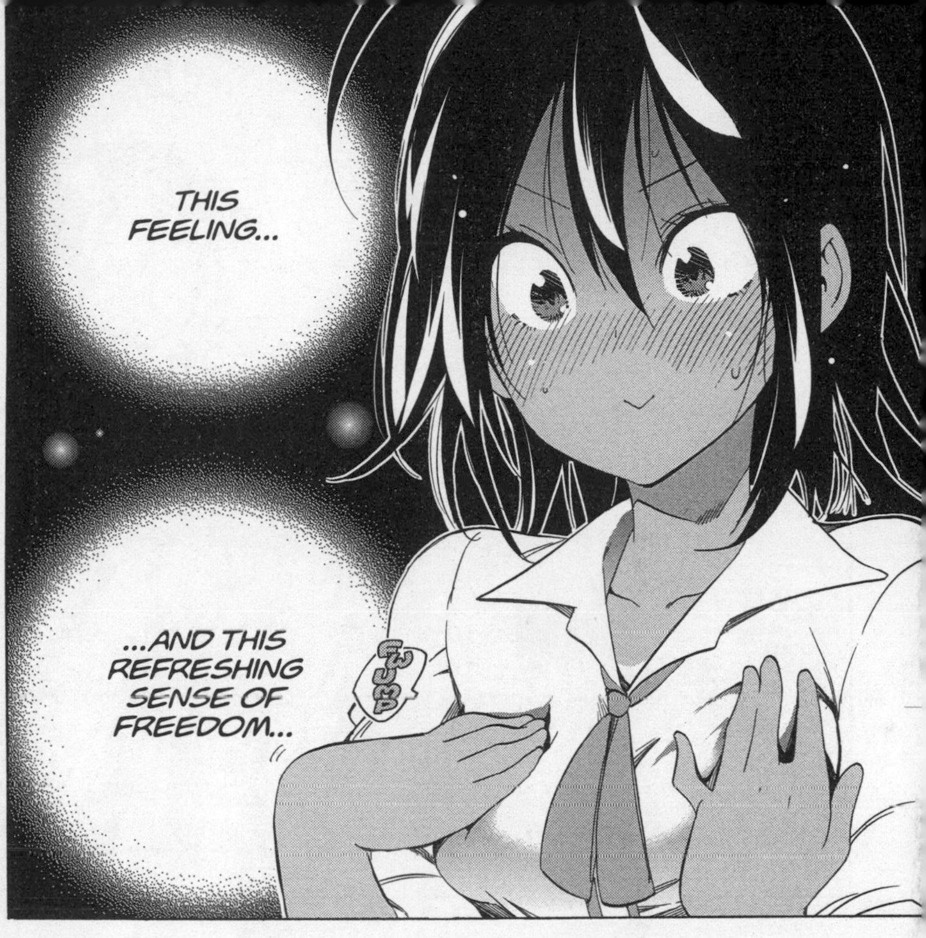
THIS FEELING...
...AND THIS REFRESHING SENSE OF FREEDOM...

Question 13: Sometimes a Genius's Panic Is Inversely Related to [X]

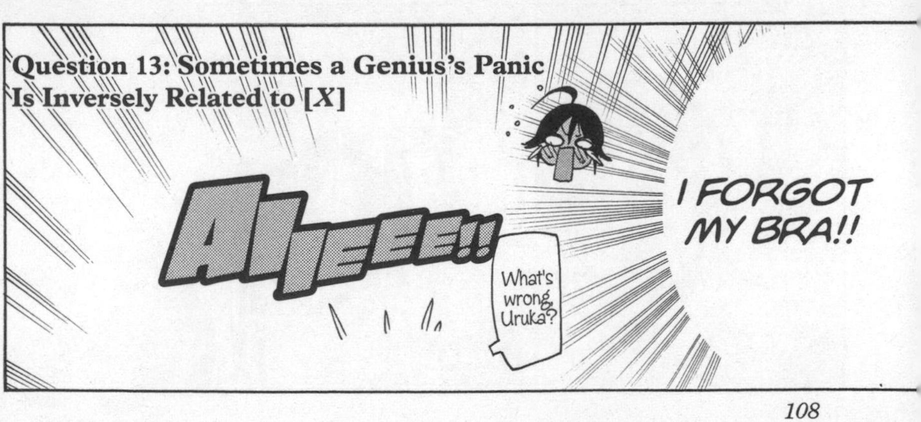
I FORGOT MY BRA!!
AHIEEE!!
What's wrong, Uruka?

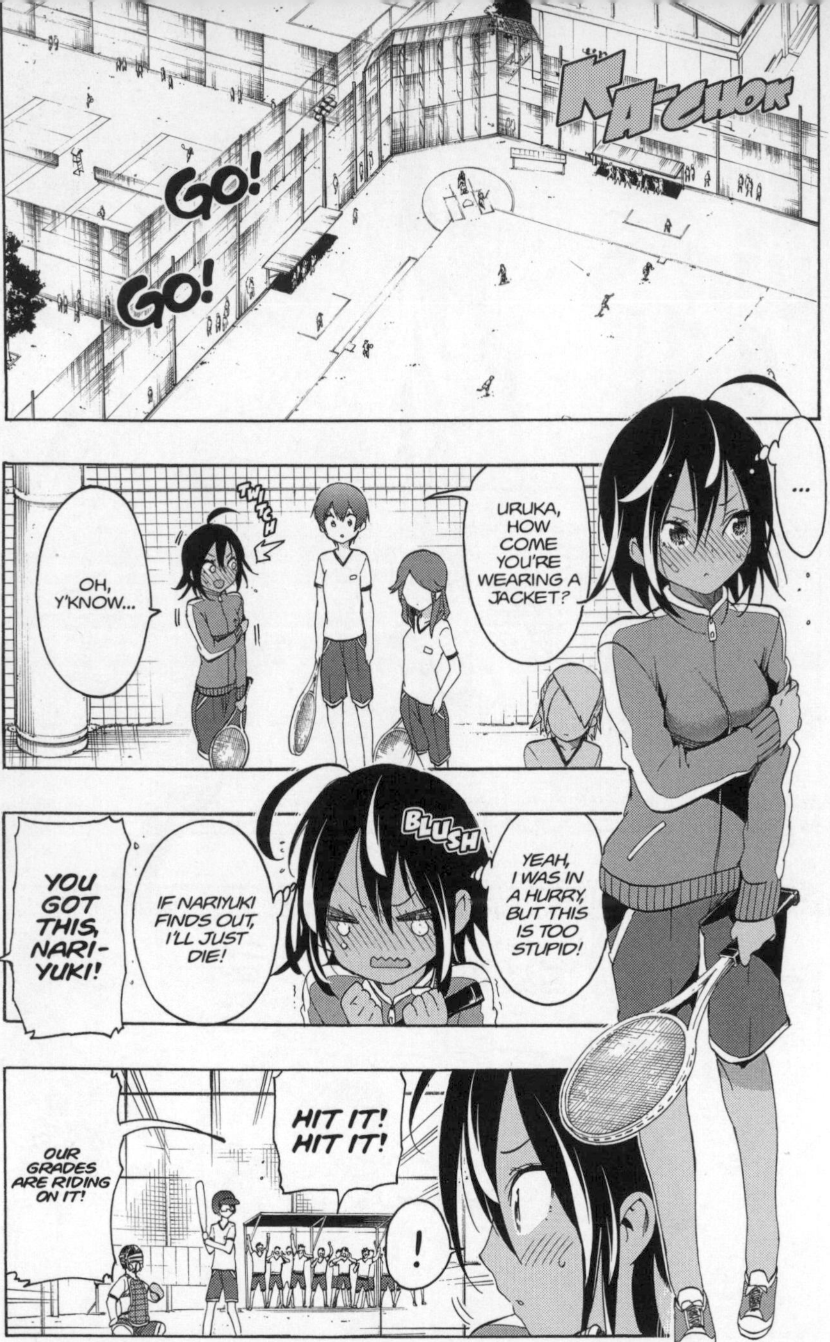
KA-CHOK
GO!
GO!
...
URUKA, HOW COME YOU'RE WEARING A JACKET?
TWITCH
OH, Y'KNOW...
YEAH, I WAS IN A HURRY, BUT THIS IS TOO STUPID!
BLUSH
IF NARIYUKI FINDS OUT, I'LL JUST DIE!
YOU GOT THIS, NARI-YUKI!
!
HIT IT! HIT IT!
OUR GRADES ARE RIDING ON IT!

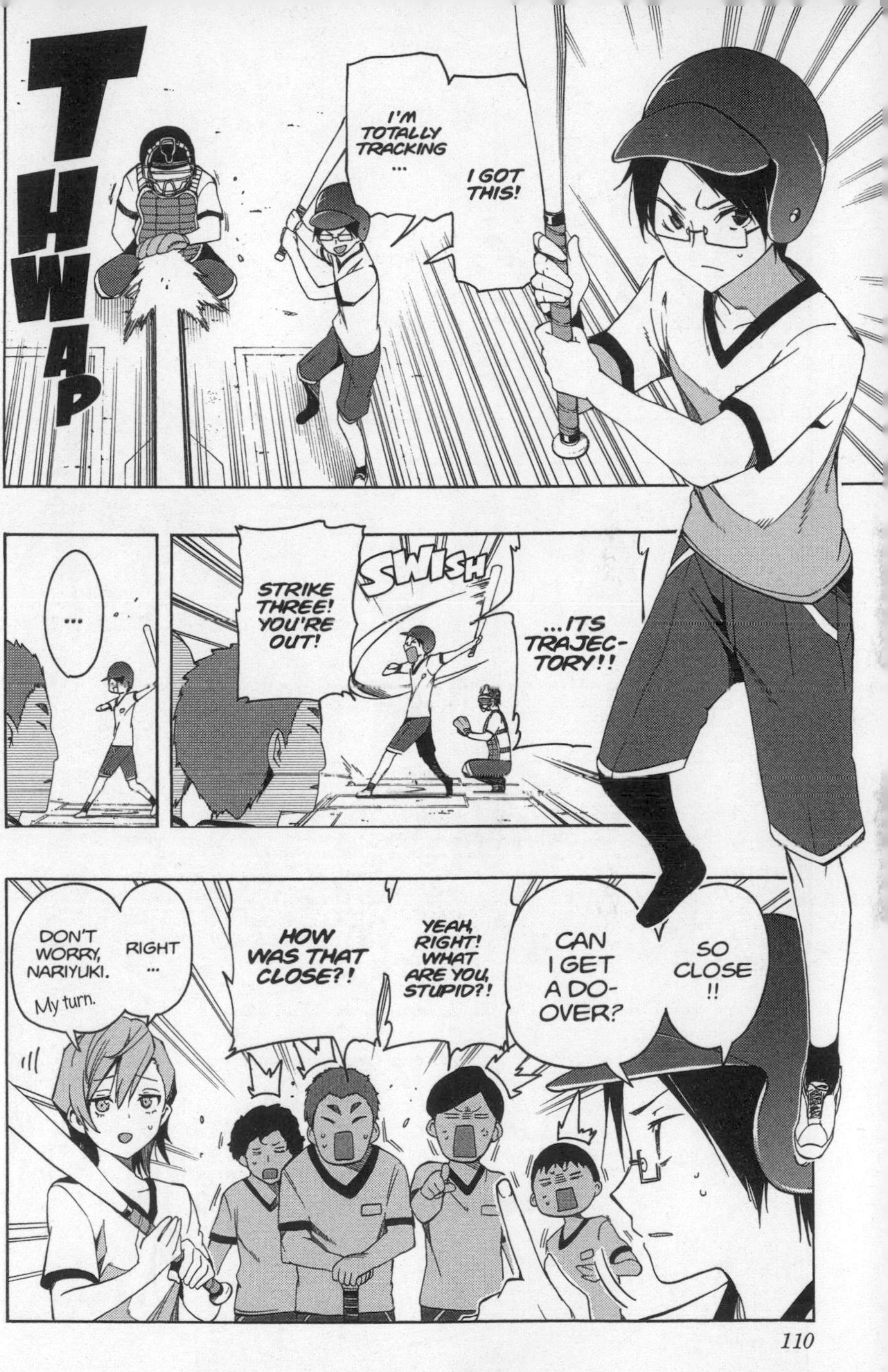
I GOT THIS!
I'M TOTALLY TRACKING ...
THWAP
...ITS TRAJECTORY!!
SWISH
STRIKE THREE! YOU'RE OUT!
...
SO CLOSE !!
CAN I GET A DO-OVER?
YEAH, RIGHT! WHAT ARE YOU, STUPID?!
HOW WAS THAT CLOSE?!
RIGHT ...
DON'T WORRY, NARIYUKI.
My turn.

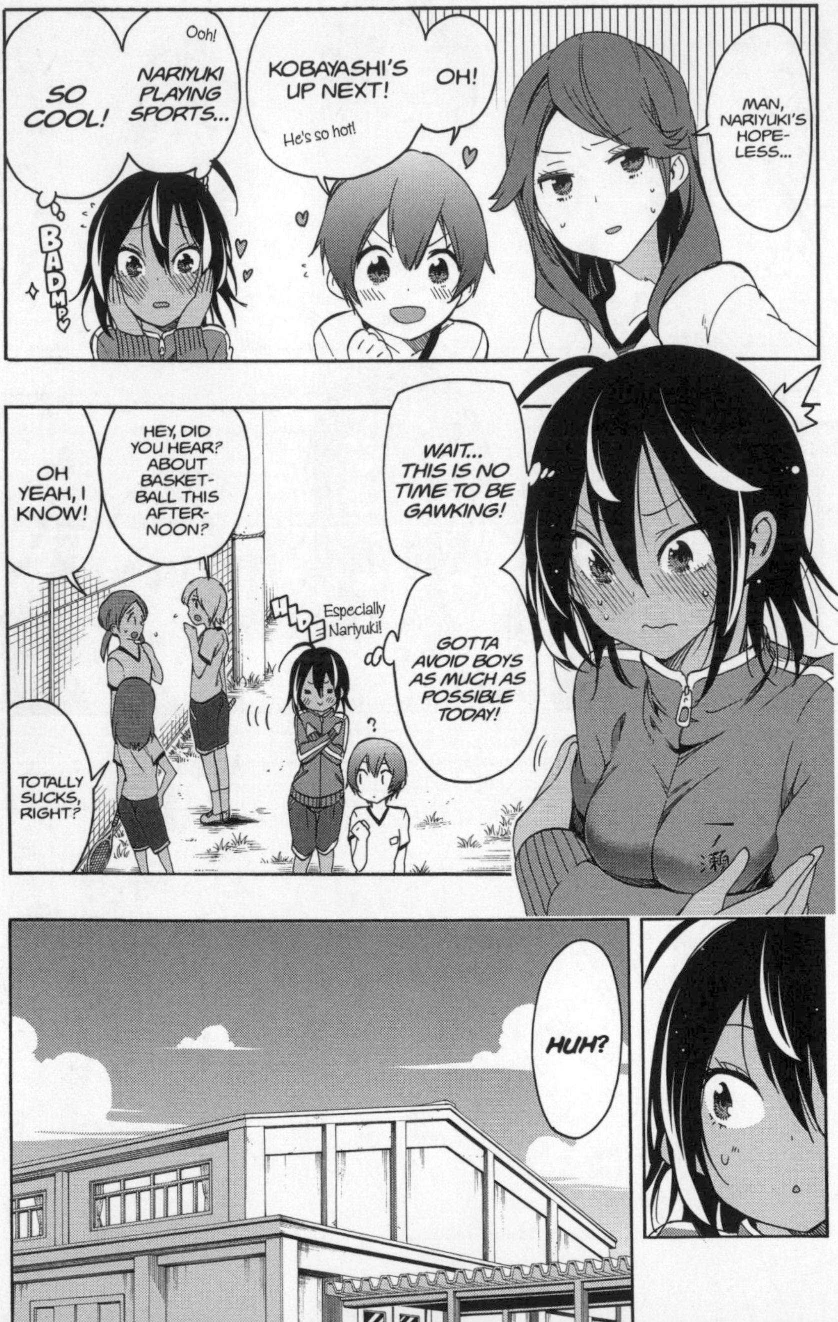
MAN, NARIYUKI'S HOPELESS...
OH!
KOBAYASHI'S UP NEXT!
He's so hot!
Ooh!
NARIYUKI PLAYING SPORTS...
SO COOL!
BADMP
WAIT... THIS IS NO TIME TO BE GAWKING!
GOTTA AVOID BOYS AS MUCH AS POSSIBLE TODAY!
HEY, DID YOU HEAR? ABOUT BASKETBALL THIS AFTERNOON?
OH YEAH, I KNOW!
HIDE
Especially Nariyuki!
TOTALLY SUCKS, RIGHT?
HUH?

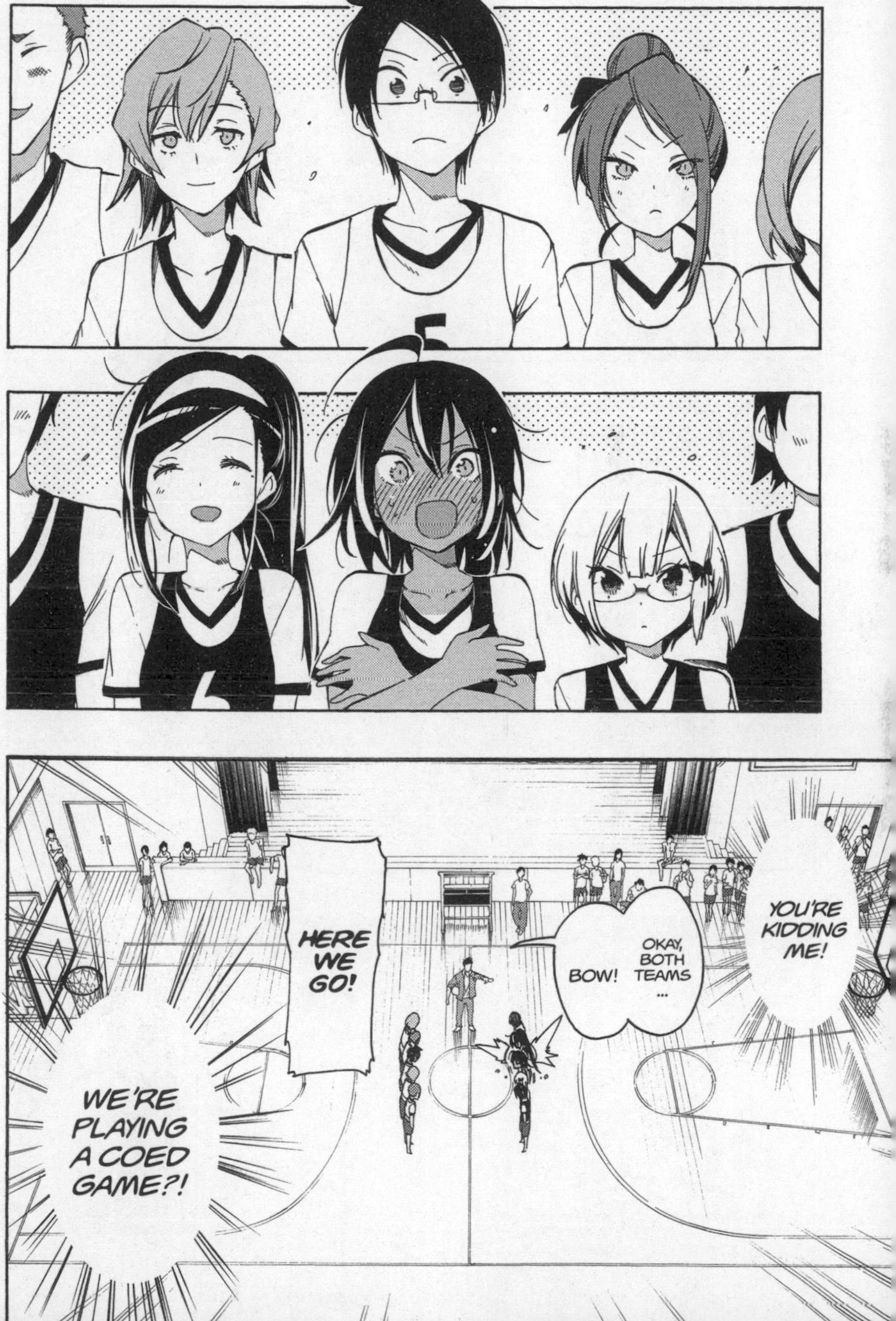
YOU'RE KIDDING ME!
OKAY, BOTH TEAMS ...
BOW!
HERE WE GO!
WE'RE PLAYING A COED GAME?!

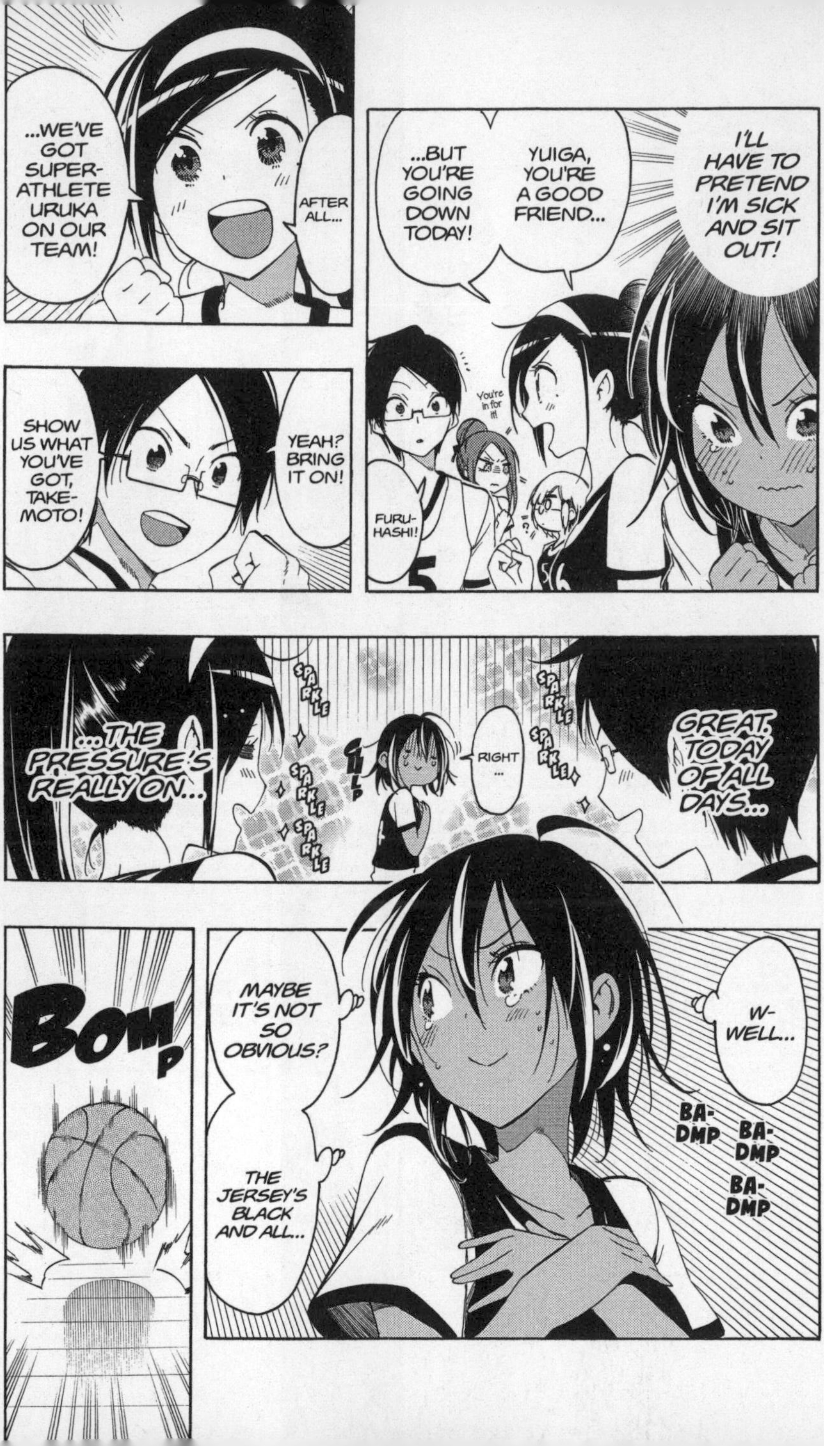
I'LL HAVE TO PRETEND I'M SICK AND SIT OUT!
YUIGA, YOU'RE A GOOD FRIEND...
...BUT YOU'RE GOING DOWN TODAY!
You're in for it!
FURU-HASHI!
AFTER ALL...
...WE'VE GOT SUPER-ATHLETE URUKA ON OUR TEAM!
YEAH? BRING IT ON!
SHOW US WHAT YOU'VE GOT, TAKE-MOTO!
GREAT. TODAY OF ALL DAYS...
SPARKLE
SPARKLE
RIGHT...
SPARKLE
SPARKLE
GULP
...THE PRESSURE'S REALLY ON...
W-WELL...
BA-DMP
BA-DMP
BA-DMP
MAYBE IT'S NOT SO OBVIOUS?
THE JERSEY'S BLACK AND ALL...
BOMP

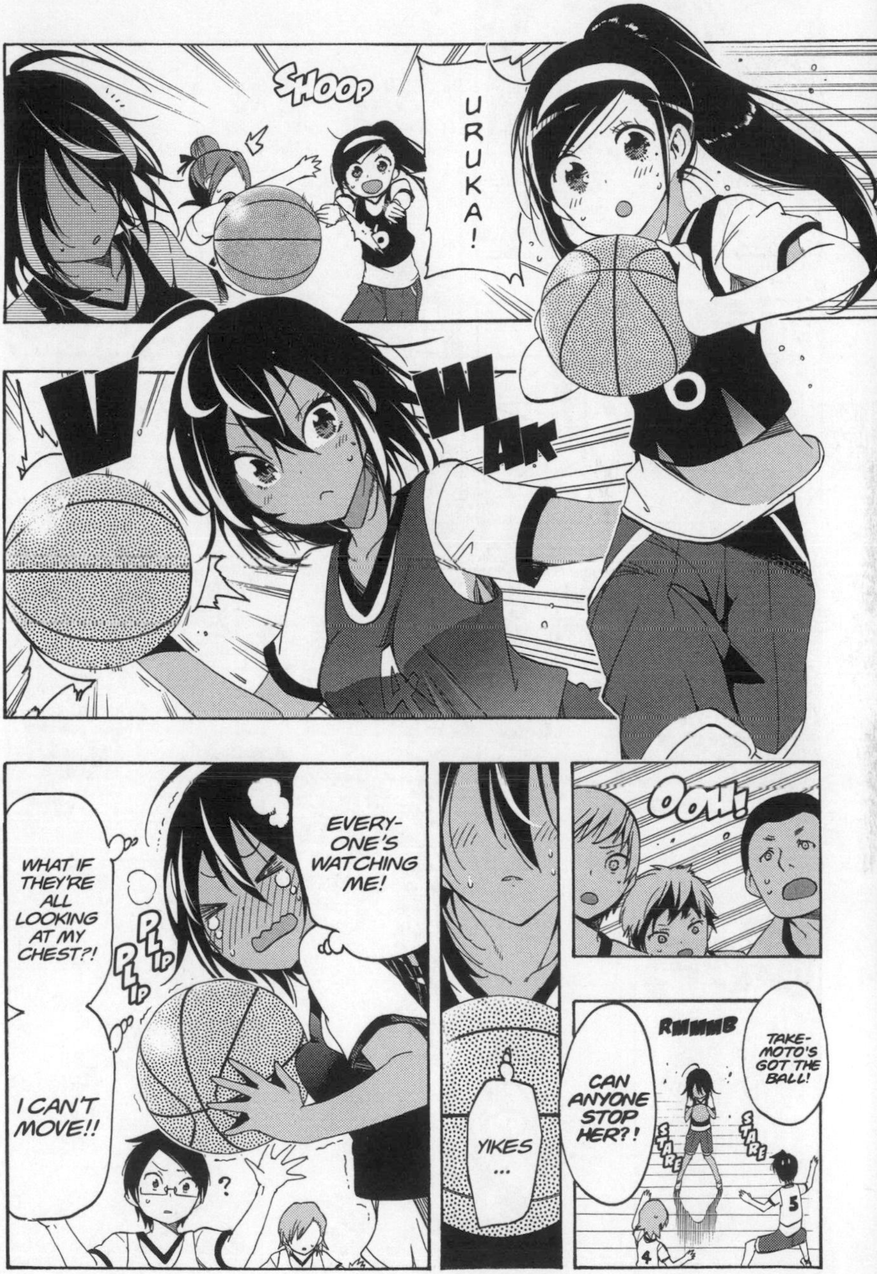
SHOOP
URUKA!
VWAK
OOH!
RMMMB
TAKE-MOTO'S GOT THE BALL!
CAN ANYONE STOP HER?!
STARE
STARE
YIKES ...
EVERY-ONE'S WATCHING ME!
WHAT IF THEY'RE ALL LOOKING AT MY CHEST?!
PLIP
PLIP
I CAN'T MOVE!!
?

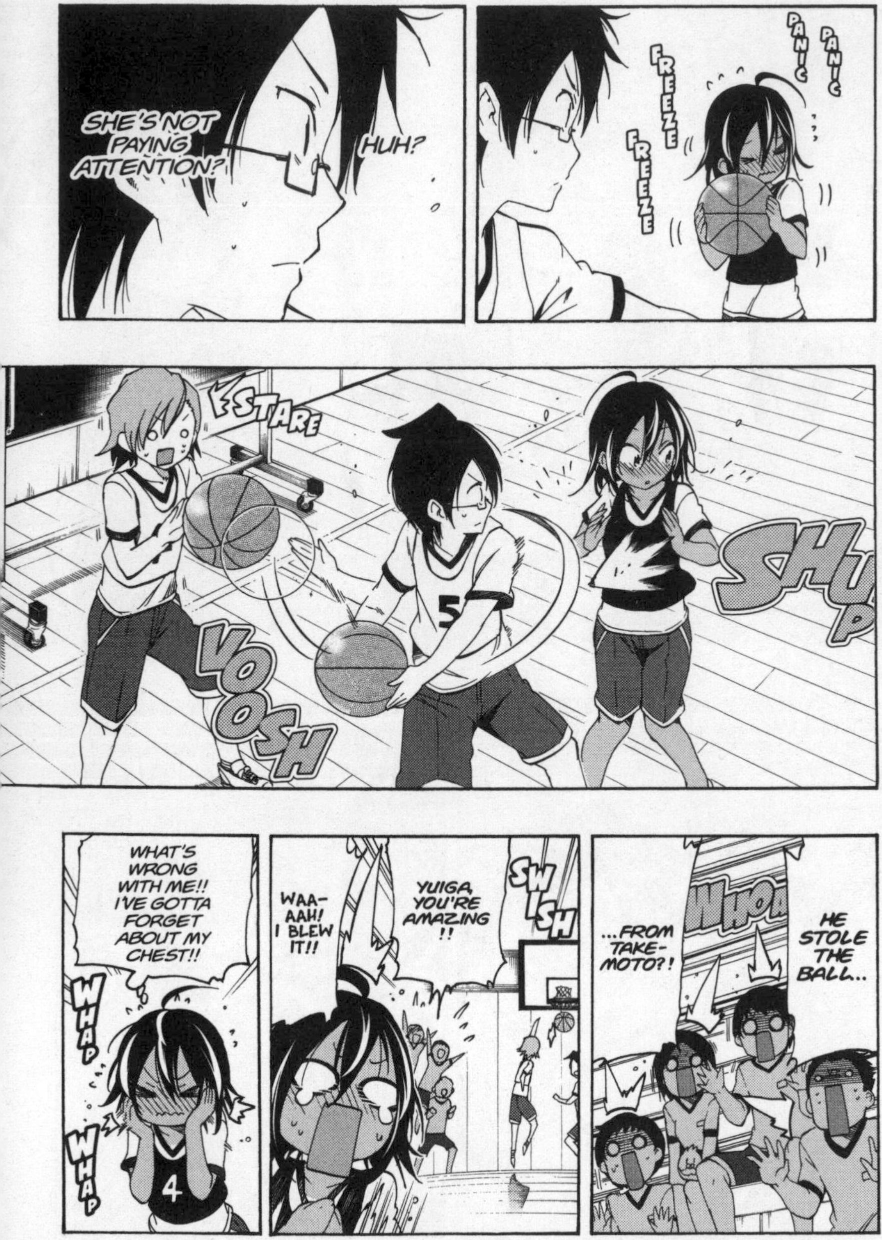
PANIC
PANIC
FREEZE
FREEZE
HUH?
SHE'S NOT PAYING ATTENTION?
STARE
SHUP
VOOSH
HE STOLE THE BALL...
...FROM TAKE-MOTO?!
SWISH
YUIGA, YOU'RE AMAZING!!
WAA-AAH! I BLEW IT!!
WHAT'S WRONG WITH ME!! I'VE GOTTA FORGET ABOUT MY CHEST!!
WHAP
WHAP

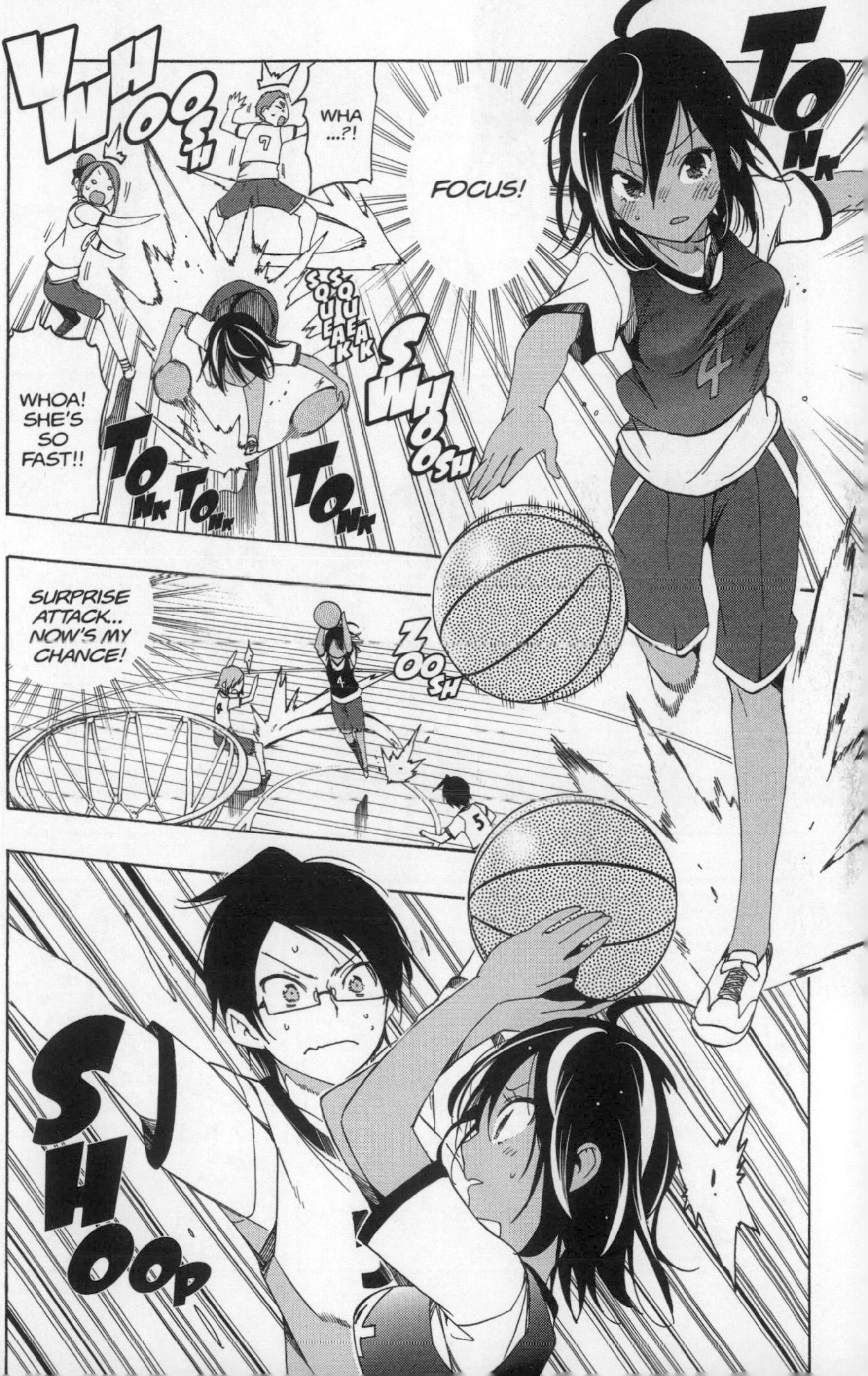
TONK
FOCUS!
WHA ...?!
WHOOSH
SQUEAK SQUEAK
SWHOOSH
WHOA! SHE'S SO FAST!!
TONK TONK TONK
ZOOSH
SURPRISE ATTACK... NOW'S MY CHANCE!
SHHOOP

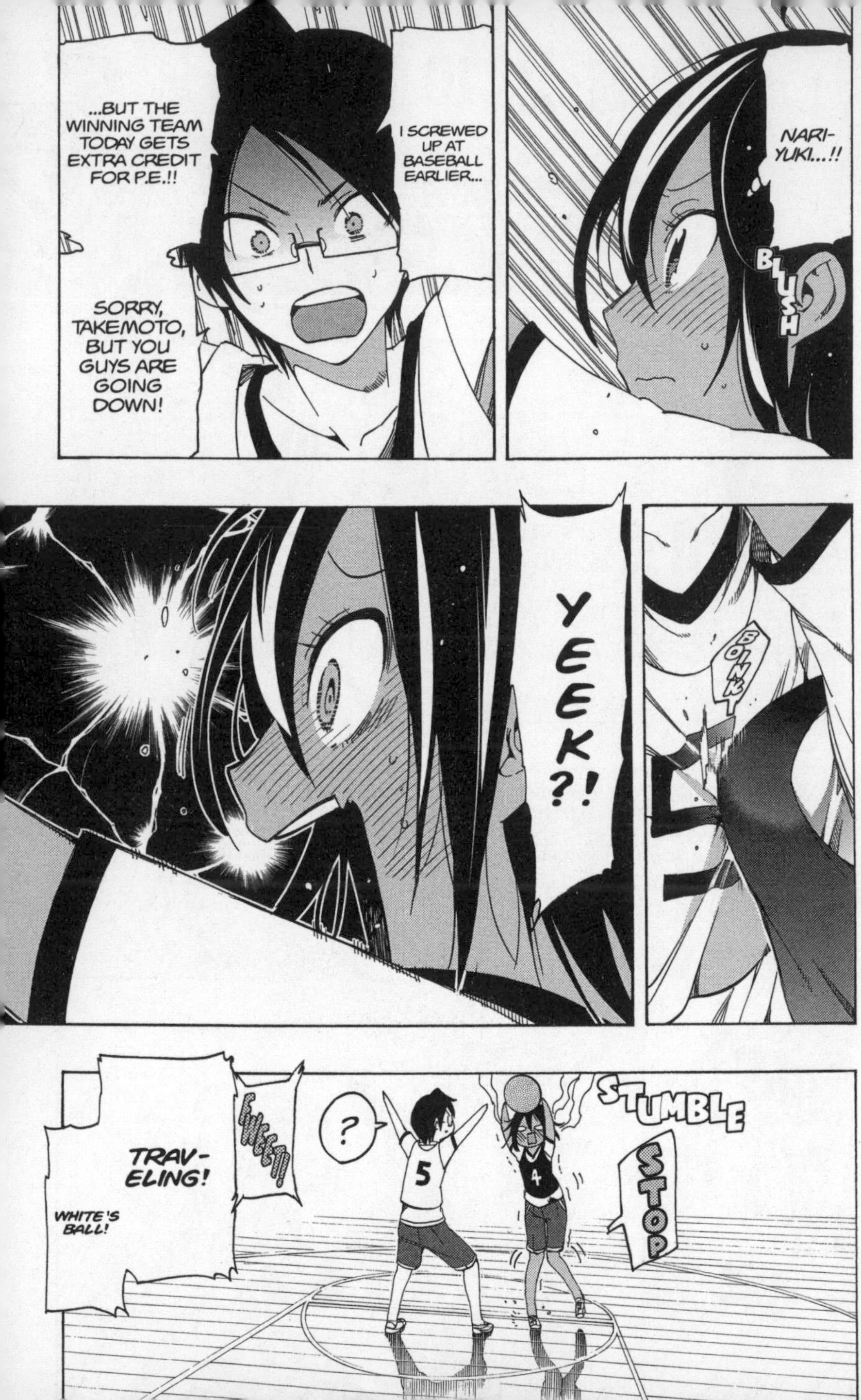
NARI-YUKI...!!
BLUSH
I SCREWED UP AT BASEBALL EARLIER...
...BUT THE WINNING TEAM TODAY GETS EXTRA CREDIT FOR P.E.!!
SORRY, TAKEMOTO, BUT YOU GUYS ARE GOING DOWN!
BOINK
YEEK?!
STUMBLE
STOP
?
FWEET!!
TRAV-ELING!
WHITE'S BALL!

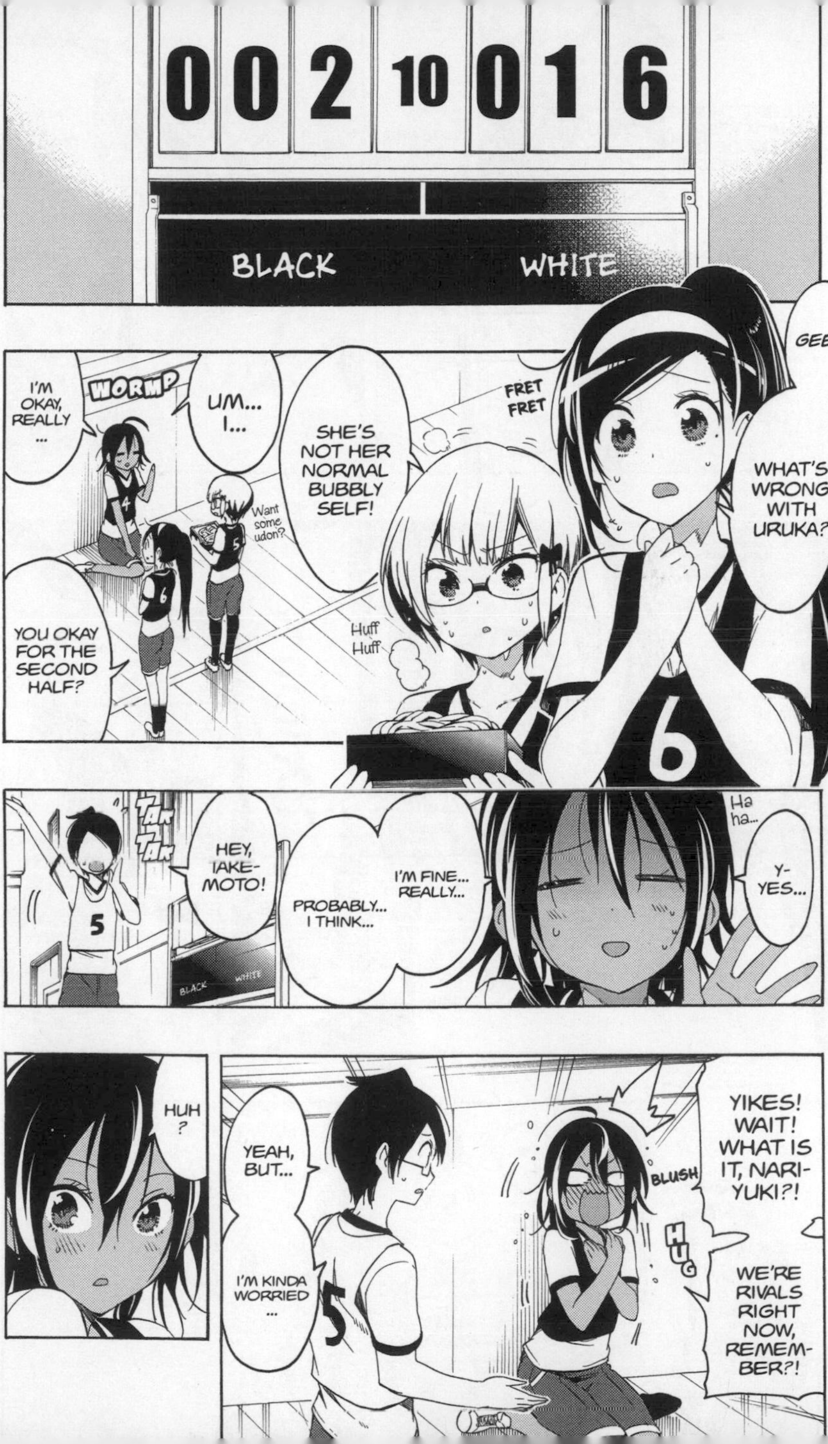
0 0 2 10 0 1 6
BLACK
WHITE
GEE...
WHAT'S WRONG WITH URUKA?
FRET FRET
SHE'S NOT HER NORMAL BUBBLY SELF!
Huff Huff
UM... I...
I'M OKAY, REALLY ...
WORMP
Want some udon?
YOU OKAY FOR THE SECOND HALF?
Ha ha...
Y- YES...
I'M FINE... REALLY...
PROBABLY... I THINK...
HEY, TAKE-MOTO!
TAK TAK
BLACK
WHITE
YIKES! WAIT! WHAT IS IT, NARI-YUKI?!
BLUSH
HUG
WE'RE RIVALS RIGHT NOW, REMEMBER?!
YEAH, BUT...
I'M KINDA WORRIED ...
HUH ?

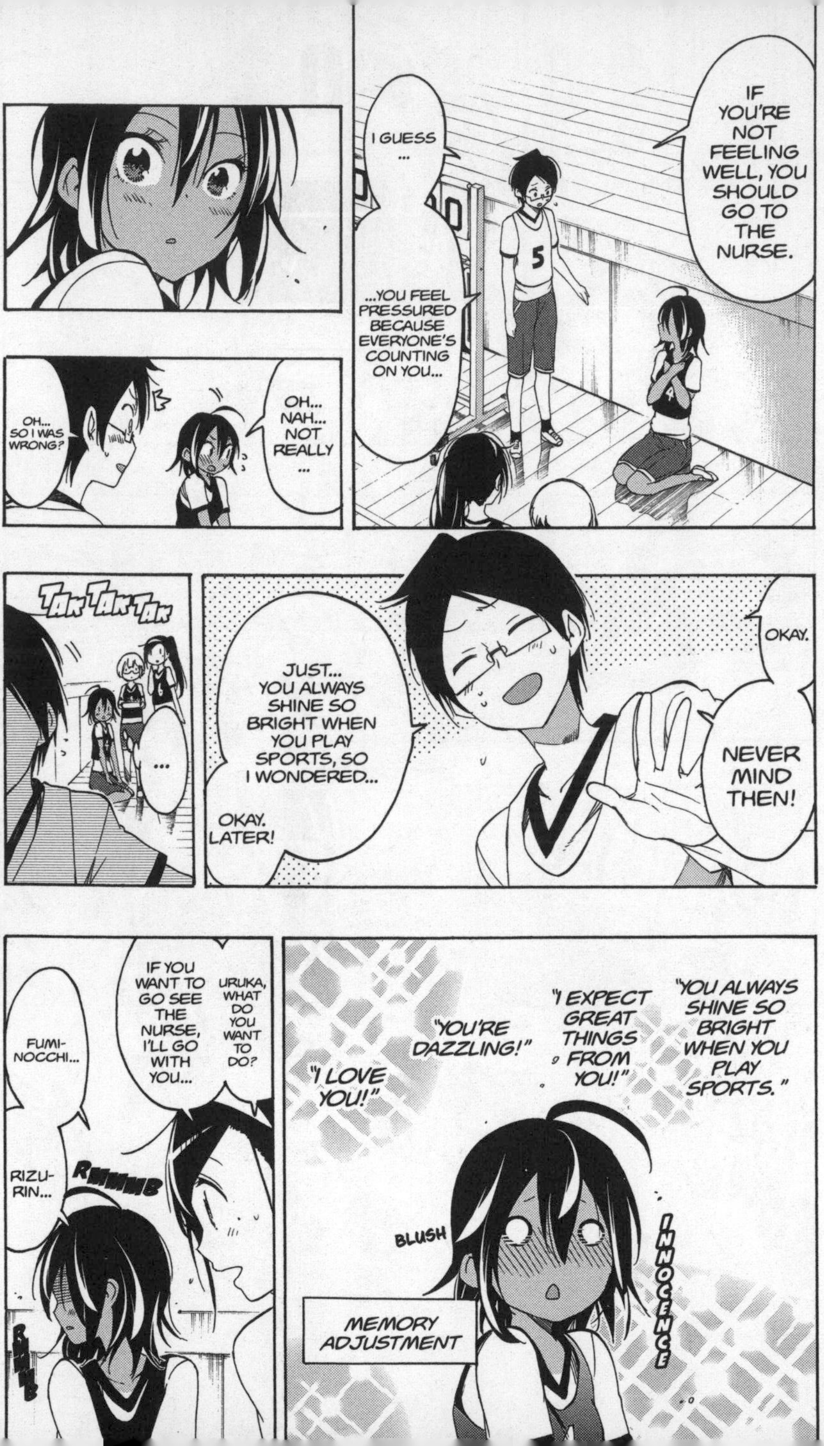
IF YOU'RE NOT FEELING WELL, YOU SHOULD GO TO THE NURSE.
I GUESS ...
...YOU FEEL PRESSURED BECAUSE EVERYONE'S COUNTING ON YOU...
OH... NAH... NOT REALLY ...
OH... SO I WAS WRONG?
OKAY.
NEVER MIND THEN!
JUST... YOU ALWAYS SHINE SO BRIGHT WHEN YOU PLAY SPORTS, SO I WONDERED...
OKAY. LATER!
TAK TAK TAK
...
"YOU ALWAYS SHINE SO BRIGHT WHEN YOU PLAY SPORTS."
"I EXPECT GREAT THINGS FROM YOU!"
"YOU'RE DAZZLING!"
"I LOVE YOU!"
BLUSH
INNOCENCE
MEMORY ADJUSTMENT
URUKA, WHAT DO YOU WANT TO DO?
IF YOU WANT TO GO SEE THE NURSE, I'LL GO WITH YOU...
FUMI-NOCCHI...
RIZU-RIN...

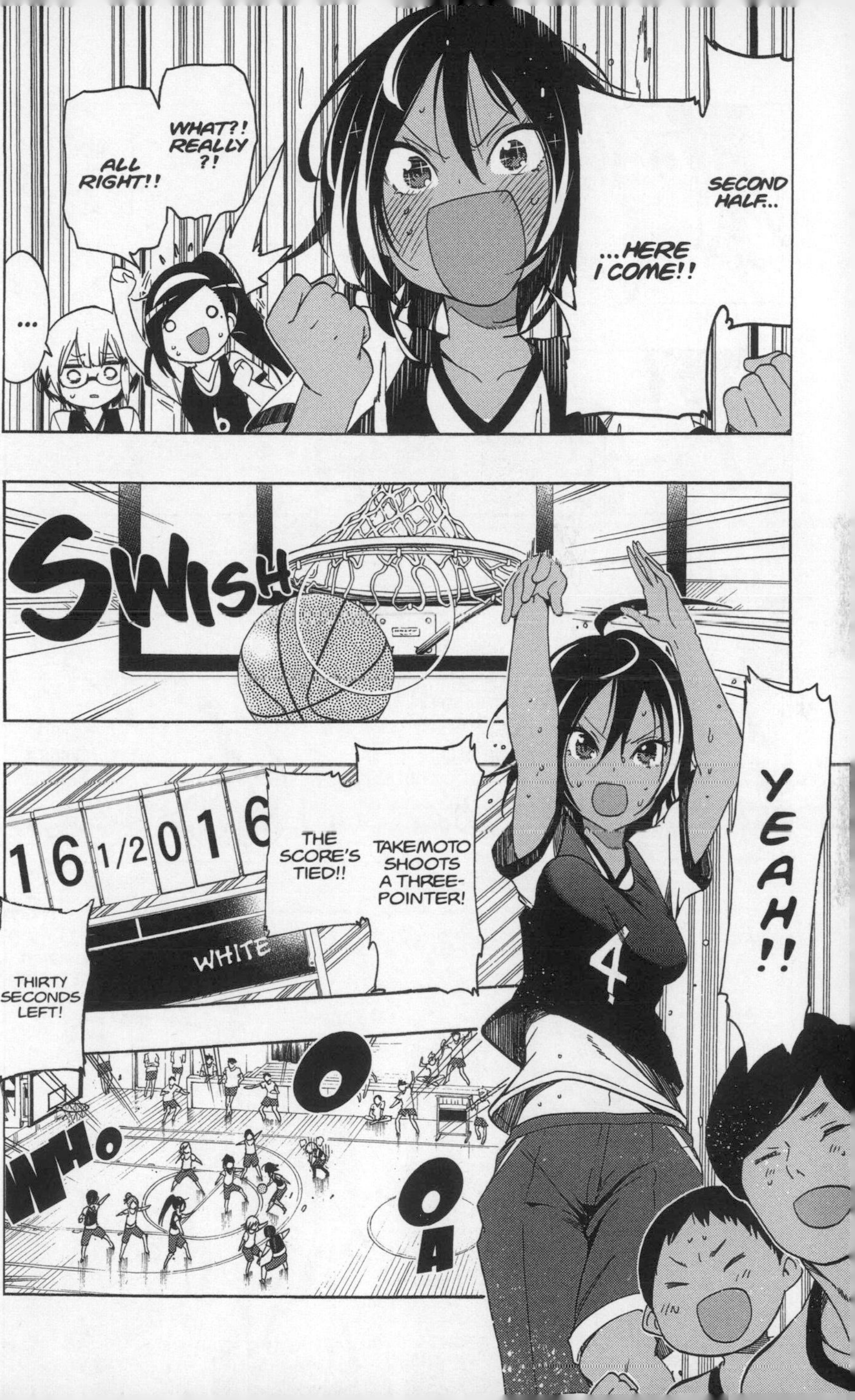
SECOND HALF...
...HERE I COME!!
WHAT?! REALLY?!
ALL RIGHT!!
...
SWISH
YEAH!!
TAKEMOTO SHOOTS A THREE-POINTER!
THE SCORE'S TIED!!
16 1/2 0 16
WHITE
THIRTY SECONDS LEFT!
WHOOOA

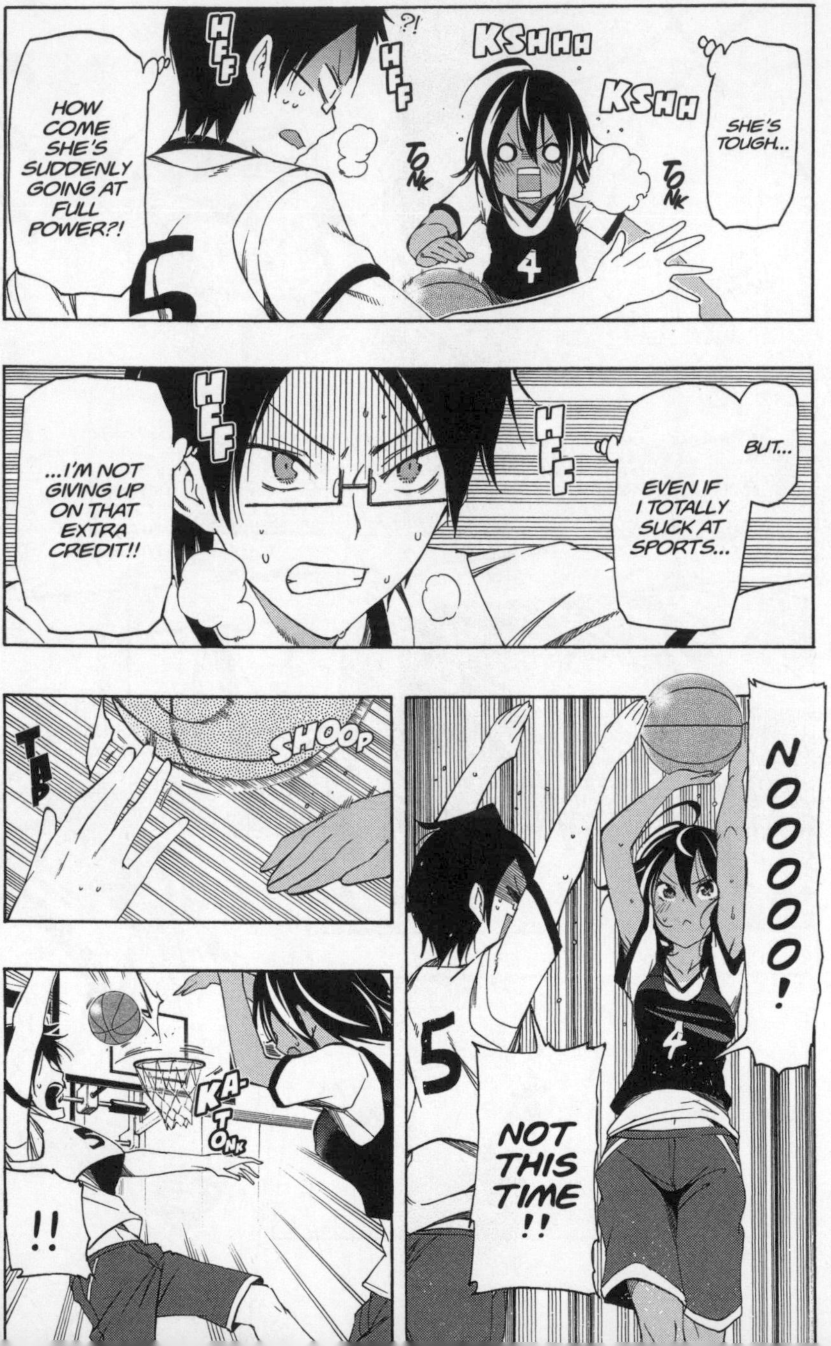
SHE'S TOUGH...
KSHH
TONK
KSHHH
?!
HFF
HFF
TONK
HOW COME SHE'S SUDDENLY GOING AT FULL POWER?!
BUT...
EVEN IF I TOTALLY SUCK AT SPORTS...
HFF
HFF
...I'M NOT GIVING UP ON THAT EXTRA CREDIT!!
NOOOOOO!
NOT THIS TIME!!
SHOOP
TAP
KA-TONK
!!

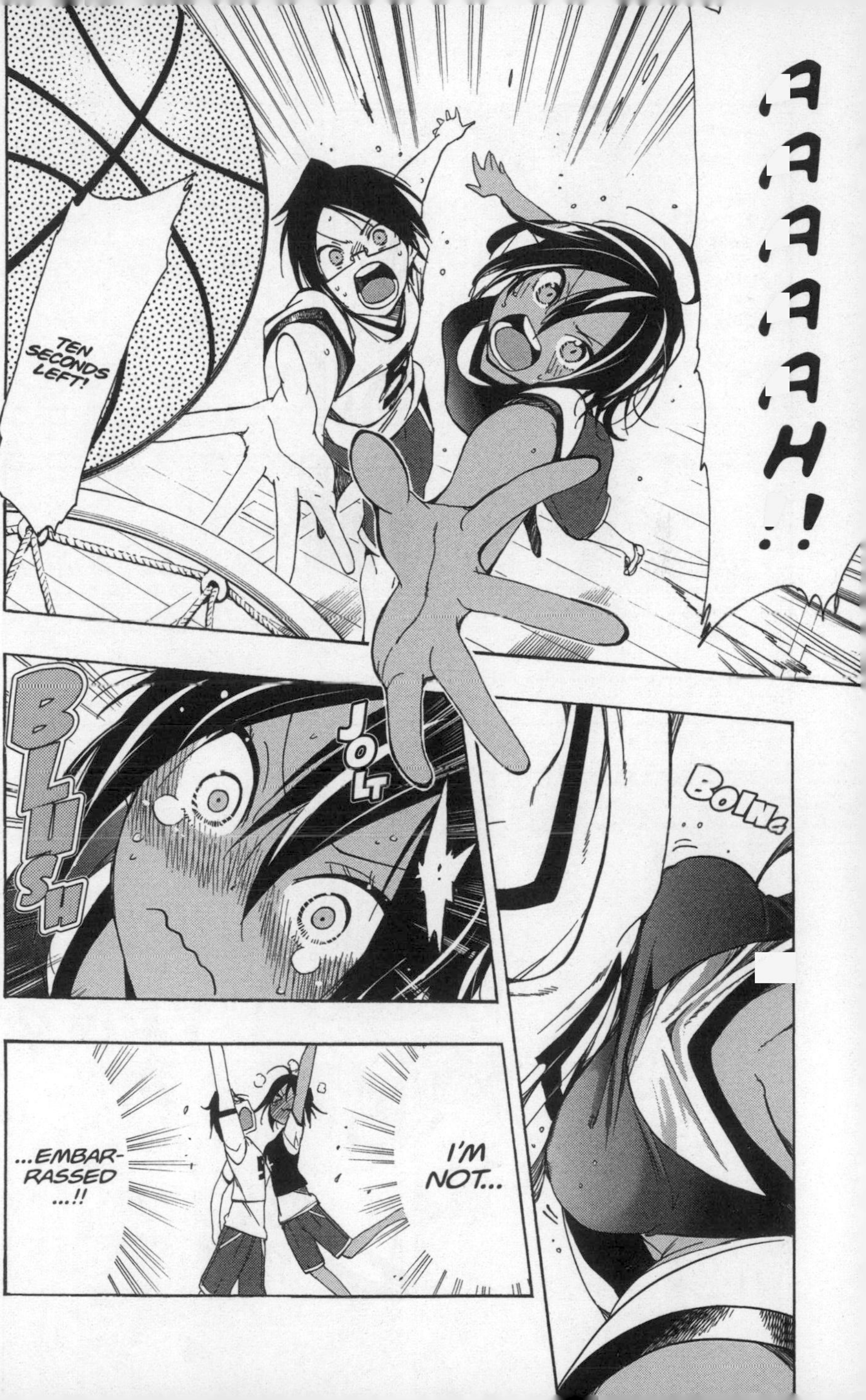
AAAAAAH!!
TEN SECONDS LEFT!
BOING
JOLT
BLUSH
I'M NOT...
...EMBAR-RASSED...!!

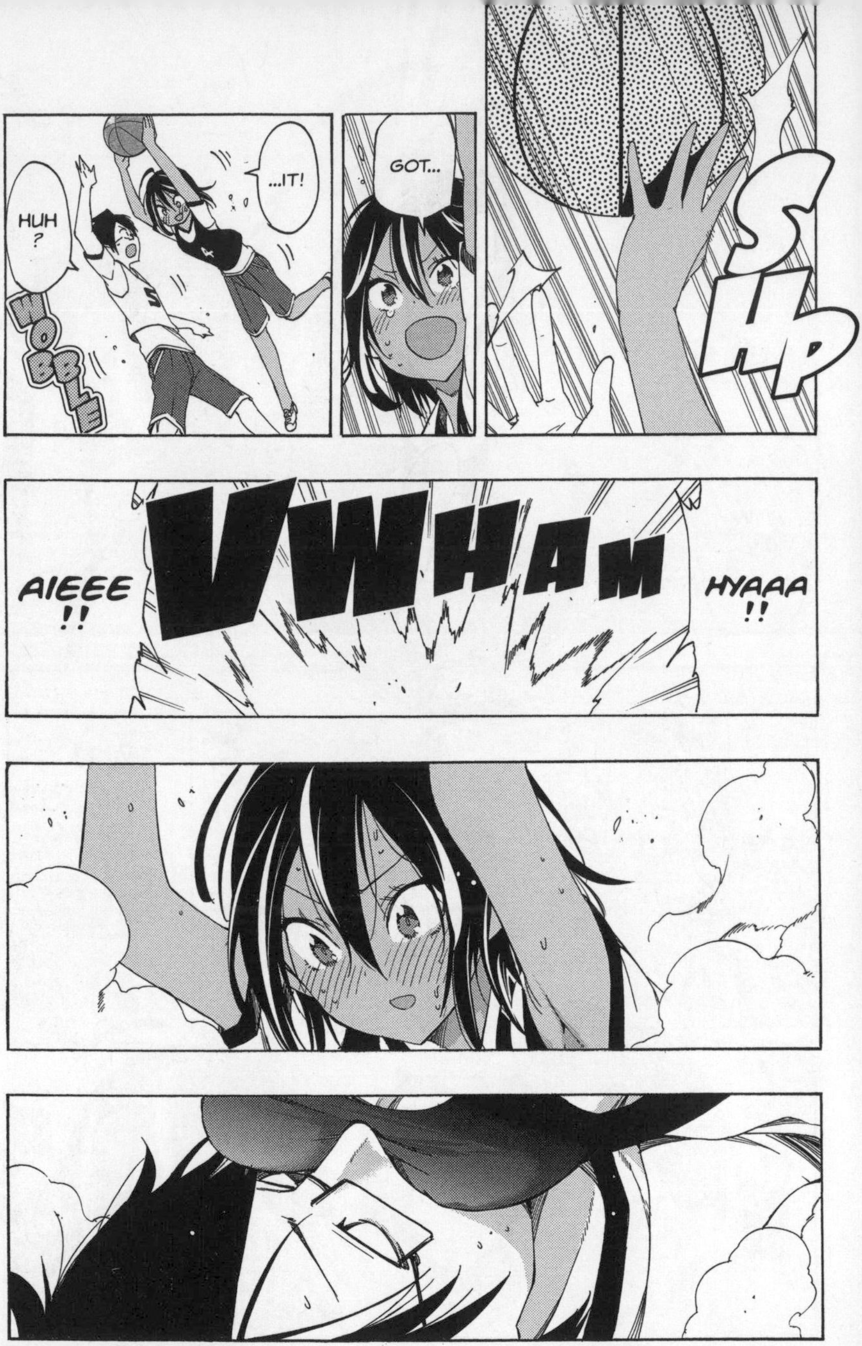
SHP
GOT...
...IT!
HUH ?
WOBBLE
HYAAA !!
VWHAM
AIEEE !!

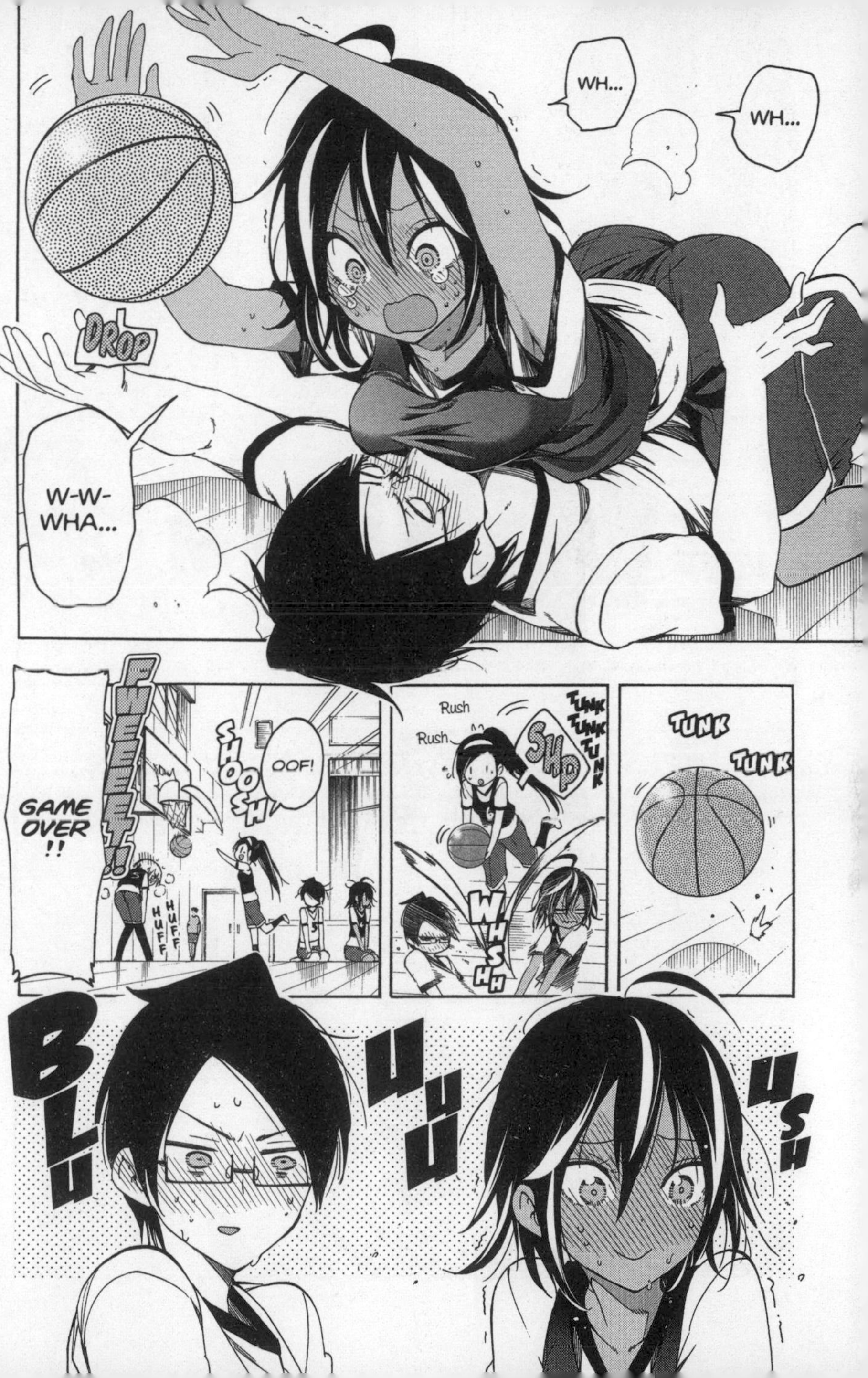
WH...
WH...
DROP
W-W-WHA...
TUNK
TUNK
TUNK TUNK TUNK
SHP
Rush
Rush
WHSHH
OOF!
SHOOSH
FWEEEET!!
GAME OVER!!
HUFF
HUFF
BLUUUUSH

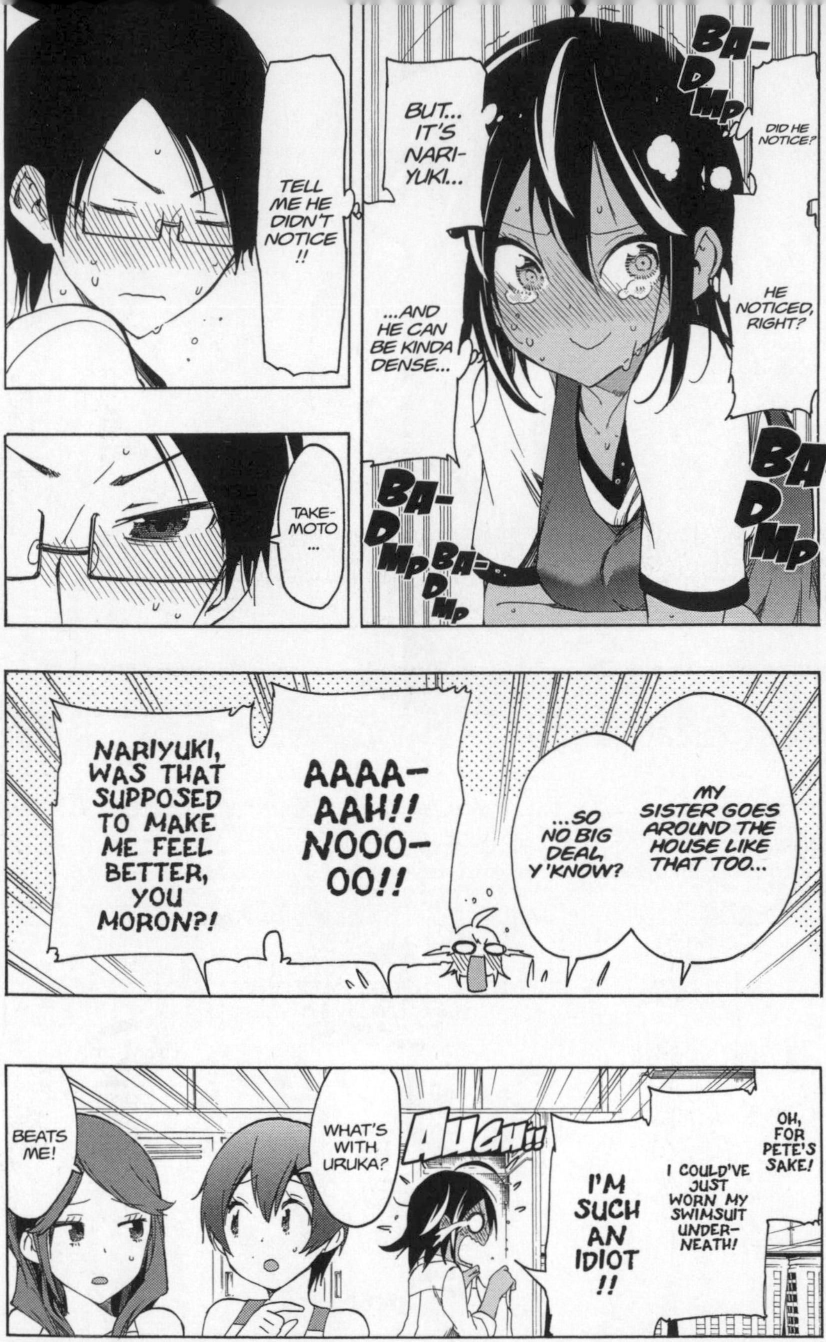
BA-DMP
DID HE NOTICE?
BUT... IT'S NARI-YUKI...
HE NOTICED, RIGHT?
...AND HE CAN BE KINDA DENSE...
BA-DMP
BA-DMP BA-DMP
TELL ME HE DIDN'T NOTICE!!
TAKE-MOTO...
MY SISTER GOES AROUND THE HOUSE LIKE THAT TOO...
...SO NO BIG DEAL, Y'KNOW?
AAAA-AAH!! NOOOO-OO!!
NARIYUKI, WAS THAT SUPPOSED TO MAKE ME FEEL BETTER, YOU MORON?!
OH, FOR PETE'S SAKE!
I COULD'VE JUST WORN MY SWIMSUIT UNDER-NEATH!
I'M SUCH AN IDIOT!!
AUGH!!
WHAT'S WITH URUKA?
BEATS ME!

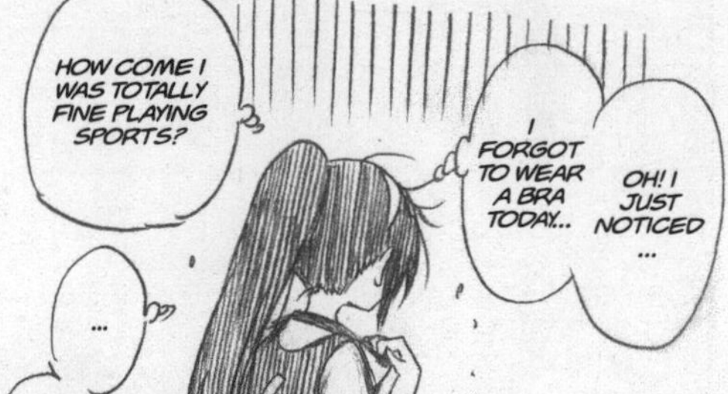
OH! I JUST NOTICED ...
I FORGOT TO WEAR A BRA TODAY...
HOW COME I WAS TOTALLY FINE PLAYING SPORTS?
...
THAT'S WEIRD... WHY'M I TEARING UP?
SNIFFLE

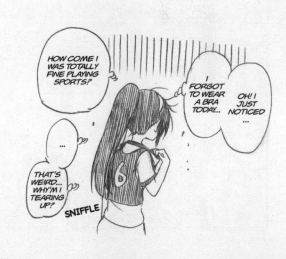

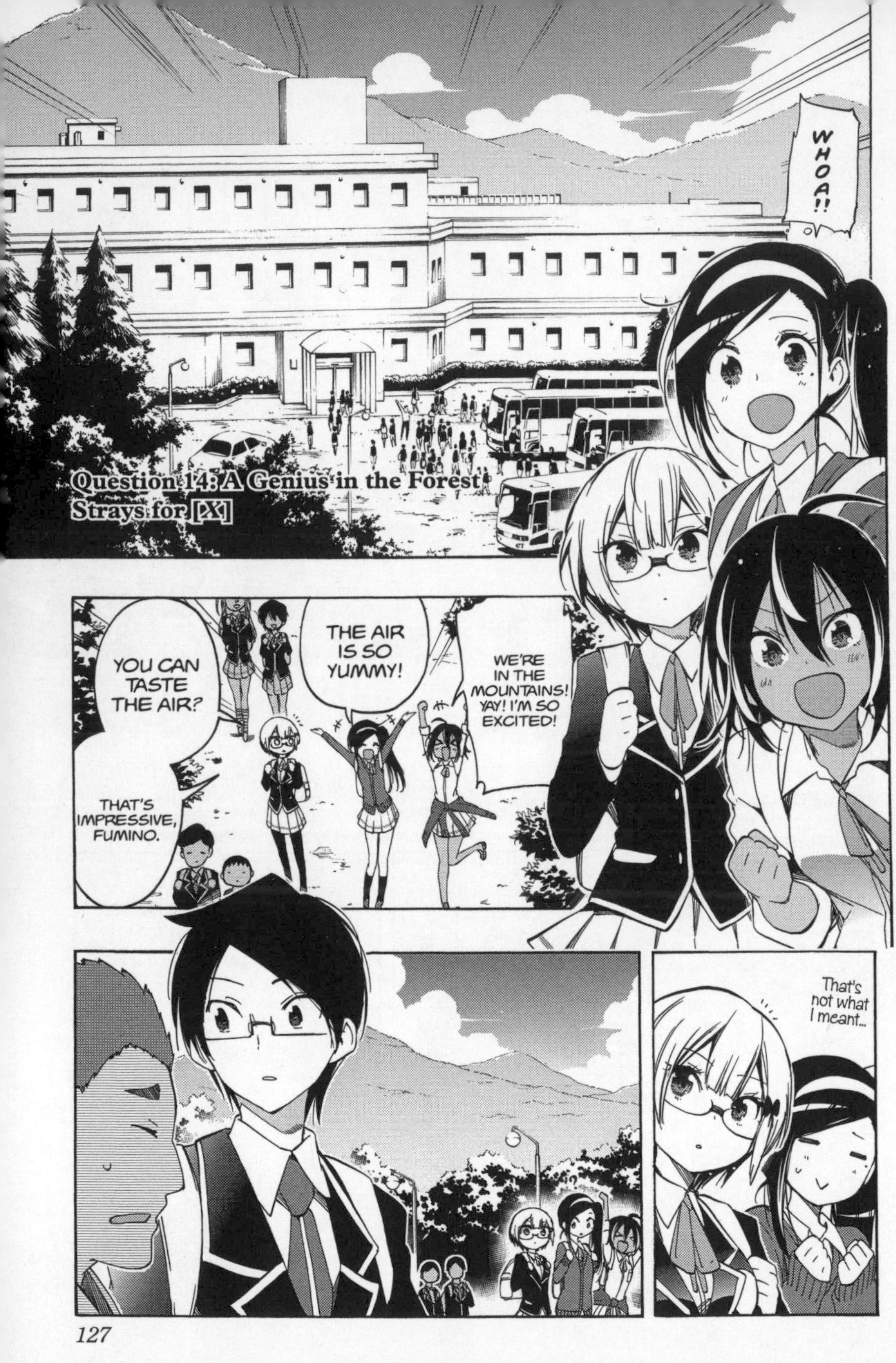
WHOA!!
Question 14: A Genius in the Forest Strays for [X]
WE'RE IN THE MOUNTAINS! YAY! I'M SO EXCITED!
THE AIR IS SO YUMMY!
YOU CAN TASTE THE AIR?
THAT'S IMPRESSIVE, FUMINO.
That's not what I meant...

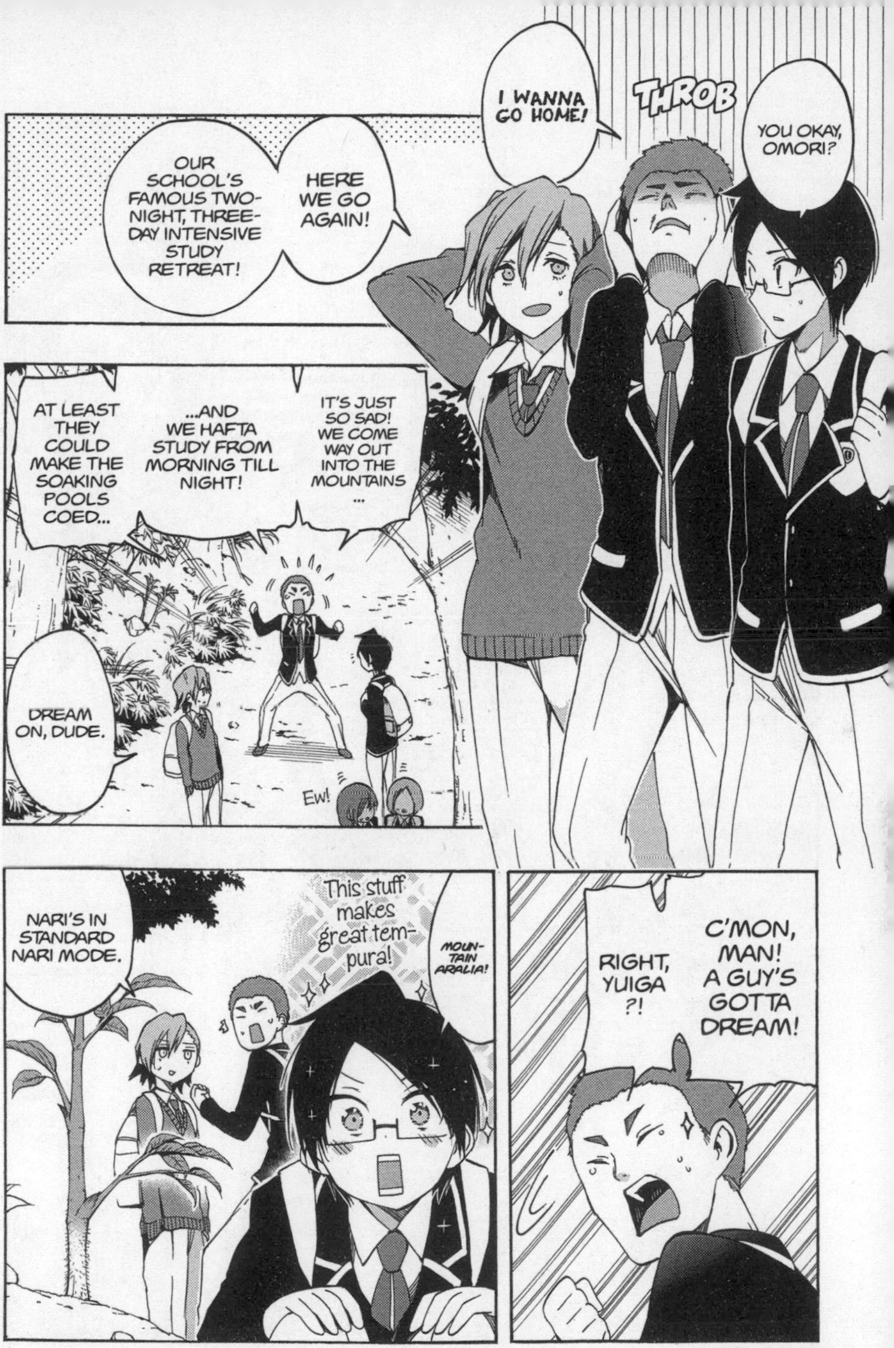
YOU OKAY, OMORI?
THROB
I WANNA GO HOME!
HERE WE GO AGAIN!
OUR SCHOOL'S FAMOUS TWO-NIGHT, THREE-DAY INTENSIVE STUDY RETREAT!
IT'S JUST SO SAD! WE COME WAY OUT INTO THE MOUNTAINS ...
...AND WE HAFTA STUDY FROM MORNING TILL NIGHT!
AT LEAST THEY COULD MAKE THE SOAKING POOLS COED...
DREAM ON, DUDE.
Ew!
C'MON, MAN! A GUY'S GOTTA DREAM!
RIGHT, YUIGA?!
MOUN-TAIN ARALIA!
This stuff makes great tem-pura!
NARI'S IN STANDARD NARI MODE.

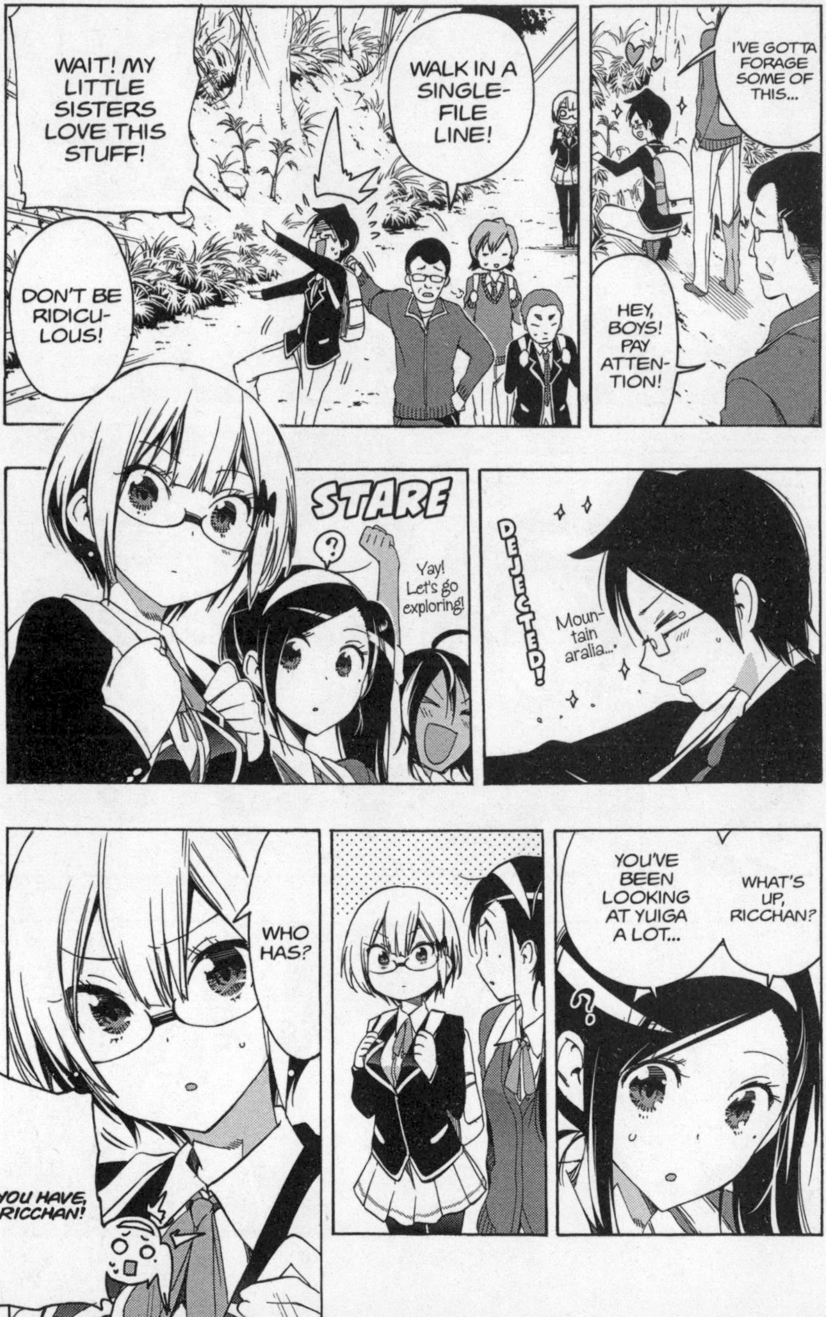
I'VE GOTTA FORAGE SOME OF THIS...
HEY, BOYS! PAY ATTENTION!
WALK IN A SINGLE-FILE LINE!
WAIT! MY LITTLE SISTERS LOVE THIS STUFF!
DON'T BE RIDICULOUS!
DEJECTED!
Mountain aralia...
STARE
Yay! Let's go exploring!
WHAT'S UP, RICCHAN?
YOU'VE BEEN LOOKING AT YUIGA A LOT...
WHO HAS?
YOU HAVE, RICCHAN!

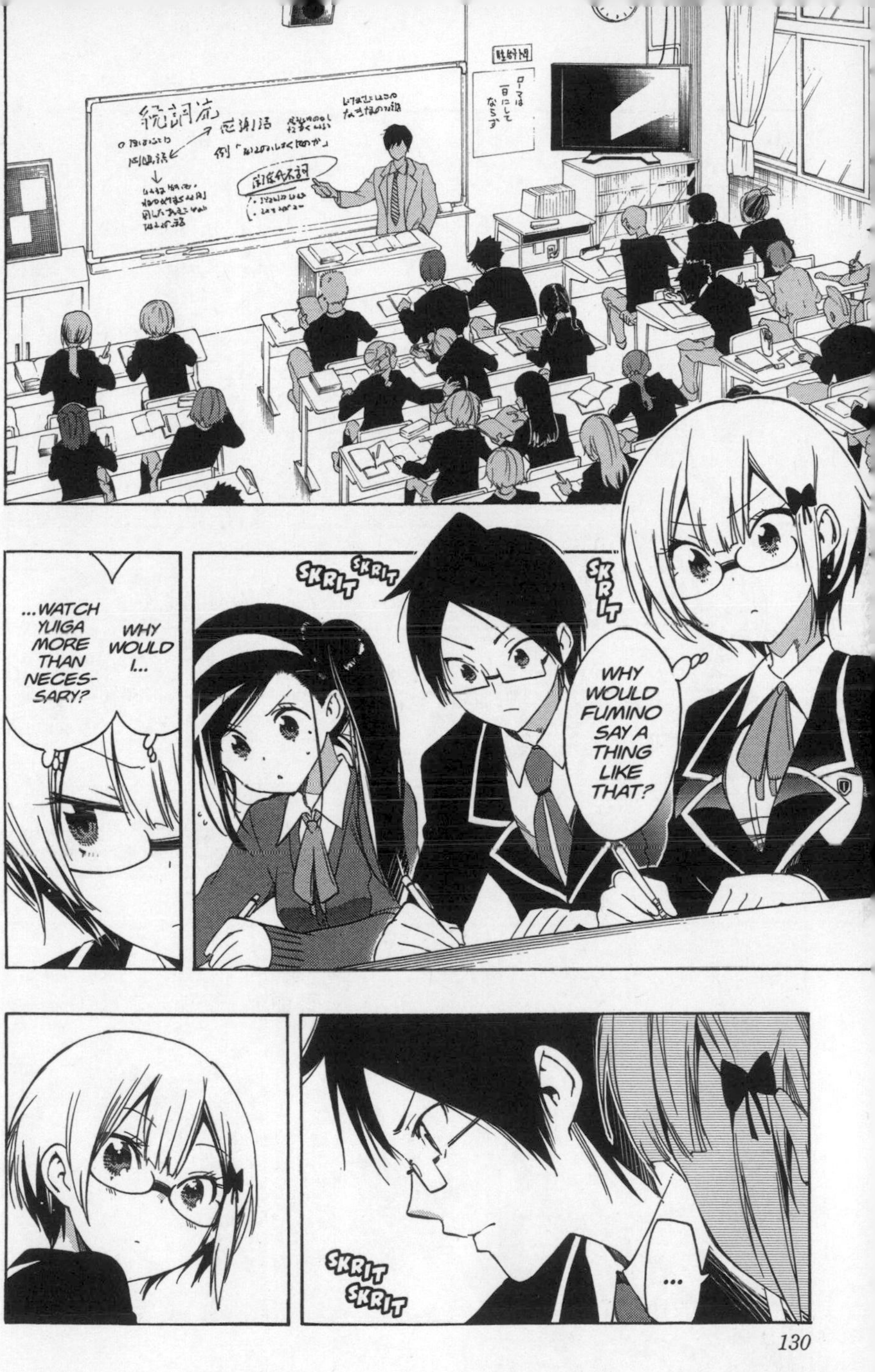
ローマは一日にしてならず
SKRIT SKRIT
SKRIT
WHY WOULD FUMINO SAY A THING LIKE THAT?
WHY WOULD I...
...WATCH YUIGA MORE THAN NECES-SARY?
...
SKRIT SKRIT

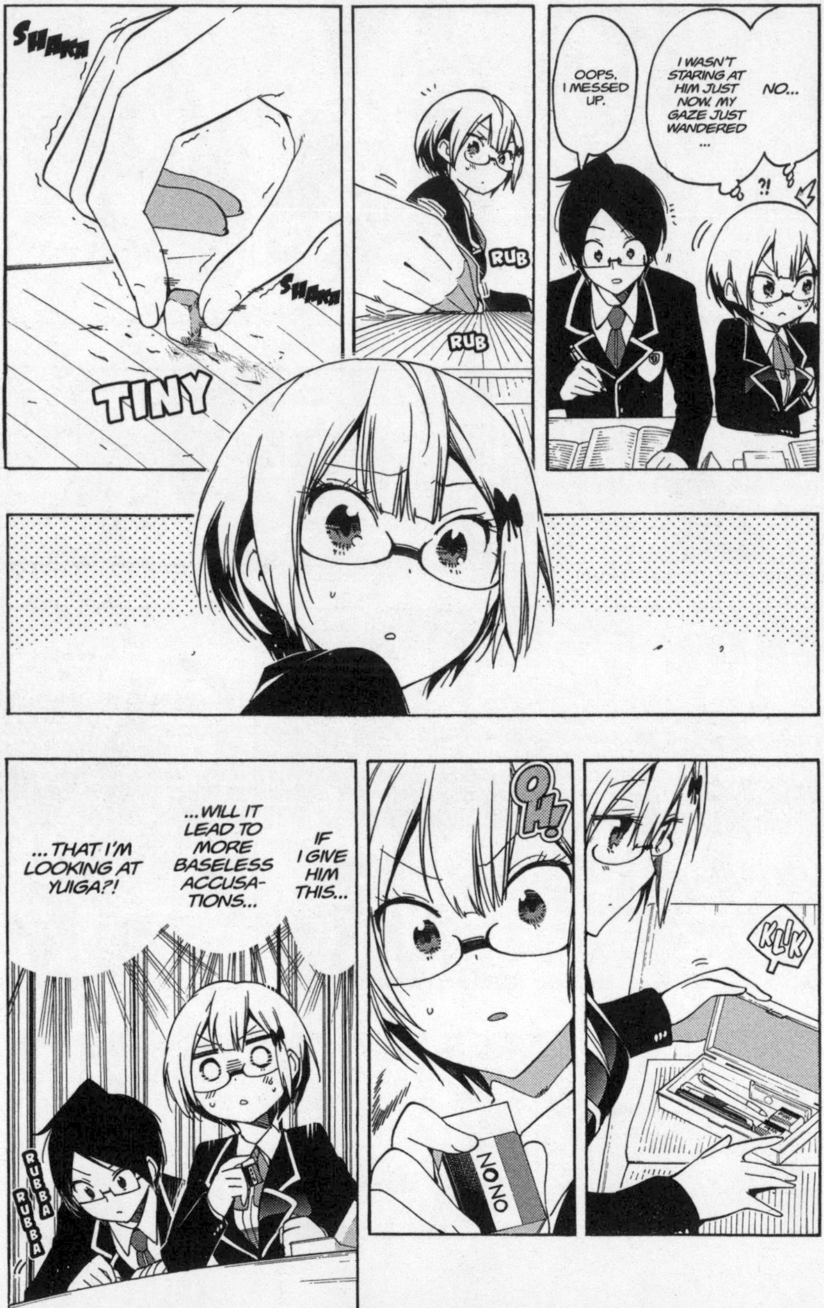
NO...
I WASN'T STARING AT HIM JUST NOW. MY GAZE JUST WANDERED ...
OOPS. I MESSED UP.
?!
RUB
RUB
SHAKA
SHAKA
TINY
KLIK
OH!
NONO
IF I GIVE HIM THIS...
...WILL IT LEAD TO MORE BASELESS ACCUSA-TIONS...
...THAT I'M LOOKING AT YUIGA?!
RUBBA RUBBA

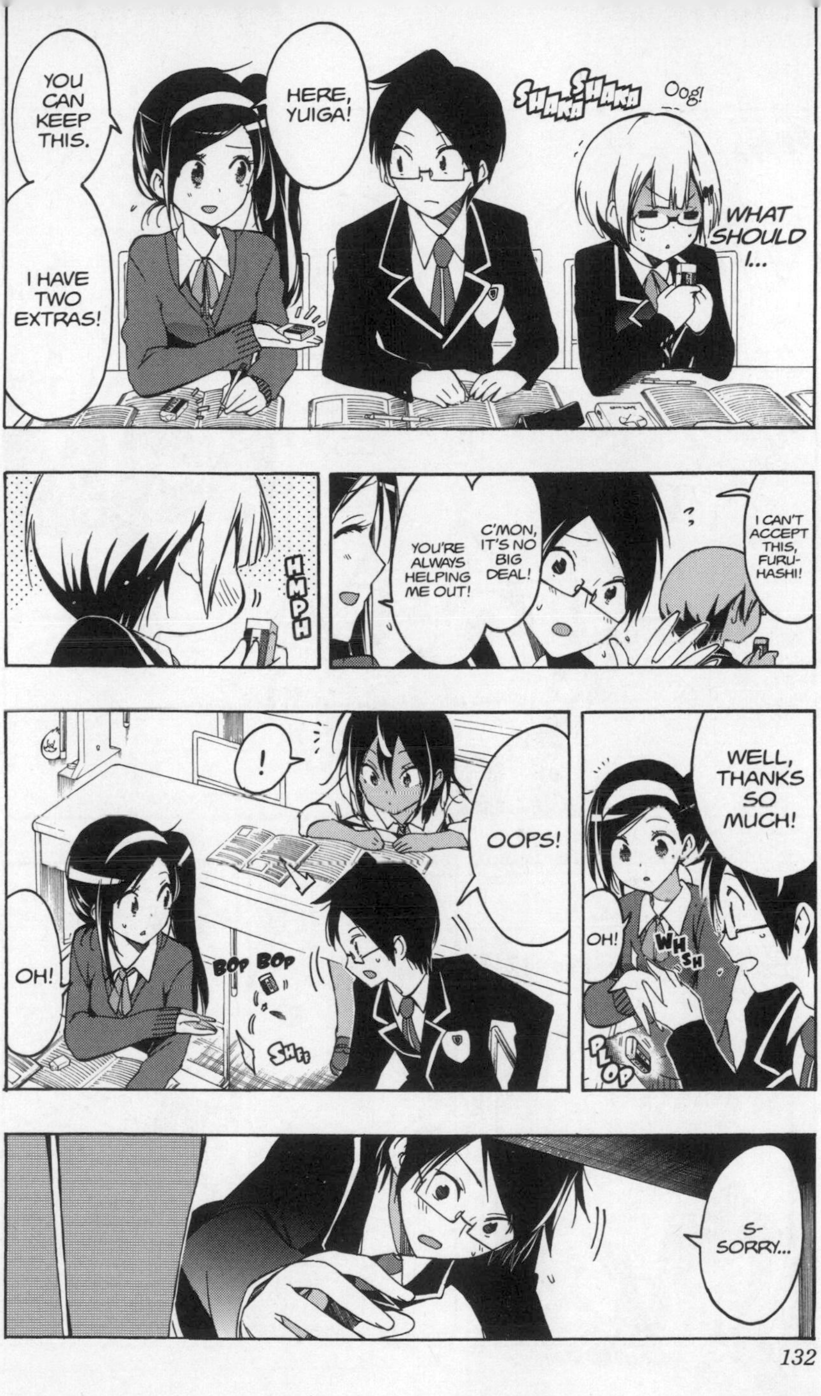
SHAKA SHAKA
Oog!
WHAT SHOULD I...
HERE, YUIGA!
YOU CAN KEEP THIS.
I HAVE TWO EXTRAS!
?
I CAN'T ACCEPT THIS, FURU-HASHI!
C'MON, IT'S NO BIG DEAL!
YOU'RE ALWAYS HELPING ME OUT!
HMPH
WELL, THANKS SO MUCH!
OH!
WHSH
PLOP
OOPS!
!
BOP BOP
SHFF
OH!
S-SORRY...

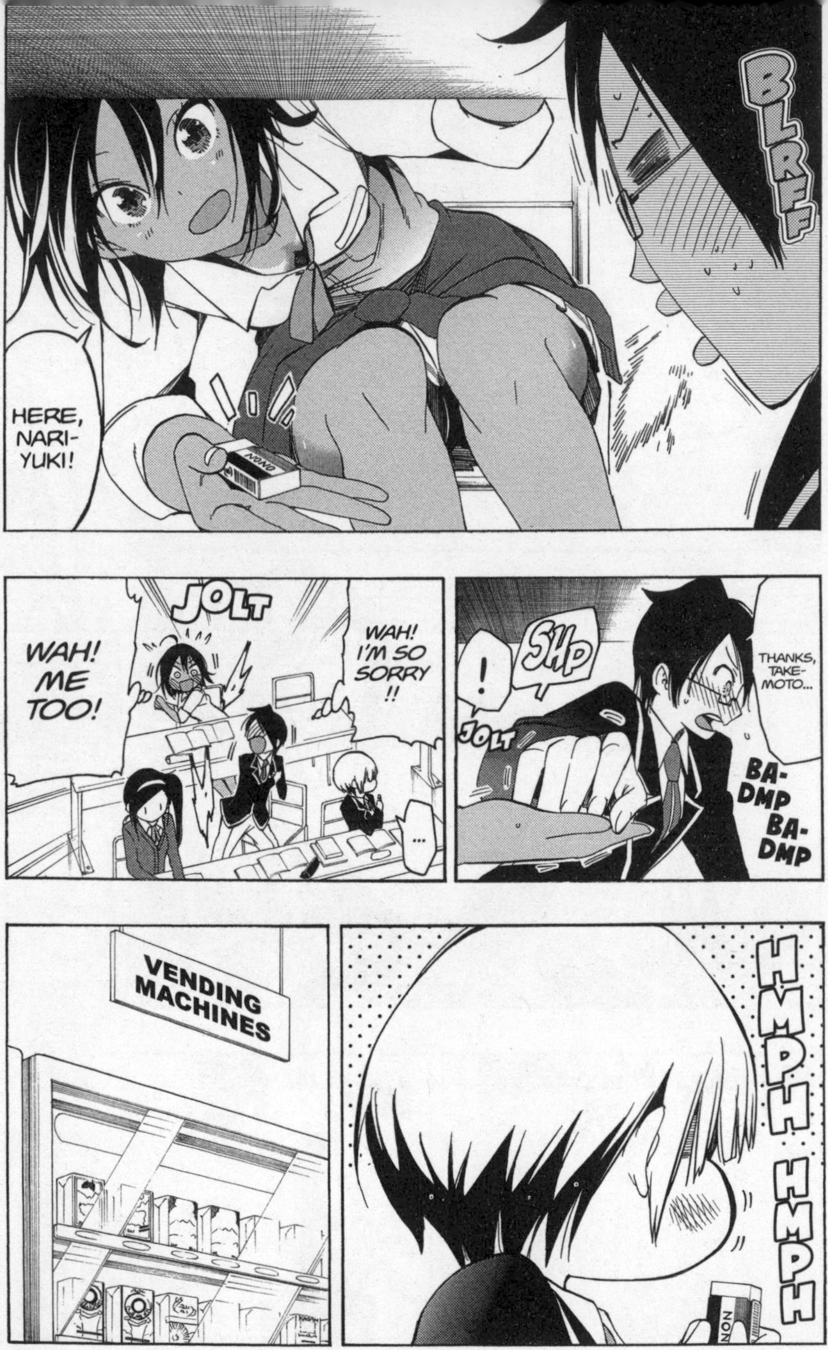
BLRFF
HERE, NARI-YUKI!
THANKS, TAKE-MOTO...
SHP
!
JOLT
BA-DMP BA-DMP
JOLT
WAH! I'M SO SORRY!!
WAH! ME TOO!
...
HMPH HMPH
VENDING MACHINES

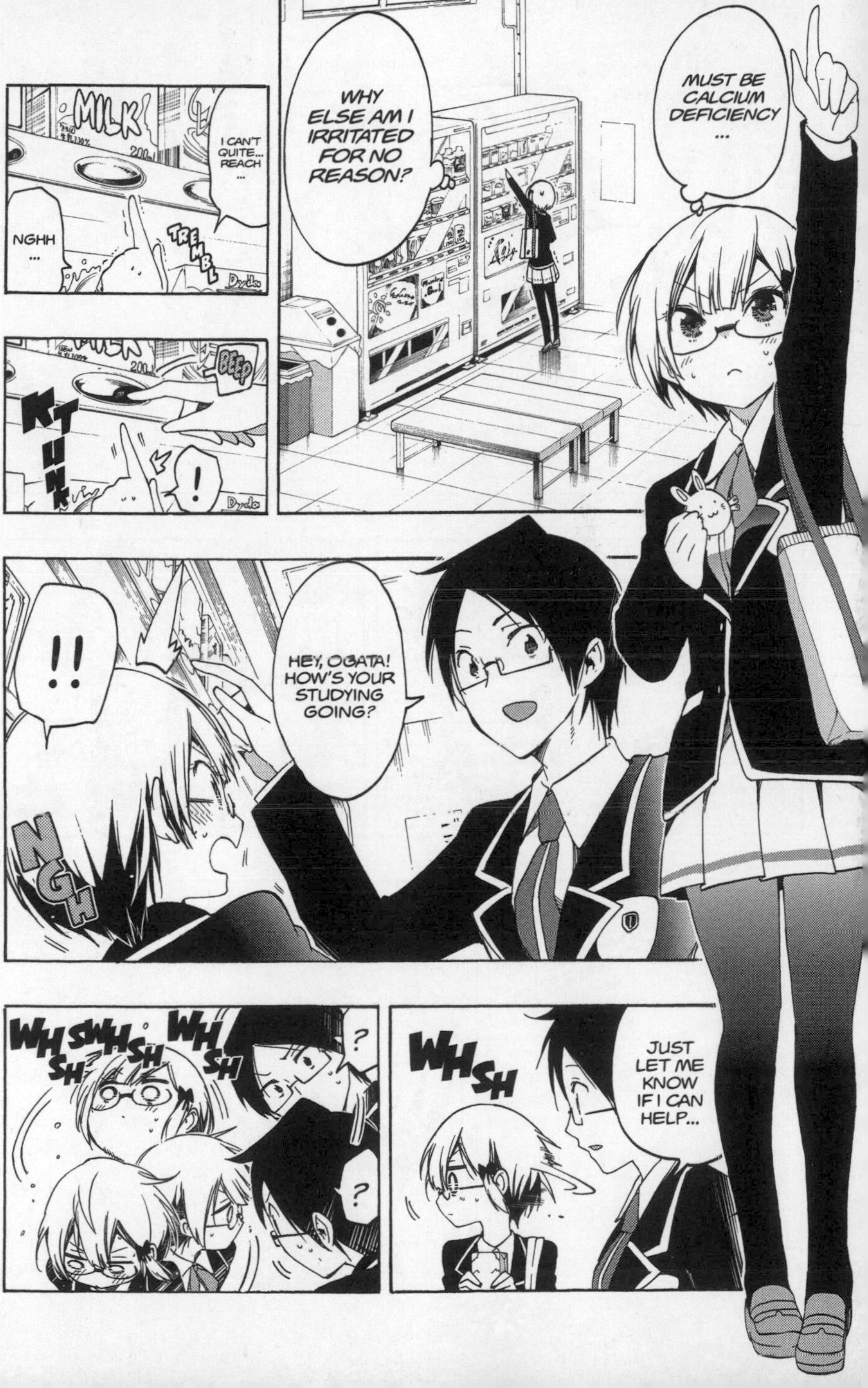
MUST BE CALCIUM DEFICIENCY ...
WHY ELSE AM I IRRITATED FOR NO REASON?
I CAN'T QUITE... REACH ...
NGHH ...
TREMBL
MILK
BEEP
KTUNK
!
HEY, OGATA! HOW'S YOUR STUDYING GOING?
!!
NGH
WHSH
JUST LET ME KNOW IF I CAN HELP...
WHSH
SWHSH
WHSH
?
?

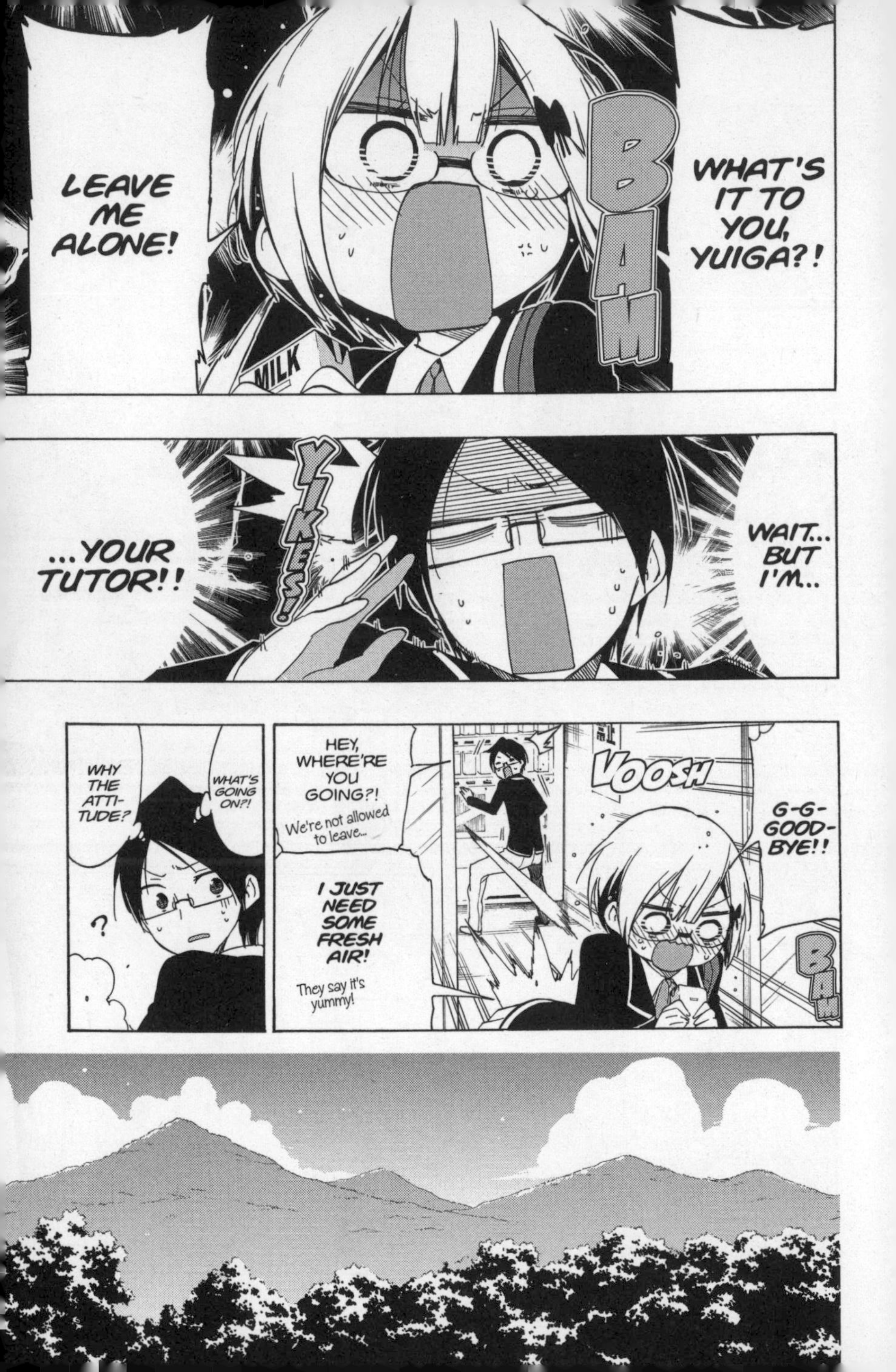
WHAT'S IT TO YOU, YUIGA?!
BAM
LEAVE ME ALONE!
MILK
WAIT... BUT I'M...
YIKES!
...YOUR TUTOR!!
G-G-GOOD-BYE!!
BAM
VOOSH
HEY, WHERE'RE YOU GOING?!
We're not allowed to leave...
I JUST NEED SOME FRESH AIR!
They say it's yummy!
WHAT'S GOING ON?!
WHY THE ATTI-TUDE?
?

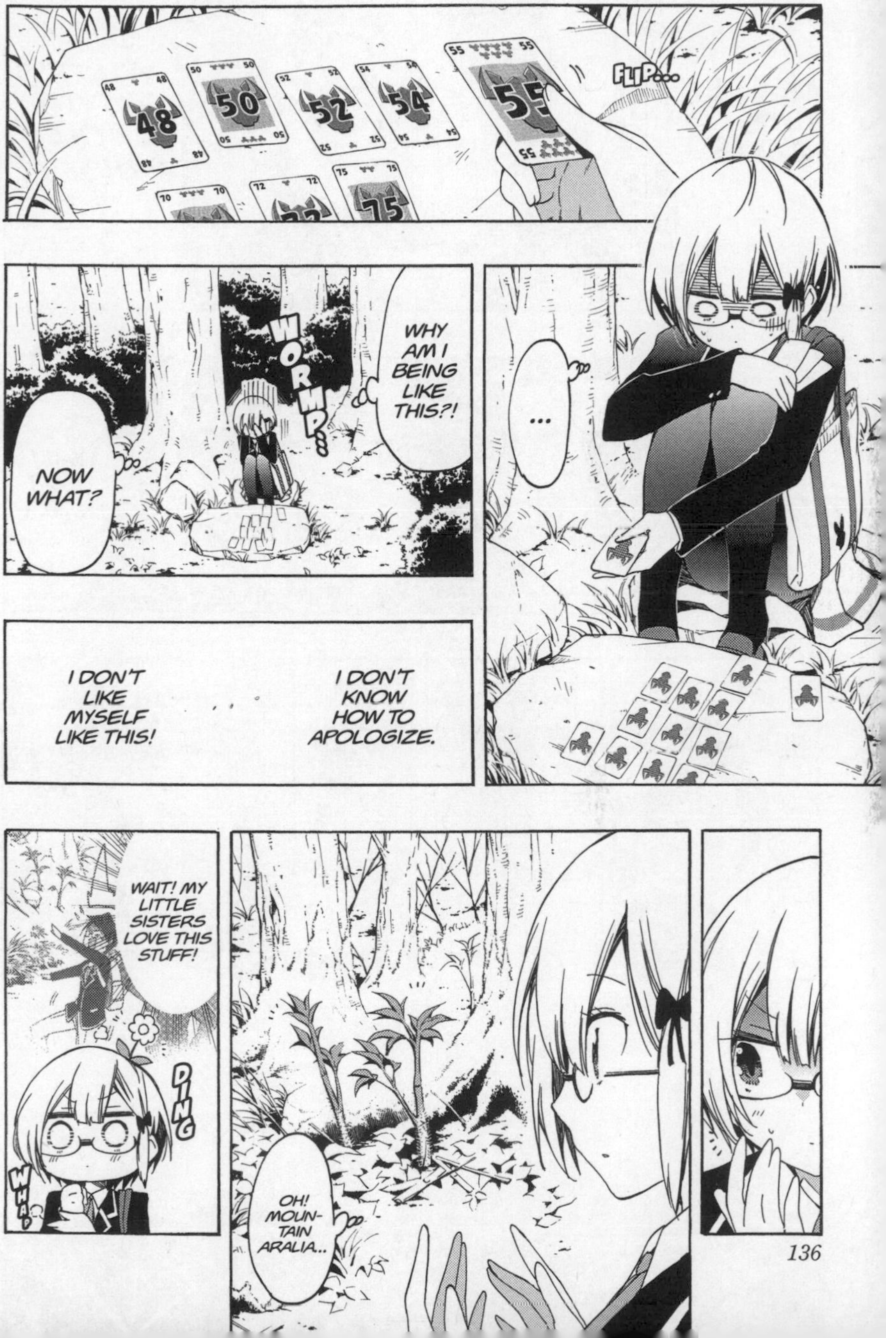
FLIP...
...
WHY AM I BEING LIKE THIS?!
WORMP...
NOW WHAT?
I DON'T KNOW HOW TO APOLOGIZE.
I DON'T LIKE MYSELF LIKE THIS!
OH! MOUN-TAIN ARALIA..
WAIT! MY LITTLE SISTERS LOVE THIS STUFF!
DING
WHAP

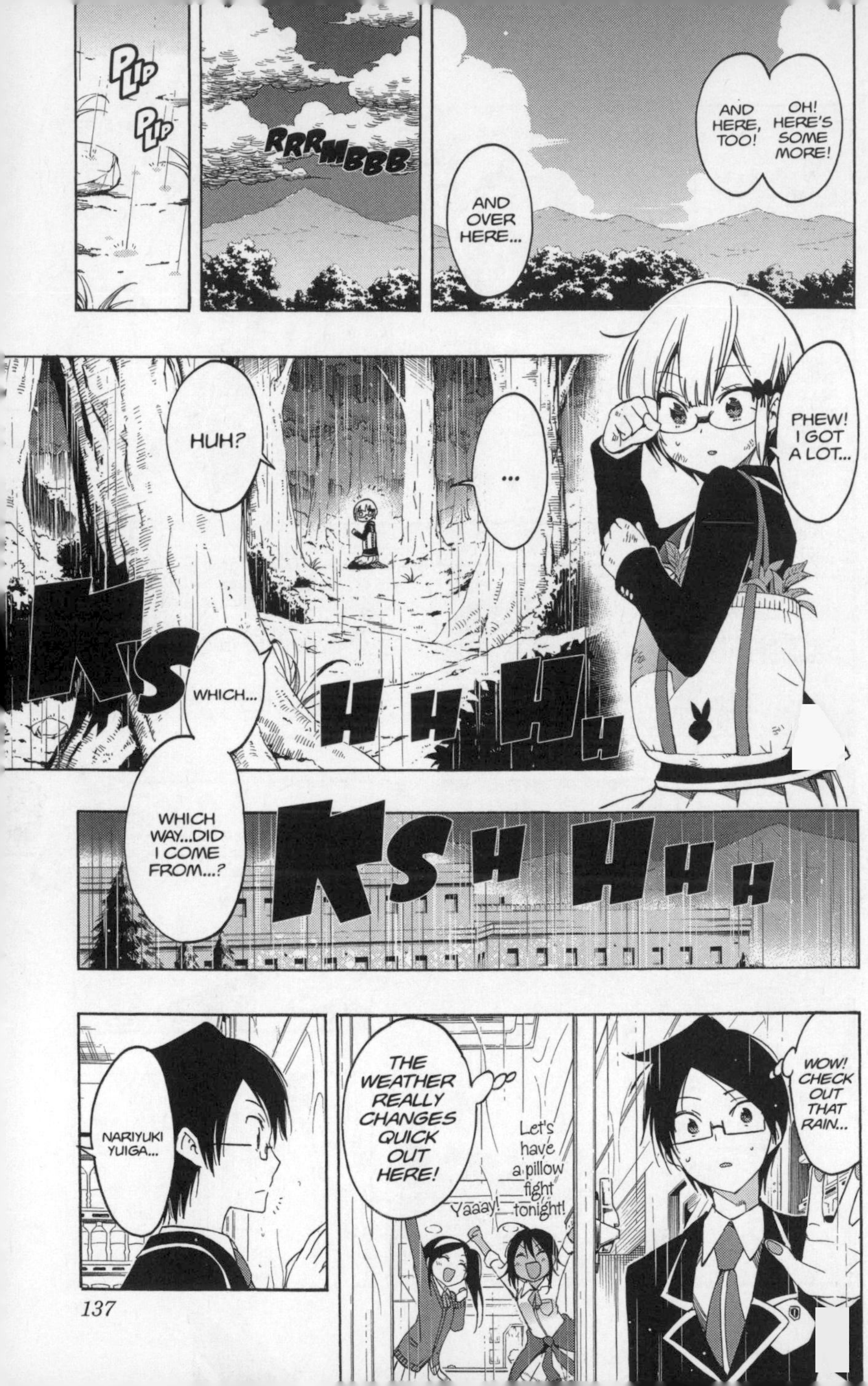
OH! HERE'S SOME MORE!
AND HERE, TOO!
AND OVER HERE...
RRRMBBB
PLIP
PLIP
PHEW! I GOT A LOT...
...
HUH?
KSHHHHH
WHICH...
WHICH WAY...DID I COME FROM...?
KSHHHHH
WOW! CHECK OUT THAT RAIN...
THE WEATHER REALLY CHANGES QUICK OUT HERE!
Let's have a pillow fight tonight!
Yaaay!
NARIYUKI YUIGA...

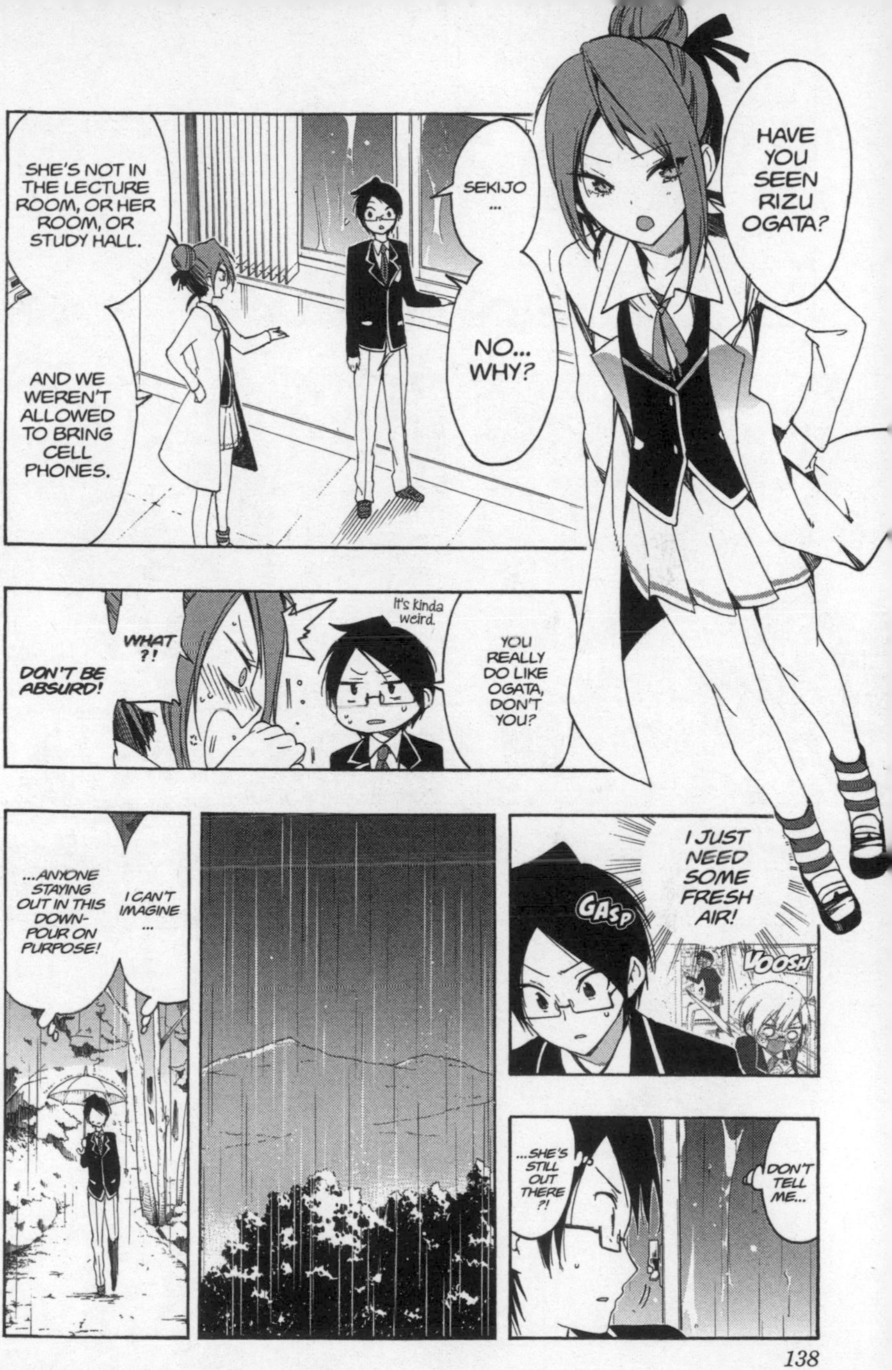
HAVE YOU SEEN RIZU OGATA?
SEKIJO ...
NO... WHY?
SHE'S NOT IN THE LECTURE ROOM, OR HER ROOM, OR STUDY HALL.
AND WE WEREN'T ALLOWED TO BRING CELL PHONES.
YOU REALLY DO LIKE OGATA, DON'T YOU?
It's kinda weird.
WHAT ?!
DON'T BE ABSURD!
I JUST NEED SOME FRESH AIR!
GASP
VOOSH
DON'T TELL ME...
...SHE'S STILL OUT THERE ?!
I CAN'T IMAGINE ...
...ANYONE STAYING OUT IN THIS DOWN-POUR ON PURPOSE!

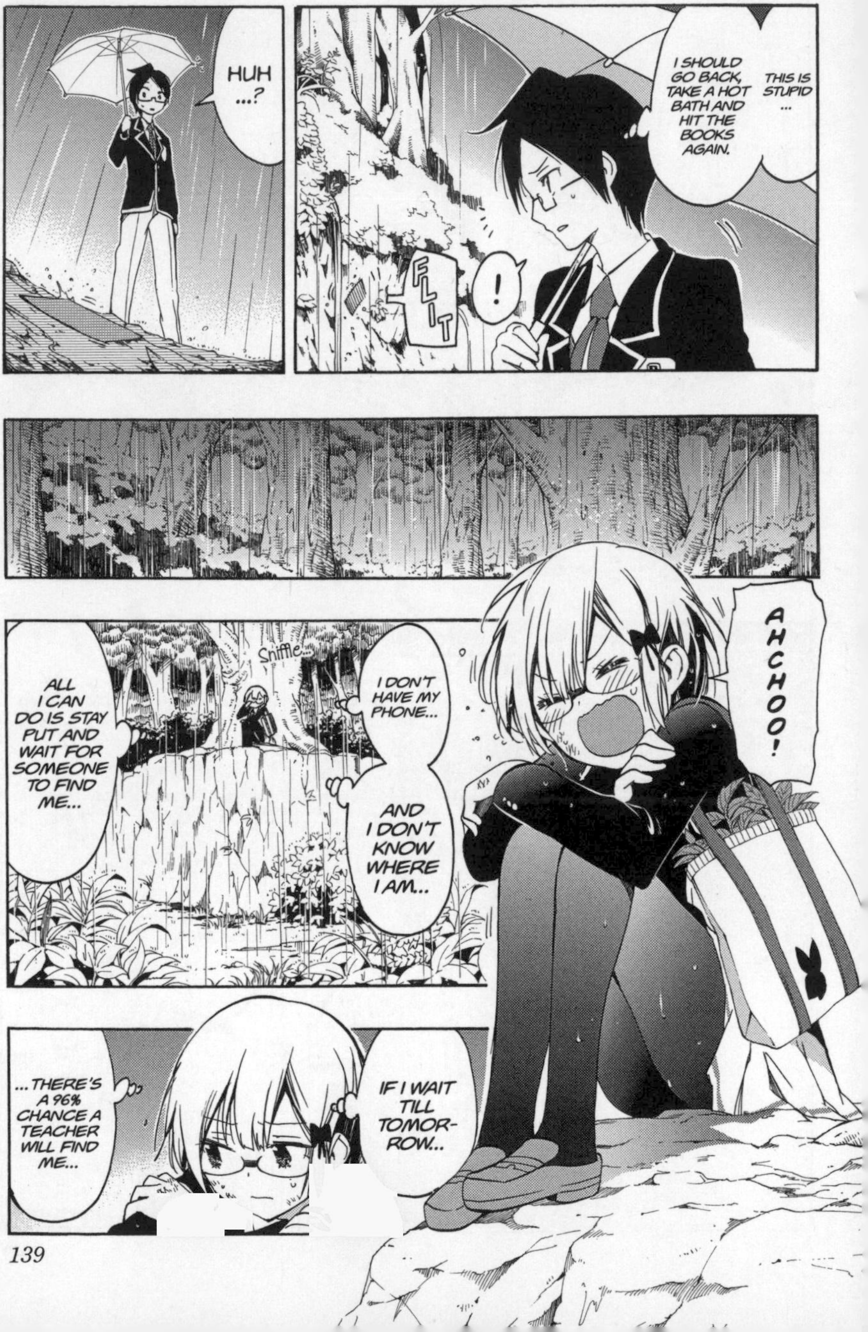
THIS IS STUPID ...
I SHOULD GO BACK, TAKE A HOT BATH AND HIT THE BOOKS AGAIN.
!
FLIT
HUH ...?
AHCHOO!
Sniffle...
I DON'T HAVE MY PHONE...
AND I DON'T KNOW WHERE I AM...
ALL I CAN DO IS STAY PUT AND WAIT FOR SOMEONE TO FIND ME...
IF I WAIT TILL TOMOR-ROW...
...THERE'S A 96% CHANCE A TEACHER WILL FIND ME...

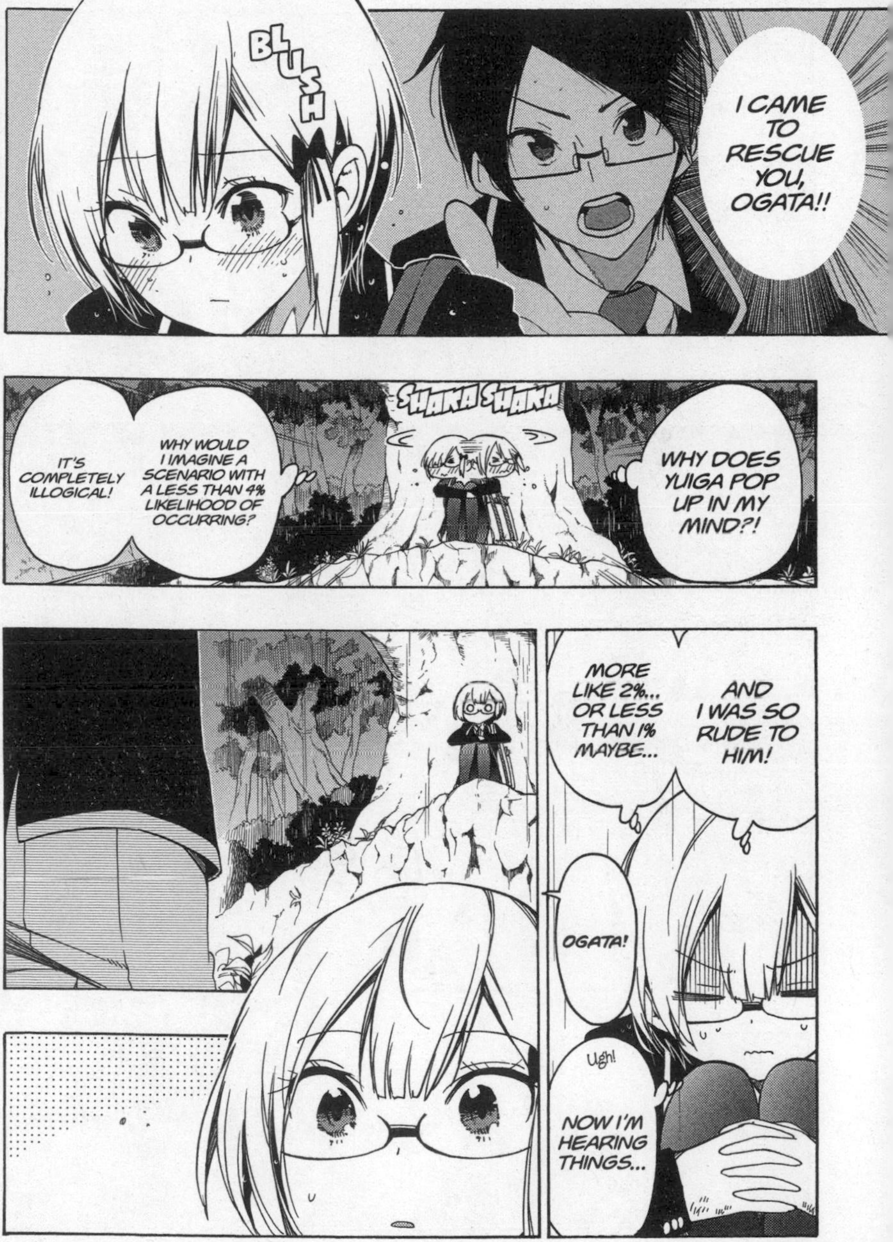
BLUSH
I CAME TO RESCUE YOU, OGATA!!
WHY DOES YUIGA POP UP IN MY MIND?!
SHAKA SHAKA
WHY WOULD I IMAGINE A SCENARIO WITH A LESS THAN 4% LIKELIHOOD OF OCCURRING?
IT'S COMPLETELY ILLOGICAL!
AND I WAS SO RUDE TO HIM!
MORE LIKE 2%... OR LESS THAN 1% MAYBE...
OGATA!
Ugh!
NOW I'M HEARING THINGS...

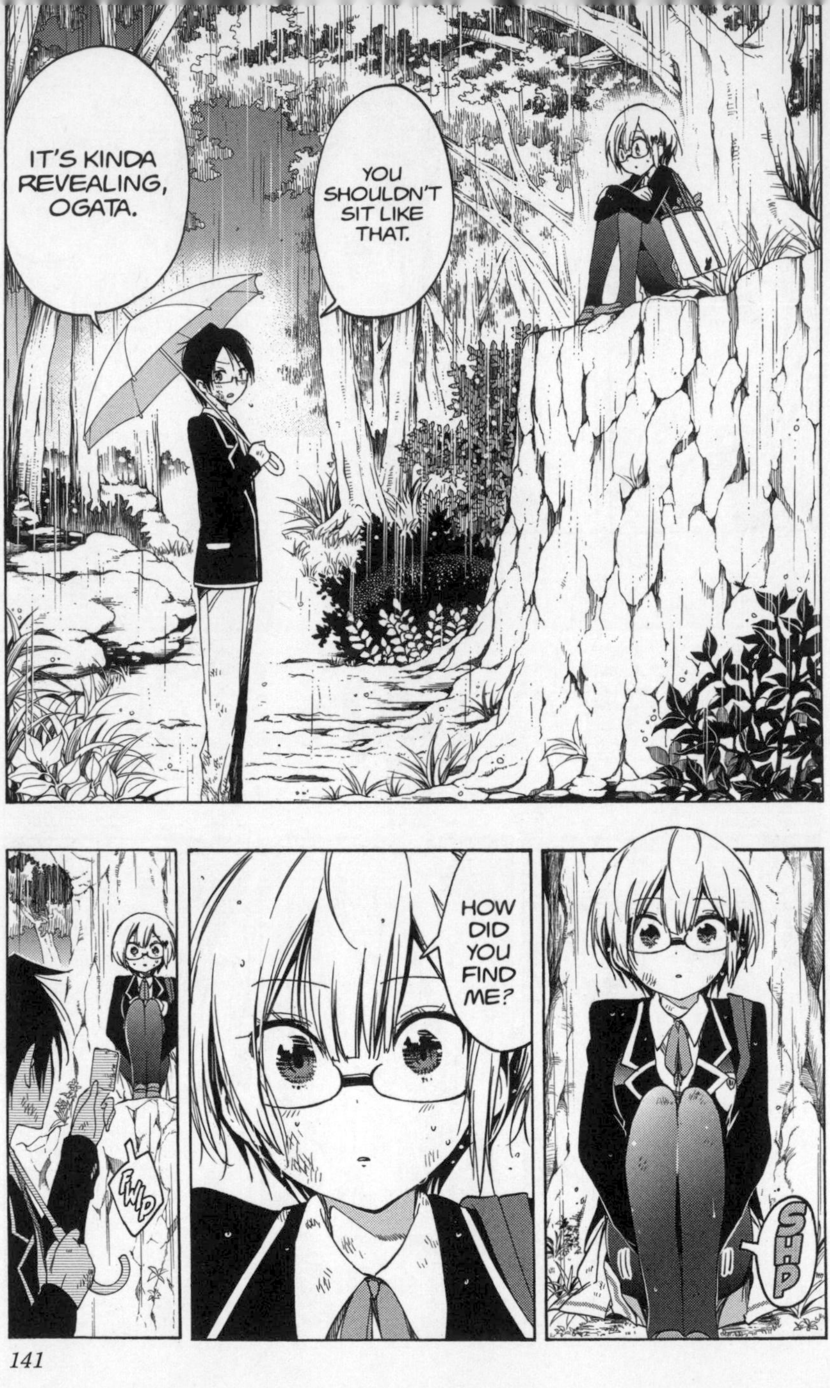
YOU SHOULDN'T SIT LIKE THAT.
IT'S KINDA REVEALING, OGATA.
SHP
HOW DID YOU FIND ME?
FWIP

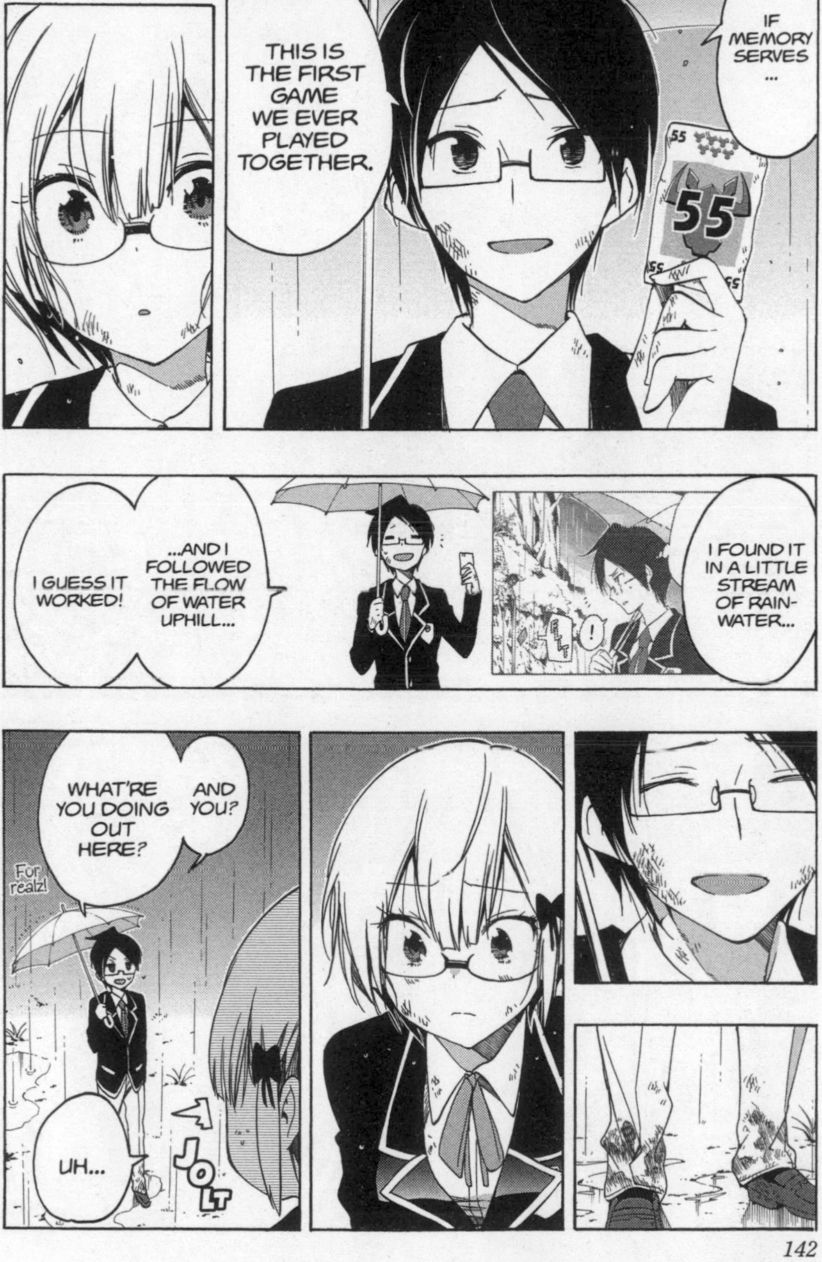
IF MEMORY SERVES ...
THIS IS THE FIRST GAME WE EVER PLAYED TOGETHER.
I FOUND IT IN A LITTLE STREAM OF RAIN-WATER...
!
...AND I FOLLOWED THE FLOW OF WATER UPHILL...
I GUESS IT WORKED!
AND YOU?
WHAT'RE YOU DOING OUT HERE?
For realz!
JOLT
UH...

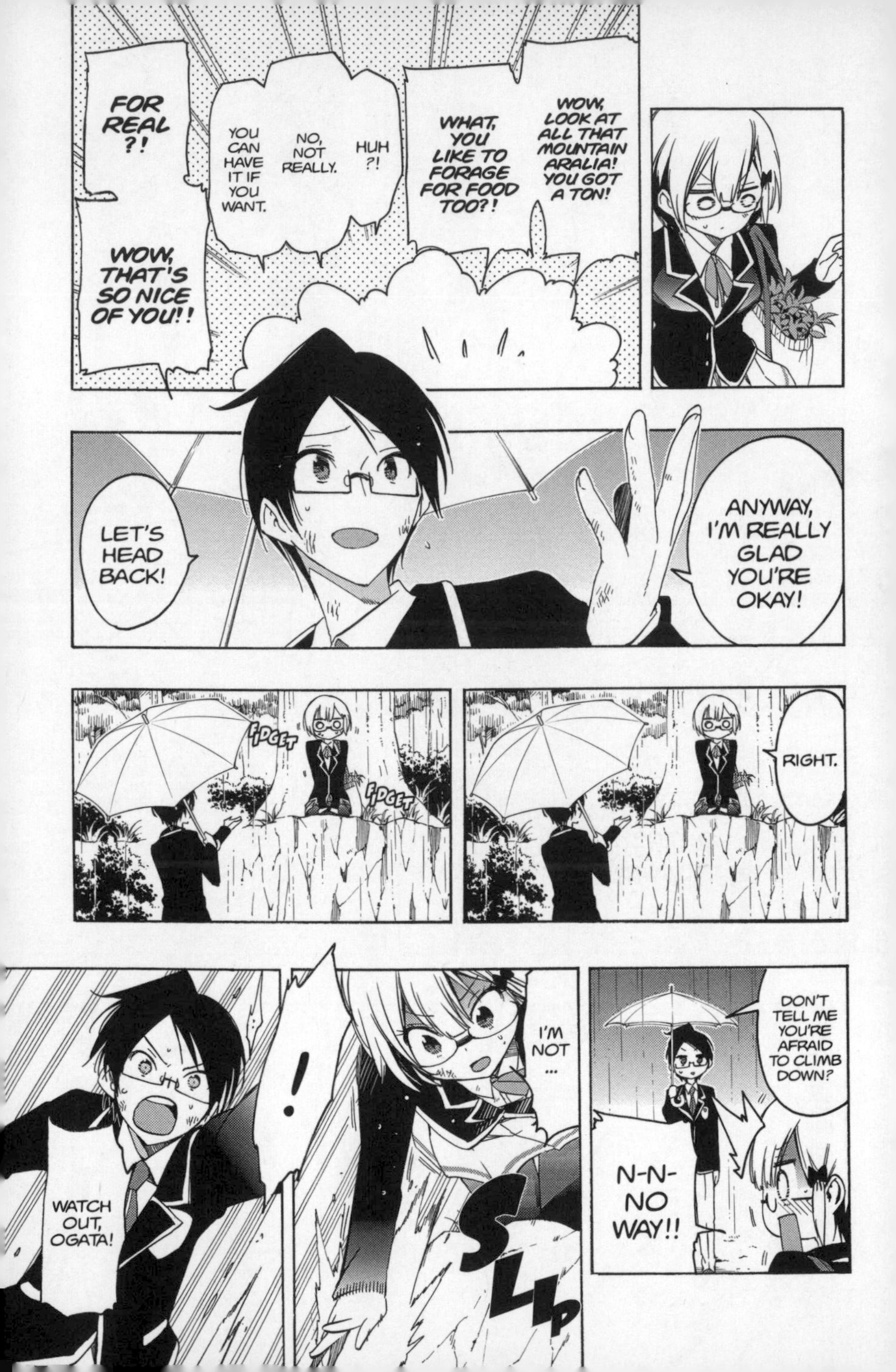
WOW, LOOK AT ALL THAT MOUNTAIN ARALIA! YOU GOT A TON!
WHAT, YOU LIKE TO FORAGE FOR FOOD TOO?!
HUH ?!
NO, NOT REALLY.
YOU CAN HAVE IT IF YOU WANT.
FOR REAL ?!
WOW, THAT'S SO NICE OF YOU!!
ANYWAY, I'M REALLY GLAD YOU'RE OKAY!
LET'S HEAD BACK!
RIGHT.
FIDGET
FIDGET
DON'T TELL ME YOU'RE AFRAID TO CLIMB DOWN?
N-N-NO WAY!!
I'M NOT ...
!
SLIP
WATCH OUT, OGATA!

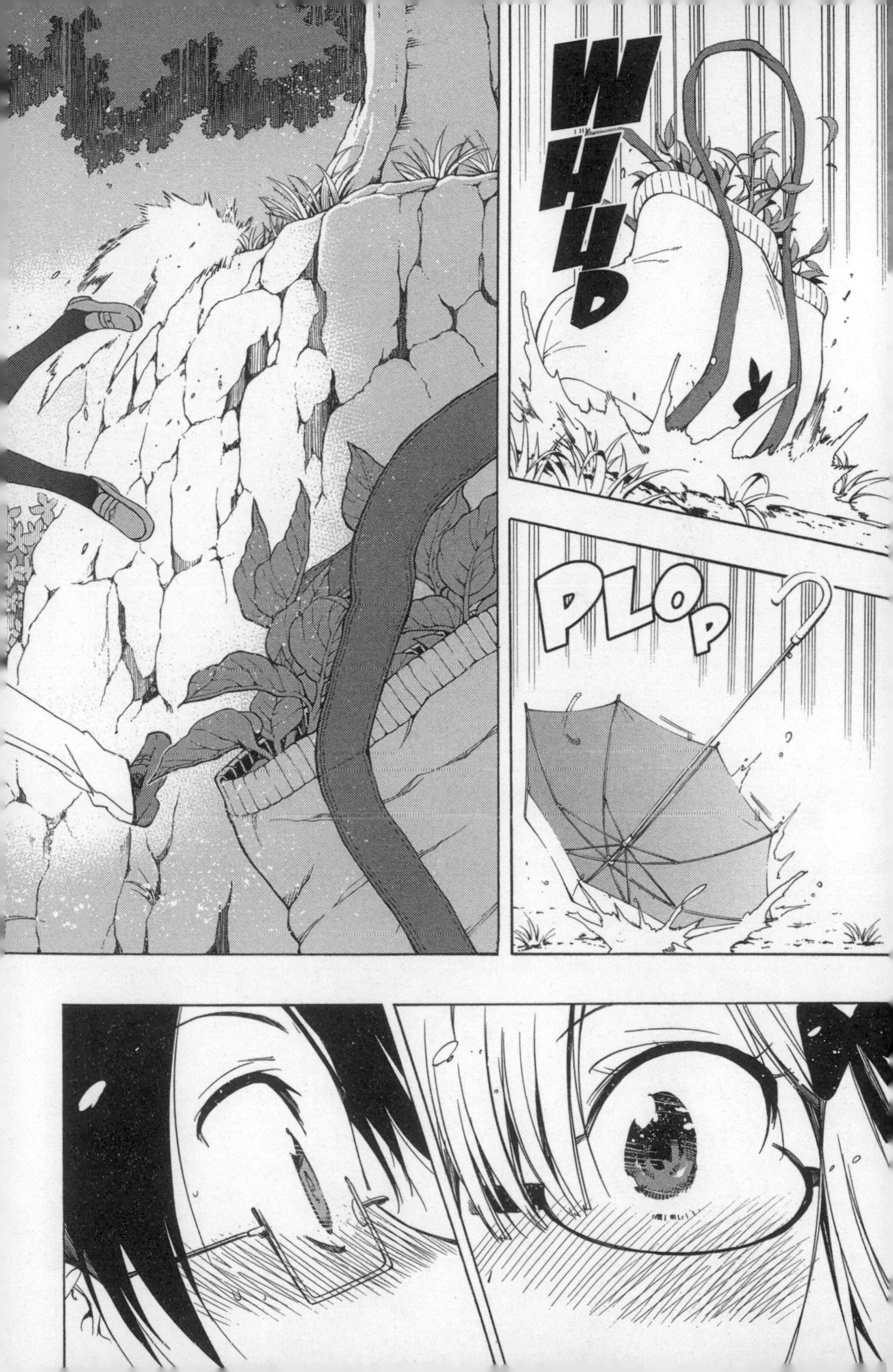
WHUD
PLOP

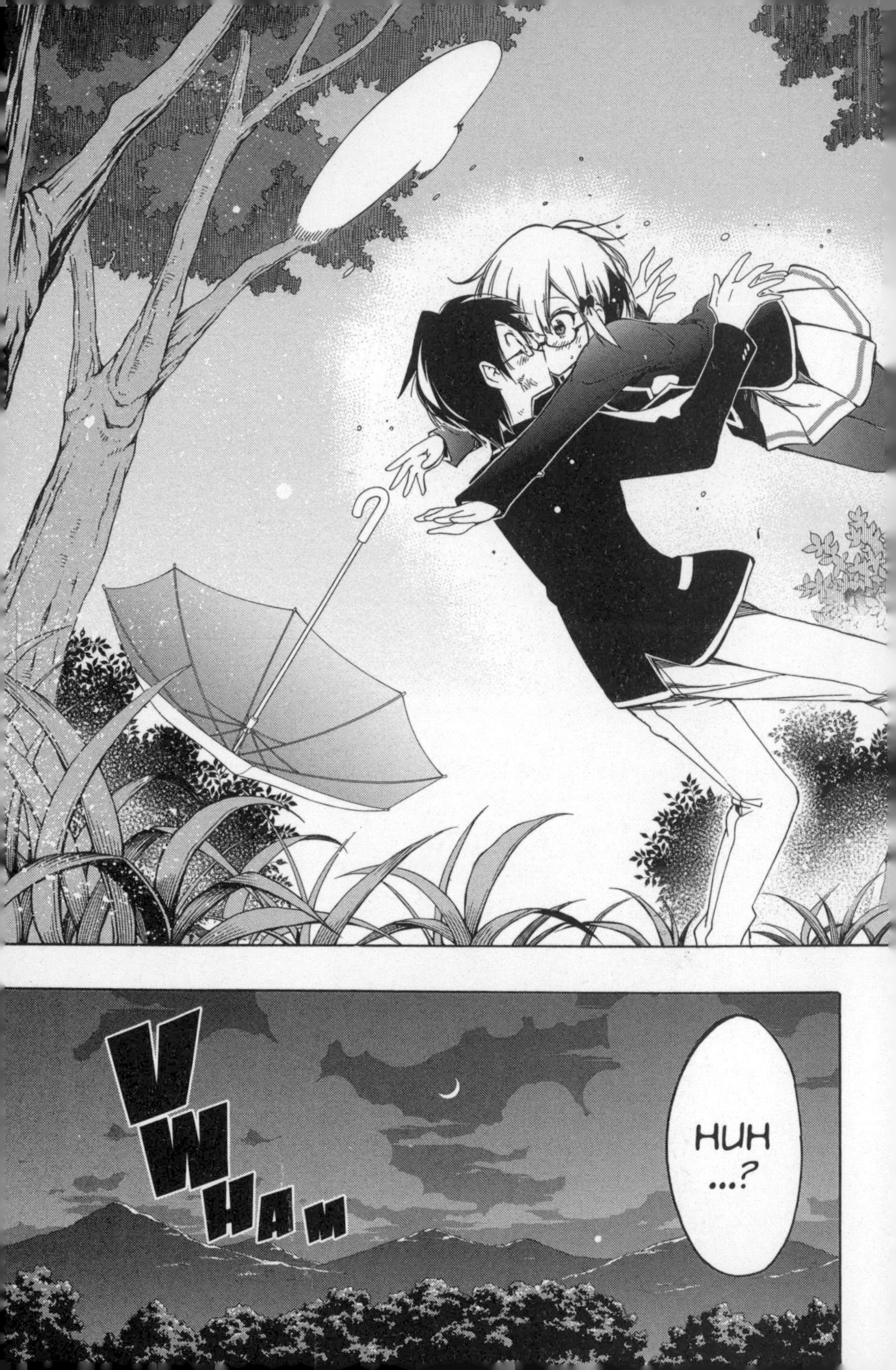
HUH ...?
VWHAM

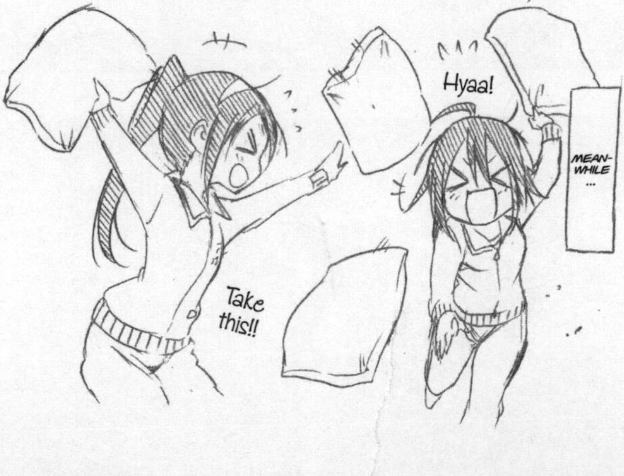
MEAN-WHILE ...
Hyaa!
Take this!!

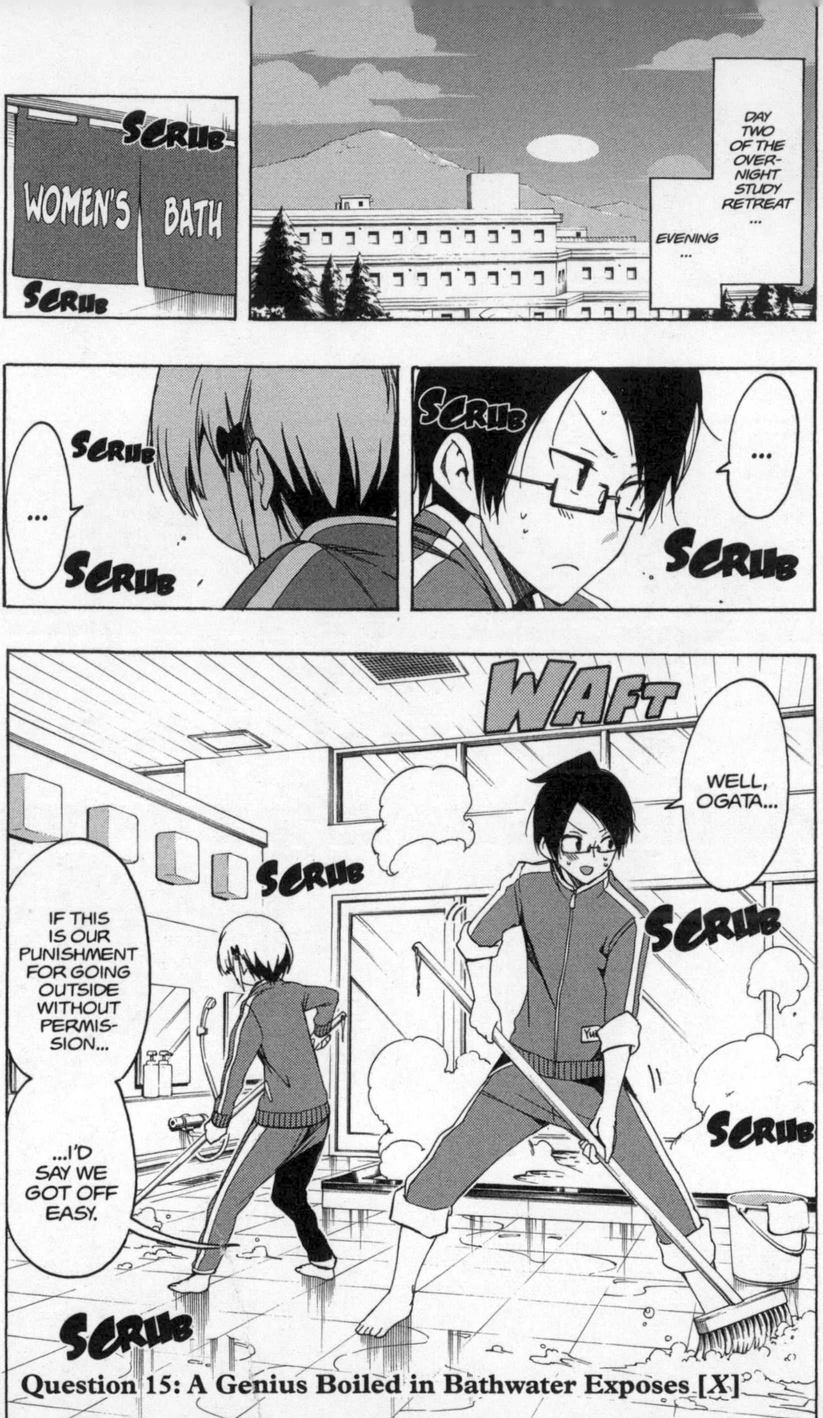
DAY TWO OF THE OVER-NIGHT STUDY RETREAT ...
EVENING ...
SCRUB
WOMEN'S BATH
SCRUB
SCRUB
...
SCRUB
...
SCRUB
SCRUB
WAFT
WELL, OGATA...
SCRUB
SCRUB
SCRUB
IF THIS IS OUR PUNISHMENT FOR GOING OUTSIDE WITHOUT PERMIS-SION...
...I'D SAY WE GOT OFF EASY.
SCRUB

Question 15: A Genius Boiled in Bathwater Exposes [X]

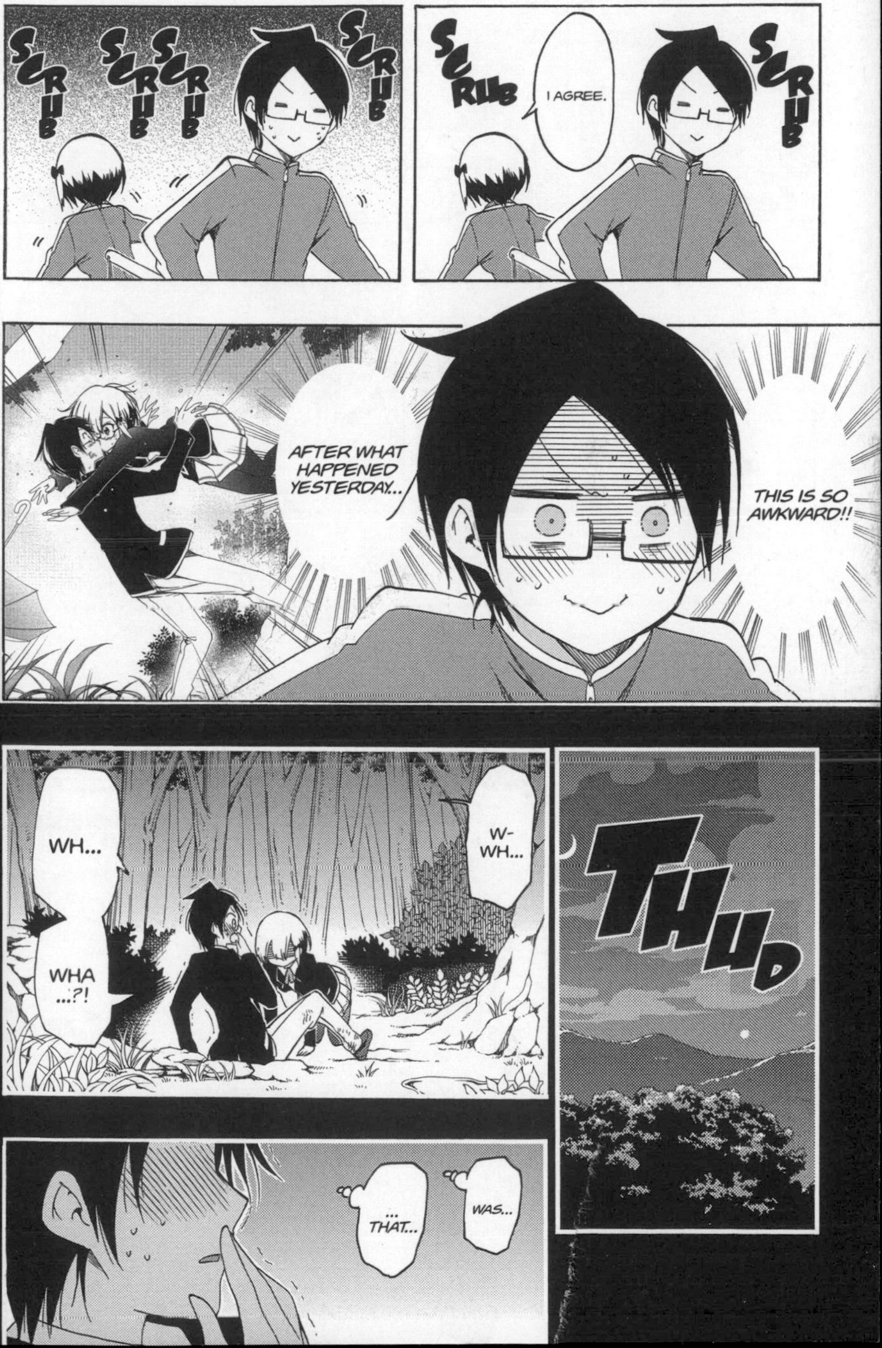
SCRUB
I AGREE.
SCRUB
SCRUB
SCRUB
SCRUB
SCRUB
THIS IS SO AWKWARD!!
AFTER WHAT HAPPENED YESTERDAY...
THUD
W-WH...
WH...
WHA ...?!
WAS...
...THAT...

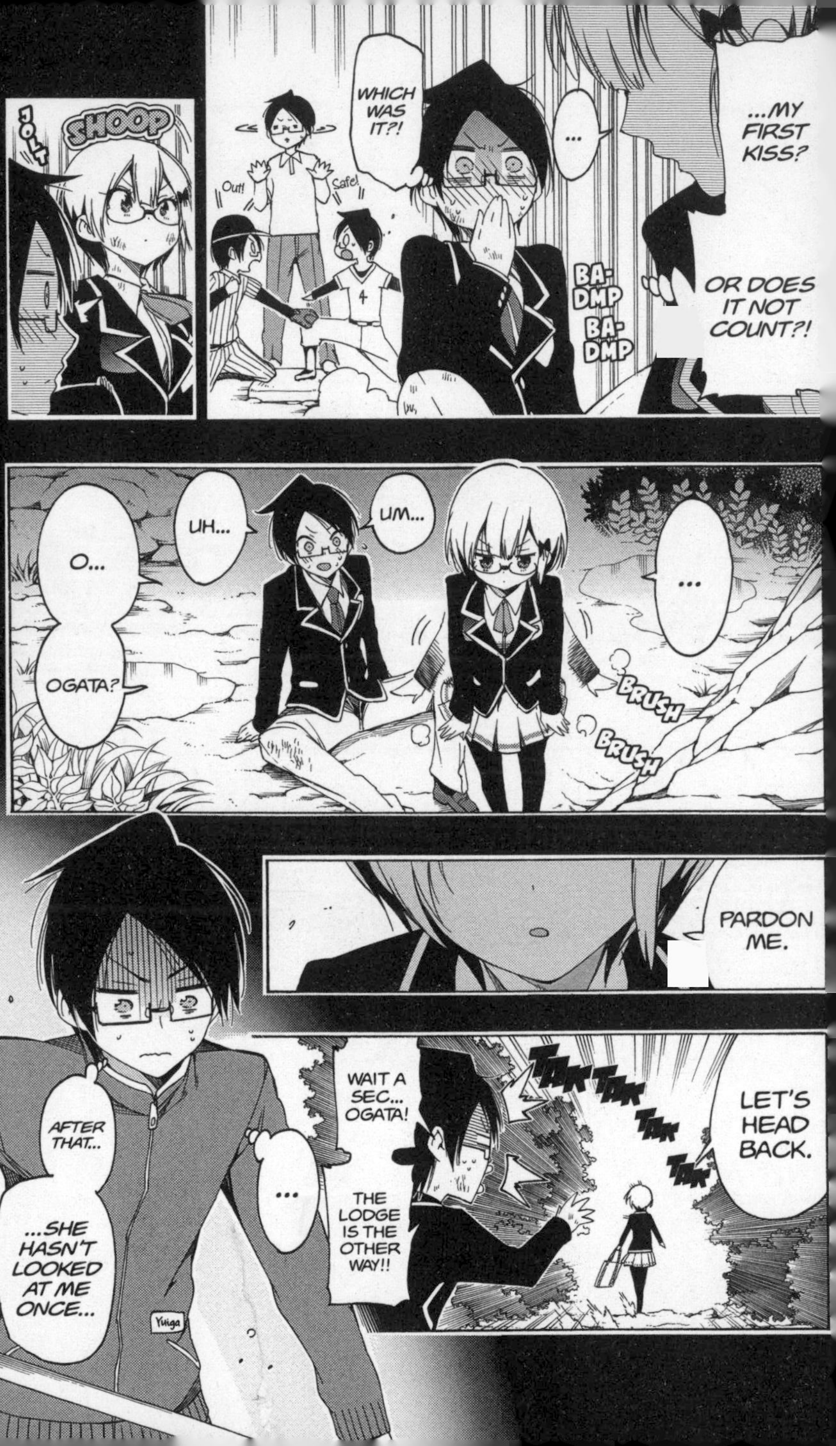
...MY FIRST KISS?
OR DOES IT NOT COUNT?!
...
WHICH WAS IT?!
BA-DMP BA-DMP
Safe!
Out!
SHOOP
JOLT
...
BRUSH
BRUSH
UM...
UH...
O...
OGATA?
PARDON ME.
LET'S HEAD BACK.
TAK TAK TAK TAK
WAIT A SEC... OGATA!
THE LODGE IS THE OTHER WAY!!
...
AFTER THAT...
...SHE HASN'T LOOKED AT ME ONCE...
Yuiga

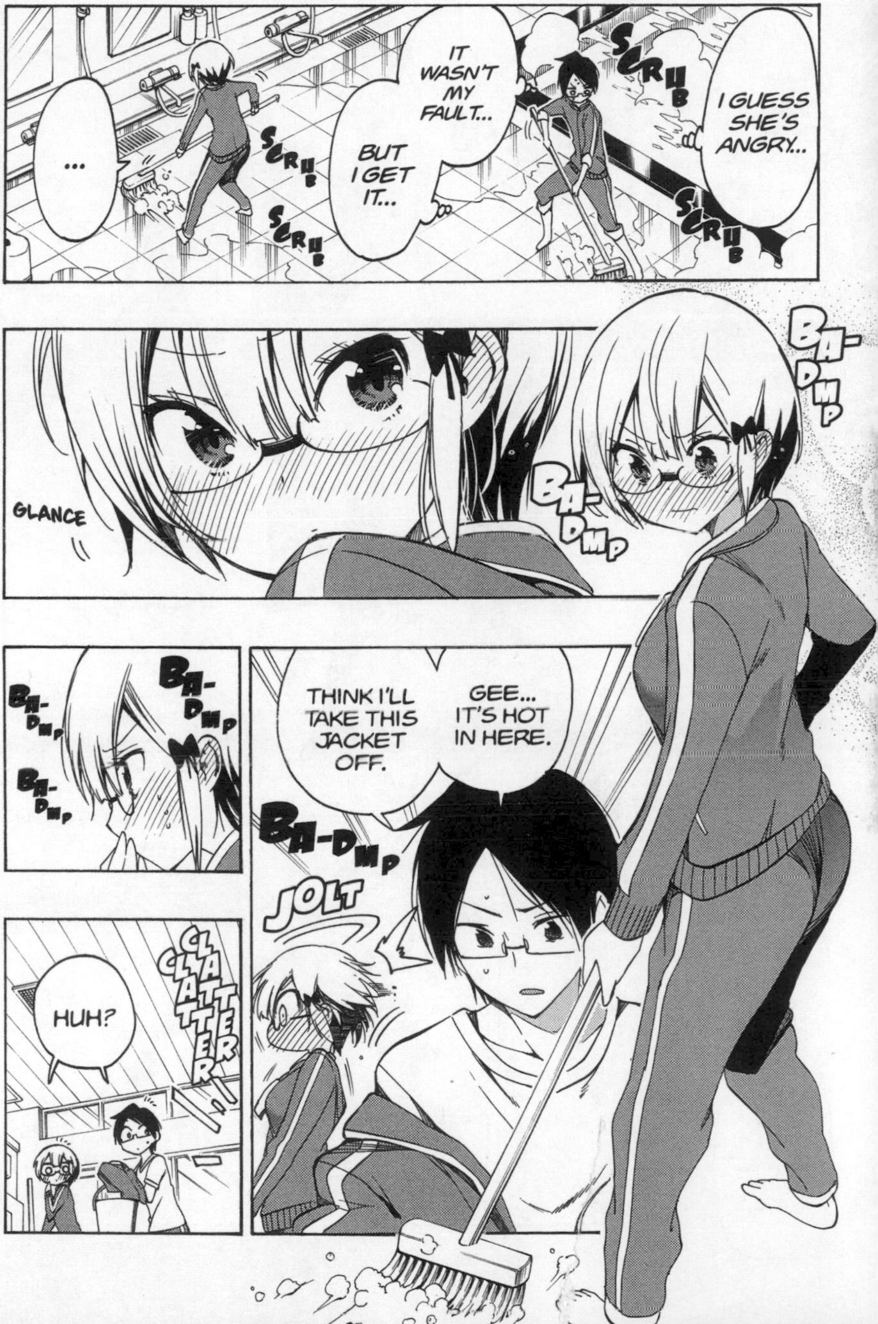
SCRUB
I GUESS SHE'S ANGRY...
SCRUB
IT WASN'T MY FAULT...
BUT I GET IT...
SCRUB
SCRUB
...
BA-DMP
BA-DMP
GLANCE
GEE... IT'S HOT IN HERE.
THINK I'LL TAKE THIS JACKET OFF.
BA-DMP
JOLT
BA-DMP
BA-DMP
BA-DMP
CLATTER
CLATTER
HUH?

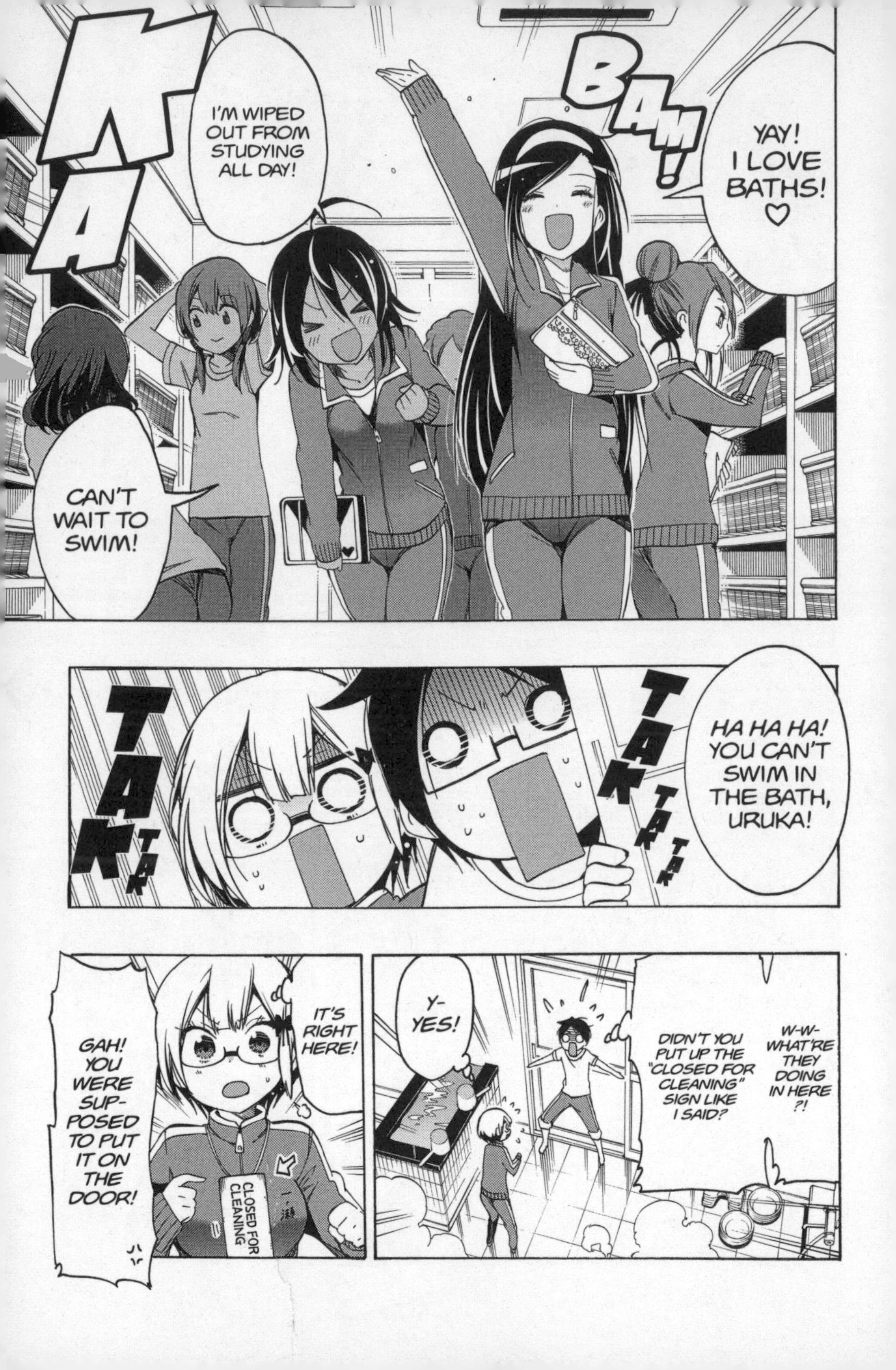
BAM!
YAY! I LOVE BATHS! ♡
I'M WIPED OUT FROM STUDYING ALL DAY!
HA
CAN'T WAIT TO SWIM!
HA HA HA! YOU CAN'T SWIM IN THE BATH, URUKA!
TAK TAK TAK
TAK TAK
W-W-WHAT'RE THEY DOING IN HERE ?!
DIDN'T YOU PUT UP THE "CLOSED FOR CLEANING" SIGN LIKE I SAID?
Y- YES!
IT'S RIGHT HERE!
GAH! YOU WERE SUP-POSED TO PUT IT ON THE DOOR!
CLOSED FOR CLEANING

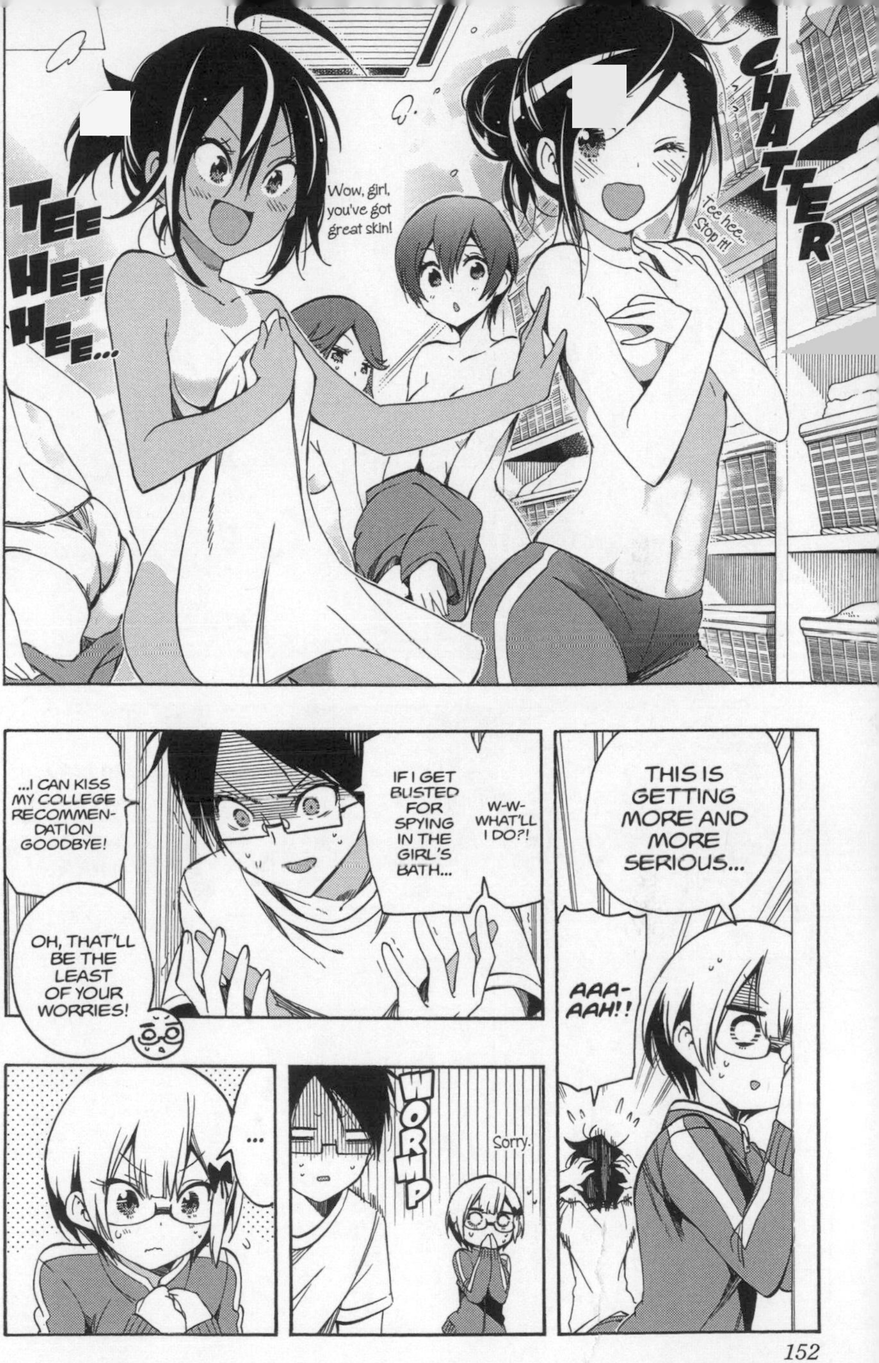
CHATTER
Tee hee... Stop it!
Wow, girl, you've got great skin!
TEE HEE HEE...
THIS IS GETTING MORE AND MORE SERIOUS...
AAA-AAH!!
W-W-WHAT'LL I DO?!
IF I GET BUSTED FOR SPYING IN THE GIRL'S BATH...
...I CAN KISS MY COLLEGE RECOMMENDATION GOODBYE!
OH, THAT'LL BE THE LEAST OF YOUR WORRIES!
WORMP
Sorry.
...

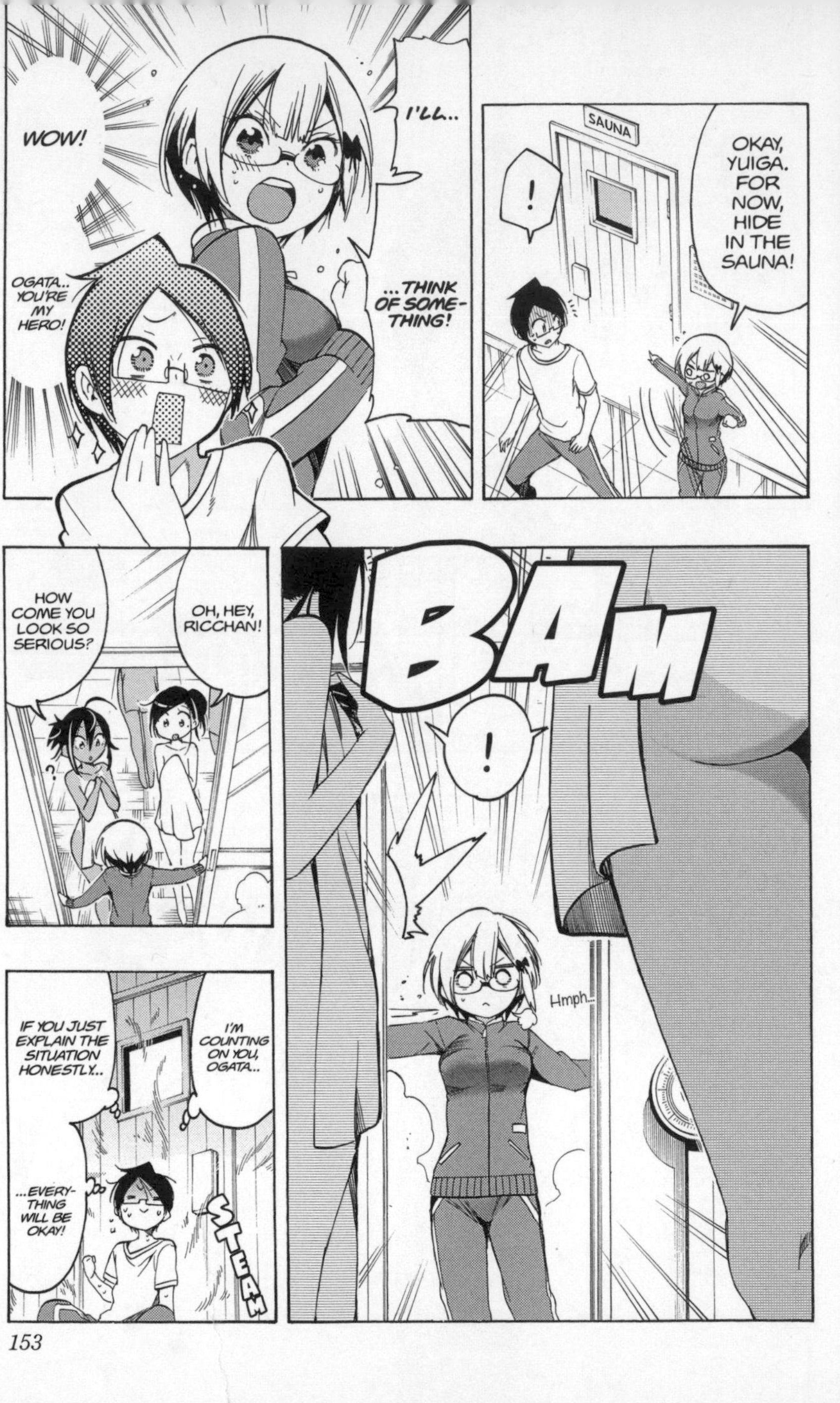
SAUNA
OKAY, YUIGA. FOR NOW, HIDE IN THE SAUNA!
!
I'LL...
...THINK OF SOME-THING!
WOW!
OGATA... YOU'RE MY HERO!
BAM
!
Hmph...
OH, HEY, RICCHAN!
HOW COME YOU LOOK SO SERIOUS?
I'M COUNTING ON YOU, OGATA...
IF YOU JUST EXPLAIN THE SITUATION HONESTLY...
...EVERY-THING WILL BE OKAY!
STEAM

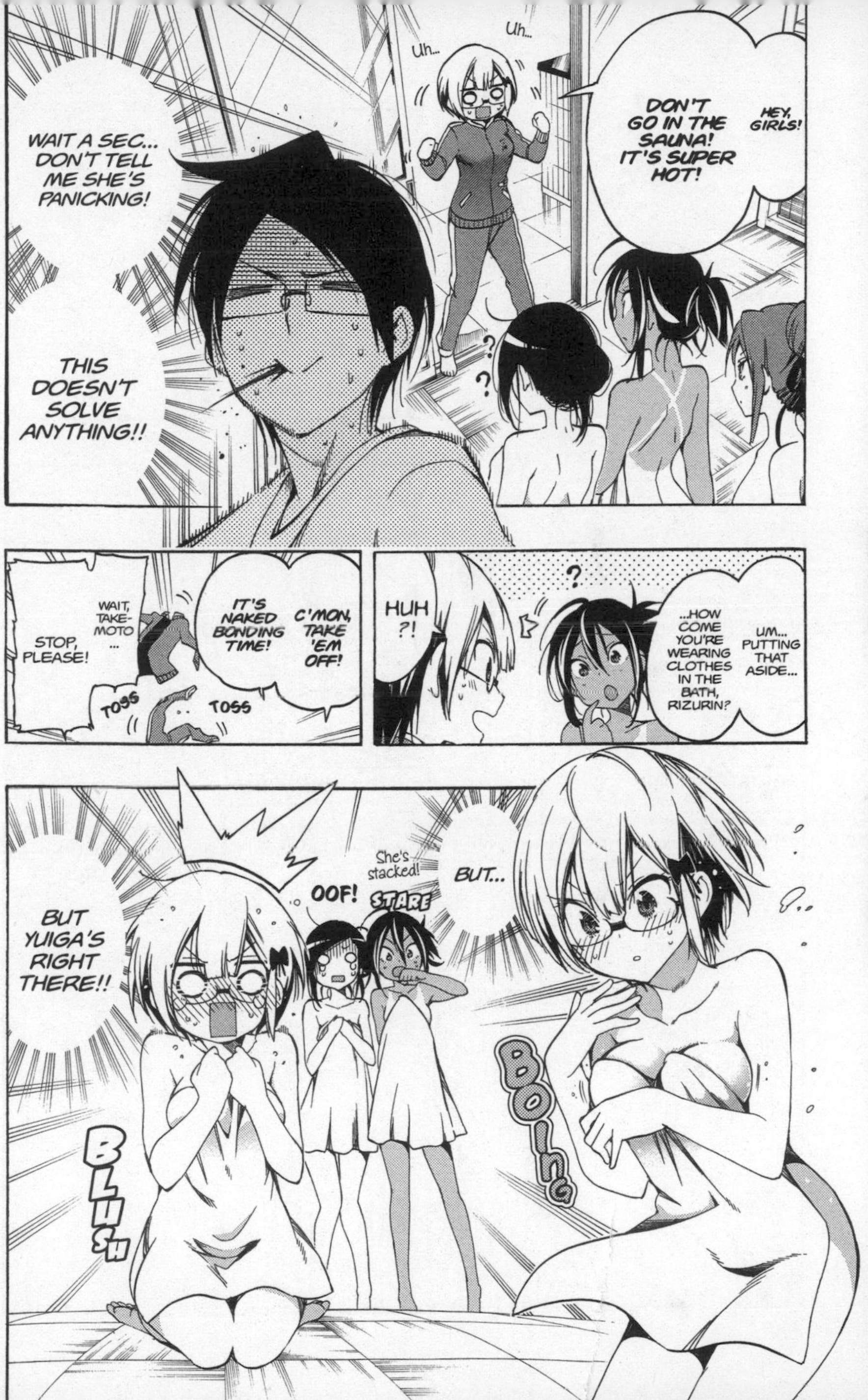
HEY, GIRLS!
DON'T GO IN THE SAUNA! IT'S SUPER HOT!
Uh...
Uh...
WAIT A SEC... DON'T TELL ME SHE'S PANICKING!
THIS DOESN'T SOLVE ANYTHING!!
UM... PUTTING THAT ASIDE...
...HOW COME YOU'RE WEARING CLOTHES IN THE BATH, RIZURIN?
?
HUH ?!
C'MON, TAKE 'EM OFF!
IT'S NAKED BONDING TIME!
WAIT, TAKE-MOTO ...
STOP, PLEASE!
TOSS
TOSS
BUT...
BOING
STARE
She's stacked!
OOF!
BUT YUIGA'S RIGHT THERE!!
BLUSH

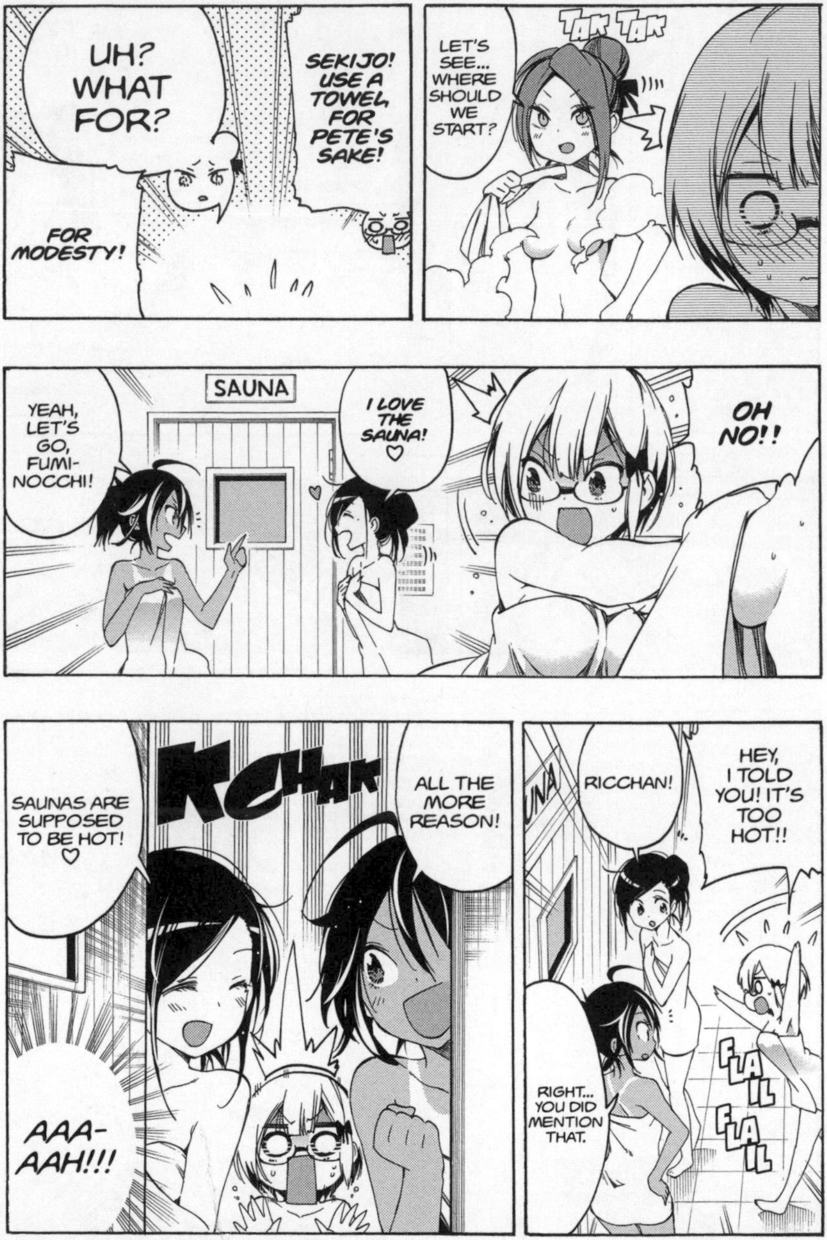
TAK TAK
LET'S SEE... WHERE SHOULD WE START?
SEKIJO! USE A TOWEL, FOR PETE'S SAKE!
UH? WHAT FOR?
FOR MODESTY!
OH NO!!
I LOVE THE SAUNA! ♡
SAUNA
YEAH, LET'S GO, FUMI-NOCCHI!
HEY, I TOLD YOU! IT'S TOO HOT!!
RICCHAN!
FLAIL FLAIL
RIGHT... YOU DID MENTION THAT.
ALL THE MORE REASON!
KCHAK
SAUNAS ARE SUPPOSED TO BE HOT! ♡
AAA-AAH!!!

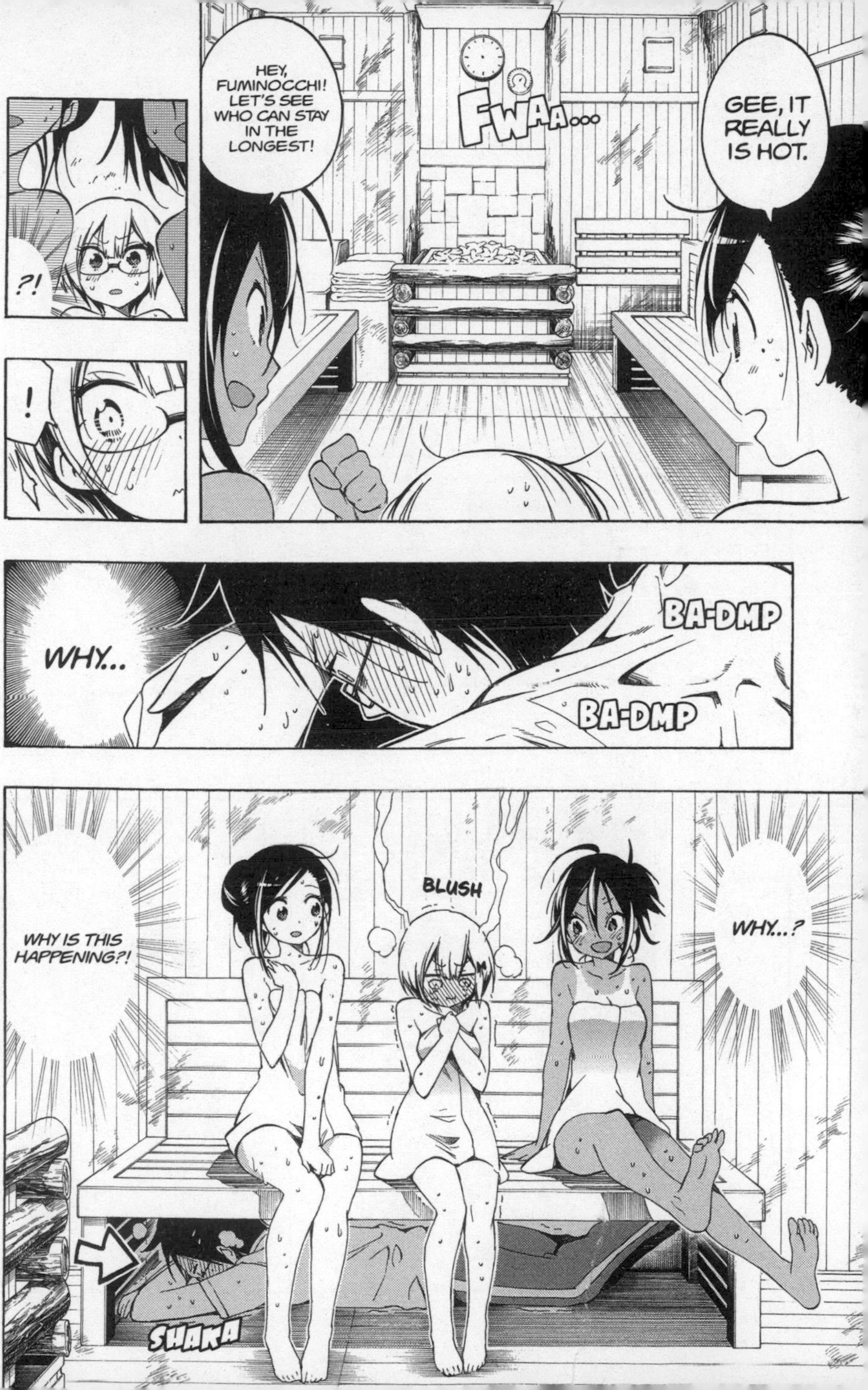
GEE, IT REALLY IS HOT.
FWAA...
HEY, FUMINOCCHI! LET'S SEE WHO CAN STAY IN THE LONGEST!
?!
!
BA-DMP
WHY...
BA-DMP
WHY...?
BLUSH
WHY IS THIS HAPPENING?!
SHAKA

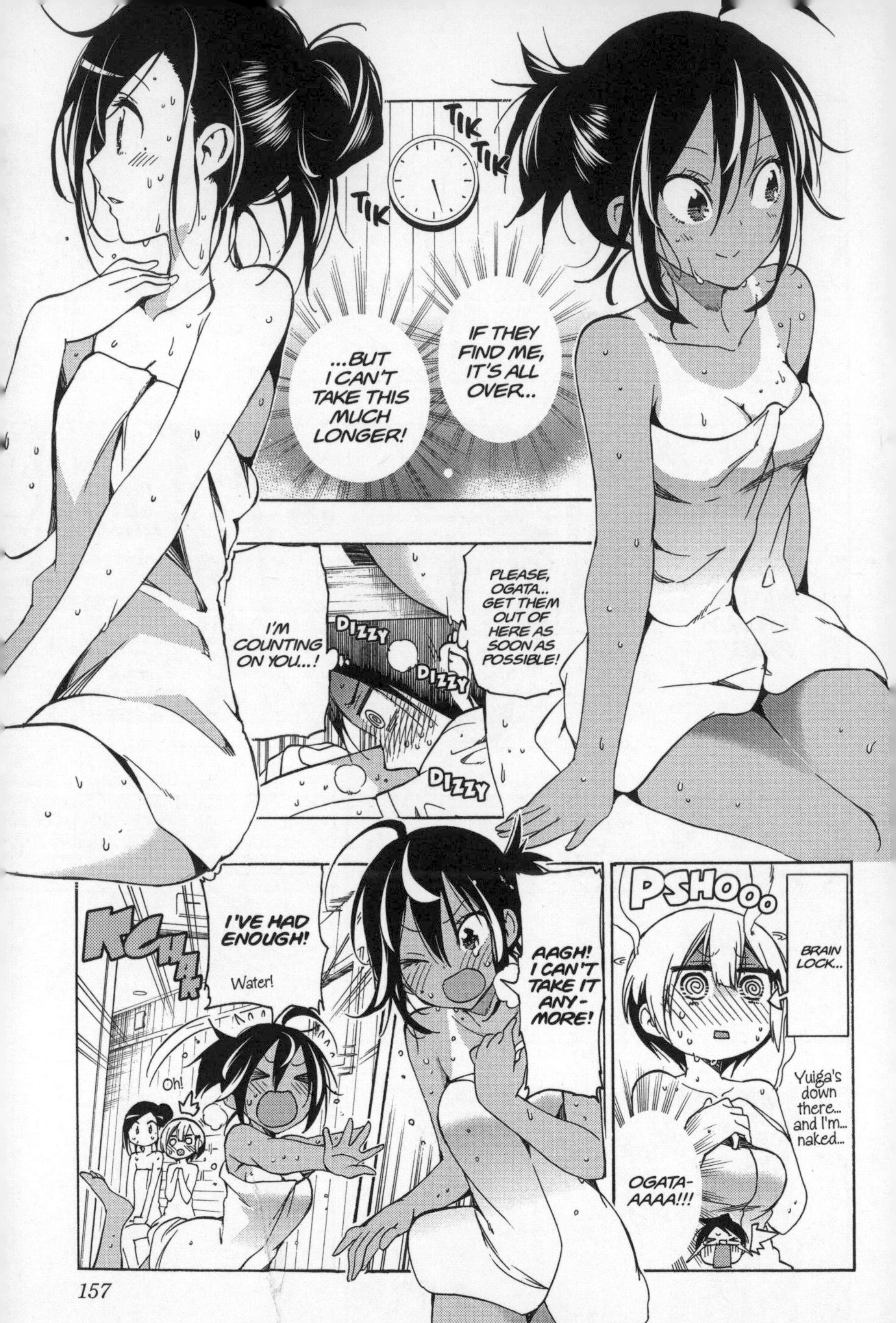
TIK TIK TIK
IF THEY FIND ME, IT'S ALL OVER...
...BUT I CAN'T TAKE THIS MUCH LONGER!
PLEASE, OGATA... GET THEM OUT OF HERE AS SOON AS POSSIBLE!
I'M COUNTING ON YOU...!
DIZZY
DIZZY
DIZZY
PSHOooo
BRAIN LOCK...
Yuiga's down there... and I'm... naked...
OGATA-AAAA!!!
AAGH! I CAN'T TAKE IT ANY-MORE!
I'VE HAD ENOUGH!
KCHAK
Water!
Oh!

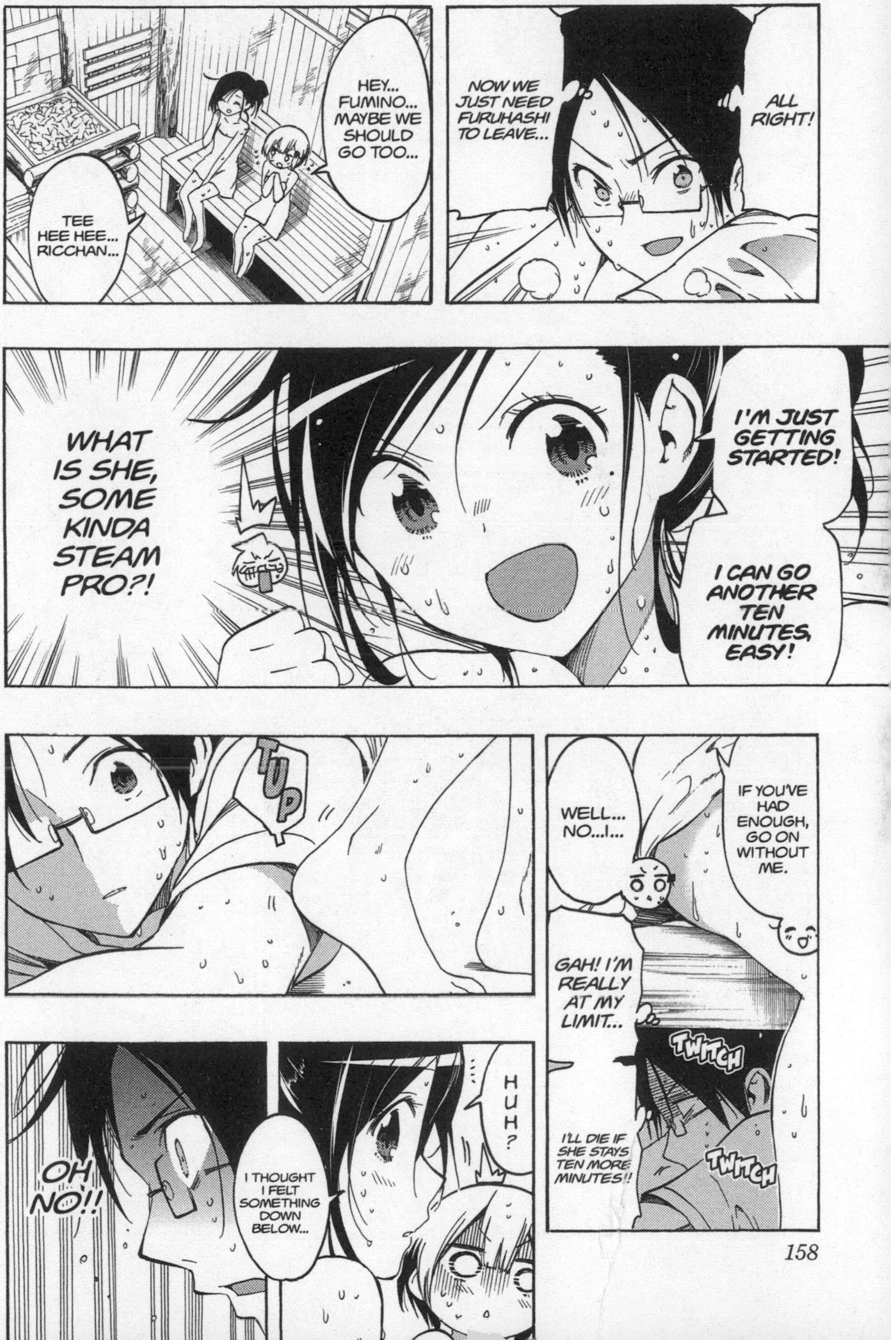
ALL RIGHT!
NOW WE JUST NEED FURUHASHI TO LEAVE...
HEY... FUMINO... MAYBE WE SHOULD GO TOO...
TEE HEE HEE... RICCHAN...
I'M JUST GETTING STARTED!
I CAN GO ANOTHER TEN MINUTES, EASY!
WHAT IS SHE, SOME KINDA STEAM PRO?!
IF YOU'VE HAD ENOUGH, GO ON WITHOUT ME.
WELL... NO...I...
GAH! I'M REALLY AT MY LIMIT...
TWITCH
I'LL DIE IF SHE STAYS TEN MORE MINUTES!!
TWITCH
TUP
HUH?
I THOUGHT I FELT SOMETHING DOWN BELOW...
OH NO!!

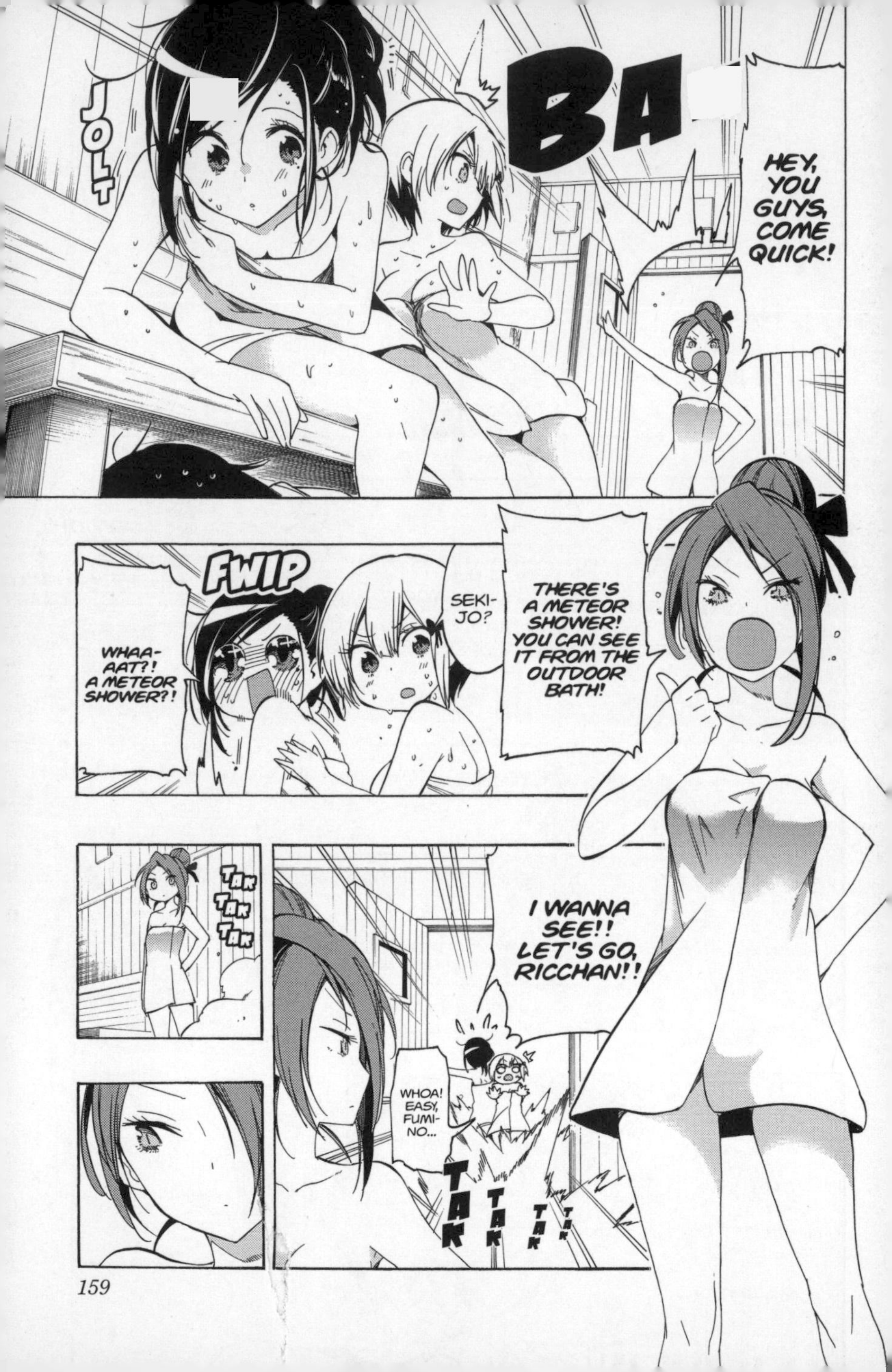
HEY, YOU GUYS, COME QUICK!
BA
JOLT
THERE'S A METEOR SHOWER! YOU CAN SEE IT FROM THE OUTDOOR BATH!
SEKI-JO?
FWIP
WHAA-AAT?! A METEOR SHOWER?!
I WANNA SEE!! LET'S GO, RICCHAN!!
WHOA! EASY, FUMI-NO...
TAK TAK TAK TAK
TAK TAK TAK

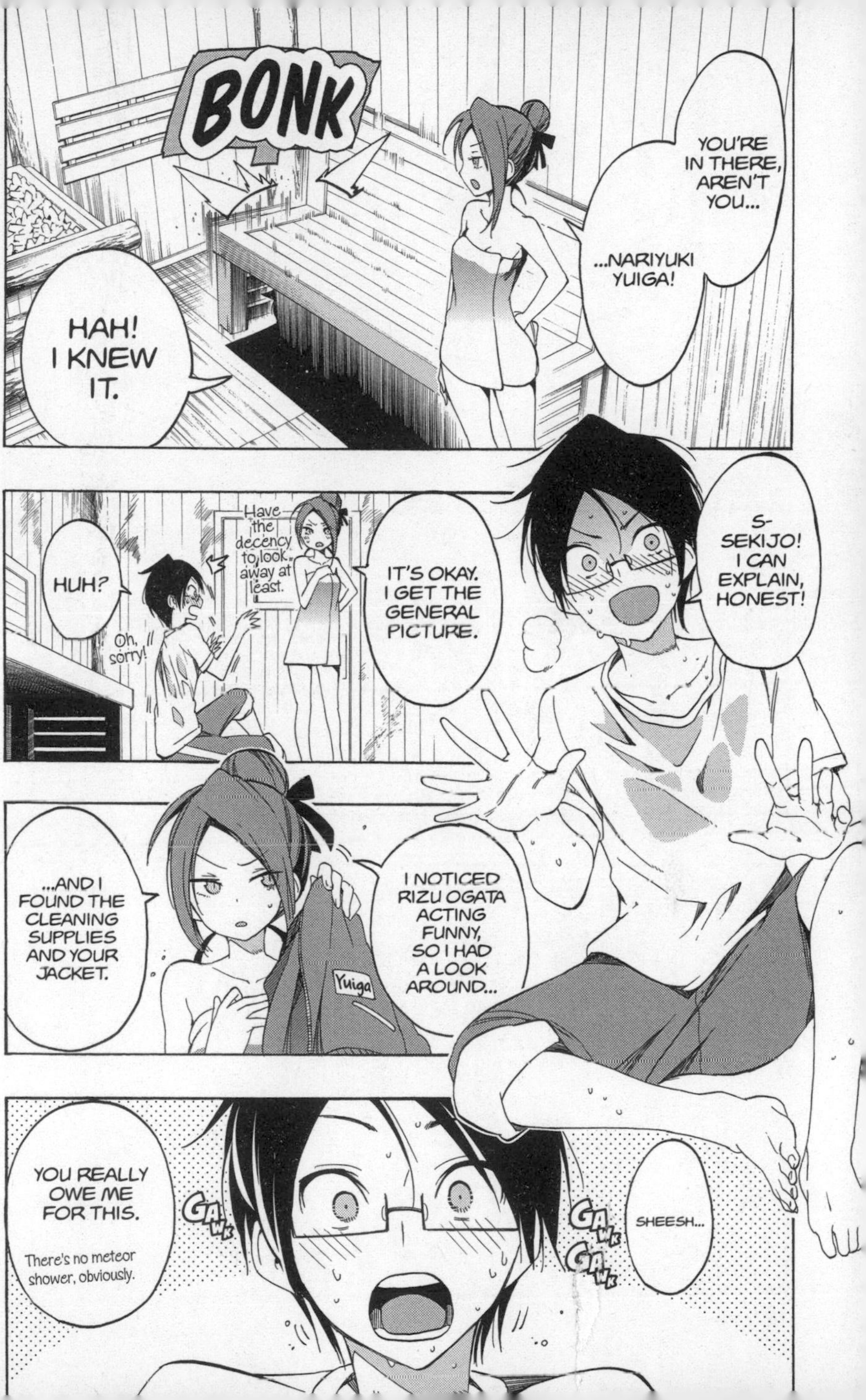
YOU'RE IN THERE, AREN'T YOU...
...NARIYUKI YUIGA!
BONK
HAH! I KNEW IT.
S-SEKIJO! I CAN EXPLAIN, HONEST!
IT'S OKAY. I GET THE GENERAL PICTURE.
Have the decency to look away at least.
HUH?
Oh, sorry!
I NOTICED RIZU OGATA ACTING FUNNY, SO I HAD A LOOK AROUND...
Yuiga
...AND I FOUND THE CLEANING SUPPLIES AND YOUR JACKET.
SHEESH...
GAWK
GAWK
GAWK
YOU REALLY OWE ME FOR THIS.
There's no meteor shower, obviously.

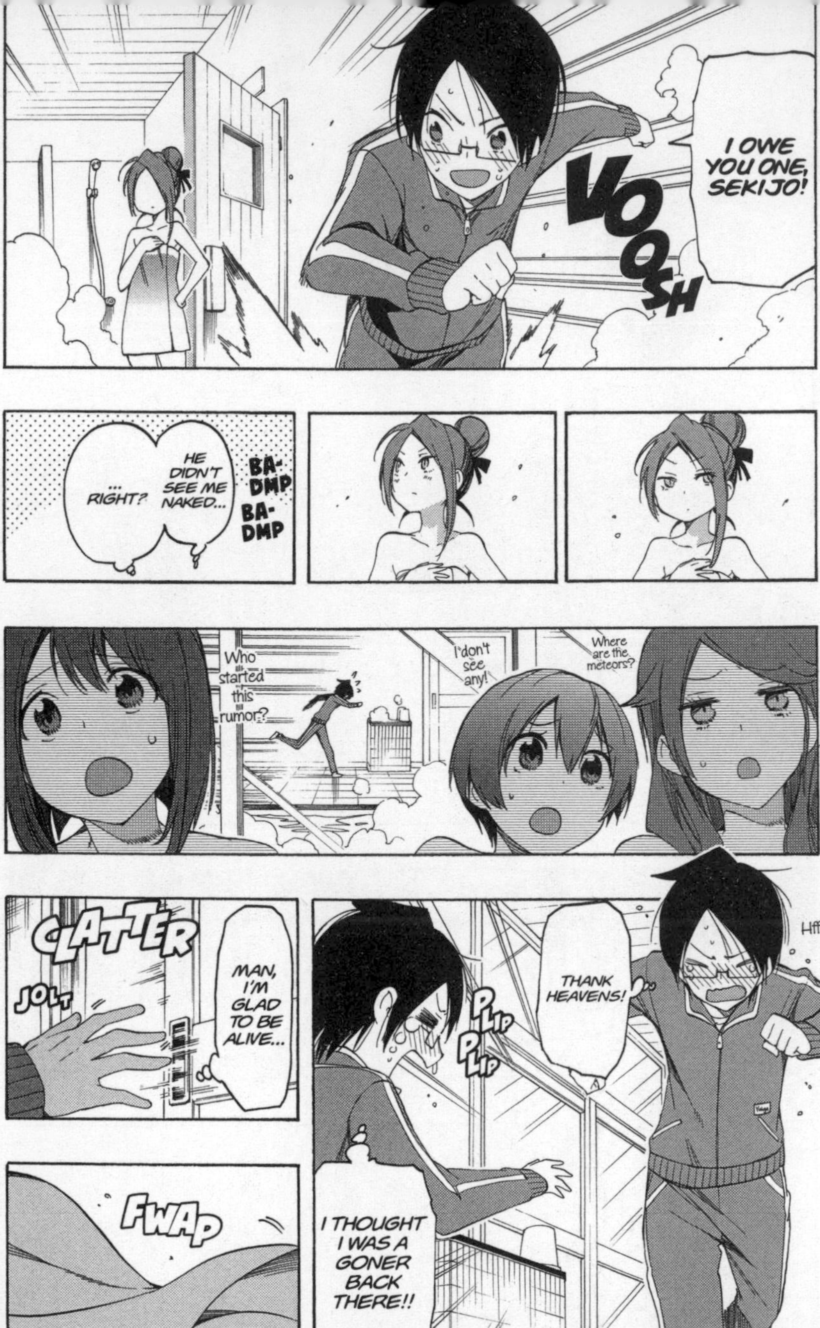
I OWE YOU ONE, SEKIJO!
VOOSH
HE DIDN'T SEE ME NAKED...
...RIGHT?
BA-DMP
BA-DMP
Where are the meteors?
I don't see any!
Who started this rumor?
Hff
THANK HEAVENS!
PLIP
PLIP
I THOUGHT I WAS A GONER BACK THERE!!
CLATTER
MAN, I'M GLAD TO BE ALIVE...
JOLT
FWAP

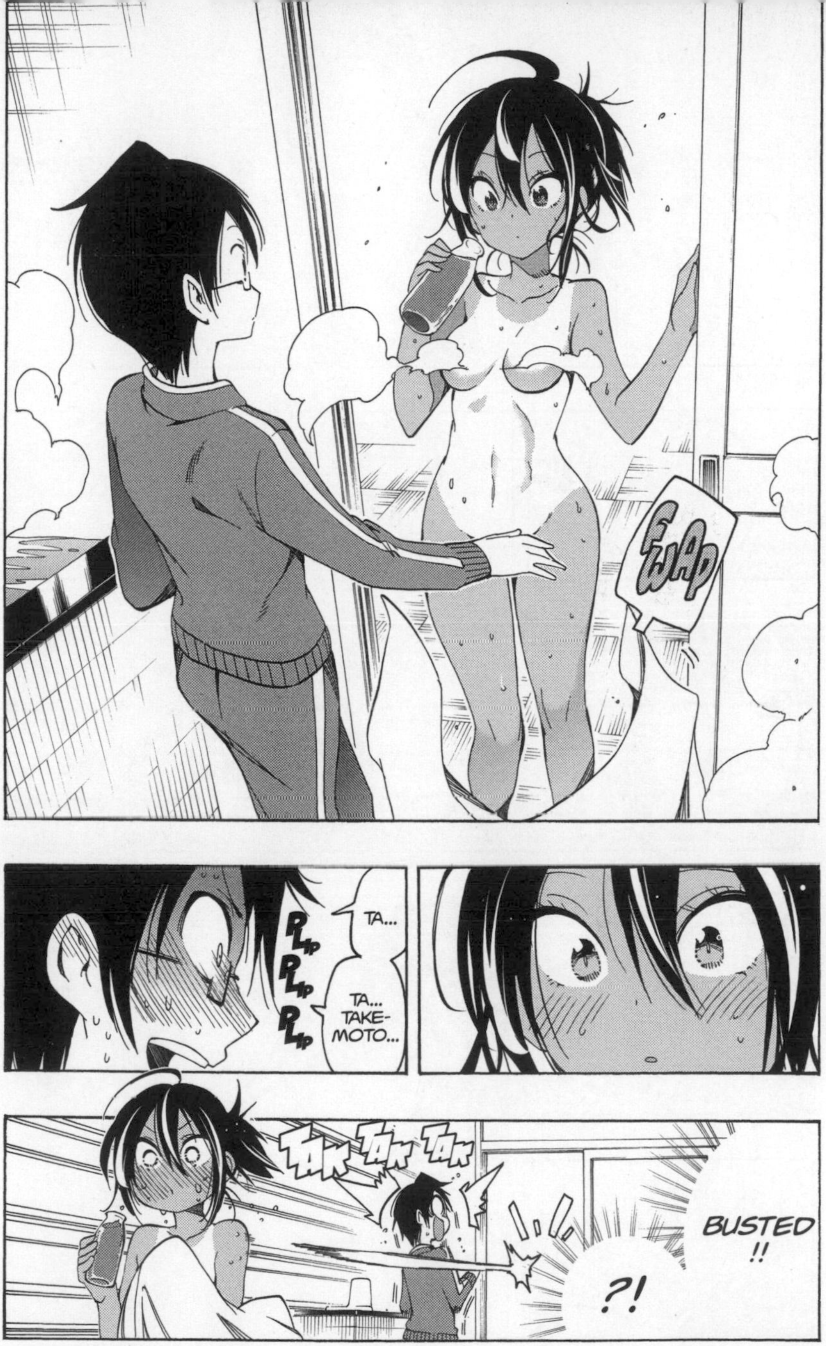
FWAP
TA...
TA... TAKE-MOTO...
PLIP PLIP PLIP PLIP
BUSTED !!
?!
!.!
TAK TAK TAK

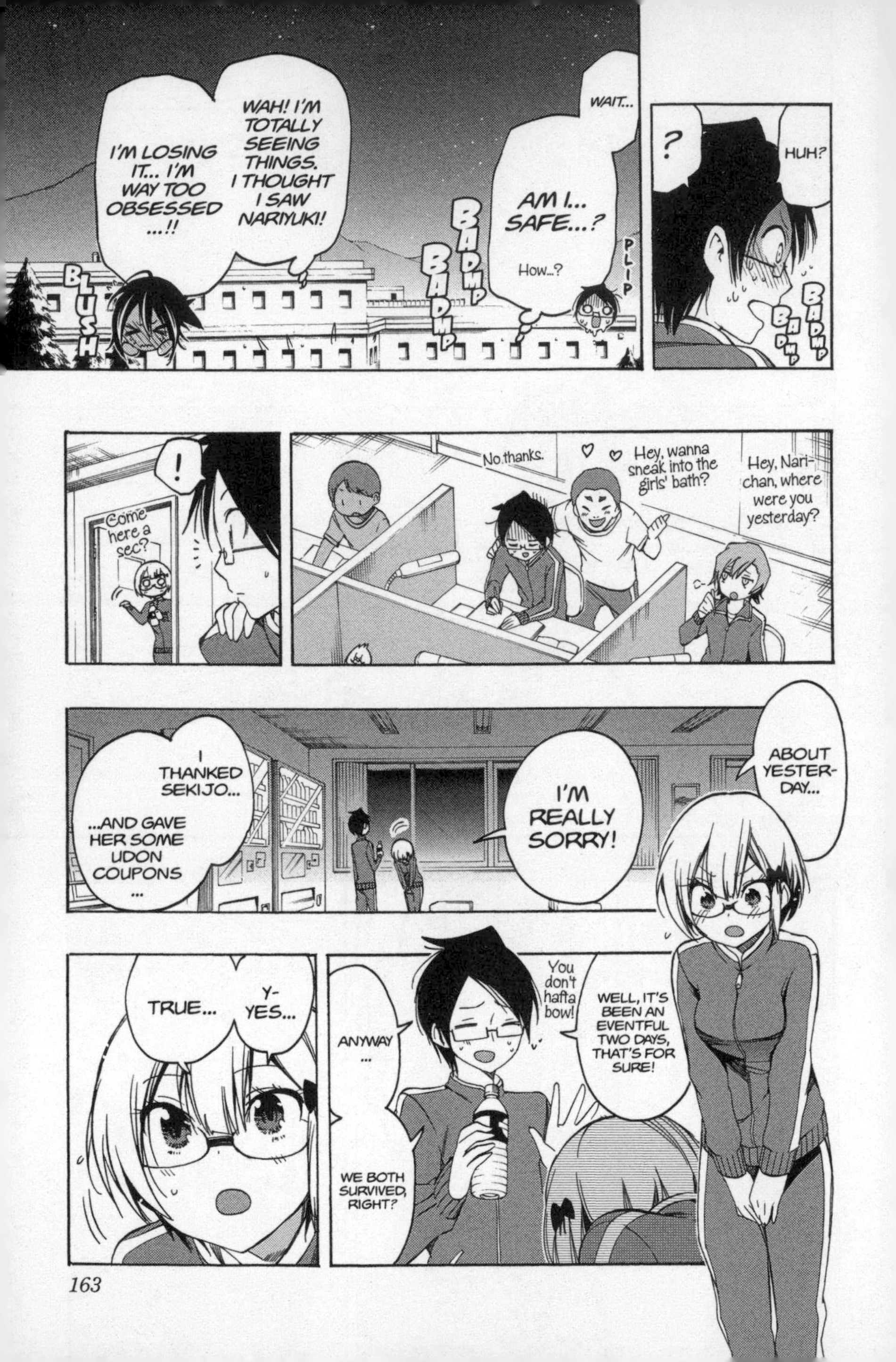
?
HUH?
BADMP BADMP
WAIT...
AM I... SAFE...?
How...?
PLIP
BADMP BADMP
WAH! I'M TOTALLY SEEING THINGS. I THOUGHT I SAW NARIYUKI!
I'M LOSING IT... I'M WAY TOO OBSESSED ...!!
BLUSH
Hey, Nari-chan, where were you yesterday?
Hey, wanna sneak into the girls' bath?
No thanks.
!
Come here a sec?
ABOUT YESTER-DAY...
I'M REALLY SORRY!
I THANKED SEKIJO...
...AND GAVE HER SOME UDON COUPONS ...
WELL, IT'S BEEN AN EVENTFUL TWO DAYS, THAT'S FOR SURE!
You don't hafta bow!
ANYWAY ...
WE BOTH SURVIVED, RIGHT?
Y-YES...
TRUE...

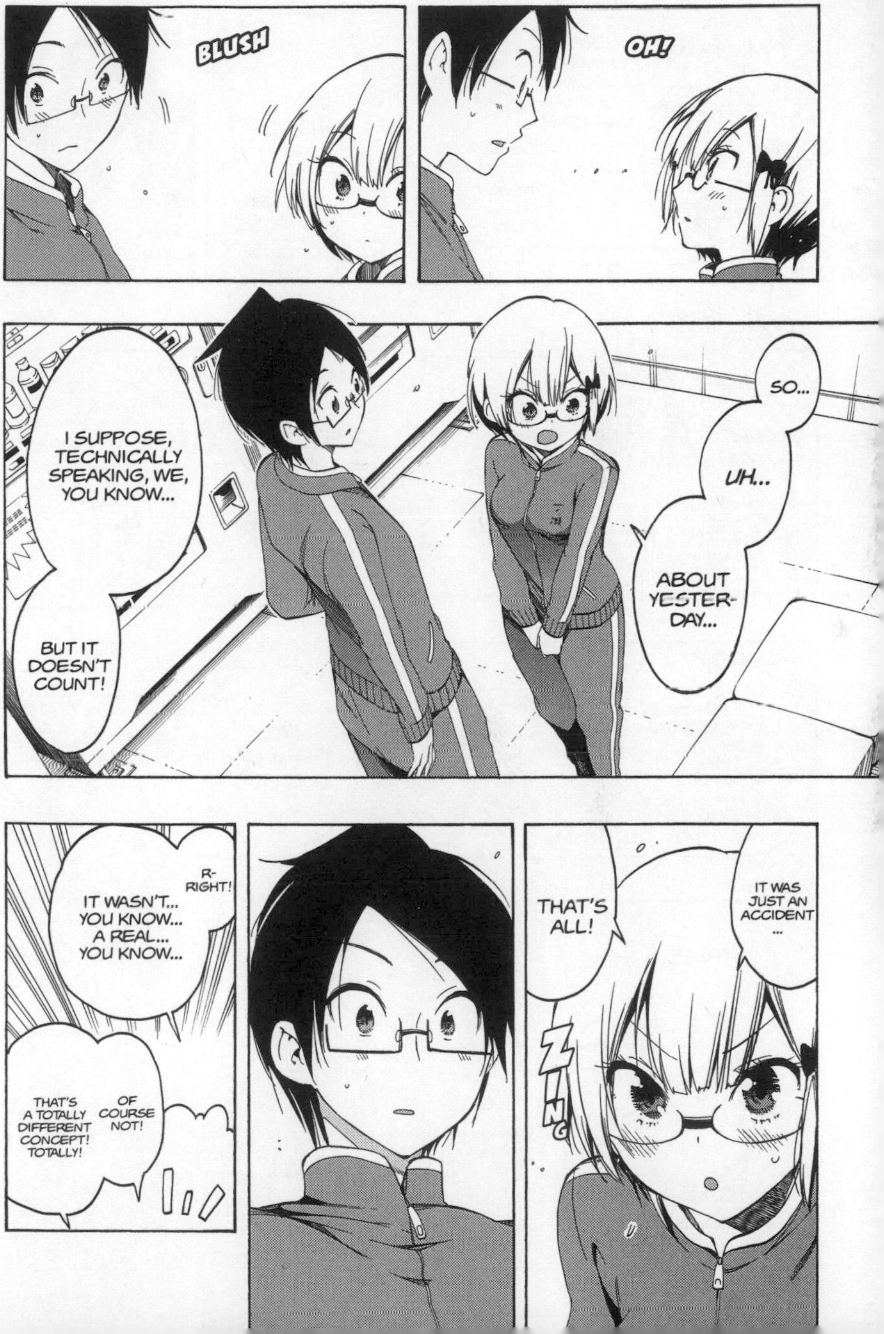
OH!
BLUSH
SO...
UH...
ABOUT YESTER-DAY...
I SUPPOSE, TECHNICALLY SPEAKING, WE, YOU KNOW...
BUT IT DOESN'T COUNT!
IT WAS JUST AN ACCIDENT ...
THAT'S ALL!
ZING
R-RIGHT!
IT WASN'T... YOU KNOW... A REAL... YOU KNOW...
OF COURSE NOT!
THAT'S A TOTALLY DIFFERENT CONCEPT! TOTALLY!

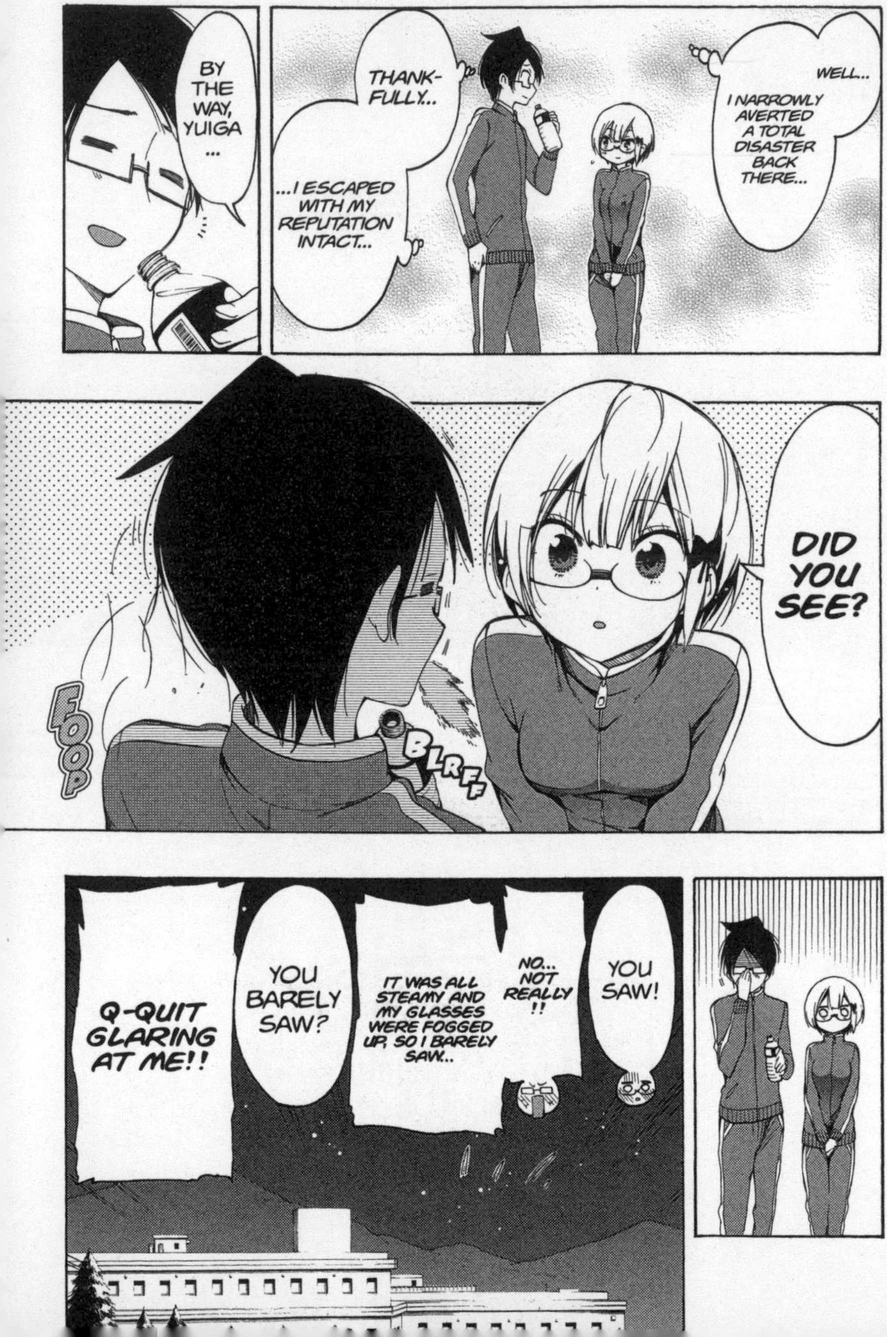
WELL... I NARROWLY AVERTED A TOTAL DISASTER BACK THERE...
THANK-FULLY...
...I ESCAPED WITH MY REPUTATION INTACT...
BY THE WAY, YUIGA ...
DID YOU SEE?
BLRFF
FOOP
YOU SAW!
NO... NOT REALLY!!
IT WAS ALL STEAMY AND MY GLASSES WERE FOGGED UP, SO I BARELY SAW...
YOU BARELY SAW?
Q-QUIT GLARING AT ME!!

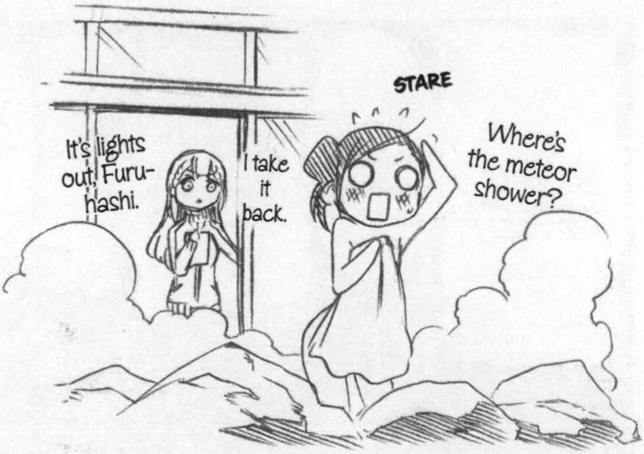
STARE
Where's the meteor shower?
I take it back.
It's lights out, Furu-hashi.

Question 16: Thus, a Predecessor Still Relates to a Genius as [X]

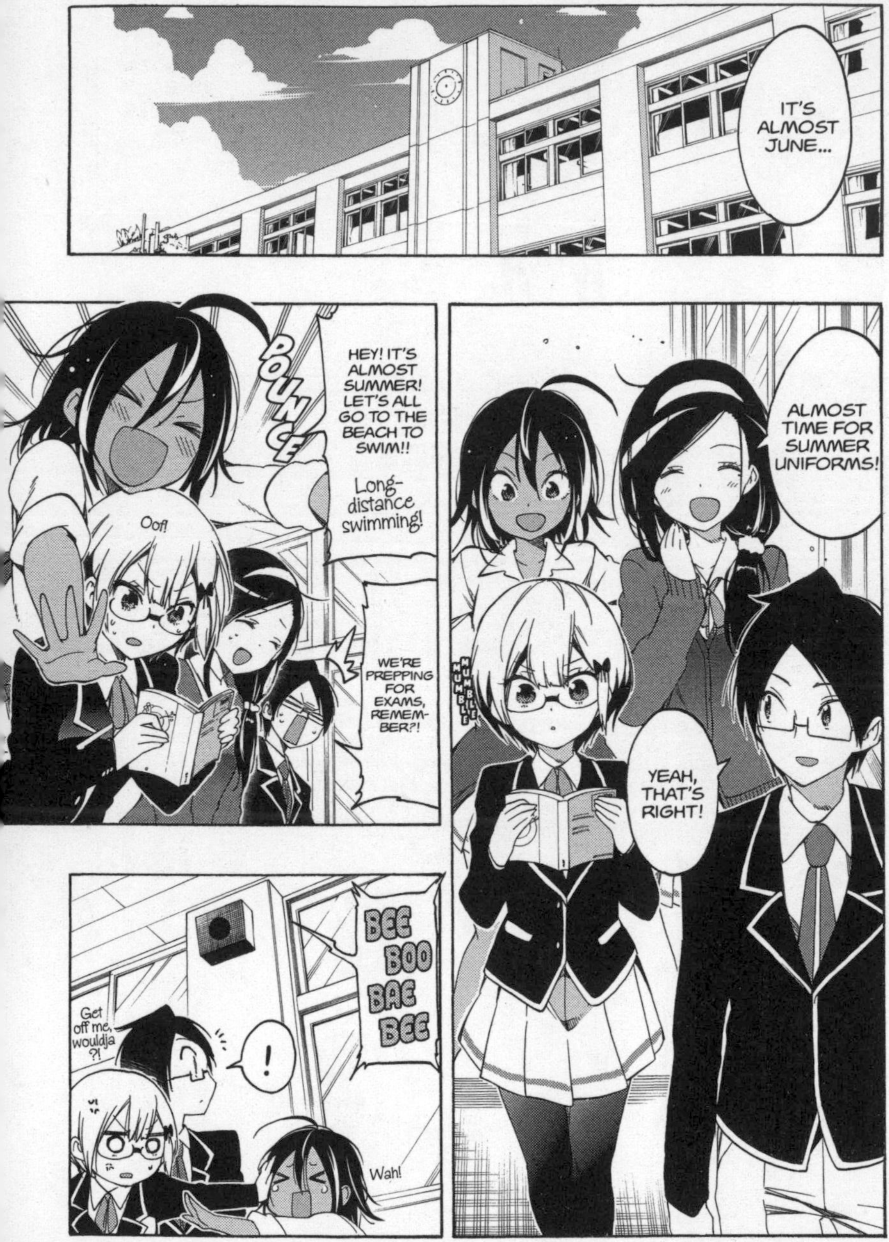

IT'S ALMOST JUNE...
ALMOST TIME FOR SUMMER UNIFORMS!
MUMBLE MUMBLE
YEAH, THAT'S RIGHT!
HEY! IT'S ALMOST SUMMER! LET'S ALL GO TO THE BEACH TO SWIM!!
Long-distance swimming!
POUNCE
Oof!
WE'RE PREPPING FOR EXAMS, REMEMBER?!
BEE BOO BAE BEE
!
Get off me, wouldja?!
Wah!

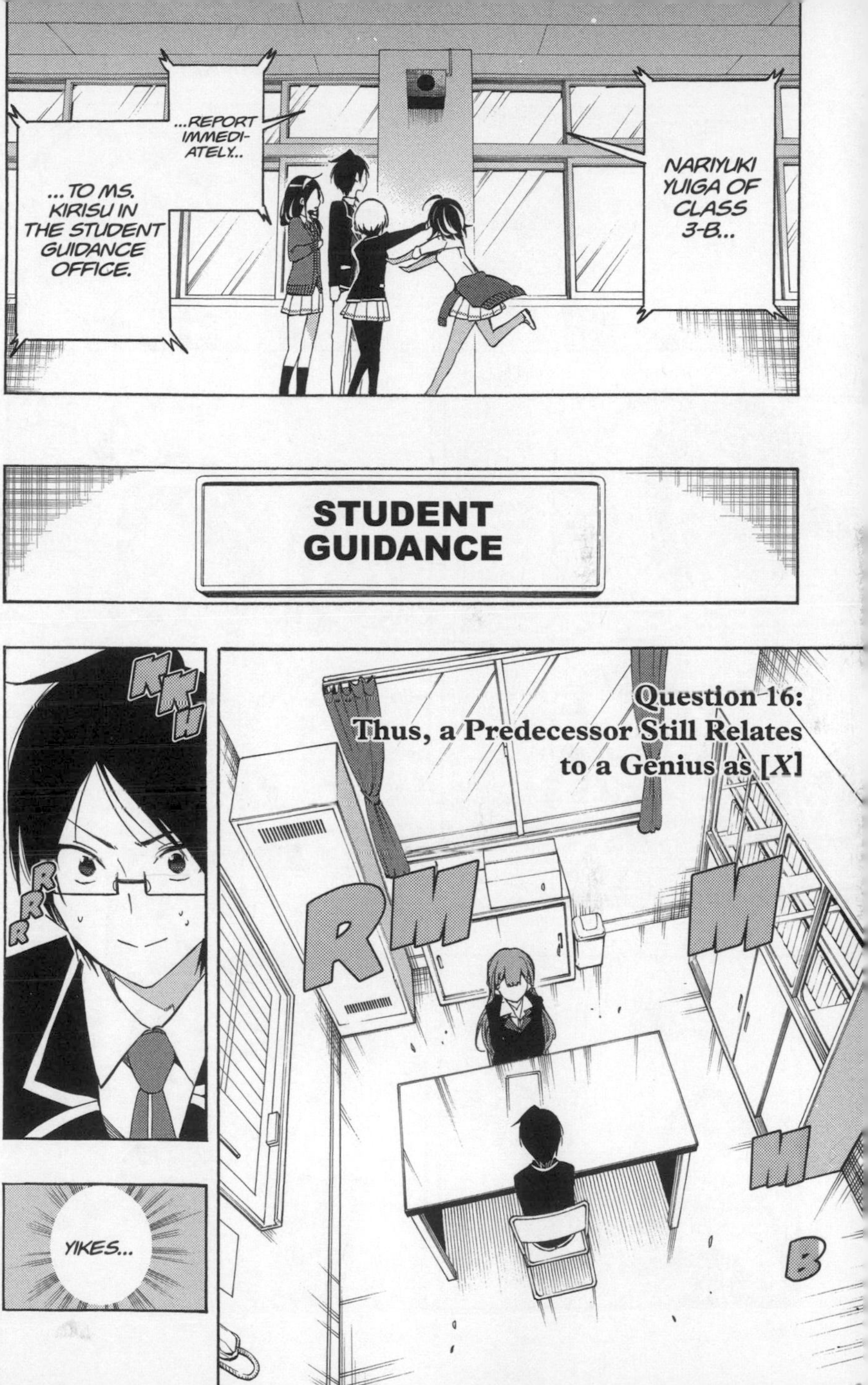
NARIYUKI YUIGA OF CLASS 3-B...
...REPORT IMMEDIATELY...
...TO MS. KIRISU IN THE STUDENT GUIDANCE OFFICE.
STUDENT GUIDANCE
Question 16: Thus, a Predecessor Still Relates to a Genius as [X]
RMMMB
RRRR
YIKES...

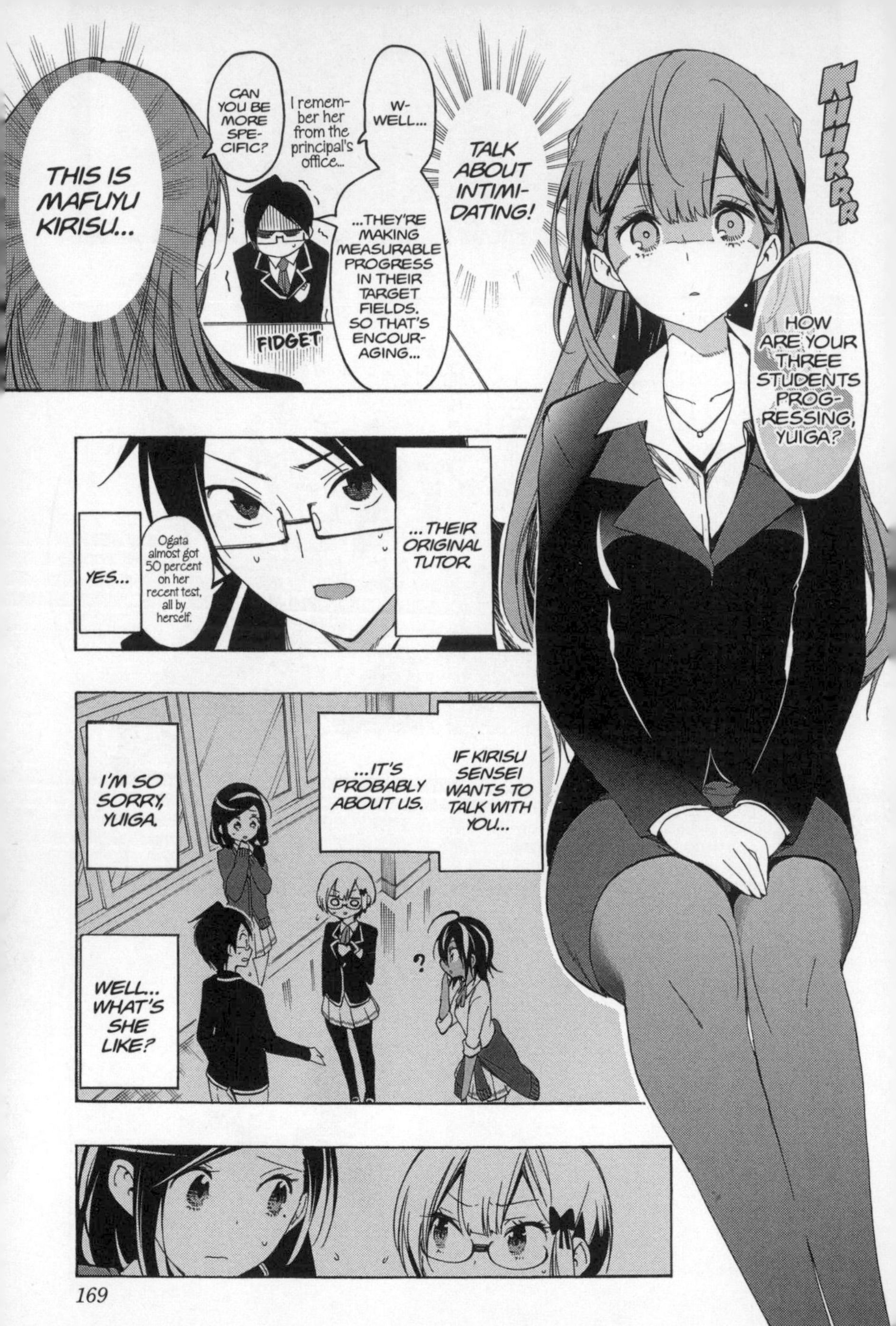
KHURRR
HOW ARE YOUR THREE STUDENTS PROG-RESSING, YUIGA?
TALK ABOUT INTIMI-DATING!
W-WELL...
...THEY'RE MAKING MEASURABLE PROGRESS IN THEIR TARGET FIELDS. SO THAT'S ENCOUR-AGING...
I remem-ber her from the principal's office...
CAN YOU BE MORE SPE-CIFIC?
THIS IS MAFUYU KIRISU...
FIDGET
...THEIR ORIGINAL TUTOR.
Ogata almost got 50 percent on her recent test, all by herself.
YES...
IF KIRISU SENSEI WANTS TO TALK WITH YOU...
...IT'S PROBABLY ABOUT US.
I'M SO SORRY, YUIGA.
?
WELL... WHAT'S SHE LIKE?

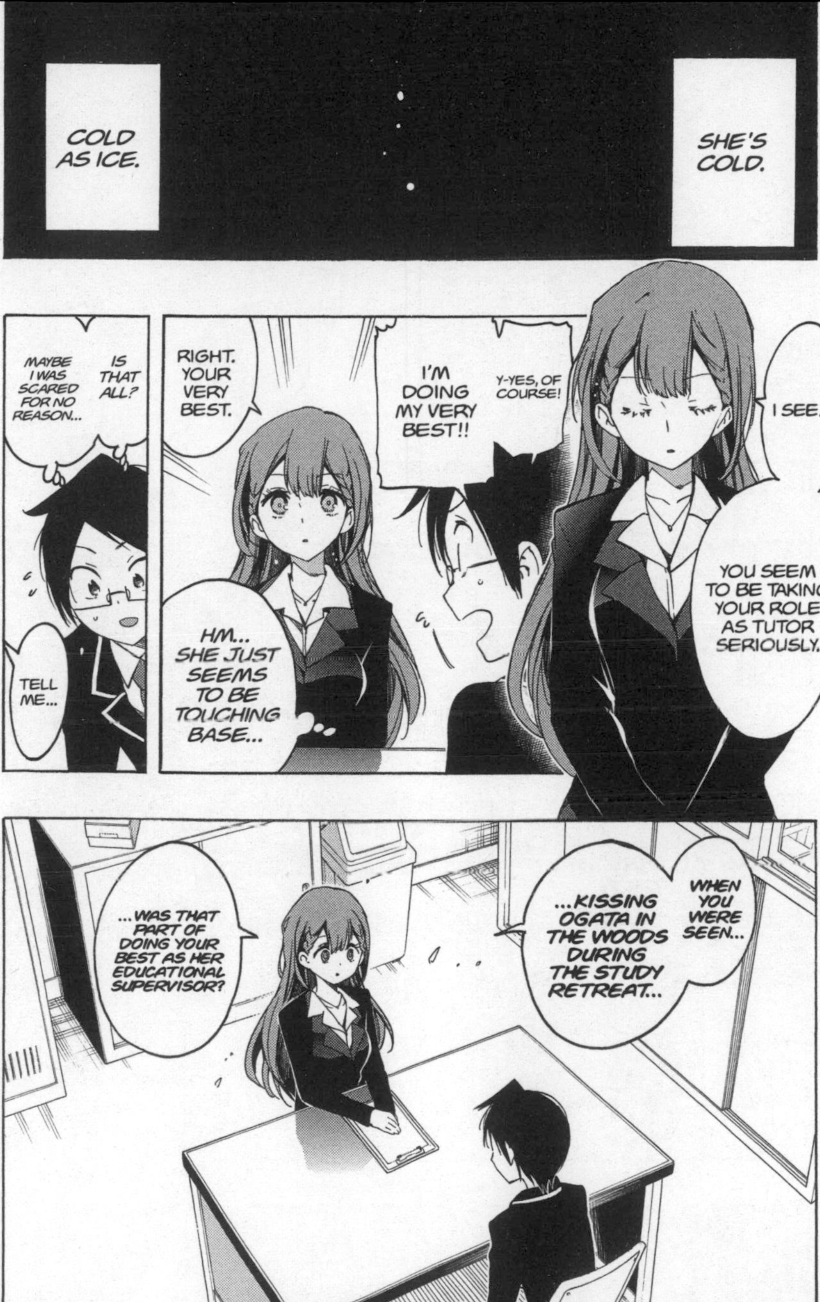
SHE'S COLD.
COLD AS ICE.
I SEE...
YOU SEEM TO BE TAKING YOUR ROLE AS TUTOR SERIOUSLY.
Y-YES, OF COURSE!
I'M DOING MY VERY BEST!!
RIGHT. YOUR VERY BEST.
HM... SHE JUST SEEMS TO BE TOUCHING BASE...
IS THAT ALL?
MAYBE I WAS SCARED FOR NO REASON...
TELL ME...
WHEN YOU WERE SEEN...
...KISSING OGATA IN THE WOODS DURING THE STUDY RETREAT...
...WAS THAT PART OF DOING YOUR BEST AS HER EDUCATIONAL SUPERVISOR?

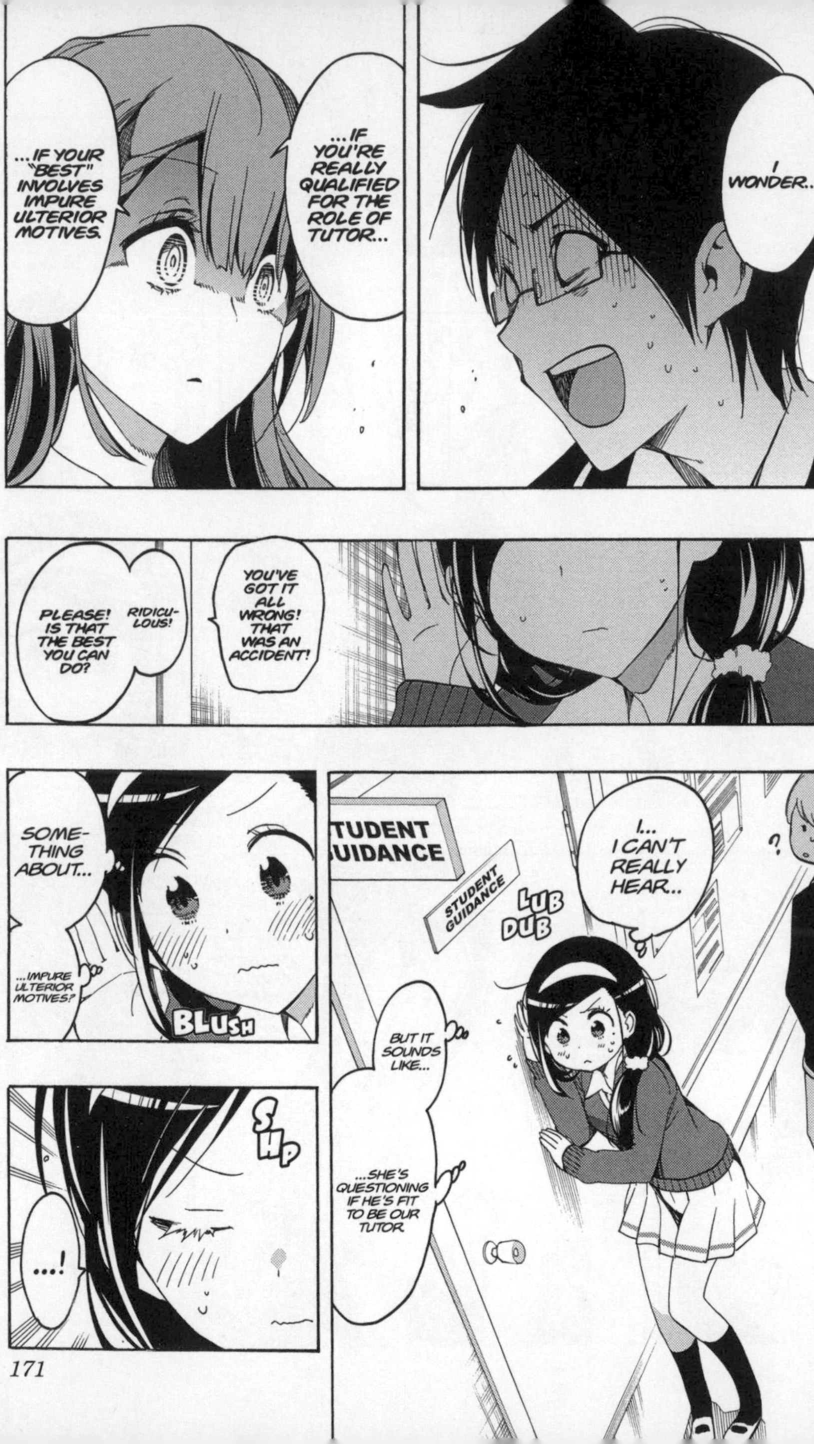
I WONDER...
...IF YOU'RE REALLY QUALIFIED FOR THE ROLE OF TUTOR...
...IF YOUR "BEST" INVOLVES IMPURE ULTERIOR MOTIVES.
YOU'VE GOT IT ALL WRONG! THAT WAS AN ACCIDENT!
RIDICU-LOUS!
PLEASE! IS THAT THE BEST YOU CAN DO?
?
I... I CAN'T REALLY HEAR...
LUB DUB
STUDENT GUIDANCE
STUDENT GUIDANCE
BUT IT SOUNDS LIKE...
...SHE'S QUESTIONING IF HE'S FIT TO BE OUR TUTOR.
SOME-THING ABOUT...
...IMPURE ULTERIOR MOTIVES?
BLUSH
SHP
...!

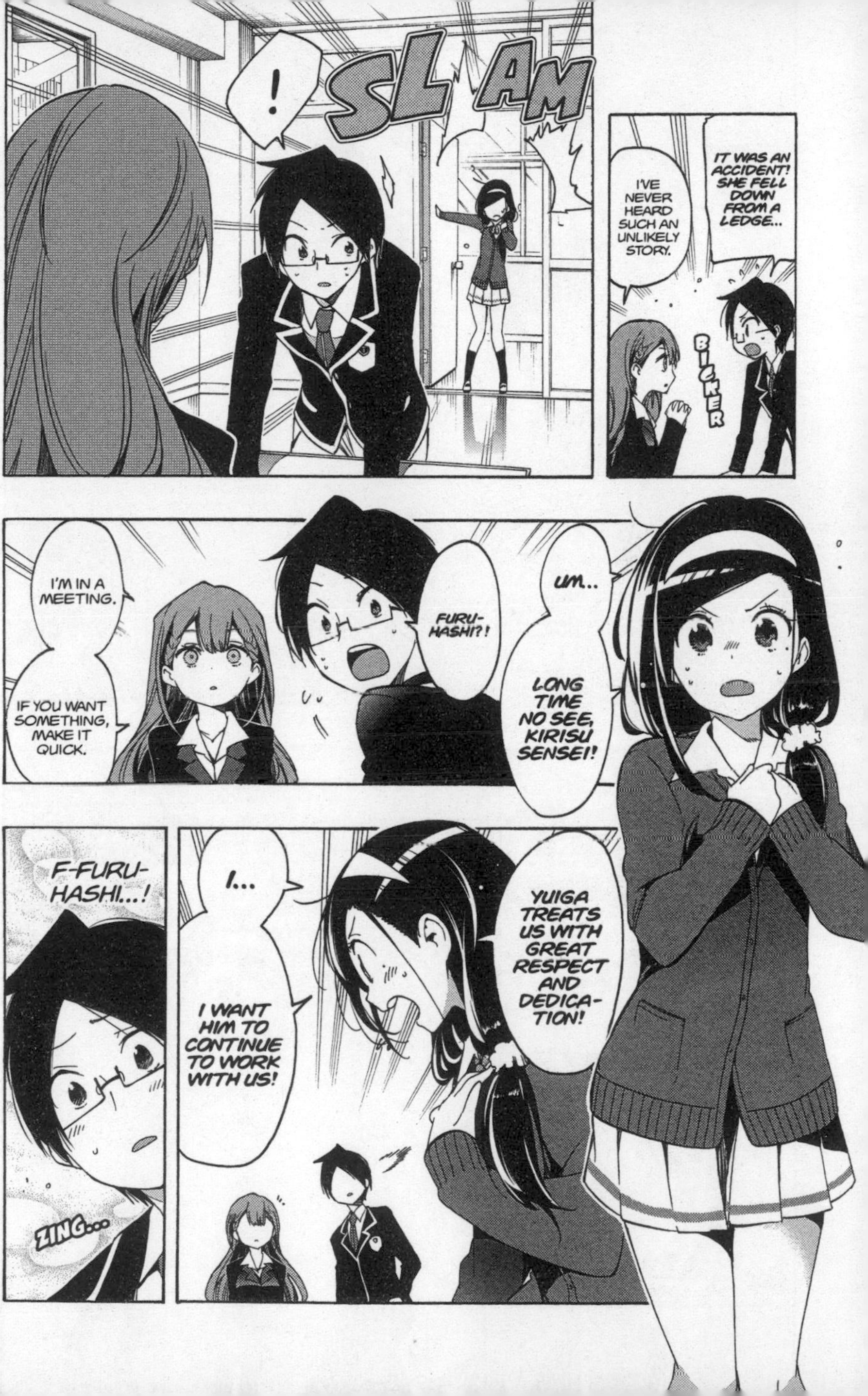
IT WAS AN ACCIDENT! SHE FELL DOWN FROM A LEDGE...
I'VE NEVER HEARD SUCH AN UNLIKELY STORY.
BICKER
SLAM
!
UM...
LONG TIME NO SEE, KIRISU SENSEI!
FURU-HASHI?!
I'M IN A MEETING.
IF YOU WANT SOMETHING, MAKE IT QUICK.
YUIGA TREATS US WITH GREAT RESPECT AND DEDICATION!
I...
I WANT HIM TO CONTINUE TO WORK WITH US!
F-FURU-HASHI...!
ZING...

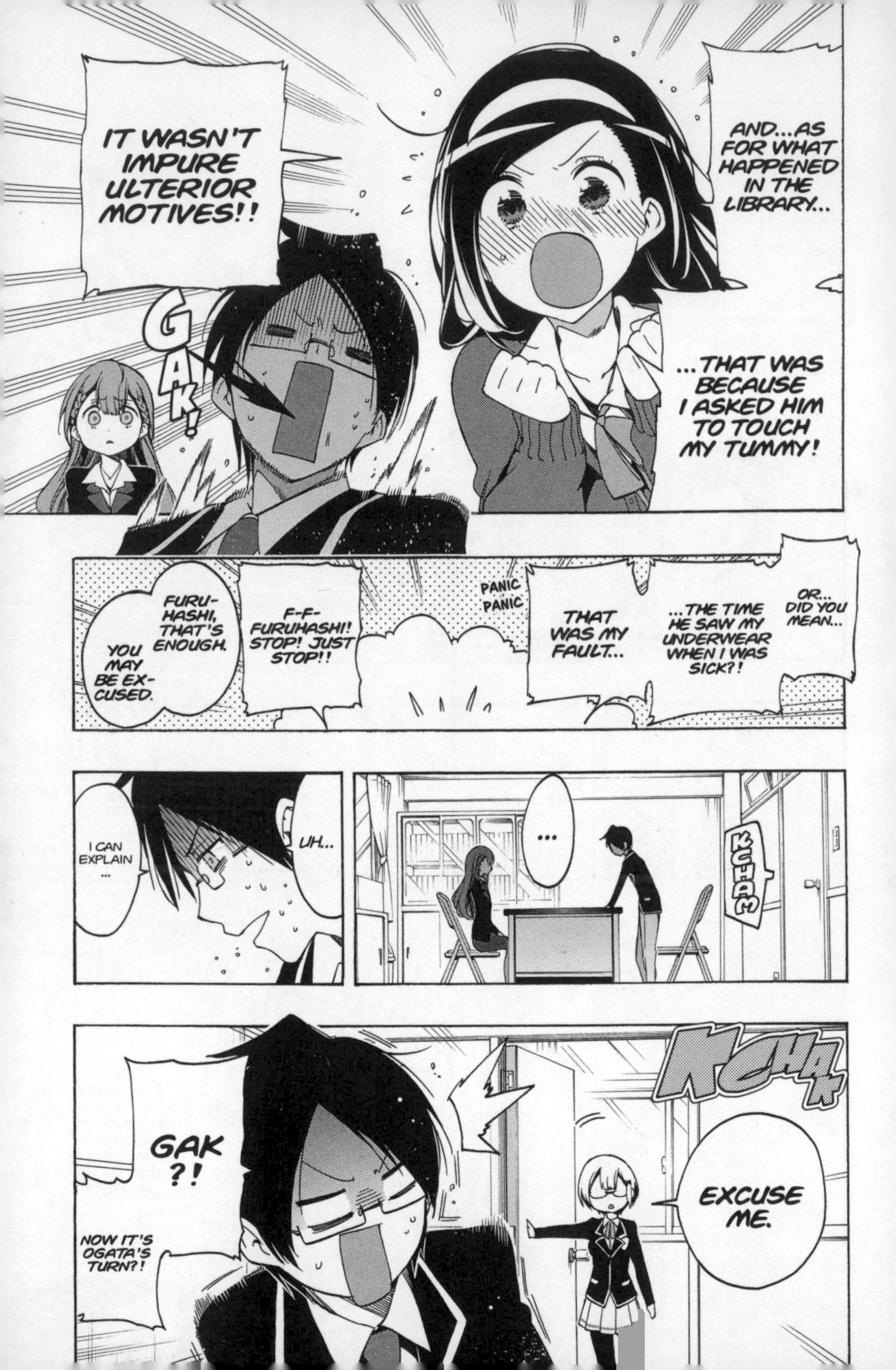
AND...AS FOR WHAT HAPPENED IN THE LIBRARY...
...THAT WAS BECAUSE I ASKED HIM TO TOUCH MY TUMMY!
IT WASN'T IMPURE ULTERIOR MOTIVES!!
GAK!
OR... DID YOU MEAN...
...THE TIME HE SAW MY UNDERWEAR WHEN I WAS SICK?!
THAT WAS MY FAULT...
PANIC PANIC
F-F-FURUHASHI! STOP! JUST STOP!!
FURUHASHI, THAT'S ENOUGH.
YOU MAY BE EX-CUSED.
KCHAM
...
UH...
I CAN EXPLAIN ...
KCHAK
EXCUSE ME.
GAK ?!
NOW IT'S OGATA'S TURN?!

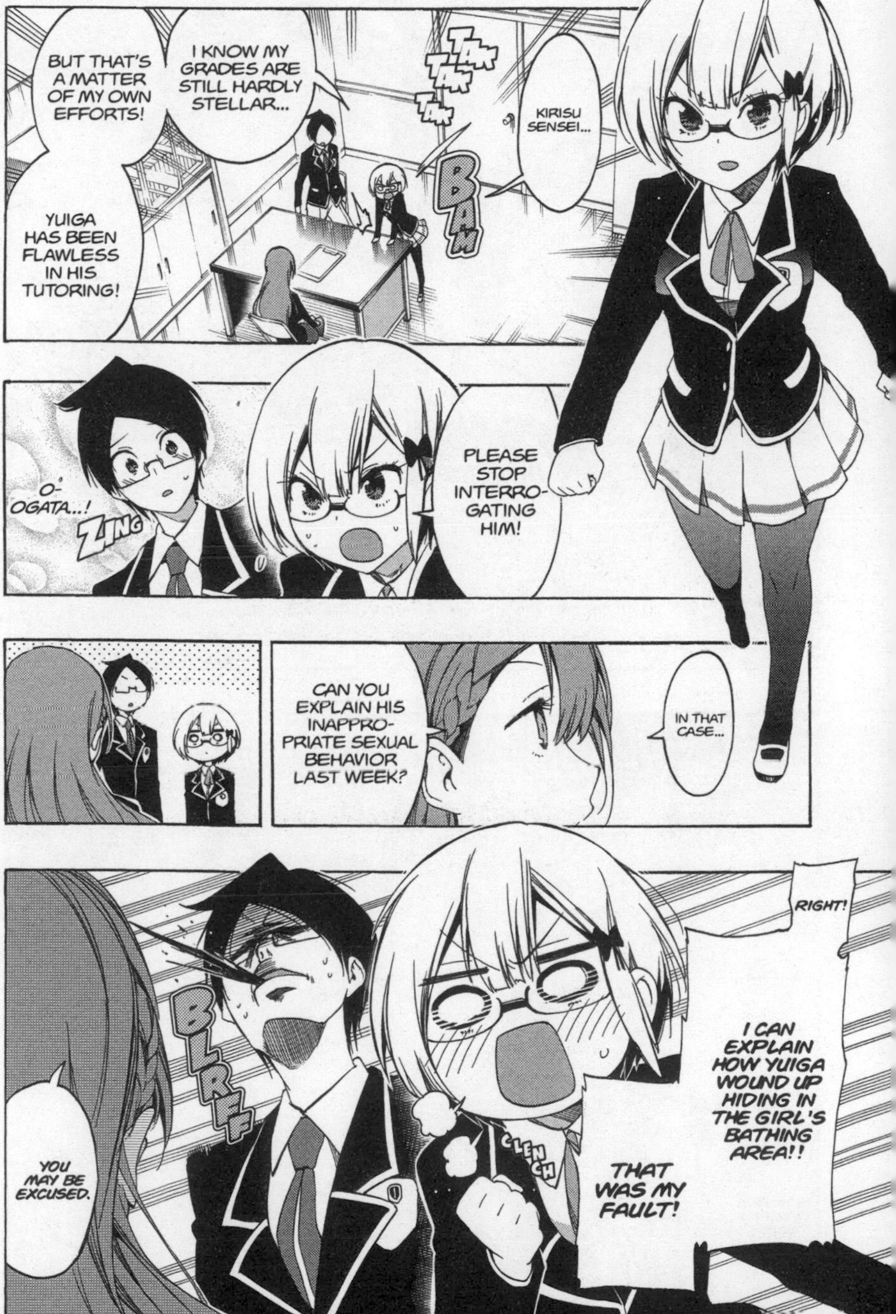
TAK TAK TAK
KIRISU SENSEI...
BAM
I KNOW MY GRADES ARE STILL HARDLY STELLAR...
BUT THAT'S A MATTER OF MY OWN EFFORTS!
YUIGA HAS BEEN FLAWLESS IN HIS TUTORING!
PLEASE STOP INTERRO-GATING HIM!
O-OGATA...!
ZING
IN THAT CASE...
CAN YOU EXPLAIN HIS INAPPRO-PRIATE SEXUAL BEHAVIOR LAST WEEK?
RIGHT!
I CAN EXPLAIN HOW YUIGA WOUND UP HIDING IN THE GIRL'S BATHING AREA!!
THAT WAS MY FAULT!
CLENCH
BLRFF
YOU MAY BE EXCUSED.

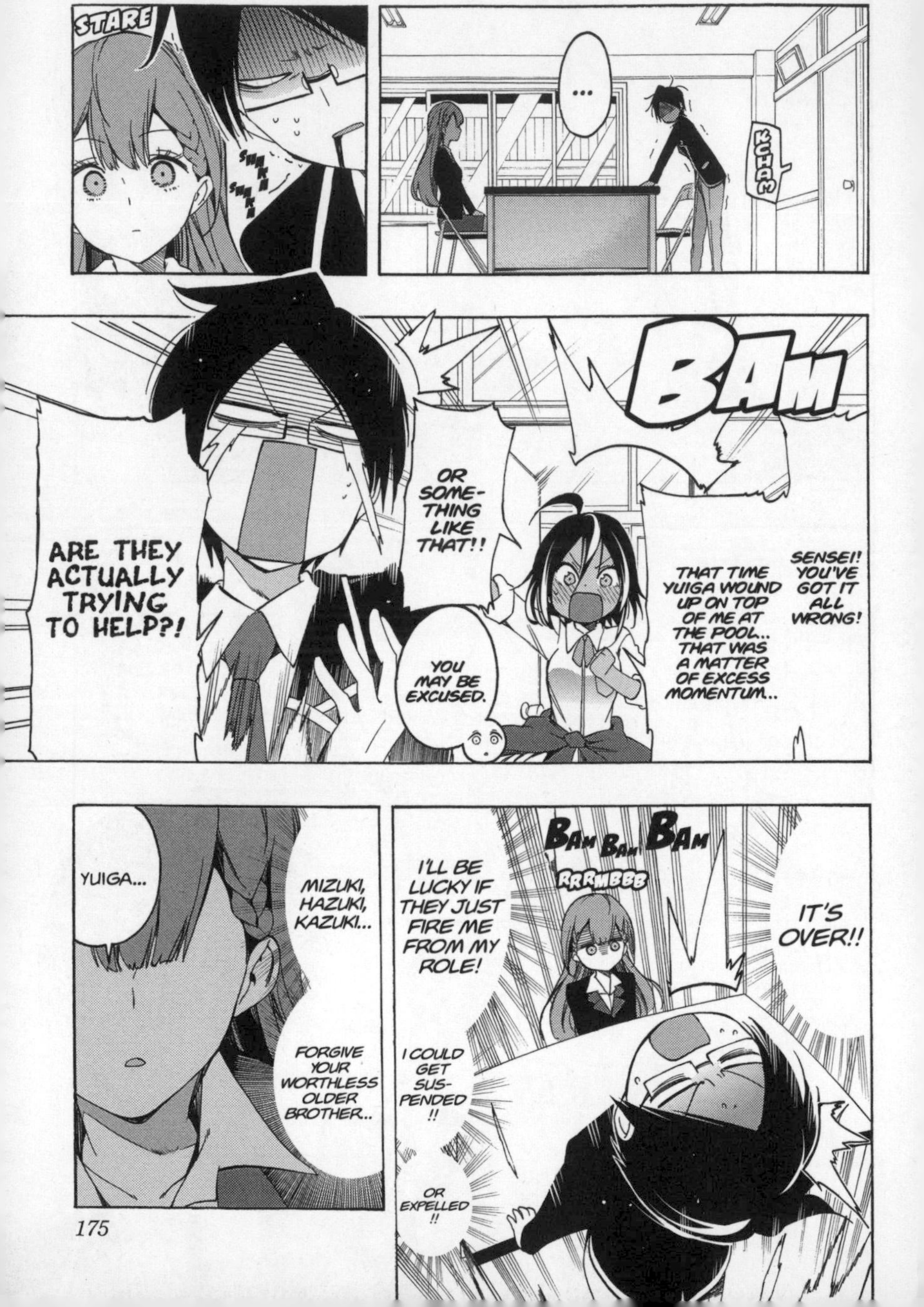
...
K'CHAM
STARE
SHAKE SHAKE
BAM
SENSEI! YOU'VE GOT IT ALL WRONG!
THAT TIME YUIGA WOUND UP ON TOP OF ME AT THE POOL... THAT WAS A MATTER OF EXCESS MOMENTUM...
OR SOME-THING LIKE THAT!!
YOU MAY BE EXCUSED.
ARE THEY ACTUALLY TRYING TO HELP?!
BAM BAM BAM
RRRMBBB
IT'S OVER!!
I'LL BE LUCKY IF THEY JUST FIRE ME FROM MY ROLE!
I COULD GET SUS-PENDED!!
OR EXPELLED!!
MIZUKI, HAZUKI, KAZUKI...
YUIGA...
FORGIVE YOUR WORTHLESS OLDER BROTHER...

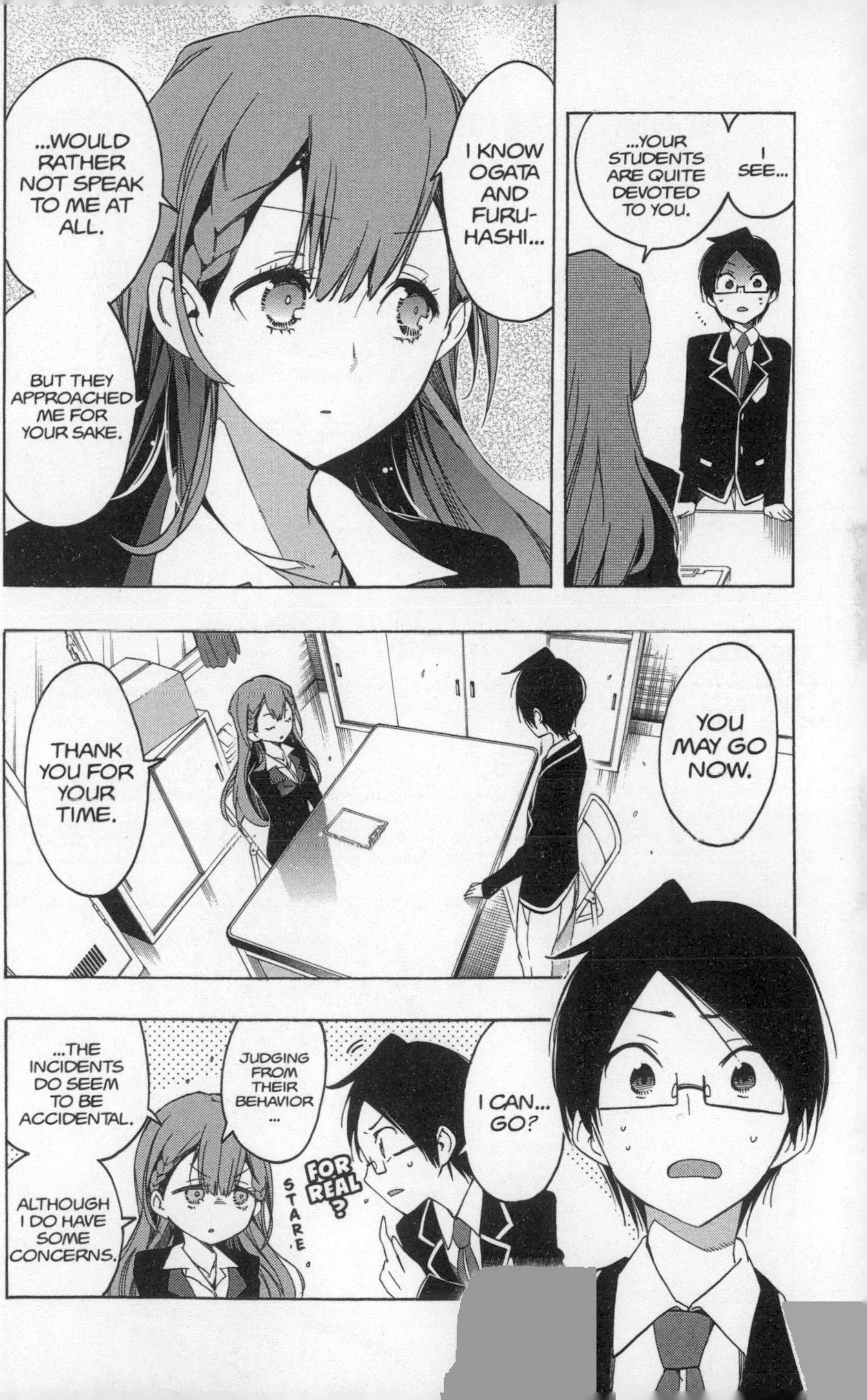
I SEE...
...YOUR STUDENTS ARE QUITE DEVOTED TO YOU.
I KNOW OGATA AND FURU-HASHI...
...WOULD RATHER NOT SPEAK TO ME AT ALL.
BUT THEY APPROACHED ME FOR YOUR SAKE.
YOU MAY GO NOW.
THANK YOU FOR YOUR TIME.
I CAN... GO?
JUDGING FROM THEIR BEHAVIOR...
...THE INCIDENTS DO SEEM TO BE ACCIDENTAL.
FOR REAL?
STARE
ALTHOUGH I DO HAVE SOME CONCERNS.

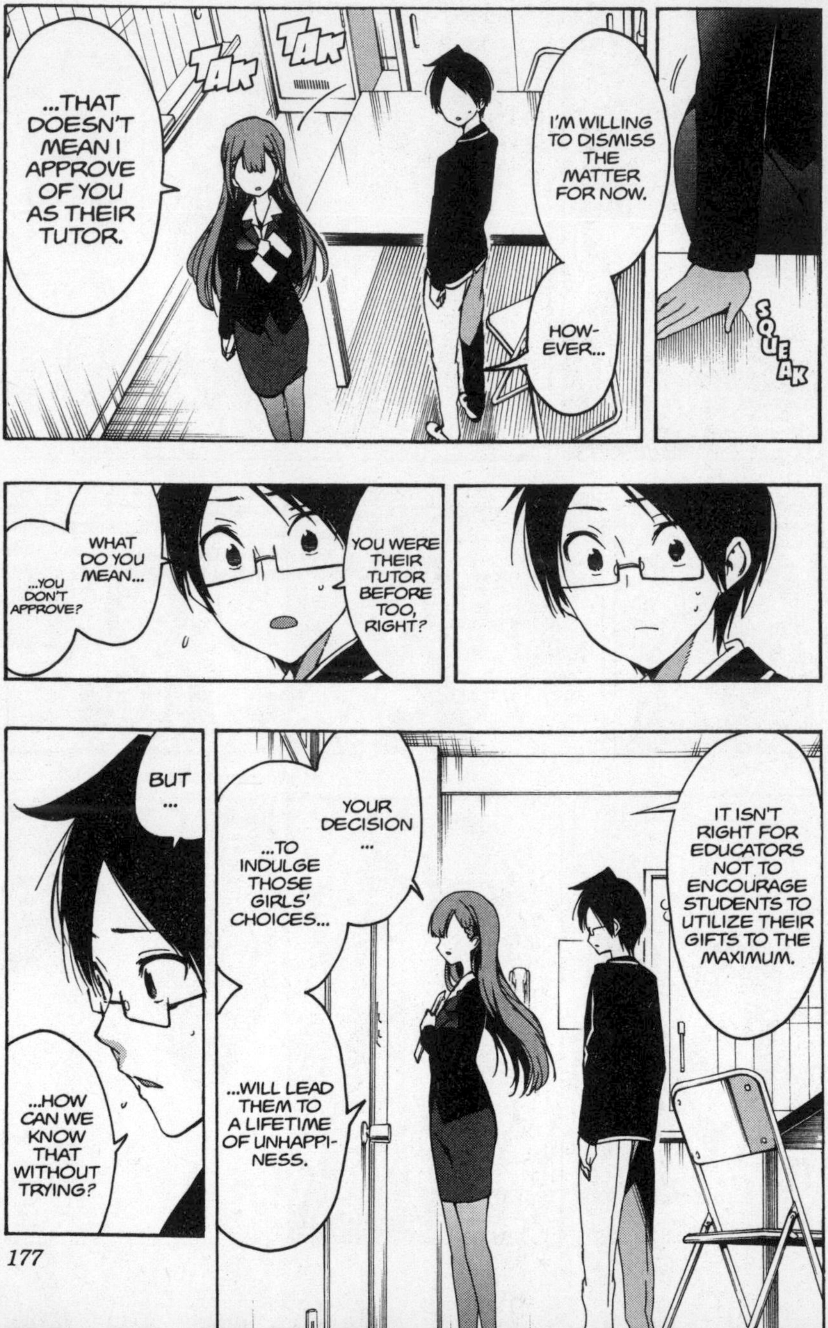
SQUEAK
I'M WILLING TO DISMISS THE MATTER FOR NOW.
HOW-EVER...
TAK
TAK
...THAT DOESN'T MEAN I APPROVE OF YOU AS THEIR TUTOR.
YOU WERE THEIR TUTOR BEFORE TOO, RIGHT?
WHAT DO YOU MEAN...
...YOU DON'T APPROVE?
IT ISN'T RIGHT FOR EDUCATORS NOT TO ENCOURAGE STUDENTS TO UTILIZE THEIR GIFTS TO THE MAXIMUM.
YOUR DECISION...
...TO INDULGE THOSE GIRLS' CHOICES...
...WILL LEAD THEM TO A LIFETIME OF UNHAPPI-NESS.
BUT...
...HOW CAN WE KNOW THAT WITHOUT TRYING?

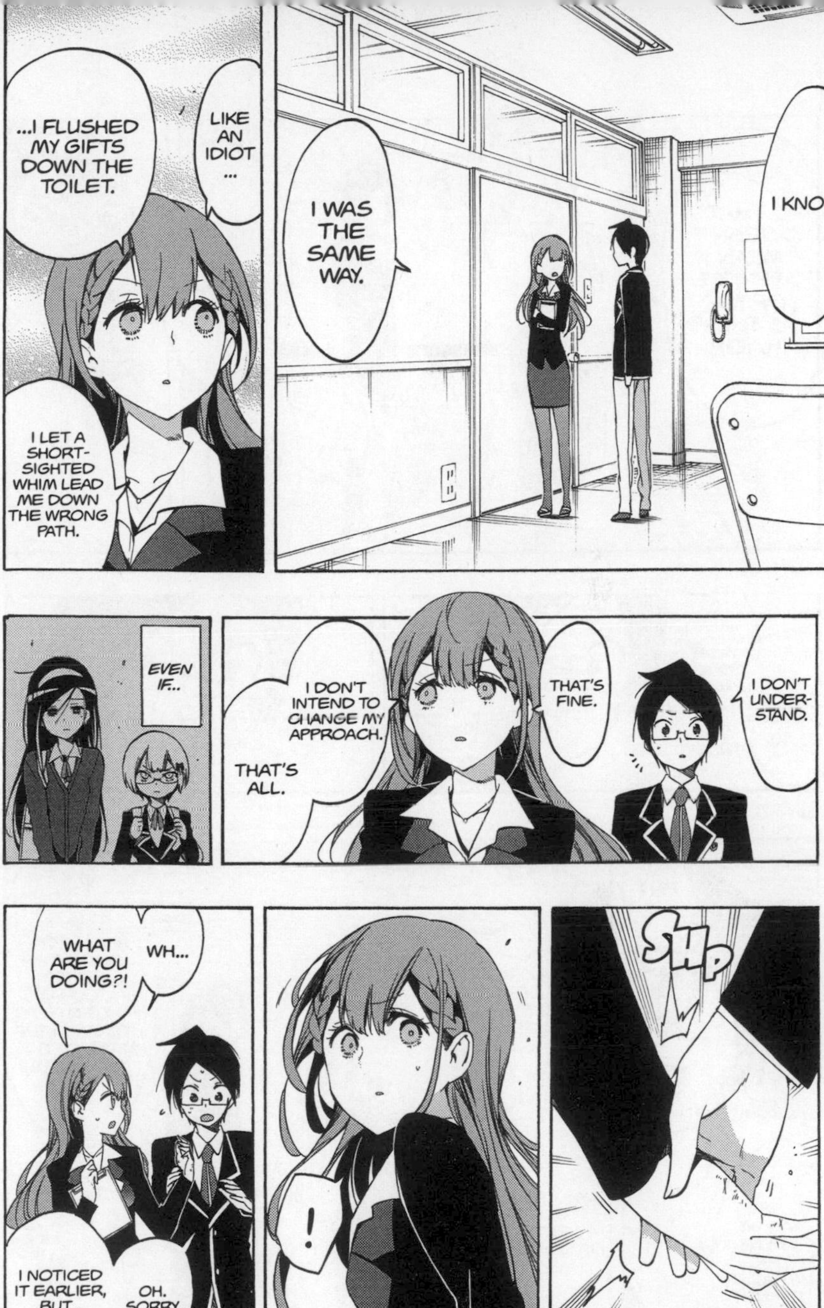
I KNOW.
I WAS THE SAME WAY.
LIKE AN IDIOT...
...I FLUSHED MY GIFTS DOWN THE TOILET.
I LET A SHORT-SIGHTED WHIM LEAD ME DOWN THE WRONG PATH.
I DON'T UNDERSTAND.
THAT'S FINE.
I DON'T INTEND TO CHANGE MY APPROACH.
THAT'S ALL.
EVEN IF...
SHP
!
WH...
WHAT ARE YOU DOING?!
OH. SORRY.
I NOTICED IT EARLIER, BUT...

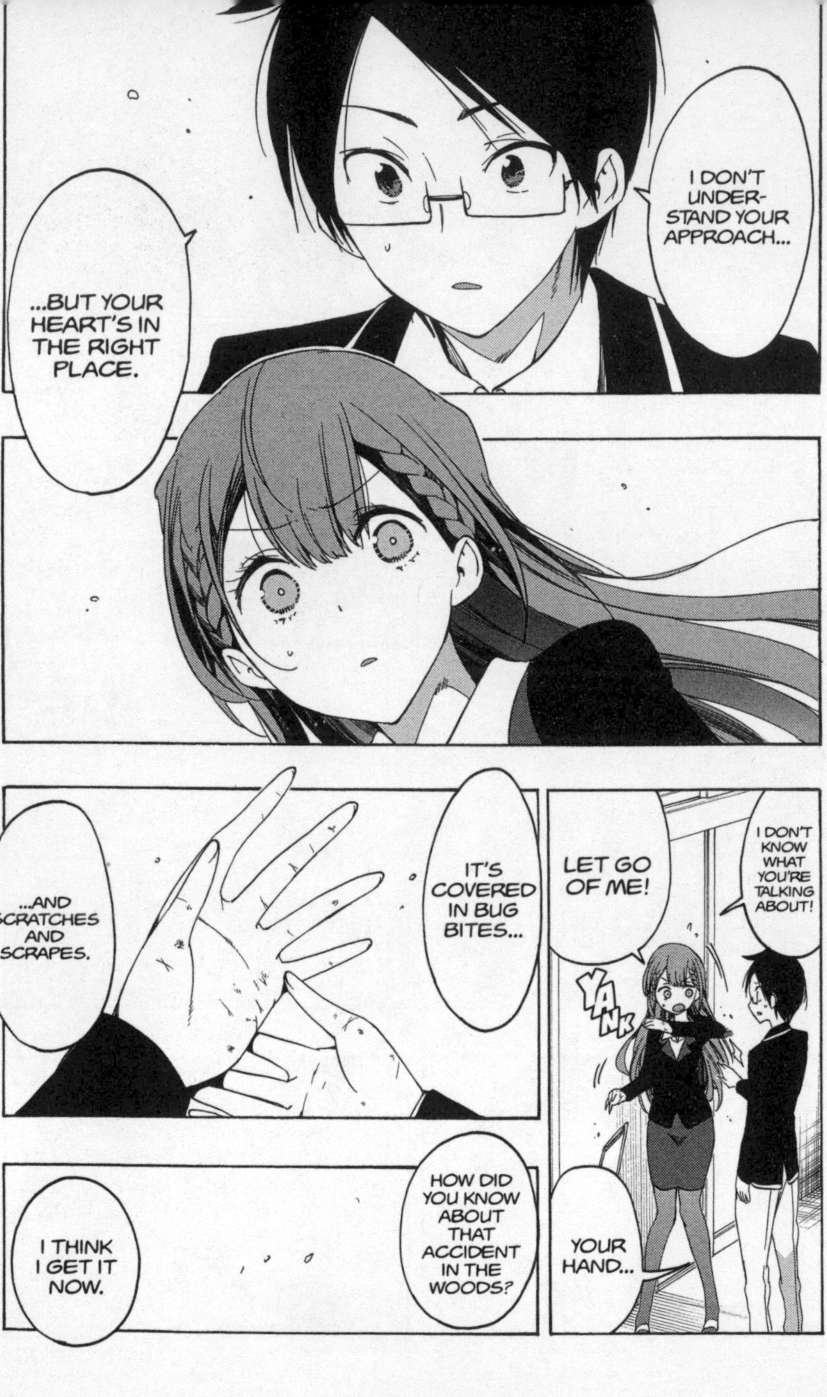
I DON'T UNDERSTAND YOUR APPROACH...
...BUT YOUR HEART'S IN THE RIGHT PLACE.
I DON'T KNOW WHAT YOU'RE TALKING ABOUT!
LET GO OF ME!
YANK
YOUR HAND...
IT'S COVERED IN BUG BITES...
...AND SCRATCHES AND SCRAPES.
HOW DID YOU KNOW ABOUT THAT ACCIDENT IN THE WOODS?
I THINK I GET IT NOW.

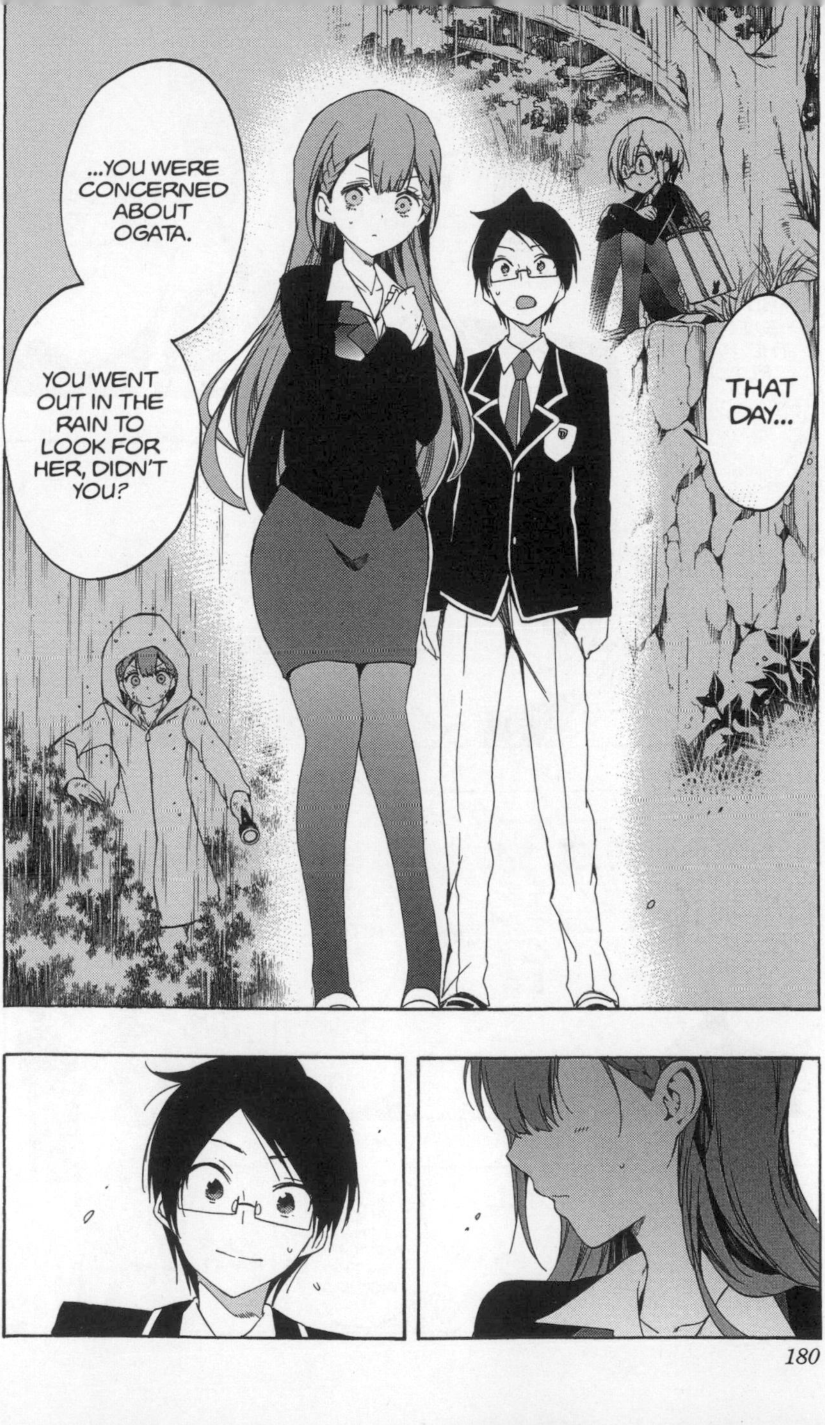
THAT DAY...
...YOU WERE CONCERNED ABOUT OGATA.
YOU WENT OUT IN THE RAIN TO LOOK FOR HER, DIDN'T YOU?

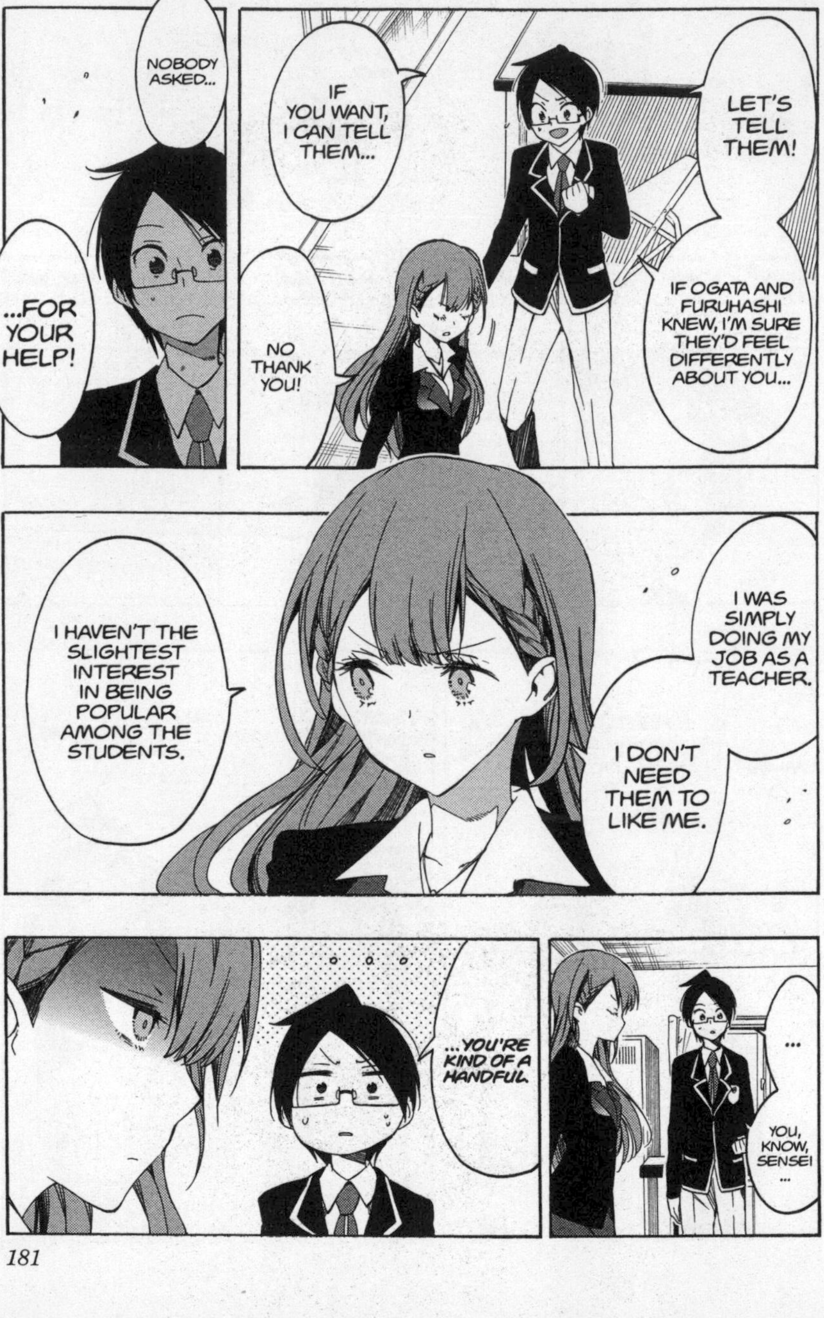

LET'S TELL THEM!
IF OGATA AND FURUHASHI KNEW, I'M SURE THEY'D FEEL DIFFERENTLY ABOUT YOU...
IF YOU WANT, I CAN TELL THEM...
NO THANK YOU!
NOBODY ASKED...
...FOR YOUR HELP!
I WAS SIMPLY DOING MY JOB AS A TEACHER.
I DON'T NEED THEM TO LIKE ME.
I HAVEN'T THE SLIGHTEST INTEREST IN BEING POPULAR AMONG THE STUDENTS.
...
YOU, KNOW, SENSEI ...
...YOU'RE KIND OF A HANDFUL.

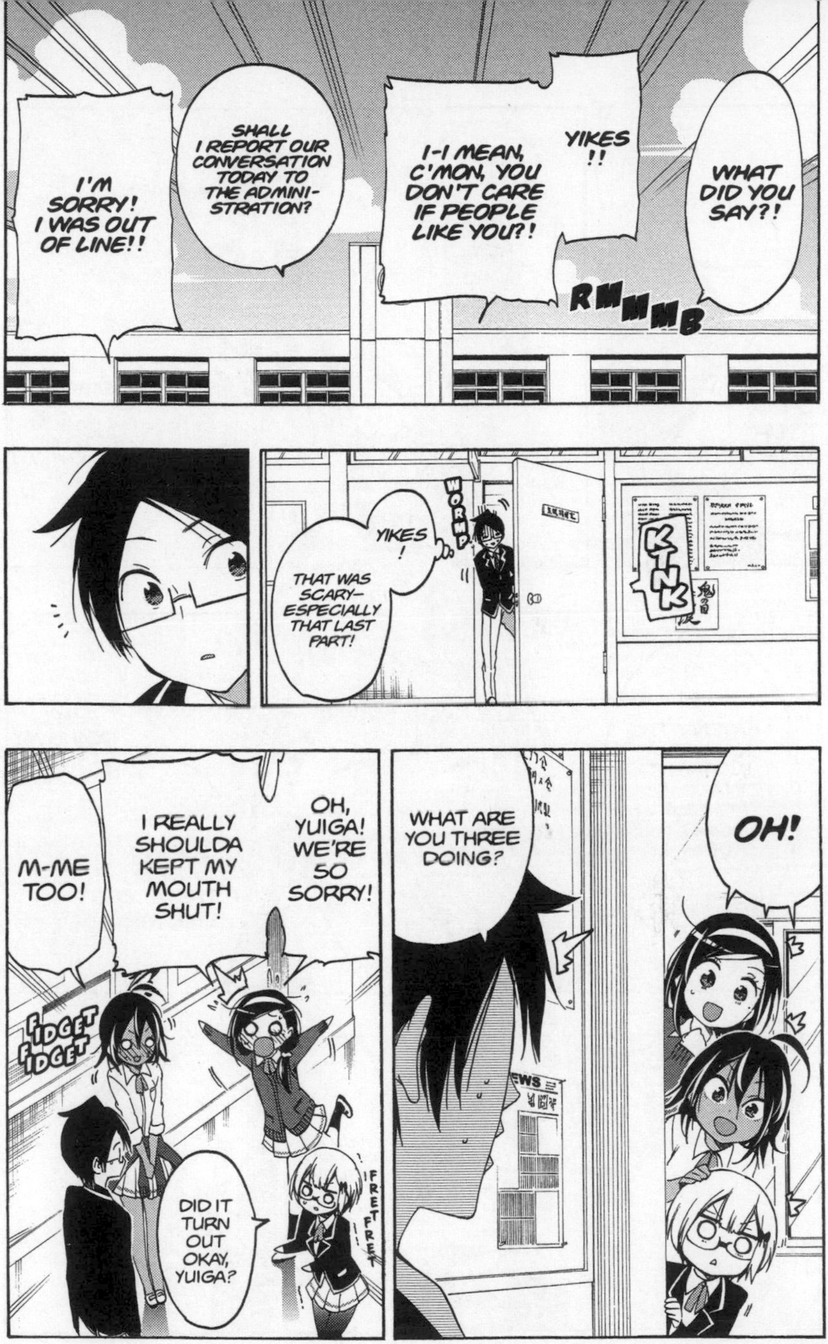
WHAT DID YOU SAY?!
RMMMB
YIKES!!
I-I MEAN, C'MON, YOU DON'T CARE IF PEOPLE LIKE YOU?!
SHALL I REPORT OUR CONVERSATION TODAY TO THE ADMINISTRATION?
I'M SORRY! I WAS OUT OF LINE!!
KTNK
WORMP
YIKES!
THAT WAS SCARY—ESPECIALLY THAT LAST PART!
OH!
WHAT ARE YOU THREE DOING?
OH, YUIGA! WE'RE SO SORRY!
I REALLY SHOULDA KEPT MY MOUTH SHUT!
M-ME TOO!
FIDGET FIDGET
FRET FRET
DID IT TURN OUT OKAY, YUIGA?

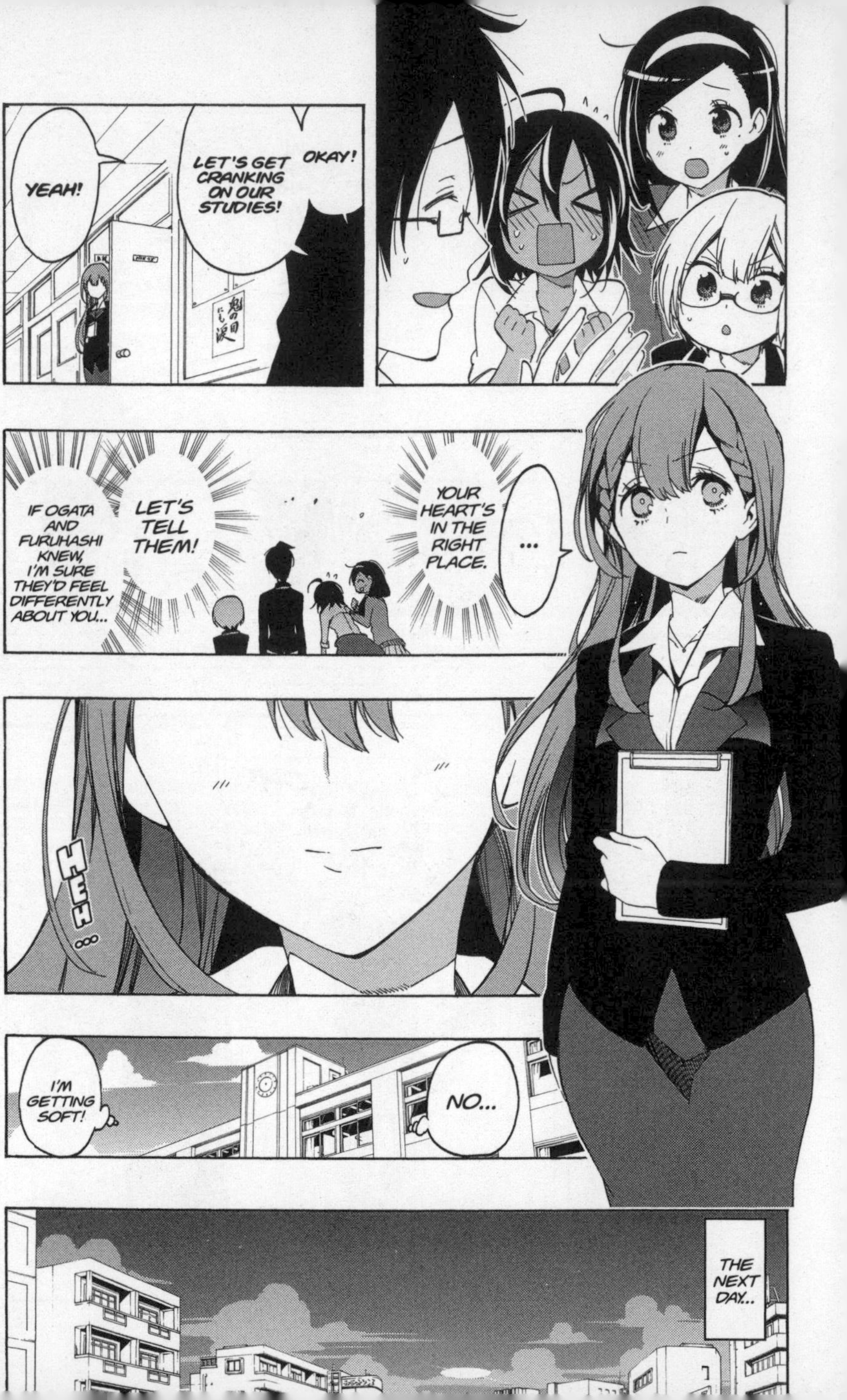
OKAY!
LET'S GET CRANKING ON OUR STUDIES!
鬼の目にも涙
YEAH!
...
YOUR HEART'S IN THE RIGHT PLACE.
LET'S TELL THEM!
IF OGATA AND FURUHASHI KNEW, I'M SURE THEY'D FEEL DIFFERENTLY ABOUT YOU...
HEH...
NO...
I'M GETTING SOFT!
THE NEXT DAY...

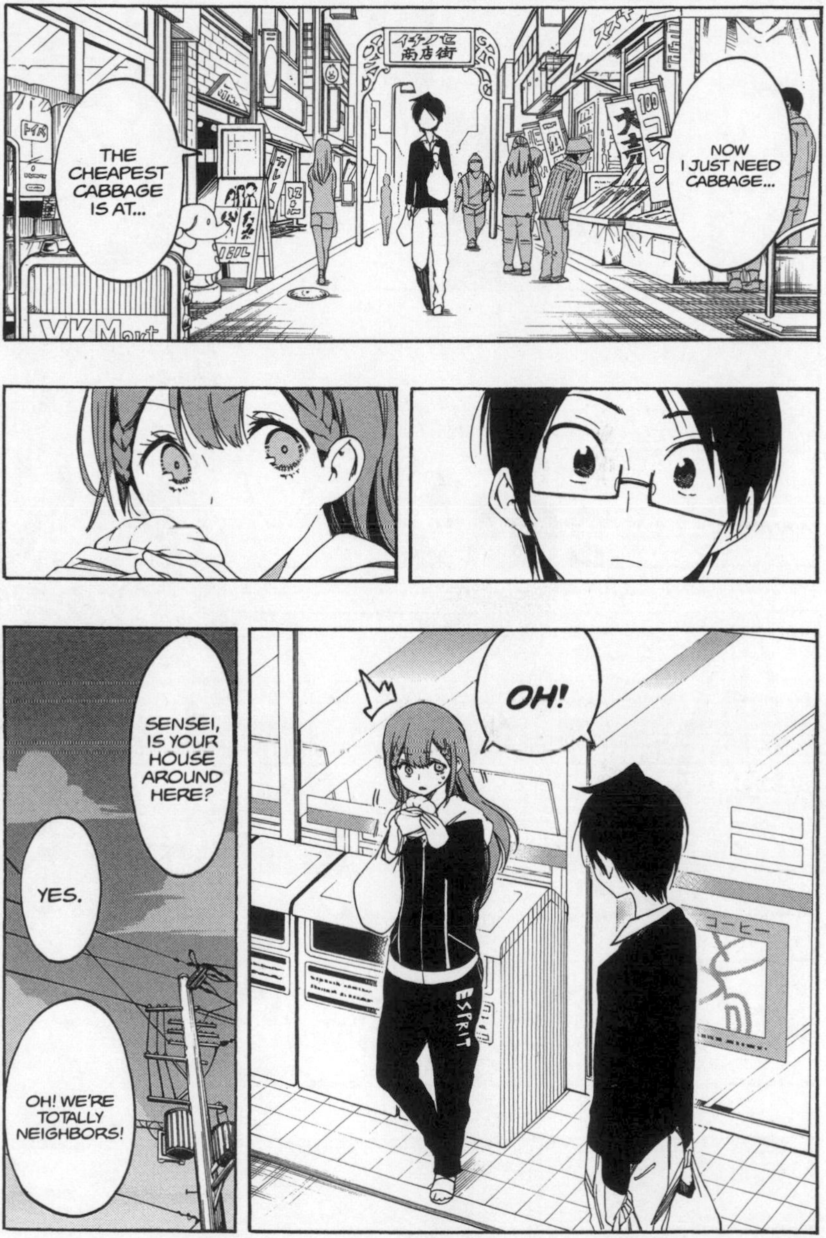
NOW I JUST NEED CABBAGE...
THE CHEAPEST CABBAGE IS AT...
OH!
SENSEI, IS YOUR HOUSE AROUND HERE?
YES.
OH! WE'RE TOTALLY NEIGHBORS!

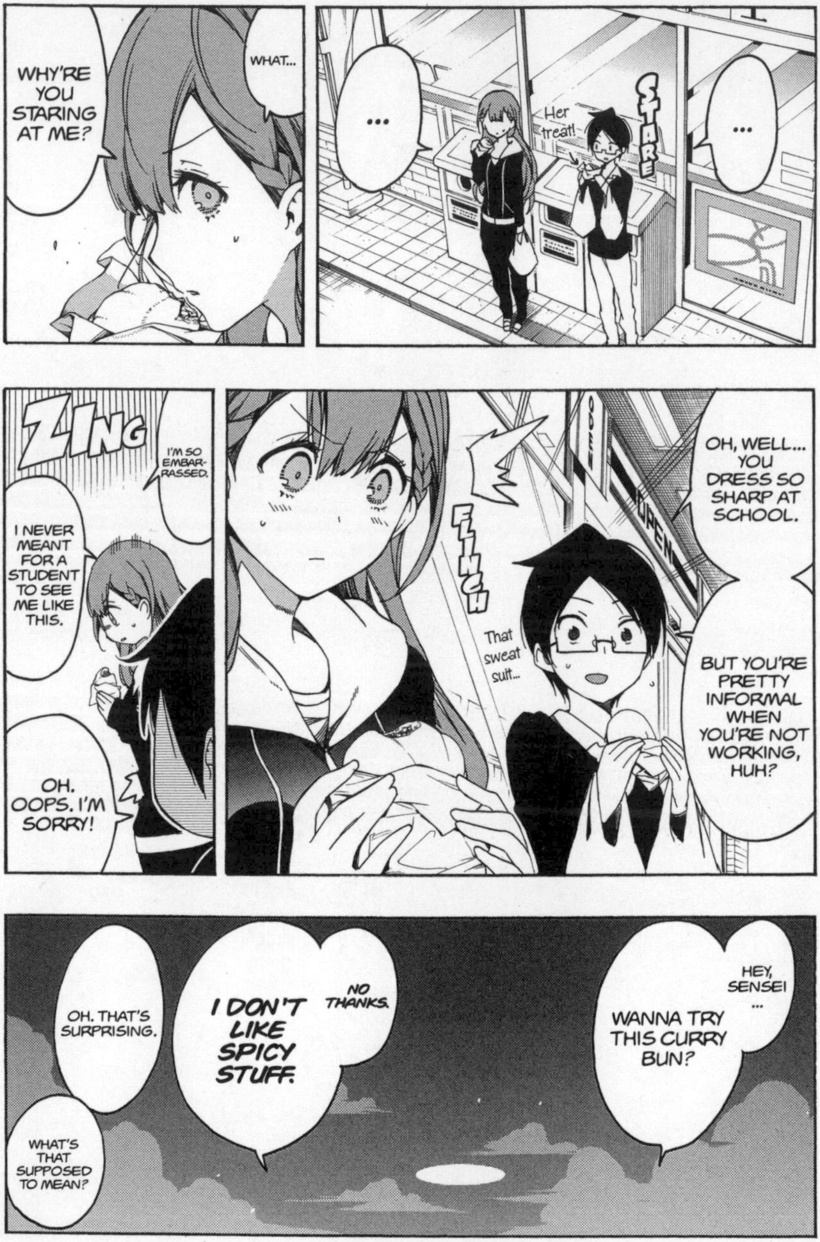
...
STARE
Her treat!
...
WHAT...
WHY'RE YOU STARING AT ME?
OH, WELL... YOU DRESS SO SHARP AT SCHOOL.
FLINCH
BUT YOU'RE PRETTY INFORMAL WHEN YOU'RE NOT WORKING, HUH?
That sweat suit...
ZING
I'M SO EMBARRASSED.
I NEVER MEANT FOR A STUDENT TO SEE ME LIKE THIS.
OH. OOPS. I'M SORRY!
HEY, SENSEI ...
WANNA TRY THIS CURRY BUN?
NO THANKS.
I DON'T LIKE SPICY STUFF.
OH. THAT'S SURPRISING.
WHAT'S THAT SUPPOSED TO MEAN?

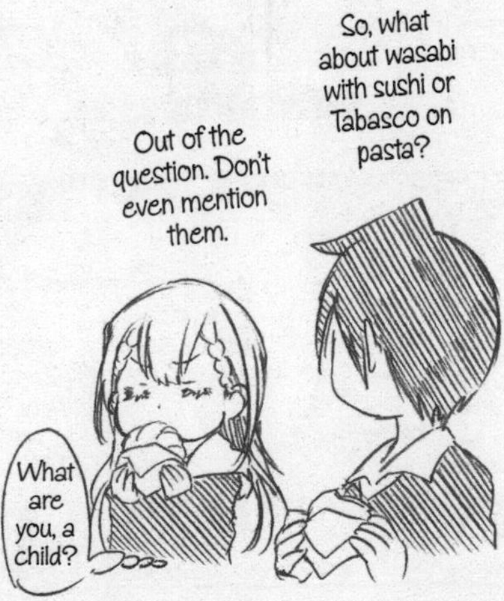
So, what about wasabi with sushi or Tabasco on pasta?
Out of the question. Don't even mention them.
What are you, a child?

Bonus Comic

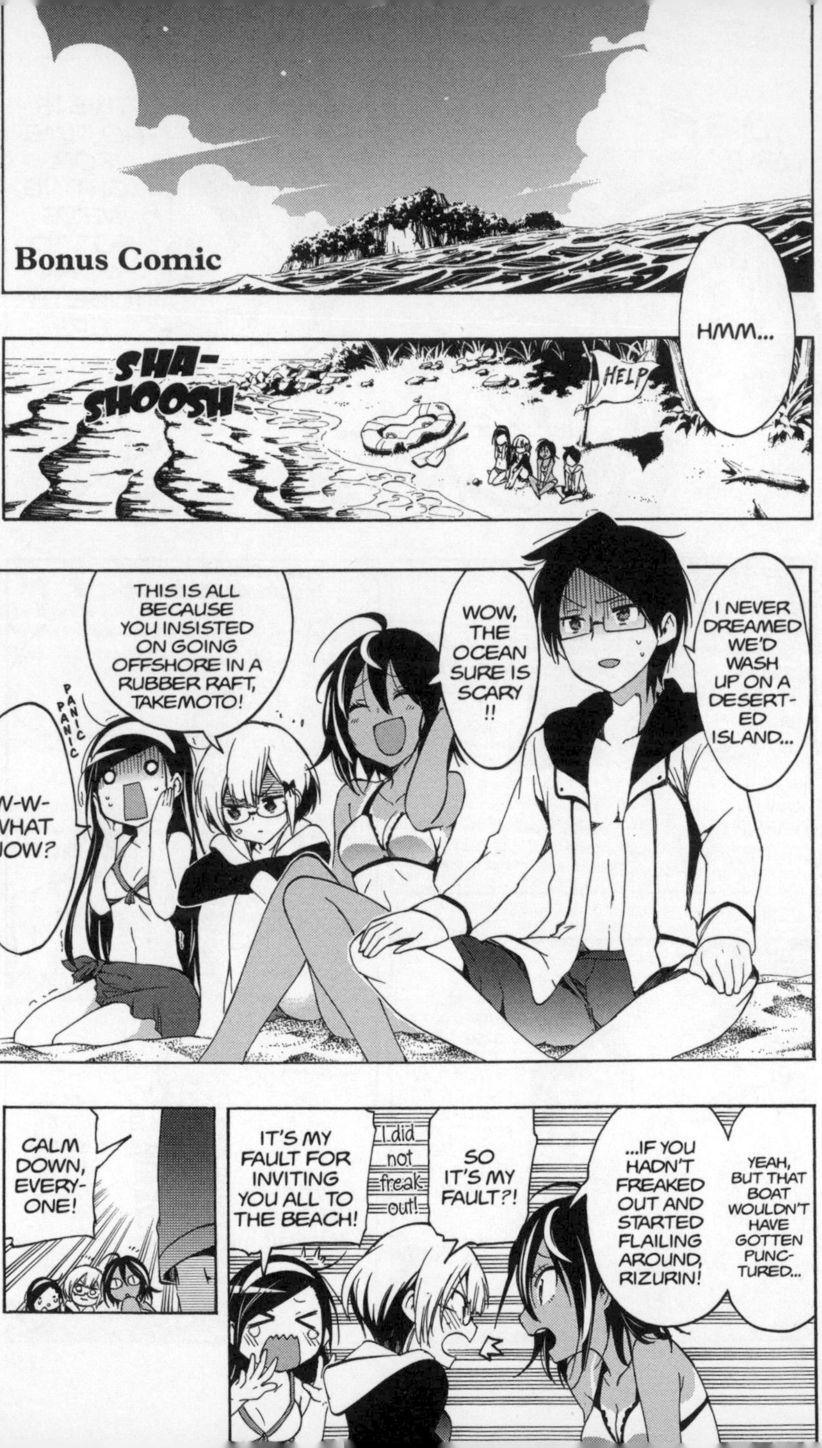
SHA-SHOOSH
HELP
HMM...
I NEVER DREAMED WE'D WASH UP ON A DESERTED ISLAND...
WOW, THE OCEAN SURE IS SCARY!!
THIS IS ALL BECAUSE YOU INSISTED ON GOING OFFSHORE IN A RUBBER RAFT, TAKEMOTO!
PANIC PANIC
W-W-WHAT NOW?
YEAH, BUT THAT BOAT WOULDN'T HAVE GOTTEN PUNCTURED...
...IF YOU HADN'T FREAKED OUT AND STARTED FLAILING AROUND, RIZURIN!
SO IT'S MY FAULT?!
I did not freak out!
IT'S MY FAULT FOR INVITING YOU ALL TO THE BEACH!
CALM DOWN, EVERYONE!

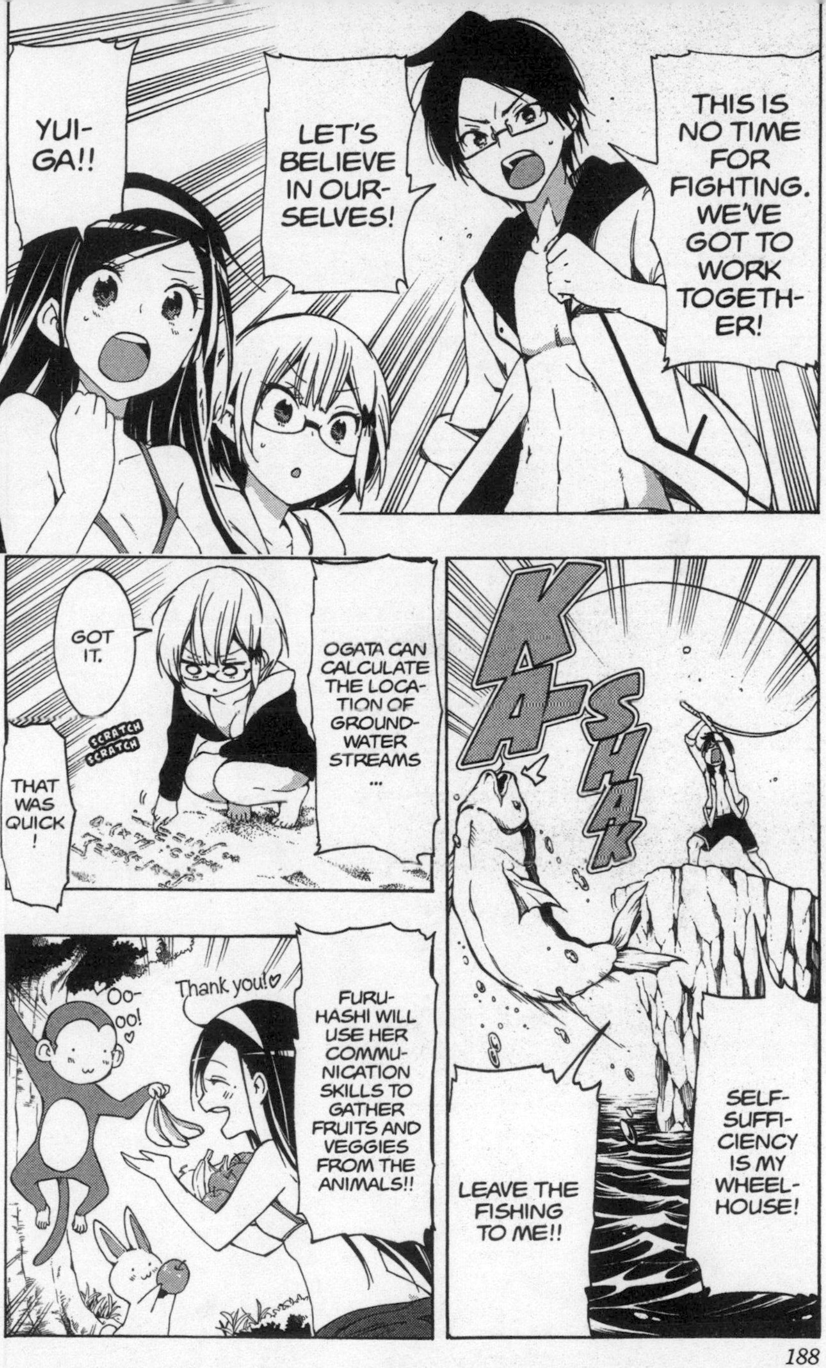
THIS IS NO TIME FOR FIGHTING. WE'VE GOT TO WORK TOGETH-ER!
LET'S BELIEVE IN OUR-SELVES!
YUI-GA!!
KA-SHAK
SELF-SUFFI-CIENCY IS MY WHEEL-HOUSE!
LEAVE THE FISHING TO ME!!
OGATA CAN CALCULATE THE LOCA-TION OF GROUND-WATER STREAMS ...
GOT IT.
SCRATCH SCRATCH
THAT WAS QUICK!
FURU-HASHI WILL USE HER COMMU-NICATION SKILLS TO GATHER FRUITS AND VEGGIES FROM THE ANIMALS!!
Thank you!♡
Oo-oo!♡

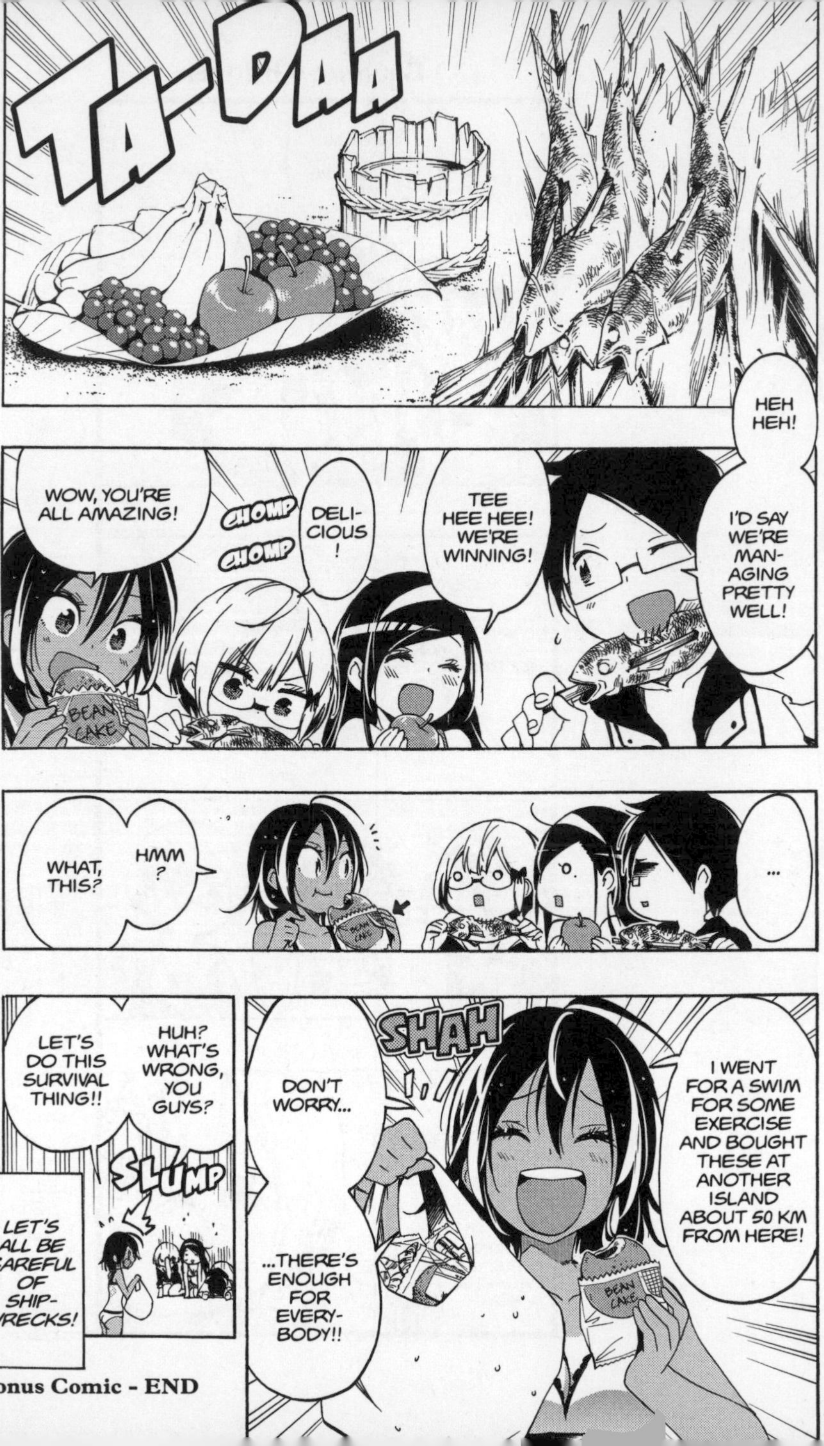
TA-DAA
HEH HEH!
I'D SAY WE'RE MANAGING PRETTY WELL!
TEE HEE HEE! WE'RE WINNING!
CHOMP CHOMP
DELICIOUS!
WOW, YOU'RE ALL AMAZING!
BEAN CAKE
...
HMM?
WHAT, THIS?
SHAH
I WENT FOR A SWIM FOR SOME EXERCISE AND BOUGHT THESE AT ANOTHER ISLAND ABOUT 50 KM FROM HERE!
BEAN CAKE
DON'T WORRY...
...THERE'S ENOUGH FOR EVERYBODY!!
HUH? WHAT'S WRONG, YOU GUYS?
LET'S DO THIS SURVIVAL THING!!
SLUMP
LET'S ALL BE CAREFUL OF SHIPWRECKS!

Bonus Comic - END

[X] Become Children

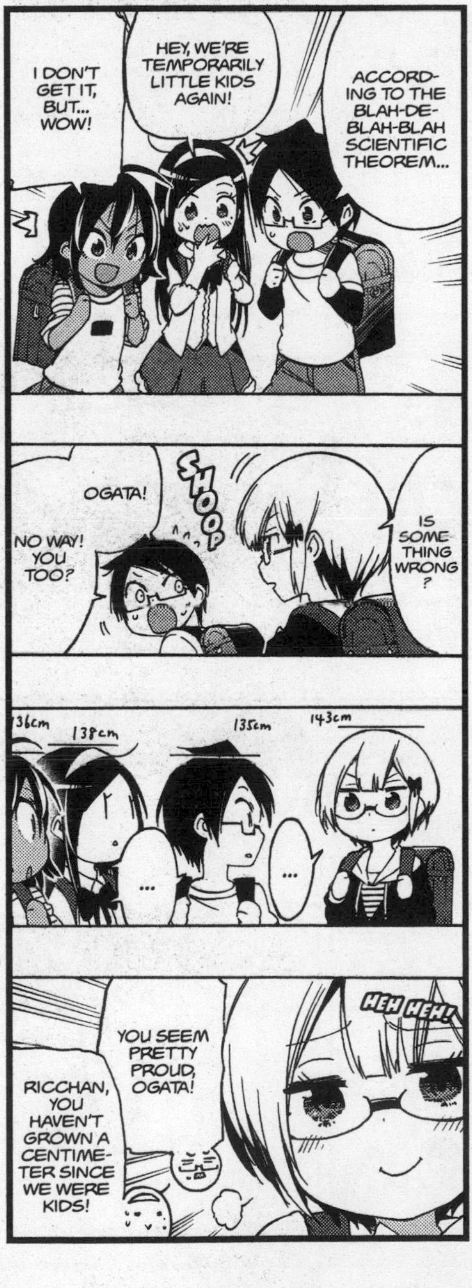
ACCORDING TO THE BLAH-DE-BLAH-BLAH SCIENTIFIC THEOREM...
HEY, WE'RE TEMPORARILY LITTLE KIDS AGAIN!
I DON'T GET IT, BUT... WOW!
IS SOMETHING WRONG?
SHOOP
OGATA!
NO WAY! YOU TOO?
143cm
135cm
138cm
136cm
...
...
HEH HEH!
YOU SEEM PRETTY PROUD, OGATA!
RICCHAN, YOU HAVEN'T GROWN A CENTIMETER SINCE WE WERE KIDS!

We Never Learn

2

 STAFF

Taishi Tsutsui

Yu Kato

Shinobu Irooki

Yuji Iwasaki

Naoki Ochiai

 HELP

Paripoi

Chisato Hatada

Chikomichi

[x] + ○

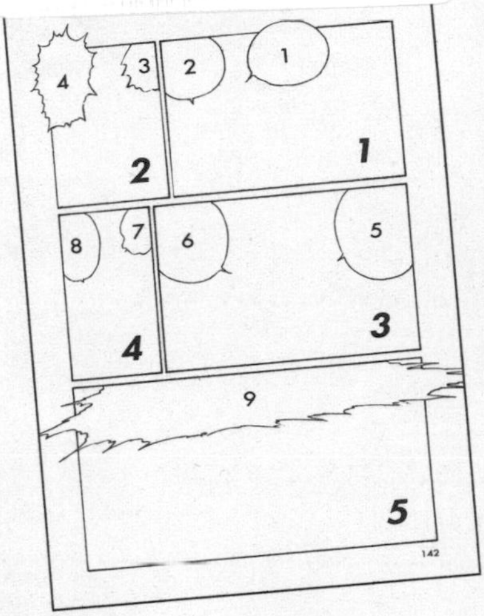

1
2
3
4
1
2
5
6
7
8
3
4
9
5
142

We Never Learn reads from right to left, starting in the upper-right corner. Japanese is read from right to left, meaning that action, sound effects and word-balloon order are completely reversed from English order.

○ ÷ ▽

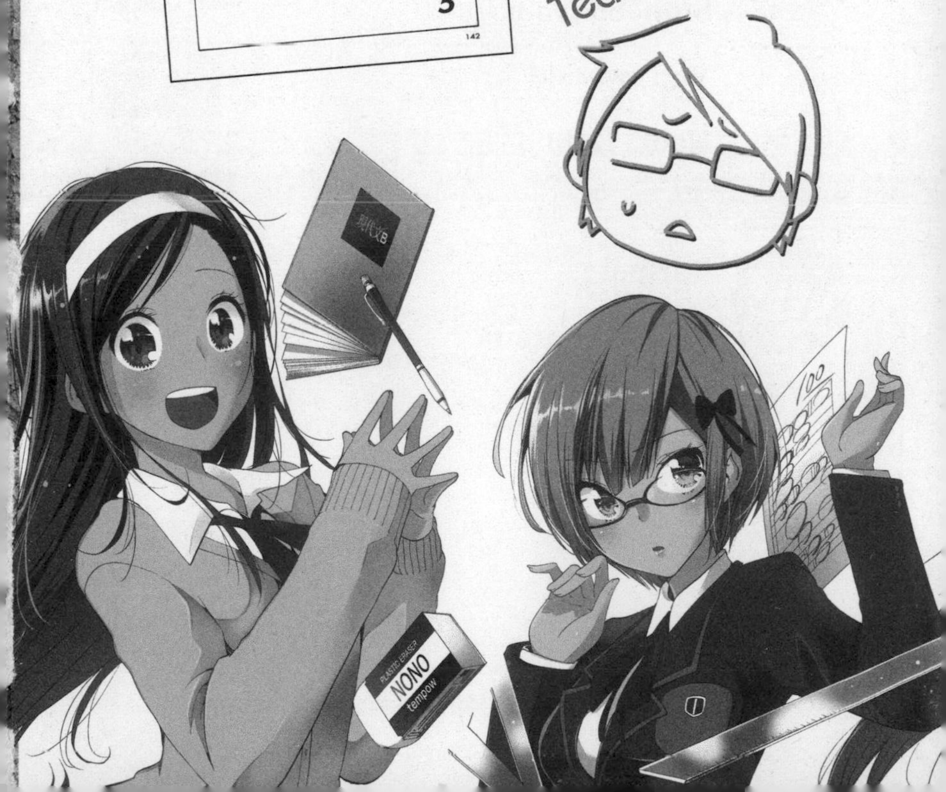

Teacher?
現代文B
PLASTIC ERASER
NONO
tempow